W9-APK-184

Politics, Parties, and Elections in America

Fourth Edition

John F. Bibby
The University of Wisconsin—Milwaukee

Australia • Canada • Denmark • Japan • Mexico
New Zealand • Philippines • Puerto Rico • Singapore
South Africa • Spain • United Kingdom • United States

Political Science Publisher: Clark Baxter
Marketing Manager: Jay Hu
Project Editor: Dorothy Anderson
Text Designer: Jane Rae Brown
Compositor: Skripps & Associates, Typographers
Cover Designer: Jane Rae Brown
Cover Images: Alicia's Dawn, *by Roland Kulla; flag photo by Jane Rae Brown*
Printer/Binder: Webcom, Ltd.

Printed in Canada
1 2 3 4 5 6 03 02 01 00 99

For permission to use material from this text, contact us:
Web: www.thomsonrights.com
Fax: 1-800-730-2215
Phone: 1-800-730-2214

Library of Congress Cataloging-in-Publication Data

Bibby, John F.
Politics, parties, and elections in America / John F. Bibby — 4th ed.
p. cm.
Includes bibliographical references and index.
ISBN 0-8304-1547-5 (alk. paper)
1. Political parties—United States
2. Elections—United States
I. Title
JK2261.B49 1999
324.7'0973—dc21 99-12827

Wadsworth/Thomson Learning
10 Davis Drive
Belmont, CA 94002-3098
USA
www.wadsworth.com

International Headquarters
Thomson Learning
290 Harbor Drive, 2nd Floor
Stamford, CT 06902-7477
USA

UK/Europe/Middle East
Thomson Learning
Berkshire House
168-173 High Holborn
London WC1V 7AA
United Kingdom

Asia
Thomson Learning
60 Albert Street #15-01
Albert Complex
Singapore 189969

Canada
Nelson/Thomson Learning
1120 Birchmount Road
Scarborough, Ontario M1K 5G4
Canada

Contents

PARTIES AND POLITICS IN AMERICA: AN OVERVIEW

CHAPTER

ONE

Anyone who seriously studies American political parties soon is confronted with a series of seeming contradictions and confusing conditions.

On the One Hand:

Prior to the 1996 elections, a majority of Americans said they believed that the U.S. should have a third party and 52 percent said that there was at least a fifty-fifty chance they would vote for it.

An overwhelming majority of Americans agree with the statement "Both political parties are pretty much out of touch with the American people."

On the Other Hand:

On election day in 1996, only 8.4 percent of the voters actually cast ballots for Ross Perot, the candidate of the Reform party, which he created to challenge the Republicans and Democrats.

Over two-thirds of the citizenry consider themselves either Republicans or Democrats, and an additional 26 percent who claim to be independents actually lean toward one of the major parties and demonstrate considerable party loyalty in the

A common complaint about American parties is that they are about as different from each other as Tweedledum and Tweedledee. That is, "there's not a dime's worth of difference between them." Thus, in a CBS/New York Times poll before the 1996 election, 43 percent said the Democrats would do a better job insuring a strong economy and 41 percent said the Republicans would.

With two-thirds of the electorate identifying with the Republican and Democratic parties, the two organizations have developed broadly based and relatively stable followings.

Only the nominees of the Republican and Democratic parties stand a reasonable chance to win the presidency, Congress, governorships, or state legislatures. Furthermore, these bodies are organized on a partisan basis with key power positions allocated to members of the majority party.

It does make a difference which party wins elections. The vast expansion of social welfare programs that occurred under President Johnson was possible only because of the Democrats' landslide victory of 1964. Similarly, President Reagan's program of lower taxes and retrenchment of domestic programs was possible because of Republicans winning the presidency in 1980 and 1984 and controlling the Senate from 1981–1986. And when the GOP won control of Congress for the first time in forty years in 1994, a Democratic president felt compelled to announce "the era of big government is over" and later after partisan confrontations the president and Congress reached a landmark agreement to balance the budget.

Few Americans have formally joined party organizations, worked for candidates, or contributed money to parties or candidates.

Elected public officials frequently deviate from the policy positions of their parties and demonstrate a marked sense of independence.

These seeming contradictions point up the unique character of American political parties. They count among their affiliates the vast majority of the voters. They nominate candidates and contest the major offices in the land. They staff formal organizational structures at the national level and in the fifty states. They organize the executive and legislative branches in Washington and the states. And they exert tremendous influence on governmental policy. Despite these signs of strength and pervasiveness, American parties have few formal members, are often undermanned and in financial straits, disunited in terms of policy direction, and fragmented in terms of power. These puzzling aspects of American political parties dramatize many of the major concerns of this book:

- the unique character of political parties as institutions for aggregating political influence
- the functions performed by political parties within the American political system
- the impact of institutional factors (e.g., separation of powers, direct primaries) on American parties.
- the relationship of parties to voters, candidates, officeholders, and interest groups
- the ongoing processes of change in the party system
- the impact of parties on governmental policy
- the changing role of parties in the American political system

The Nature of Politics

What is politics? In common usage, it is the unseemly machinations of the ambitious and self-serving to gain advantage over others; it is the subverting of the public welfare for group or partisan advantage; it is the never ending struggle between the Republicans and the Democrats; and it is what happens in government—in Washington or the statehouses of Sacramento, Harrisburg, Springfield, Baton Rouge, or Cheyenne. Generally, when one is accused of acting politically, there is a suspicion that less than wholesome activities are afoot.

But when these pejorative connotations are removed, the essence of politics is *power*—the ability of one person to get another person to behave in a desired manner. Politics and the use of power inevitably involve *conflict* because what people want from life differs—they have different values—and because there is a scarcity of life's prized objectives (e.g., wealth, security, prestige, and power). In its most basic sense, then, politics is concerned with "Who Gets What, When, and How."[1]

Whether a political system works depends to a large degree upon whether society's inevitable political conflicts among competing interests can be resolved and managed via bargaining and compromise. If the processes of bargaining and compromise enable competing interests to get enough of what they want, it is possible for these interests to continue to cooperate and not disrupt the whole legal structure of government. Politics, therefore, can be viewed as a process of conflict management.

The political process, however, involves more than keeping the lid on the passions of social conflict. It is also the process through which individuals and groups organize and act collectively to achieve social goals—individual freedom, public health, quality education, national security, economic opportunity, clean air and water.

When politics is stripped of its unsavory normative connotations and viewed in its essentials, it can be seen as a basic social process involving (1) the acquisition, retention, and exercise of power; (2) the expression and management of conflicts; and (3) collective action. In each of these aspects of politics, political parties play a central role. Parties help determine who governs, who wins or loses public policy disputes, and the extent of the win or loss.

The Nature of Party

In spite of their acknowledged impact on American government, political parties have proved to be elusive creatures for social commentators to define. One famous characterization was that of Edmund Burke, the British philosopher and member of Parliament, who in 1770 offered a classic ideologically oriented definition: "Party is a body of men united, for promoting by their joint endeavors the national interest, upon some particular principle in which they are all agreed."[2] Whatever relevance this conception of party had for eighteenth century England, it is clearly inappropriate for American political parties, which have never been noted for their ideological purity. Conservatives, moderates, and liberals are found in both the Republican and Democratic parties, albeit not in the same proportions. Furthermore, it is not uncommon for senators and representatives to vote in opposition to their party colleagues in excess of 40 percent of the time. Definitions stressing organizational structure (i.e., the existence of a hierarchy of organizations—county committees, state central committees, and national committees) are also inadequate because parties include masses of voters as well as dues-paying members, officials or staff, candidates, their supporters, campaign consultants, and government officials.

A definition of parties better adapted to the modern American and Western democratic contexts is that provided by political scientist Leon D. Epstein: "*Any group, however loosely organized, seeking to elect government officeholders under a given label.*"[3] This definition allows for the lack of ideological and policy unity so apparent in American parties. It also accommodates the wide variety of party organizations in the country, which range from the disciplined urban machines of the Mayor Richard J. Daley era in Chicago to the well-financed and professionally staffed Republican National Committee, to the under-financed and disorganized, but loyal, bands of volunteers who man local party organizations in regions where their party has virtually no chance of winning elections. The Epstein conception of party also takes into account two special aspects of parties: (1) their preoccupation with contesting elections, and (2) the fact that it is only parties that run candidates on their own labels.

As V. O. Key, Jr., pointed out, "the fundamental difficulty about the term 'political party' is that it is applied without discrimination to many groups and near groups."[4] He therefore urged students of parties to recognize them as tripartite social structures composed of the following elements (figure 1.1):

The party in the electorate: voters with a sense of loyalty to and identification with the party

The party organization: party officials, committees, volunteer workers, and paid staff

The party in government: party candidates for governmental office and public officeholders at the local, state, and national levels.

American parties, therefore, are structures that contain a variety of components: from the weakly committed voter who usually supports the party's candidates to the dedicated activist

Figure 1. 1
THE TRIPARTITE STRUCTURE OF AMERICAN POLITICAL PARTIES

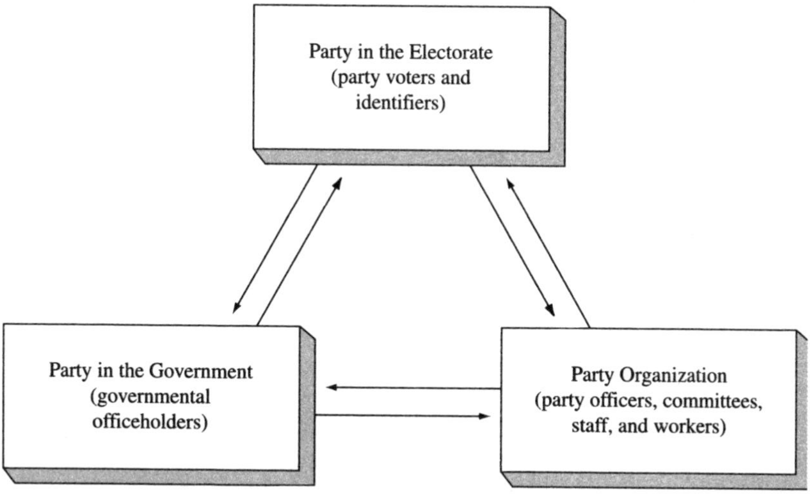

Source: Paul Allen Beck, *Party Politics in America*, 8th ed. (New York: Longman, 1997), p.12.

with an ideological commitment who volunteers time and treasure; from the party boss seeking to run a disciplined patronage dispensing organization to the public official who, while elected on a party level, seeks to project an image independent of party. As Paul Allen Beck has noted, the political party "embraces the widest range of involvement and commitment."[5]

The Functions of Parties

Serving as Intermediaries

Wherever free elections have been conducted on a continuing basis at the national or regional level, political parties exist. This basic fact is suggestive of the fundamental role of parties in a democratic society. They are intermediary or linkage mechanisms between the mass of the citizenry and their government. Parties function as institutions to bring scattered elements of the public together, to define objectives, and to work collectively to achieve those objectives through governmental policy. Parties, therefore, are involved in aggregating societal interests, recruiting leadership, compromising competing demands, contesting elections, and seeking to organize governments.

Parties developed as the old bases of governmental authority (e.g., divine right of kings) crumbled before the democratic revolutions of the eighteenth and nineteenth centuries and governments were seen as deriving their powers from the people. To legitimize their positions, leaders were compelled to appeal to the voters. Such appeals required the development of organizations to communicate with and mobilize the masses. V. 0. Key, Jr., summarized the process of party development in the Western democracies as follows:

> As democratic theory spread, those dissatisfied with the old order rallied the masses . . . against the established holders of authority. In effect the outs played demagogue, lined up the unwashed in their support, and, at the elections, by superiority of numbers and organization they bested those dominant in government. Those who suffered such indignities were compelled in self-defense to defer to the people, no matter how distasteful it was, and to form organizations to solicit electoral support.[6]

As will be discussed in the following chapter, the development of American parties generally follows the pattern Key outlined. America was the first nation to transfer executive power from one faction to another via an election (the election of 1800) and this feat was accomplished by a political party. The United States, thereby, became the first nation with modern political parties organized on a national basis with broad membership, in contrast to the parliamentary factions that existed in Great Britain.

Many political scientists believe that parties are the principal intermediary between the citizens and their government. E. E. Schattschneider, for example, opened his 1942 classic study with the assertion that "political parties created democracy and modern democracy is unthinkable save in terms of parties."[7] And more recently Samuel Huntington, in a cross-national study, observed that parties were distinctive institutions of the modern state whose function "is to organize participation, to aggregate interests, to serve as the link between social forces and the government."[8] Even if such statements overstate the role of parties, parties do permeate every aspect of national and state government and politics. As Sarah McCally Morehouse has reminded us, it is Republicans and Democrats who "make the major decisions regarding who pays and who receives."[9]

In their role as intermediaries, parties must compete with other institutions. They share the linkage functions with interest groups, which exist in infinite variety—labor unions; business and trade associations; professional organizations; racial, ethnic, and religious groups; single issue groups; ideological groups. The mass media, especially with the advent of television, also functions as an intermediary between government and the people. The party's place in the political system as an intermediary institution is illustrated in figure 1. 2.

Figure 1. 2
POLITICAL PARTIES AS INTERMEDIARIES

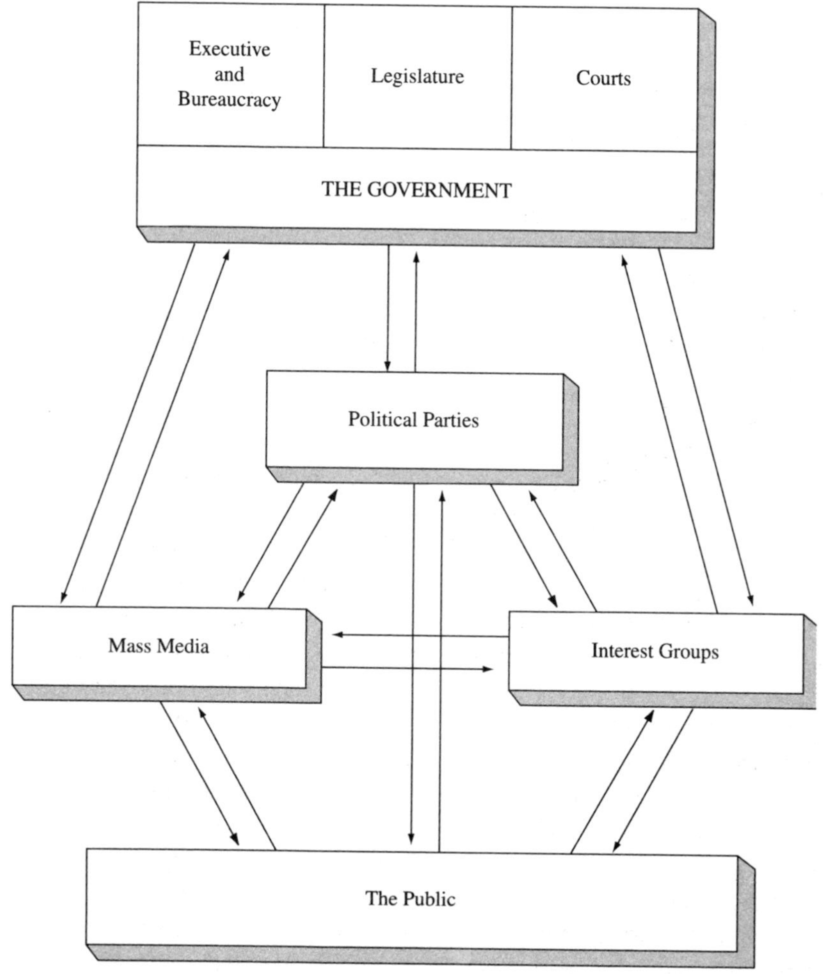

Nominating Candidates

The determination of which names shall appear on the general election ballot—the narrowing of the voter's choice—is a critical stage in the electoral process. The nominating process controls the voter's range of choice and thus severely limits who is eligible for public office. For the candidate —both incumbent and challenger—the nomination is a hurdle that must be cleared if entry into elective politics is to be achieved. In the United States, all national and most major state elected officials are nominated by political parties. So crucial is the nomination process to the parties that Schattschneider concluded:

> Unless the party makes authoritative and effective nominations, it cannot stay in business. . . . The nature of the nominating procedure determines the nature of the party; he who can make nominations is the owner of the party.[10]

While interest groups, political action committees (PACs), pollsters, campaign consultants, and candidate organizations seek to influence nominating decisions, it is ultimately the party that makes nominations. And without a party nomination, the record demonstrates that it is virtually impossible to gain major elected office. No one has been elected president since the development of modern parties in the early 1800s without a partisan nomination. Following the 1998 elections, all members of the House and Senate except independent Representative Bernard Sanders (Vt.) were either Democrats or Republicans. Since 1942, only five persons have been elected governor as independents or minor party candidates; and after the 1998 elections, only 20 state legislators among a national total of 7,375 (.003 percent) were neither Republicans nor Democrats (excluding Nebraska's nonpartisan legislature).

The outcome of partisan nominations can dramatically influence a party's electoral prospects and its future course of development. For example, the Democrats' 1972 nomination of Senator George McGovern (S.D.), who was widely perceived to be way to the left of the average Democratic voter and American citizen, doomed the party to a landslide defeat and sowed the seeds for continuing divisiveness between liberals and moderates that contributed to ensuing losses of the presidency.

Similarly, Senator Barry Goldwater's (Ariz.) capture of the 1964 Republican nomination led to the party's disastrous defeat, as the nominee was seen by voters to be substantially more conservative than they were. His nomination, however, signalled the growing conservative movement within the party. This movement helped develop the cadre of rank and file workers devoted to conservative ideology that made it possible for Ronald Reagan to challenge incumbent President Gerald R. Ford for the 1976 GOP nomination and then easily win the 1980 nomination. In nominating Ronald Reagan for president, the Republican party significantly altered the course of American history because he was the first post-New Deal president to seriously attempt to limit the growth of government domestic programs and expenditures.

The impact of the nomination process upon the House of Representatives during the 1980s and 1990s has been striking. As the South became more competitive between the Republican and Democratic parties, conservatives increasingly were drawn to the GOP. At the same time, the Voting Rights Act of 1965 made it possible for black voters, who are overwhelmingly Democratic, to participate in the electoral process. The net effect of these changes was to make the Democratic party in the South more liberal than in the past and, therefore, it nominated congressional candidates who reflected the national party's policy orientation instead of the traditional southern conservative view. The nomination and election of these moderate to liberal southern Democrats gave the Democratic party in the House increased unity in roll call votes and enabled it to control the chamber's agenda and policy output from the mid-1980s until 1995.[11] At the same time, the infusion of white southern conservatives into the Republican nominating primaries has resulted in GOP nominees with decidedly conservative policy views. As the electoral realignment of the region progressed in the 1990s, these conservatives were elected in larger and larger numbers, thereby creating a Republican party in the House characterized by an overwhelmingly conservative policy orientation and a top leadership corps from the South after the 1994–1998 elections.

Control of the party nominating process has gradually shifted from the hands of the party organization to the party in the electorate. Nominations for congressional and state office since the 1920s have been made via the direct primary, in which party voters select the nominee. In presidential nominations, the party leadership's voice has similarly been diminished with the rise of the presidential primary as the principal method of selecting national convention delegates.

Contesting Elections and Channeling the Vote

In the general election stage, the parties mobilize the electorate and channel it normally either to the Democratic or Republican candidate. Given the physical size of the country, the masses of people involved, the diverse interests at stake, the number of states, the pace of social change, and the variety of political cultures, it is quite remarkable how successful the parties are in channeling the vote. Despite assertions of party decline and evidence of fewer Americans—especially young people—professing an identification with either party, the Republicans and Democrats can rely upon the partisan commitment of most voters to guide their election day choices. The parties, of course, cannot rely only on latent partisanship among the electorate. Partisans must be activated to turn out and actually vote; independents must be won; and opposition party identifiers must be wooed and at least temporarily converted. In these activities, parties play a central role, but they are not exclusively party tasks. These responsibilities are shared with interest groups, candidate organizations, campaign technicians, and consultants.

Organizing the Government

For governmental institutions to operate with at least a modest degree of effectiveness, they require a division of labor, leadership, and rules; that is, they must be organized. The job of organizing government has fallen to the political parties. For example, Congress and most state legislatures are organized on a partisan basis. (Exceptions include the Nebraska nonpartisan legislature and some legislatures heavily dominated by one party.) With their majority status following the 1998 elections, only Republicans held the leadership roles of Speaker of the House, Senate Majority Leader, committee chairmen, and subcommittee chairmen and thereby largely determined the agenda and decisions of the chamber. Similarly, the executive branch is also organized on a primarily partisan basis. Presidential appointments go almost exclusively to members of the president's party. Indeed, most policy making officers of the executive branch must gain a clearance from party officials at the national, state, and local levels prior to their appointment.

The constitutional separation of powers was intended by the Founders to encourage tension between the Congress and president so that neither branch would become too powerful and threaten individual liberties. However sound the Founders' theory may have been, it is also clear that modern government requires legislative-executive coordination if societal needs and international obligations are to be met. An important source of such policy coordination is the tie of partisanship. Presidents tend to work primarily through their fellow partisans in Congress to achieve their policy goals. At the same time, leaders of the president's party in Congress, lacking formal power to control their party members, rely on the prestige and influence of the White House to exert leverage for party unity on roll call votes. Presidential influence on his congressional party is normally at its zenith during the first two years of the term, when his popularity is highest and fellow party members are seeking to enhance his record for the next election. The impact of presidential leadership can be impressive. For example, President Lyndon Johnson wielded heavy Democratic congressional majorities to enact his Great Society social welfare program after the 1964 election, and in 1981 Ronald Reagan worked through a Republican majority in the Senate to set a conservative agenda for Congress. Even a president whose party does not control the House or Senate counts upon the loyalty of fellow partisans in Congress to achieve his policy goals. Presidents George Bush and Bill Clinton, for example, have relied upon congressional partisans to sustain their vetoes in order to achieve bargaining leverage on legislation with the opposition party leaders. Of course, the president's ability to rely upon his fellow partisans in Congress varies with conditions—especially the popular support enjoyed by the president. When that support diminishes, so does his capacity to hold his party together in support of his programs in Congress, as the first two years of the Clinton administration demonstrated.

Providing Public Accountability

Democratic governments derive their powers from the people. Fred I. Greenstein, therefore, has suggested a simple and workable definition of democracy as a political system in which "citizens have a relatively high degree of control over their leaders."[12] Parties provide voters with a means to hold public officials accountable for the actions of government. They, therefore, make a contribution to citizen control of government.

The contemporary political world is incredibly complex. The

array of issues and candidates upon which the model citizen should be informed in a general election is almost mind-boggling. Political power in the United States is divided among the legislative, executive, and judicial branches and among national, state, and local governments. The voter, therefore, is expected to make informed choices for officials at all levels and in several branches of government. There are choices for offices from president to county registrar of deeds, and issues from U.S.–Russia relations to the administration of county courts. Fortunately, the voter can respond to these tangled questions in terms of a few simple criteria and is not required to spend all available time studying politics.

Party labels enable voters to sort out this complexity and vote for the candidates of their preferred party—the party which they perceive to be closest to their interests. Because each major elected official wears a party label—a type of political brand name—voters can also assign to the party in power either credit or, more likely, blame for the state of the union. Without party labels to sort out the candidates and issues, the average voter would be at sea with no compass for a guide.

Additionally, parties can contribute to citizen control of government because they are forced to advocate policies that will retain the support of their traditional constituencies, while at the same time seeking additional votes among the unaffiliated or the disaffected members of the opposition party. The very uncertainty of electoral outcomes works against parties becoming excessively complacent because retention of office requires a constant reassessment of public sentiments. As a result, parties and candidates spend millions of dollars in both election and nonelection years on public opinion surveys of voter sentiments.

The process of citizen control of government to which parties contribute is indirect, of course, and imperfect in nature. It is not a matter of voters instructing their leaders on the specific policies that they want the government to follow. Rather, periodic elections using party labels give the voters a chance to register their general reaction to a party's stewardship in office. The voters' judgment can either be positive, as in the case of Ronald Reagan's (1984) and Bill Clinton's reelection (1996) victories, or be negative—witness the voter's rejection of reelection bids by Jimmy Carter (1980) and George Bush (1992). There is scant evidence, however, that in these elections voters were voting for specific governmental policies advocated by the winning candidates. They were rendering a general verdict on the incumbents' performance in office and, based upon past performance, their likely ability to deal with future problems.[13]

Managing Conflict

Because people vary in their goals and values and because what people want is often in short supply, conflict is inevitable in society. A stable governmental order, therefore, requires mechanisms for compromising competing group demands. Conflict must be managed and American parties have traditionally played a significant role in reconciling competing group demands.

Winning elections within a two-party system requires building broadly based coalitions. Inevitably elements of the coalition will have somewhat divergent objectives. For example, the dominant Democratic New Deal coalition forged by President Franklin D. Roosevelt during the 1930s contained such contentious elements as white Protestant southerners, blacks, northern urban Catholics, blue-collar workers, Jews, and marginal farmers. The conflicts inherent in this alignment have been juggled with varying degrees of success since the 1930s. Within the Congress, for example, the Democrats have practiced the politics of "inclusive compromise" in which Democratic representatives from urban areas have supported farm price supports, while rural Democrats have voted for federally subsidized housing and urban development programs, and both groups have backed federal water projects for their party members from the arid Western states.[14] Uneasy alliances also exist within the GOP, which during the 1980s and 1990s has sought to accommodate the interests of business-oriented economic conservatives as well as the social policy concerns of religious conservatives. As these examples suggest, within the American political system many group conflicts in society have been settled *within* the parties.

Parties as Competitors for Political Influence

As prominent as parties are in the American political order, they do not have the field to themselves. They must compete for political influence with candidate organizations, campaign consultants, interest groups, and the mass media. In recent years, the ability of parties to compete for a place in the campaign process has been weakened by the growing role of a professional corps of consultants and experts skilled in the latest campaign techniques and technologies. To a significant degree, these professional consultants operate outside the regular party organizations and are closely tied to the organizations of individual candidates. Even well financed and professionally staffed party organizations at the national, state, and local levels find it impossible to provide their candidates with all the technical assistance—media experts, pollsters, direct mail specialists, campaign managers—that they require. Recognizing the value of these specialists, the candidates, therefore, often seek to employ this type of talent using funds which have been raised independently of the parties. In the process, the candidates have become less dependent upon their party organizations at election time. This sense of independence from party is often reflected in the behavior of candidates after they have won public office.

Parties also face stiff competition from organized groups in terms of funding campaigns. Election costs are constantly and dramatically rising and the parties cannot fund (and are often forbidden by law from funding) all or even major shares of the costs of campaigns. Increasingly, interest groups, through political action committees (PACs), have come to play a larger role in funding candidates. Even the national government and the states are now competitors of the parties for a role in campaign finance. Since 1976, presidential campaigns have been funded primarily with taxpayer money and an increasing number of states have public funding programs designed to limit the role of the parties and PACs in elections.

The mass media, especially television, are also competitors with the parties for political influence. To a large degree, political reality for most Americans is what they see on the network news programs anchored by Dan Rather, Tom Brokaw, or Peter Jennings. Americans get their news mainly from television. Television, therefore, has come to play a major role in politics and especially in presidential nomination contests.

By the 1970s the bulk of the national convention delegates were chosen in presidential primaries—mass elections that by 1996 attracted 24.5 million voters. In the sequence of presidential primaries that run from February to June of presidential election years, it is essential that a candidate establish the image of a winner, that is, momentum. Being interpreted as the winner of an early primary is necessary to gain media coverage, achieve standing in the polls, and raise funds for the next in a long series of primaries. But as Austin Ranney has pointed out, "doing best in the early primaries is not simply a matter of getting more votes than the other candidates; it is getting substantially more votes than expected."[15] And it is the news media—especially television commentators—who decide what is expected. For example, in the 1972 New Hampshire primary, Democratic Senator Edmund Muskie (Maine) came in first with 46 percent of the votes compared to Senator George McGovern's (South Dakota) second place finish with 37 percent. But the media had previously announced that Muskie was expected to receive at least 50 percent of the vote in his neighboring state of New Hampshire. Therefore, McGovern, who had done better than expected, was declared the winner by the media. Muskie lost momentum and McGovern's campaign received a tremendous boost that carried him to the presidential nomination. Similarly, the media declared Jimmy Carter the winner of the 1976 Democratic primary in New Hampshire when he placed first in a multicandidate field with only 28 percent of the vote. With this "win," he was on his way to the nomination.

In effect, what has been happening in presidential politics is that the traditional role of screening the candidates is being shifted away from party leaders—governors, members of Congress, state and local party chairmen, and mayors—to the mass media and the participants in presidential primaries. For example, the news media in reporting and interpreting the 1992 New Hampshire presidential primary tended to discount former Massachusetts Democratic senator Paul Tsongas's neighboring state victory in the Democratic primary, while emphasizing Pat Buchanan's strong showing against President Bush in the Republican primary. The impact of Bill Clinton's loss of front-runner status, due to media reports concerning allegations of his marital infidelity and draft avoidance during the Vietnam war, was thereby lessened, and Clinton was able to continue his candidacy. The party role in presidential nominations has not been eliminated, but the age of party leadership domination of presidential nominations has clearly passed. Television has become a powerful, competing intermediary institution.

Some observers viewing the rise of campaign consultants, PACs, and television have predicted a bleak future for American parties. There have even been apocalyptic visions of partyless politics. But the parties have demonstrated qualities of adaptability, durability, and resilience. As succeeding chapters will demonstrate, the three elements of the party retain significant influence: the party in the electorate retains the allegiance of over 60 percent of the voters who identify with one of the two major parties; the party in government dominates decision-making in the Congress; and there are signs of renewed strength in both national and state party organizations.

Parties and Interest Groups: There Is a Difference!

Interest groups engage in many of the same activities as political parties. They seek to *influence nominations, elect favored candidates, influence the appointment* of officials to the executive branch, and *influence governmental decisions*. While there are surface similarities, parties are unique institutions that can be distinguished from interest groups.

Parties Run Candidates under Their Own Labels

No matter how much interest groups may concern themselves with elections through endorsements and support of candidates in primaries and general elections, it is only the parties that run candidates on their own labels. There are no candidates for major office that run under the label of the AFL-CIO, U.S. Chamber of Commerce, NAACP, American Bar Association, or Methodist Church. Only parties assume responsibility for the candidates that run under their banners and act as agents of public accountability for the actions of their affiliated officeholders.

Parties Have Broad Issue Concerns

Interest groups reflect the concerns of persons who share a common viewpoint or set of attitudes and wish to further those interests through government policy. Normally these interests are quite narrow in scope, reflecting the special concerns of the membership and not the full gamut of governmental policies. The National Association of Home Builders, for example, is primarily concerned about federal housing policy and interest rates; the Tobacco Institute worries about regulation of smoking; the American Legion seeks benefits for former members of the armed forces and advocates a strong defense; the Wildlife Federation seeks sanctuary for wildlife through environmental protection, and so on. Most interest groups have clear priorities in terms of the issues to which they devote attention and they do not strain the unity of their organizations or their treasuries by getting involved in issues of only marginal interest to the membership. Even broadly based organizations like the AFL-CIO, which seeks to influence a wide range of governmental policies, have clear priorities that reflect the bread and butter concerns of union members.

Political parties, by contrast, take stands on the whole spectrum of issues with which government deals—foreign, fiscal, welfare, education, transportation, health, racial, environmental, science, energy, and social policy. No other political organization has a breadth of policy concerns comparable to that of political parties.

Parties Give Priority to Controlling the Personnel of Government

However broad the policy concerns of parties may be, they tend to give priority in the United States to winning elections. Parties want to control the personnel of government. To achieve this end, American parties have shown great flexibility in terms of their policy positions and willingness to accommodate a wide variety of different views in their midst. While Republican and Democratic members of Congress as a group show distinctly different voting patterns on major issues, it is also true that each party contains significant though differing proportions of conservatives, moderates, and liberals. Ideological purity takes a backseat to winning elections for American parties. By contrast, interest groups are concerned first and foremost with government policy. Most groups are concerned about who is elected or appointed only because of the policies these officeholders will promulgate, not out of a desire to put fellow group members in public office. As a result, most interest groups support candidates in both parties whom they see as capable of advancing group aims.

Parties Are Quasi-Public Organizations

Interest groups like the American Bankers Association, American Farm Bureau Federation, the Teamsters, Common Cause, or the American Library Association are private associations. They operate under minimal governmental regulation and enjoy all the protections of the First Amendment. Parties are quite different organizations. In the United States they are heavily regulated by federal and especially state statutes. These statutes provide legal definitions of parties, mandate organizational structures and procedures, define membership, and specify how certain party functions like nominating candidates will be carried out. American parties are, therefore, quasi-public institutions, whereas interest groups are private associations.[16]

Parties Have a Unique Relationship to Their Clientele
Parties have a unique relationship to their clientele—the party in the electorate. As Paul Allen Beck has observed, other political organizations, like interest groups, seek to attract the support of persons beyond their membership, but such persons always remain outside the group. But the persons in the electorate being wooed by parties are permitted to take part through the direct primary in the most important activities of the party—the nomination of its candidates and the selection of its leadership. "The American party is an open, inclusive, and semipublic political organization composed of its own clientele, a tangible organization, and personnel in government. As such it stands alone and unique in the American political system."[17]

Party Government and the Peaceful Transfer of Governmental Authority

"Democracy involves a balance between the forces of conflict and consensus."[18] Institutional structures are needed to reflect and articulate the attitudes and demands of various elements of society. But conflict must be held within reasonable bounds if the political order is to have any stability and continuity. Structures for achieving agreement and consensus are required. As the discussion of party functions has demonstrated, parties are central to these seemingly conflicting requirements of a democratic order. They both reflect the conflicts in society and they are involved in the bargaining and negotiation needed to achieve conflict resolution.

As is discussed in chapter 2, the party conflict has been institutionalized in the United States. Americans expect electoral contests between two parties, with the victorious party organizing the government, and the opposition party maintaining a steady barrage of criticism. Changes in the personnel of government are in reality shifts in party control of the presidency or Congress. This process of displacement from power via the election of partisan majorities, of course, is taken for granted by Americans. But it is, in fact, a fundamentally different way of replacing officeholders than the common practices of the not too distant past in Western nations. Party displacement of governments is "a substitute for revolt and insurrection and a new means for determining succession of authority."[19]

Governmental succession through changes in party control is possible only when the notion of the *loyal opposition* is accepted. Loyal opposition involves opposing and criticizing the policies of the government-of-the-day (those currently in office) and standing ready to take its place. But it also requires acceptance of the basic structure of the government and the processes under which it operates. In other words, acceptance of a loyal opposition party requires that those in power and their supporters recognize that to oppose the policies of the government is not treason and advocacy of revolution. In the United States, it took a long time to establish the principle that assaults on the government by the "outs" were to be expected and tolerated. In his Farewell Address, Washington, for example, warned against a spirit of party that he feared would arouse the rabble against the government. And after the Federalists lost the election of 1800, they were so bitter that in the secret Hartford Convention (1814) they advocated the secession of the New England states from the Union, even though the country was at war. Wilfred Binkley has pointed out that from 1816 to the 1830s, most Americans believed that "there could be but one party—the Republicans—and that all of them belonged to it."[20] It was not until the 1840s that the "idea of loyal party opposition . . . [received] acceptance and approval from Americans."[21] Acceptance of the notion of loyal opposition made possible the institutionalization of party conflict which in turn made possible the achievement of public office for the "outs" by nonrevolutionary means.

Suggestions for Further Reading

Aldrich, John H. *Why Parties? The Origin and Transformation of Party Politics in America.* Chicago, Ill.: University of Chicago Press, 1995.

Beck, Paul Allen. *Party Politics in America.* 8th ed. New York: Longman, 1997.

Eldersveld, Samuel J. *Political Parties in American Society.* New York: Basic Books, 1982.

———*Political Parties in the American Mold.* Madison: University of Wisconsin Press, 1986.

Epstein, Leon D. *Political Parties in Western Democracies.* New York: Praeger, 1967.

Herring, Pendleton. *The Politics of Democracy.*New York: Rinehart, 1940.

Patterson, Kelly D. *Political Parties and Maintenance of Liberal Democracy.* New York: Columbia University Press, 1996.

Ranney, Austin, and Kendall, Willmoore. *Democracy and the American Party System.* New York: Harcourt, Brace, 1956.

Ware, Alan. *Political Parties and Party Systems.* Oxford: Oxford University Press, 1996.

Notes

1. Harold Lasswell, *Politics: Who Gets What, When, and How* (New York: McGraw-Hill, 1936).

2. Edmund Burke, "Thoughts on the Cause of Present Discontents," in *The Works of Edmund Burke*, vol. 1 (Boston, Mass.: Little, Brown, 1871), p. 151.

3. Leon D. Epstein, *Political Parties in Western Democracies* (New York: Praeger, 1967), p. 9.

4. V. O. Key, Jr., *Politics, Parties, and Pressure Groups*, 5th ed. (New York: Crowell, 1964), p. 163.

5. Paul Allen Beck, *Party Politics in America*, 8th ed. (New York: Longman, 1997), p. 13.

6. Key, *Politics, Parties, and Pressure Groups*, p. 201.

7. E. E. Schattschneider, *Party Government* (New York: Holt, Rinehart and Winston, 1942), p. 1.

8. Samuel Huntington, *Political Order in Changing Societies* (New Haven, Conn.: Yale University Press, 1980), p. 91.

9. Sarah McCally Morehouse, *State Politics, Parties and Policy* (New York: Holt, Rinehart and Winston, 1981), p. 29.

10. Schattschneider, *Party Government*, p. 64.

11. David W. Rohde, "Something's Happening Here; What It Is Ain't Exactly Clear: Southern Democrats in the House of Representatives," in Morris P. Fiorina and David W. Rohde, eds., *Home Style and Washington Work: Studies in Congressional Politics* (Ann Arbor: University of Michigan Press, 1989), pp. 137–163; and Nicol E. Rae, *Southern Democrats* (New York: Oxford University Press, 1994).

12. Fred I. Greenstein, *The American Party System and the American People*, 2nd ed. (Englewood Cliffs, N.J.: Prentice-Hall, 1970), p. 2.

13. Paul R. Abramson, John H. Aldrich, and David W. Rohde, *Change and Continuity in the 1996 Elections* (Washington, D.C.: CQ Press, 1998), pp. 146–150.

14. David Mayhew, *Party Loyalty among Congressmen: The Differences between Democrats and Republicans, 1947–1962* (Cambridge, Mass.: Harvard University Press, 1966).

15. Austin Ranney, *Channels of Power: The Impact of Television on American Politics* (New York: Basic Books, 1983), p. 95.

16. See Leon D. Epstein's discussion of political parties as public utilities in his *Political Parties in the American Mold* (Madison: University of Wisconsin Press, 1986), ch. 6.

17. Beck, *Party Politics*, p. 13.

18. Samuel J. Eldersveld, *Political Parties in American Society* (New York: Basic Books, 1982), p. 15.

19. Key, *Politics, Parties, and Pressure Groups*, p. 205.

20. Wilfred E. Binkley, *American Political Parties: Their Natural History* (New York: Knopf, 1944), p. 152.

21. Austin Ranney and Willmoore Kendall, *Democracy and the American Party System* (New York: Harcourt, Brace, 1956), p. 110.

2 THE PARTY BATTLE IN AMERICA

CHAPTER TWO

Organized partisanship was an unplanned development. In their plan for the Republic, the framers of the Constitution did not envision a president nominated by party conventions, partisan slates of presidential electors, or a Congress organized on the basis of partisanship. Early leaders like Washington, Hamilton, and Madison believed that parties would be divisive and undermine the public interest. Their grand design was not to create "a system of party government under a constitution but rather a constitutional government that would check and control parties."[1] Fearing the impending rise of parties, Washington's Farewell Address in 1796 sounded a warning call against parties.

> [The Spirit of party] serves always to distract the Public Councils and enfeeble the Public administration. It agitates the Community with illfounded jealousies and false alarms, kindles the animosity of one party against another, foments occasional riot and insurrection. It opens the door to foreign influence and corruption, which find a facilitated access to the government itself through the channels of party passions. . . .

Such misgivings about parties have remained a persistent element of the American political culture. Early in the twentieth century, when party conflict had been institutionalized, progressive reformers succeeded in imposing upon parties severe regulations which have stripped them of such functions as control of the nominating process. In the 1970s, Congress passed legislation that aided their rivals—the political action committees. A strong strain of apprehension and dissatisfaction concerning the role of political parties continues to flourish among the citizenry. A 1996 Voter

News Service (VNS) exit poll found that 56 percent of Americans preferred to have the presidency and Congress controlled by different parties. And in a 1994 National Election Study, almost 40 percent of respondents said they would prefer having candidates run without party labels.[2] Thus from the beginning of the Republic to the present, political parties have functioned in an environment that is not altogether hospitable. American parties may have evolved into durable institutions that command substantial numbers of adherents, but the public retains a feeling of distrust, or at least suspicion.

The First Party System 1788–1824: Federalists, Republicans, and One Party Factionalism

American parties were born in the policy conflict between Hamilton and Jefferson during the Washington administration. As their disputes intensified, each turned to his supporters within the Congress, and factional alliances between leaders of the executive and legislative branches developed. The emerging parties, therefore, developed out of national divisions, not state politics. It was, however, the Jeffersonians who first sought to broaden their operations beyond the nation's capital by endorsing candidates for Congress and presidential elector. Later they developed slates of candidates for state offices.[3] The Federalists, led by Hamilton and Adams, were forced to follow suit and compete for support within the mass electorate. The Federalists, however, were reluctant party organizers whose initial reaction to the party organizing activities of Jefferson's Democratic-Republicans was to bemoan their rivals' appeals to the public. As Hamilton noted, the Federalists "erred in relying so much on the rectitude and utility of their measures as to have neglected the cultivation of popular favor by fair and justifiable expedients."[4] Historians are in general agreement that the dramatic extension of party organizations at the local level in the election of 1800 and the aggressive organizing of the Democratic-Republicans in support of Jefferson contributed to his election over John Adams.[5] The nomination of presidential candidates by party caucuses in Congress is further evidence of the emergence of party organizations.

The Federalists were advocates of a positive national government capable of nation building and the protection of American

Table 2.1
Party Systems in American History

Party System	Dates	Competing Parties	Characteristics/Comments
First Party System	1788–1824	Federalist vs. Democratic-Republicans	Parties emerge in 1790s. One party factionalism within Democratic-Republican party after 1820.
Second Party System	1828–1854	Democrats vs. Whigs	Balanced two party competition, with Democrats the dominant party.
Third Party System	1856–1896	Republicans vs. Democrats	Republican dominance from 1862–1874, balanced two party competition from 1874–1896. Sectionalism in political conflict.
Fourth Party System	1896–1928	Republicans vs. Democrats	Republican dominance except for period of intraparty schism in 1912. Continued sectionalism.
Fifth Party System	1932–1968	Republicans vs. Democrats	Democratic dominance and formation of the New Deal Democratic coalition; in the 1950s, the coalition starts to fray and the era of divided party control of the government begins.
Sixth Party System	1968–		Weakened partisanship among the voters; candidate-centered politics; blacks becoming overwhelmingly Democratic; southern whites shift to the Republicans; split ticket voting; divided government; after the 1994 elections, the Republicans regain control of Congress for the first time since 1954.

business interests. In foreign affairs, they sided with the British against the revolutionary regime of France. In terms of electoral bases of support, the Federalists tended to be the established leadership strata in most of the states, while their challengers were Jeffersonians. Federalists were distinguished by being persons of old wealth, respectable occupations, and higher levels of formal education. By contrast, the Democratic-Republicans tended to draw support from less elite elements of society. They were fearful of the strong national government emerging under the Federalists and were protectors of agricultural interests. They were aligned with the French in foreign affairs.

Federalist electoral support suffered a precipitous decline after their defeat in 1800. This decline is related to their failure, as the party of the American elite, to respond in as timely a manner as the Democratic-Republicans to the popular and democratic style of politics that was developing.[6] After 1816, the Federalists disappeared as a national political party capable of contesting for the presidency and competed only in a few states such as Massachusetts and Delaware. The Jeffersonians were triumphant and the first era of partisan competition was over. The "Era of Good Feeling" which followed was a period of partyless politics characterized by factionalism among leaders all of whom claimed to be Republicans. Since all elected officials belonged to one party, it was impossible for President James Monroe to exercise any party discipline over Congress and coherent action by Congress became impossible to achieve.

Factionalism within the dominant Democratic-Republican party led to the collapse of the congressional caucus system of presidential nominations. Since there was no opposition party, the winner of the caucus nomination was assured of election. The congressional caucus, however, had never been popular. It was seen more and more as an undemocratic device as the franchise was extended to all white males due to the dropping of property owning restrictions on voting by the states. In 1824, when the congressional caucus nominated William Crawford for president, it was inevitable that other ambitious politicians would challenge Crawford in the general election. The 1824 election became a four way contest between Crawford, John Quincy Adams, Andrew Jackson, and Henry Clay. As a result, no candidate received a majority in the electoral college. The House of Representatives, after much bickering and maneuvering, finally chose Adams. His administration was characterized by intense intraparty conflict between his followers and those of Jackson. The "Era of Good Feeling" was at an end and the expanded electorate stood ready for political mobilization by political parties.

As Everett Carll Ladd has noted, this First Party System was differentiated from those which have followed by the fact that neither Federalists nor Democratic-Republicans were born into families with these affiliations. There were no traditional party loyalties upon which to build electoral support and sustain parties. Political activists had not had their party identification passed on to them by parents and friends through reinforcing patterns of interaction.

> . . . The absence of inherited loyalties in the new party system of the first period, together with the rudimentary character of party organization and the prevailing tendency to see party as, at best, a necessary evil, made the new party growth relatively superficial. The roots of party simply did not run deep.[7]

The Second Party System, 1828-1854: Democrats versus Whigs in Two Party Competitive Politics

Andrew Jackson, the popular hero of the Battle of New Orleans, defeated Adams in 1828 and gained reelection over Clay in 1832. These elections were fought in a transitional era of bifactional politics within the dominant Democratic-Republican party. Jackson and Adams in 1828 both used variations on the Republican name as their party labels as did Clay in 1832, when Jackson switched to the Democratic label. By 1834 the amalgam of forces and groups opposed to Jackson's policies had coalesced sufficiently to form an opposition party, the Whigs. An era of unusually close two party competition followed.

This Second Party System came into being during a period when American political life was democratized: slates of presidential electors were popularly elected; property qualifications for voting were dropped; and electoral participation increased dramatically. For example, voter turnout increased from 26.9 percent of eligible voters in 1824 to 78.9 percent in 1848.[8] Party nominating procedures were also opened to wider participation as the congressional caucus was replaced by the national convention.

In the two decades that followed Jackson's reelection in 1832, the Whigs and Democrats were engaged in an intense struggle for the newly expanded electorate. They engaged in popularized campaigning—torchlight parades, rallies, picnics, campaign songs, and slogans like "Tippecanoe and Tyler too." Both parties organized state and local parties and ran full slates of candidates under a party label. In this atmosphere of partisan mobilization, voters began to see themselves as either Whigs or Democrats.[9] Unlike the Federalists, who had been reluctant to court popular support, the Whigs did so with zeal. As the national minority party, one of their favorite techniques was to run military heroes with an appeal above party for president. They did this in four of six elections and were successful twice—in 1840 with William Henry Harrison and in 1848 with Zachary Taylor. In nine of eleven elections, however, the majority Democrats won control of the Congress.

Both the Democrats and the Whigs were truly national parties which engaged in relatively close competition not only at the national level but also in each region and in most states. For example, such old bastions of Jefferson's as Georgia, North Carolina, Louisiana, and Tennessee divided their support quite evenly between the Whigs and Democrats as did the Middle Atlantic states. Ladd has observed that in the 1836–1852 period, the "United States had less regional variation in voting than at any other time in history."[10] This lack of sectionalism in American politics was a tribute to the skills of Democratic and Whig leaders in balancing the interests of farmers, manufacturing and mercantile interests, nativists, immigrants, Catholics, and Protestants. Both parties were broad coalitions which sought backing throughout the country, with the Whigs attracting proportionately more support from manufacturing and trading interests, planters, and old Protestant stock, while the Democrats did well among newly enfranchised voters, western farmers, Catholics, and new immigrants.

The absence of highly salient issues that might have divided the nation along sectional lines also contributed to the ability of the two parties to compete in all regions. However, when the racial and slavery issues reached crisis proportions in the 1850s, the Whigs and Democrats were confronted with a nation divided along sectional lines. This national schism was reflected in the parties which split on a North-South axis because neither was able to satisfy both regions. America then entered its Third Party System.

The Third Party System, 1856–1896: Ascendant Republicans versus Democrats

Culturally and economically the South became increasingly distinct from the rest of the nation during the 1840s and 1850s. While abolitionist sentiment gained support in the North, demonstrating the force of a compelling moral issue, the South continued to harbor the institution of slavery. In addition, the two regions' economies were developing quite differently. The South concentrated almost exclusively on agriculture, especially cotton, while the North was becoming more industrial, urban, and mixed in its ethnic composition. In addition, the population and wealth of the North were growing at a much more rapid rate than those of the South. These economic and cultural differences inevitably led to political conflicts over the direction of national policy. The sectional rivalries created by those differences came into their sharpest conflict because of the ceaseless westward expansion of the nation. Western settlement required the Congress and the parties to confront the issues of whether slavery would be permitted in the territories and whether the new states would be admitted as slave or free states. Any change in the number of free and slave states threatened to upset the delicate balance of power in the national government. Both the Whigs and Democrats were unable to reconcile the sectional conflicts within their ranks and as a result the electorate went through a major realignment in the 1850s and 1860s.

The Democrats' situation was made difficult by the powerful position occupied by its southern wing. In Congress, the Democrats were dominated by southerners determined to maintain the institution of slavery and protect the political position of the South by insisting that the balance of free and slave states not be upset when new states were admitted to the Union. The South was also strengthened by the two-thirds rule used by the Democratic national nominating conventions. This procedure guaranteed the South a veto over the selection of presidential nominees. As a result, the party could only agree to nominate weak "neutralist" or "doughface" candidates like Franklin Pierce (1852) and James Buchanan (1856). With weak presidents and a southern led Congress, it was not possible for the government to resolve the slavery issue.

In the midst of this sectional turmoil over the extension of slavery, the Whig party dissolved. The Whigs had traditionally been the party of national integration and accommodation between the North and South. But with the intensification of northern hostility toward slavery and heightened sectional sentiments in the South, the Whigs' position was undermined in both regions. Faced with declining electoral support, a schism between its northern and southern wings, and the emergence of the antislavery Republican party in the North, the Whig party ceased to be a major electoral force after the elections of 1854.[11]

There was a transition period toward two party competition between the Republicans and Democrats between 1854 and 1860. In the presidential election of 1856, the new Republican party—composed of abolitionists, Free Soilers, and dissident northern Whigs and Democrats—came in second to Democrats, as James Buchanan defeated General John C. Fremont. The remaining Whigs nominated former President Millard Fillmore under the American party banner and came in a dismal third. No candidate received a majority of the popular vote. The deterioration of the old party system continued in 1860. In the North, the election was a contest between the nominee of Northern Democrats, Stephen A. Douglas, and former Whig, Abraham Lincoln, the Republican nominee; while in the South, southern Democrat John C. Breckenridge contested a former southern Whig, John Bell. Again, no candidate received a popular vote majority, though Lincoln was able to gain 59.4 percent of the electoral vote with 39.8 percent of the popular vote.

The period of 1864–1874 was a period of Republican dominance. The successful prosecution of the Civil War identified the GOP with the Union, patriotism and humanitarianism. But Republican strength did not rest on emotionalism alone. The party forged an alliance of farmers through the Homestead Act and free land in the West, business and labor through support for a high protective tariff, entrepreneurs through federal land grants to build transcontinental railroads linking the West and North (and bypassing the South), and veterans through pensions. By imposing Reconstruction upon the South, the post–Civil War Radical Republicans in Congress sought to control the South through black votes and the support of carpetbaggers. Both parties were sectional parties. The GOP was dominant in the North and West, but it had little popular support in the South. The Democrats, by contrast, were a southern based party. The party's addiction to free trade did, however, give it some northern business allies among those who shared its views on trade.[12] In addition, the Democrats gained substantial support among Roman Catholic immigrants in cities of the North. After 1874 and the end of Reconstruction, the Republicans and Democrats started to compete on a more even basis up until 1896. They alternated control of the presidency and Congress, but the post-Civil War period was primarily an era of Republican dominance in national political life.

In addition to the disappearance of the Whigs and the emergence of the Republicans as the dominant political party, two other significant developments came from the era of the Third Party System. One was the growth, particularly in the middle Atlantic and some midwestern states and cities, of patronage-based party organizations or machines that were extremely effective in controlling nominations and mobilizing party votes on election day.[13] Ironically, the Third Party System was also the era that ushered in the party machine weakening reform of the Australian ballot (ballots printed at government expense instead of party printed ballots, and provision for casting one's vote in secret). The Australian ballot movement gave the voter new independence from parties in making electoral choices. It was no longer public knowledge how people voted and using government provided ballots made it easier for citizens to split their ballots and vote for candidates of differing parties.

The Fourth Party System, 1896–1928: Republican Dominance Renewed

The period following the Civil War was a period of immense social and economic change with far-reaching consequences for electoral politics. It was a time when the United States ceased to be a primarily agrarian society and became an industrialized and urban nation. By 1890 more people were employed in manufacturing than in agriculture, and by the end of the 1920s only one family in four was involved in agriculture. On the eve of the Civil War, no American city had contained a million people, but by the close of the 1920s cities with a population in excess of a million inhabitants were becoming commonplace—New York, Chicago, Philadelphia, and Los Angeles. Transportation advances, like the completion of the great transcontinental railroads, linked the East and West and made the nation more interdependent. Rail mileage grew from 8,500 in 1850 to 193,000 in 1900. This was also the era of the rise of the corporation—mammoth enterprises like Standard Oil and U.S. Steel. The ethnic makeup of the population also changed as waves of immigrants entered the country from non–English-speaking nations of Europe.

The economic and social revolution that was transforming America posed new problems for the political system. Radical agrarian movements swept the nation (e.g., the Grangers Farmers' Alliance, and Greenbackers). Third party movements also formed. The most significant was the People's party (Populist), which in 1892 garnered over one million votes and twenty-two electoral votes on a radical platform that demanded the inflation of the currency through unlimited coinage of silver, nationalization of railroads and telephone/telegraph companies, and instituting an income tax. These movements reflected the economic dislocations that were occurring and agrarian discontent with the growing power of corporations and the frequently depressed state of the farm economy. The late 1800s also witnessed the rise of labor organizations which mirrored the discontent of urban workers with their status in the new industrial order.

Neither the dominant Republicans nor the "me too" Democrats were responsive initially to these popular protest movements. In 1896, however, the forces of agrarian radicalism captured the Democratic presidential nomination for William Jennings Bryan, whose platform was a challenge to the existing industrial order. A key plank in the Democrats' platform was a call for free and unlimited coinage of silver and gold at a ratio of sixteen to one. In adopting this position, the Democrats appropriated the principal program of the Populists and made a dramatic appeal to farmers, debtors, and western mining interests. The Democrats were also the party of a low tariff.

Seeking to bolster their post–Civil War coalition, the Republicans countered by advocating the gold standard and opposition to the inflationary free coinage of silver; and they maintained their position as the party of the high protective tariff. Their stand on the silver issue cost them the support of western states, but the high protective tariff position brought them renewed support among urban workers, who blamed the depression of the 1890s on the low tariff policies of the Democratic Cleveland administration. William McKinley, the Republican candidate, was able to run on the themes of "Prosperity—Sound Money—Good Markets and Employment for Labor—A Full Dinner Bucket." Mark Hanna, the Ohio industrialist and skilled Republican campaign manager, also mobilized business interests terrified by Bryan and his policies to give generous and overwhelming support to the GOP issue.

The election of 1896 transformed the political landscape and realigned the electorate. The Republican coalition forged during and after the Civil War received an infusion of support, especially among urban dwellers of the Northeast. McKinley carried the nation's ten largest cities and increased the GOP vote in working, middle, and upper class wards. Bryan was the sectional candidate of the agrarian South, the Plains, the silver mining states of the West. He had little appeal to the industrializing East and Middle West, where the bulk of the population and electoral votes were located. V. O. Key has observed that the Democratic loss of 1896 "was so demoralizing and so thorough that the party made little headway in regrouping its forces until 1916."[14] Indeed, the Democrats elected only one president in the period between 1896 and 1928, and Woodrow Wilson's 1912 election was possible only because of a major schism within the dominant Republican coalition.

In that year, the festering internal Republican conflict between the traditional conservatives of the industrial-financial centers of the Northeast and the Progressive reformers of the Middle West and West broke wide open. Theodore Roosevelt, after failing to capture the GOP nomination from President William Howard Taft, ran as a candidate of the Progressive party. Roosevelt split the Republican vote and actually outpolled Taft in popular votes (27.4 percent to 23.2 percent). This division permitted a brief Democratic interlude under Wilson. After World War I, the fire was out of the progressive movement and Americans yearned for normalcy. In this postwar atmosphere, the Republicans asserted their dominance with impressive victories in 1920, 1924, and 1928. Although the Republicans won the election of 1928, the election returns gave evidence of expanding Democratic strength. The Democratic percentage of the popular vote jumped from 28.8 in 1924 to 40.8 in 1928, and the party's presidential ticket carried Massachusetts and Rhode Island, an indication of its approval to

Sectionalism in American Politics during the Post–Civil War Era and Early Twentieth Century

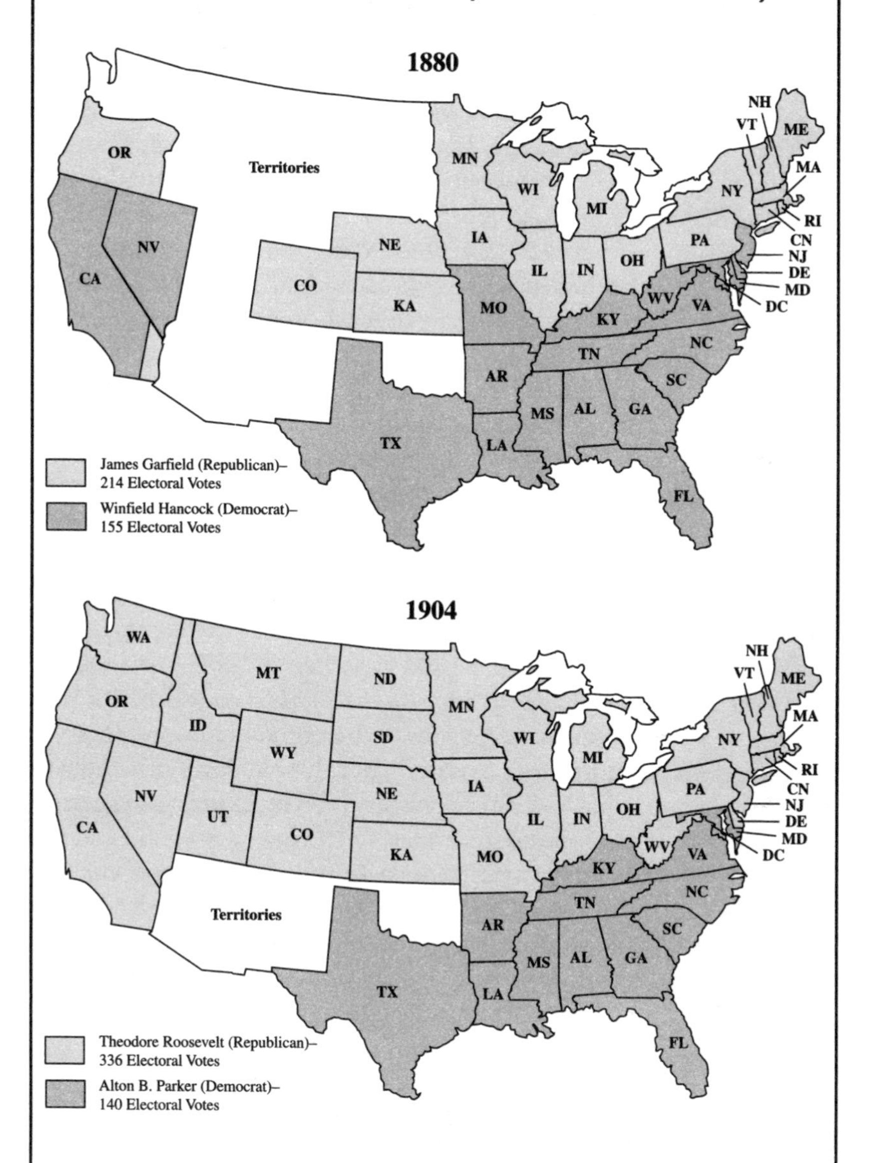

As these maps showing the outcomes of the presidential elections in 1880 and 1904 demonstrate, the legacies of the Civil War and Reconstruction plus the distinctive cultures and economies of the North and South helped to forge a party system characterized by *sectionalism.* The South was a one party Democratic region, and the Republicans tended to be dominant in the North.

voters in Catholic, urban, and industrial centers. Democratic support was thus developing in the growing metropolitan and manufacturing centers, while the GOP tended to be dominant in northern and eastern rural precincts.[15]

The Fourth Party System was an era of diminished interparty competition. In the seven presidential elections after 1896, the average Republican share of the national two party vote was 57.7 percent, while the Democrats received 42.3 percent. In four of these elections the gap between the Republican and Democratic vote exceeded ten percentage points—the usual definition of a landslide. This was in sharp contrast to the evenness of competition between 1876 and 1896, when in 1880, 1884, and 1892, less than one percentage point separated the two parties' share of the popular vote for president. The post-1896 lack of competitiveness was also reflected in state elections. Regional voting patterns were sharply differentiated. The South, especially after the disenfranchisement of blacks via devices like the poll tax and white primary, became even more overwhelmingly Democratic. In the rest of the nation, however, the Republicans were dominant. In 22 states of the North and West, the Republicans received more than 60 percent of the vote on average in the presidential elections from 1896 to 1928.[16]

The Progressive reform movement of this period had a profound impact on American parties, even though the progressives never succeeded in forming a major party. It was during the Fourth Party System era that the direct primary was instituted as the principal method of nominating candidates. The primary weakened the capacity of parties to control the nominating process and enabled candidates to make direct appeals to the voters. The presidential primary was also born in this period. Another major change in the legal environment of parties was the imposition of governmental regulation, primarily by the states. Primary laws frequently regulated party organizational structure, and campaign finance was also brought within the purview of the law. Parties became quasipublic agencies subject to legislative control.[17]

The Fifth Party System, 1932–1968: The Democratic New Deal Era

President Herbert Hoover had been in office less than a year when the stock market crash signaled the beginning of the Great

Depression of the 1930s. The election of 1932 was a major benchmark in American political history. It marked a realignment of the electorate from a Republican to a Democratic majority. The New Deal coalition that supported Franklin D. Roosevelt was formed. Like the old Republican coalition, the new Democratic majority was an amalgam of disparate and sometimes conflicting elements. White southerners, still wedded to the cause of white supremacy, were a core group, as were Catholic urban workers, mostly recent immigrant stock from eastern and southern Europe, who had been socialized to political life by the urban political machines. These Catholic voters had also been drawn to the Democratic banner by the antiprohibitionist candidacy of a coreligionist, Governor Al Smith of New York, in 1928. Blue collar workers, especially organized labor, rallied to support Roosevelt in the face of rising unemployment. Blacks forsook the party of Lincoln to back the Democrats, since the already economically depressed black society was severely rocked by the Depression. Jews, who heretofore had been predominantly Republican, also became identified with the Democratic party because of the Depression and Roosevelt's leadership against Nazi Germany. In addition, young people entering the ranks of the electorate in the 1930s and 1940s became Democrats. The Democrats were riding a wave of demographic change. Urban ethnics, Catholics, blue collar workers, and blacks were becoming a more and more significant proportion of the electorate; while the traditional Republican base of white Protestants, small town residents, farmers, and middle class businessmen constituted a shrinking share of the population.

Franklin Roosevelt's election and his New Deal social welfare policies, which instituted an American version of the welfare state, had long-run weakening consequences for the traditional, patronage based, urban party organizations. New social insurance programs (like Social Security and unemployment compensation) were effectively insulated from patronage-type politics and served as models for later federal grant-in-aid programs that emphasized professionalism in state and local government.[18] The New Deal social welfare programs not only weakened the patronage base of the machines, they also took from the machines their traditional function of providing welfare services to the deprived urban populations.

The New Deal Democratic electoral coalition forged by Roosevelt proved to be an enduring alliance. Between 1932 and

1948, the Democrats won the White House all five times and only lost control of the Congress once, in 1946. Divisions within the dominant coalition, however, appeared as early as the late 1930s when conservative southern Democratic representatives and senators began to dissent from Roosevelt's social welfare policies. The North-South split within the party became even more pronounced after 1948 and into the 1960s when northern Democratic leaders like Senator Hubert Humphrey (Minn.) led the party into taking a strong stand on civil rights issues.

Throughout the period since the 1930s, the Republican party has remained the minority party. At least twice, after electoral disasters in 1936 and 1964, it was written off by political commentators as terminally ill. Its obituaries were prepared prematurely, however, because each time the party staged a timely comeback demonstrating the resiliency of two party competition in the United States. In 1952, Republicans used a strategy long favored by minority parties to help them win the presidency and Congress. Like the Whigs of 1840 and 1848, the GOP nominated a national hero, General Dwight D. Eisenhower, the charismatic commander of Allied forces in Europe during World War II. Running on the slogan "I like Ike," the Republicans made major inroads into all elements of the New Deal coalition, while holding the traditional Republican vote. Particularly noteworthy was Eisenhower's support in the heretofore solidly Democratic South, where he carried such states of the old Confederacy as Virginia, Texas, Florida, and Tennessee. The Eisenhower years proved to be a period of consolidation in American politics. The new Republican administration and Congress did not move to repeal the policies of the New Deal. Rather, they accepted the New Deal programs and made only minor modifications. With this Republican acceptance, the Roosevelt New Deal legacy ceased to be the divisive force in American politics that it had been. One of Eisenhower's Republican successors, Ronald Reagan, could even be heard praising and quoting Roosevelt in the 1980s.

Running on a theme of "Peace and Prosperity," Eisenhower swept to an even more overwhelming victory in 1956. The election, however, confirmed the continuing minority status of the GOP, which lost seats in the House and Senate despite the landslide election of the President. The normal Democratic majority reasserted itself in 1960 and 1964 with the elections of John F. Kennedy and

Lyndon B. Johnson. The huge congressional majorities which Johnson carried into office with him in 1964 enabled the party to enact his Great Society programs—a massive expansion of social welfare assistance, which was carried out largely through extensive grant-in-aid programs to state and local governments. After the Democrats' landslide win of 1964, however, the divisions within the Democratic party intensified as the party split over such issues as race relations, the Vietnam war, defense policy, crime and civil disorder, and social policy.

The Sixth Party System: 1968–? The Post–New Deal Era—Weakened Partisanship, Candidate-Centered Politics, and Divided Government

The period from 1964 through 1968 was a transition period into a post–New Deal party system. Between 1952 and 1964, there was little change in the aggregate distribution of partisanship among the electorate. This steady state of electoral partisanship, however, underwent significant changes during the mid to late 1960s. Among the significant changes were the following: (1) black voters increased their political participation levels and increased their affiliation with the Democratic party, resulting in the virtual disappearance of Republican identification as Democratic presidents endorsed civil rights legislation and the 1964 GOP presidential nominee, Barry Goldwater, opposed it; (2) partisanship declined as more voters identified themselves as independents and tended not to see the relevance of parties; (3) white southerners, once a mainstay of the Democratic electoral coalition, moved into the Republican fold; and (4) support for the Democrats declined among its other traditional support groups such as Catholics and blue collar workers.[19] In addition, television, an information source that tends to discourage rather than encourage stable party loyalties, became the dominant campaign medium.[20]

The coming together of these forces in the 1960s helped to create and institutionalize, in the 1980s and 1990s, a *candidate-centered party system,* in which neither the Republicans nor the Democrats constituted a true majority party, and voters were heavily guided by candidate appeals. The Democrats lost the majority status they had from the New Deal to President Lyndon Johnson's Great Society era in the early 1960s; and the Republicans, while having staged a comeback, were not able to pick up the majority party mantle from the Democrats.

This absence of a party commanding the loyalties of a majority of voters sets the current party system apart from previous party systems that did have dominant majority parties among the voters. The declining impact of partisanship within the electorate can be seen in a comparison of pre- and post-1960s eras. Thus, an analysis of presidential elections from 1840 until 1960 shows that changes in the vote from one election to the next were due primarily to differences in the ability of the parties to mobilize their partisan identifiers rather than the conversion of voters from supporting one party to supporting the other.[21] Beginning in the 1960s, however, such conversions became the principal force causing interelection vote shifts. This change has been attributed primarily to the ability of candidates to appeal directly to the public and to woo voters away from the opposition. The candidate-centered nature of elections is also clearly in evidence at the congressional level. Students of congressional elections have found that up until 1960, there was no systematic personal advantage attached to being an incumbent. However, after 1960 there has been sustained advantage attached to incumbency.[22] Indeed, in House elections at least 90 percent of the incumbents normally win reelection, and Senate incumbents' reelection statistics are not far below those of their House colleagues.

An additional indicator of the weakening of party ties among voters has been the emergence of unusually strong third party and independent candidates in four presidential elections during the post–New Deal era. Even before Ross Perot became a household word in 1992 (capturing the largest vote percentage of any non–major party candidate since Theodore Roosevelt in 1912) and 1996, there was Governor George Wallace's (Ala.) 1968 run for the presidency, which garnered 13.5 percent of the vote and carried five deep South states with forty-six electoral votes, as well as Representative John B. Anderson's (Ill.) 1980 independent candidacy that netted 7.1 percent of the voters but no electoral votes.

With voters guided less than in the past by partisanship, split-ticket voting has become commonplace and divided party control of the presidency and Congress a regular occurrence. Thus, in twenty of the thirty years between Richard Nixon's first election in 1968 and the mid-point of Bill Clinton's second term in 1998, different parties have controlled the White House and at least one chamber of the Congress. A similar pattern has emerged at the state level, where divided government also occurs on a regular basis.

In this era of candidate-centered politics, party organizations neither control the nomination process nor run their nominees' campaigns. Rather, the parties play the role of providing services, particularly money, to their candidates. As result, the sixth American party system has been characterized by political scientist John H. Aldrich as one in which the parties operate in service to their candidates.[23]

Minor Parties in American Politics

The presidential candidacies of Ross Perot in 1992 and 1996 and the formation of his Reform party plus the election of non–major party governors in four states during the 1990s have sparked renewed interest in minor parties. These events are a reminder that the United States does not have a pure two-party system, since in every election year minor parties run candidates for president (fourteen in 1996). Some of these parties have long histories, for example, the Socialist and Prohibition parties. However, such doctrinal parties are not operating elements of the party system. They are, instead, like "rivulets alongside the main stream of party life" maintaining an "isolated existence."[24] Similarly, the so-called new parties, such as the Green, Libertarian, and Right-to-Life parties, which have distinctive cultural orientations, also operate largely outside the mainstream of American politics. There has been, however, a steady current of "recurring short-lived, minor party eruptions" that have been closely tied to the party system.[25] Only the Republican party, which replaced the Whigs between 1854 and 1856, when the nation was in the throes of a sectional split over slavery, has ever achieved major party status. Most have been short-lived, and none has had a realistic chance of electing a president. The most successful third party or independent presidential candidacies were those of Theodore Roosevelt (Progressive party, 27 percent of vote) in 1912; Ross Perot (independent, 18.9 percent of the vote) in 1992, and George Wallace (American Independent party, 13.5 percent of the vote) in 1968.

Significant Third Party Eruptions and Independent Candidates

Since the early days of the republic, there have been periodic third party eruptions that have raised important issues and affected future electoral alignments, election outcomes, and the nature of the party system. Although frequent, these third party movements have been short-lived, and only one, the Republican party, which emerged between 1854 and 1856, achieved major party status. Few had success winning more than a small number of electoral votes. In the post–World War II years, there has been an increase in the number of independent presidential candidates, and even candidates who have formed third parties have run highly personalized campaigns without a real party organization supporting them or a full slate of candidates for other offices.

Anti-Masonic Party. The Anti-Masons were America's first third party and an early manifestation of fundamentalist Christian distrust of the establishment and secularism. The party is best remembered for instituting the national convention in 1831 as the method for nominating presidential candidates. In 1833, it merged with the National Republicans to form the Whig party.

Free Soil Party. Formed in 1848, the Free Soilers opposed the extension of slavery in newly acquired territories and advocated a homestead act to provide free land to settlers. By 1854, the party had been absorbed into the newly formed Republican party.

American (Know Nothing) Party. This was an anti-immigrant and anti-Catholic party that achieved electoral successes at the state level in 1854 as the old Democratic-Whig party system was collapsing. Amid the sectional turmoil of the pre–Civil War period, it quickly faded out of existence.

Constitutional Union Party. An offshoot of the Whig party composed of conservatives opposed to the candidacy of Abraham Lincoln in 1860, the Constitutional Union party carried three southern states and then dissolved amid secession of the South and the Civil War.

Southern Democratic Party. This was a splinter party reflecting the schism between the northern and southern wings of the Democratic party in 1860. Its presidential nominee carried most of the southern states and garnered seventy-two electoral votes. The party dissolved after the secession of the South.

Liberal Republican Party. As a party of dissident Republican reformers opposed to Reconstruction and the corruption of the Grant administration, the Liberal Republicans nominated *New York Tribune* editor Andrew Greeley as their presidential nominee. Greeley was also endorsed and nominated by the Democrats, but the alliance's weak showing in 1872 led to its breakup and the disbanding of the Liberal Republicans.

People's (Populist) Party. As an agrarian radical movement that swept across the West and South during the farm depression of the 1890s, the Populists called for government ownership of railroads, free coinage of silver, an income tax, and an eight-hour work day. Its presidential candidate carried five states in 1892. Four years later Populists captured control of the Democratic national convention and nominated William Jennings Bryan.

Progressive (Bull Moose) Party of 1912. The Bull Moose Progressive party was Theodore Roosevelt's vehicle to regain the presidency after he was denied the GOP nomination by President William Howard Taft. Roosevelt's candidacy reflected the split between the progressive and stalwart wings of the Republican party. By coming in second in the popular voting, Roosevelt split the Republican vote and enabled the Democratic candidate, Woodrow Wilson, to be elected with 42 percent of the vote. Roosevelt returned to the GOP four years later.

Progressive Party of 1924. Led by Senator Robert La Follette of Wisconsin, the Progressives sought to build a base of farmer and labor supporters with a program calling for government ownership of railroads, protection for organized labor, direct primaries, and approval of wars by referendums. La Follette carried only his home state and died shortly after the election. His party died with him.

continued ➔

Significant Third Party Eruptions and Independent Candidates (continued)

States' Rights Party of 1948. The so-called Dixiecrats were a splinter group of southern Democrats opposed to their party's strong civil rights plank. They made no attempt to organize a separate party but, instead, used the existing southern Democratic state party machinery. The Dixiecrats returned to the Democratic fold after the election, in which they carried four states.

American Independent Party of 1968. With the Democratic party wracked by internal dissension over civil rights, law and order, and the Vietnam War, Alabama Governor George Wallace emerged as the candidate of segregationist, traditionalist, and anti-Washington elements of the electorate. He won five southern states and made inroads among blue collar workers, but in 1972 he returned to the Democratic party.

Independent John B. Anderson of 1980. After failing to win the Republican nomination, the moderate GOP congressman from Illinois ran as an independent seeking to be a centrist candidate between Republican Ronald Reagan on the right and Democrat Jimmy Carter on the left. Even though he lacked an organization, adequate financing, and a compelling issue, he won 6.6 percent of the vote. He retired from politics after the election.

H. Ross Perot, Independent in 1992 and Reform Party Candidate in 1996. Taking advantage of public disenchantment with the major party nominees in 1992, the Texas billionaire mounted a personally financed campaign for the presidency that emphasized the dangers of a huge federal budget deficit. He collected the largest percentage of popular vote (18.9) since Teddy Roosevelt in 1912, but he did not win a single electoral vote. For the 1996 campaign, Perot created and funded his own party, the Reform party, but saw his popular vote fall to 8.4 percent.

Source: John F. Bibby and L. Sandy Maisel, *Two parties—Or More? The American Party System* (Boulder, Colo.: Westview Press, 1998).

The Impact and Role of Minor Parties

Third party protests have been closely associated with the early stages of every major electoral realignment since the 1830s and hence have been called a "protorealignment phenomenon."[26] On these occasions, the rise of third parties has reflected the inability of the major parties to meet expectations of large segments of the public. Thus, the Free Soil (1848) party arose prior to the collapse of the Whigs and the emergence of the Republicans; the Populist eruption in 1892 occurred before the landmark realigning election of 1896 between McKinley and Bryan; the La Follette Progressive movement of 1924 was a precursor to the creation of the New Deal Democratic coalition in the 1930s; and the Dixiecrat (States' Rights party) revolt of southern Democrats in 1948 and George Wallace's run for the presidency as the American Independent party candidate in 1968 foreshadowed the weakening of the New Deal Democratic coalition and the beginning of the sixth party system.

Third party and independent candidates have also helped to give prominence to certain issues and forced these issues onto the public agenda when the major parties were unwilling to confront them. For example, the Free Soilers on the slavery issue; the Populists on the plight of farmers of the Great Plains and West; the Progressives of 1912 and 1924 on the economic dislocations created by industrialization and urbanization; and Perot (1992) on huge federal budget deficits. However, it is possible to overstate the extent to which third parties advocate and build public support for causes that the major parties are then forced to adopt as their own. Thus, it is commonly asserted that the Socialist party's advocacy of such policies as a minimum wage law for over twenty years led to its becoming a part of Franklin Roosevelt's New Deal program. Yet, as Paul Allen Beck has observed, "Unfortunately, there is no way of testing what might have happened had there been no Socialist party," and one of the lessons of party history is that "major parties grasp new programs and proposals in their 'time of ripeness' when large numbers of Americans have done so and when such a course is therefore useful to the parties."[27]

Furthermore, new issues in their incubation period do not depend exclusively upon minor parties. Interest groups, the mass media, prominent citizens, and factions *within* the parties can also be more effective than minor parties in issue advocacy. It is widely accepted, for example, that an interest group, the Anti-Saloon

League, was a far more powerful force in the enactment of Prohibition than was the Prohibition Party.[28]

Minor Parties at the State Level

The partisan alignment of voters at the state level has tended to follow the national pattern. During the long domination of electoral politics by the Republicans and Democrats since the 1850s, state politics has been a struggle mainly between the Democrats and the GOP just as it has been for the presidency and Congress. State party organizations, though primarily concerned about winning state level offices, have made effective use of their parties' national followings in state races. However, there have been several minor parties of consequence existing on their own local bases of support rather than as extensions or offshoots of minor parties at the national level. In several instances, these parties achieved electoral success before withering or being absorbed into the major parties.

Minnesota's Farmer-Labor Party. This party was created in the 1920s by Populists who mobilized hard-pressed farmers and laborers to challenge the state's dominant Republican party. It was so successful that it temporarily replaced the Democrats as the Republicans' principal opposition, thereby creating a three-party system in the states. In 1930, the Farmer-Labor alliance even won the governorship. However, in the 1940s, the pull of national political alignments overcame the party, and after suffering successive defeats, it merged with the Democrats to form the Democratic Farmer-Labor (DFL) party.

Wisconsin's Progressive Party. Like Minnesota, Wisconsin also had a brief interlude when a third party, led by the sons of Robert La Follette, the 1924 Progressive presidential candidate, emerged to challenge the Republicans and Democrats. Between 1934 and 1946, the state had a three-party system in which the most meaningful competition took place between the Republicans and the liberal Progressives, who succeeded in winning gubernatorial, senatorial, and congressional elections along with control of the state legislature. Just as the tides of national politics swept over Minnesota in the 1940s, as liberal and labor elements of the electorate were attracted to the national Democratic party, the Progressives found themselves steadily losing supporters. Facing likely defeat for reelection as a third party candidate and in the face of a projected Republican electoral sweep, Senator Robert M. La Follette, Jr., in 1946, decided that pragmatism dictated that the Progressives should disband and move back into the Republican party.

New York's Multiparty System. A distinctive party system has developed in the Empire State due to a type of election law that enhances the status of minor parties and institutionalizes their existence. New York permits candidates to receive the nomination of more than one party. Candidates' names can appear on the ballot under the label of multiple parties. This "cross-filing" or "fusion ticket" arrangement has encouraged various interests to seek leverage over the major parties by creating minor parties. Among the options available to minor parties under cross-filing are nominating the candidate of an allied major party and thereby gaining influence within the major party by providing votes crucial for victory. With the potential to affect election outcomes, the minor parties can pressure an allied party to nominate a favored candidate or face the prospect of the minor party either running a candidate of its own, thereby taking votes away from their normally allied party's nominee. Minor parties in New York also have the option of nominating the candidate of the party with which they are not normally allied. Through the use of these tactics, the Liberal party has exerted substantial influence over its customary ally, the Democrats. The Conservative party and, to a lesser degree, the Right to Life party have become forces to be reckoned with in state Republican politics.

Third Party Governors in the 1990s

In 1990, two well-known former Republican officeholders, Walter Hickel (Ala.) and Lowell Weicker (Conn.), were elected governor in their states on minor party tickets. In spite of these breakthroughs, both men found the problem of sustaining a third party challenge to the major parties a feat bordering on the impossible. Parties such as Hickel's Alaska Independence party and Weicker's A Connecticut party lacked an organizational infrastructure and were overly dependent upon a single, prominent, maverick politician. When these two former Republicans were not on the ballot in 1994, their parties floundered and sank.

Again in 1998, a minor party candidate, Jesse "The Body" Ventura, a former professional wrestler, actor, and suburban mayor, emerged to capture the Minnesota governorship by upsetting the major party nominees, an incumbent Democratic attorney general and a Republican mayor of St. Paul. Ventura's populist, straight talking rhetoric, tough guy image, and showmanship enabled Ross Perot's Reform party to gain its first major electoral victory. However, like the other minor party governors of the 1990s, Ventura faced a legislature controlled by the major parties, a reflection of minor parties' difficulty in recruiting a full slate of credible candidates for the numerous offices below the level of governor.

Some Lessons from Party History

Although this has been but an overview of party history in the United States, it does provide the main contours of party development and permit observations about the nature of the American party system.

The Two Party System: Some Explanations

Although there have been transitional periods characterized by factionalism within the dominant party (1824–1832) and interludes when third parties or independent candidates posed a major threat to the major parties (1892, 1912, 1924, 1992), party competition in the United States has been predominantly of the two party variety. Even when one of the major parties disintegrated, the two party division reestablished itself. And although one party frequently has been overwhelmingly dominant in the national government, the opposition party has been able to retain the loyalty of a sizable segment of the electorate. Despite the prevalence of this pattern of two party competition, scholars have had difficulty explaining the persistence of dualism. Certainly, there is no one cause of the phenomenon.

The Institutional Explanation. The standard American arrangement for electing national and state legislators is the single member district system—whoever receives a plurality of the vote is elected. In contrast to proportional representation, which utilizes multimember districts and rewards all serious parties with its proportionate share of the legislative seats, the single member system permits only one party to win in any given district. It is a system that permits only two parties to have a reasonable chance of victory. Third or minor parties are normally condemned to perpetual defeat—not a prescription for longevity—unless they can combine forces with a larger party. The single member system certainly creates incentives for two broadly based parties capable of winning legislative district pluralities. Experience of other nations—the Third Republic of France, Canada, and the United Kingdom—suggests that single member districts by themselves are not a sufficient answer to the question of why America has two parties. The single member district can only encourage this type of competition.[29]

Two party competition is encouraged by the electoral college system for choosing presidents. Election as president requires an absolute majority of the electoral votes. This requirement makes it unlikely that a third party can ever achieve the presidency without combining with or absorbing another major party. In addition, the states' electoral votes are allocated under a winner-take-all arrangement. All that is required to capture a state's electoral votes is a plurality of the vote in that state. Like the operation of the single member district, this system works to the disadvantage of third parties which have little chance of winning any state's electoral votes, let alone a sufficient number of states to elect a president.

Over and above the formidable difficulties imposed by single member districts and the electoral college stand an array of additional barriers to viable third parties. A particularly imposing barrier is created by the direct primary and the presidential primary systems for nominating candidates. One of the consequences of these highly participatory nominating systems is to channel dissent into the major parties.[30] Unlike other democracies, insurgents and dissidents do not need to form their own parties. Rather, they can avoid these difficulties by running candidates in the primaries of the major parties and through this "burrowing from within" strategy often achieve major party nominations, elective office, and intraparty influence.

The Federal Election Campaign Act (FECA) tends to benefit the major parties at the expense of minor parties. Public funding at the maximum level is available to the presidential nominees of the major parties (defined by the FECA as parties whose candidates received at least 25 percent of the vote for president in the previous election). This amounted to $61.8 million per candidate in 1996. However, minor parties receive a much smaller allocation of public funds for their nominees (e.g., Reform party candidate Ross Perot received $29 million in 1996) and then only if the party received at least 5 percent of the vote in the previous presidential election. In addition, the major parties receive a federal grant to cover the cost of their national conventions.

State regulations and laws can also inhibit minor parties. The Republican and Democratic parties are assured of automatic ballot access (each party's name and candidates appear on the general election ballot) because of their prior success in winning votes. But for new parties and independent candidates, ballot access is anything but automatic. They are required to submit petitions signed by a large number of voters just to get their candidates' names on the ballot. An unusually high hurdle to ballot access was imposed by Pennsylvania in 1997 when it enacted a law requiring a new party to secure over 99,000 signatures on a petition in a fourteen-week period. A large number of states also have "sore loser" laws that prevent candidates who lose primary elections from then running as independent candidates in the general election. Minor parties at the state level are also inhibited by the widespread practice of selecting local candidates through nonpartisan elections in which candidates run without party labels. This weakens the capacity of minor parties to build a local base of support. Nonpartisan local elections were instituted as part of a late nineteenth and early twentieth century reform movement that sought to weaken corrupt local political machines. An additional motive in some states was to thwart the new Socialist parties that were electing mayors in various cities during the first decades of the twentieth century.[31]

Institutional barriers have clearly helped to institutionalize two party electoral competition in the United States. However, this should not obscure a basic political truth: "No electoral system protects major political parties from the electorate."[32] This is a lesson that was forcefully brought home to Canada's Progressive Conservatives after the 1993 election, when they went from being the majority party in the national legislature to minor party status with only two legislative seats. In spite of the fact that Canada, like the United States, uses single member districts to elect its national legislature, America's neighbor to the North has a thriving multiparty system. The Republican party's displacement of the Whigs during the 1854–1860 period demonstrates that a new party can overcome institutional barriers by changing the nation's political agenda. It is, of course, fortunate for the republic, though unfortunate for third parties, that since the 1850s no issue as divisive as slavery has restructured American politics.

The Historical Explanation. This explanation emphasizes the impact of the special circumstances of the initial political conflicts in the new nation and the tendency for human institutions to perpetuate themselves and preserve their initial form. The initial confrontation that the country faced was the issue of ratification of the Constitution, an issue of a yes-no character that tended to divide the nation in a dual manner. The small farmers and debtors of the interior were pitted against the mercantile and financial interests of the coastal regions. The initial lines of cleavage were built upon two great complexes of interests—the agricultural interests and the financial/mercantile interests. Such a dual split was possible because the social and economic structure of society was far less complex and specialized than that of today. Partisan conflict thus began in an era when a dualist cleavage existed. The pattern of two party politics persisted, however, even though the society changed. As V. O. Key has observed:

> The great issues changed from time to time but each party managed to renew itself as it found new followers to replace those it lost. The Civil War, thus, brought a realignment in national politics, yet it re-enforced the dual division. . . . As memories of the war faded new alignments gradually took shape within the matrix of the preexisting structure, with each party hierarchy struggling to maintain its position in the system.[33]

The Cultural Explanation. American society has not been characterized by blocs of people irreconcilably attached to a particular ideology or creed. Racial, religious, and ethnic minorities, though often encountering discrimination, have generally been able to find a niche in society and have not tended toward separatism. Religious tensions have existed, but open conflict has never been common and First Amendment rights have generally enjoyed protection. Nor has class consciousness been as common in the United States as in European nations. Labor parties have had little appeal to American working men and women. In addition, there has been widespread acceptance of the constitutional order and a capitalist economic system.

While diversity abounds within American society, the ingredients for multiparty politics have largely been lacking. No group is seeking to restore the prerogatives of the Church as a state religion; no major group is seriously advocating monarchy, socialism, or communism; a labor party would have few adherents; serious advocates of giving over the ownership of factories and large farms to the workers are scarce. Should such groups exist in significant numbers, multiparty politics would be possible. But in their absence, two party politics is feasible. It is possible for one party to be slightly to the left of center—liberal—and the other to be slightly right of center—conservative—and still gain widespread electoral support. Thus the Democrats and the Republicans can attract divergent cores of support that have quite different policy viewpoints and still compete for the vote of the vast majority of Americans who consider themselves to be middle-of-the-roaders.

It is difficult to assign weights to the three explanations of two party politics that have been discussed above. Clearly, America's form of competition is the result of a combination of forces that have conspired to produce dualism.

Parties as Coalitions

Throughout their history, American parties have been broadly based coalitions. Both majority and minority parties have attracted to their banners significant support from virtually every element of society, but the core of support for the major parties has consistently differed. The New Deal coalition that so dominated the political scene for thirty years was composed of white southerners, blacks, blue collar workers, urban Catholics, ethnic minorities, and Jews. By contrast, the core of GOP strength was northern white Protestants, business and professional people, small town residents, suburbanites, and midwestern farmers. Party coalitions change over time, however, in response to new crises and issues that test the ability of party leaders to hold the diverse elements within their coalitions. The test for today's Republican leaders, who were successful in the presidential elections of the 1980s, involves holding together a diverse three-headed coalition composed of (1) traditional middle- and upper-middle-class economic conservatives, (2) the social conservatives of the Christian Right, and (3) former Democratic conservatives, primarily white southerners.

The coalition nature of the parties means that intraparty conflicts can be of crucial importance in shaping the direction of governmental policy and the nature of party competition. For example, during the first part of the century, when the GOP was dominant, the struggles between the Stalwart and Progressive Republicans were in reality contests over the direction of national policy and the nature of the governing coalition. The battles between southern conservatives and northern liberal Democrats for that party's soul since 1937 have heavily influenced the scope and nature of governmental actions as well as the character of interparty competition. Similarly in the 1980s and 1990s, the struggles within the GOP between Christian Right social conservatives and traditional economic conservatives (who tend to be moderate on social issues) had a major impact upon governmental policy during the Reagan-Bush administration and also affected GOP presidential and congressional nominating politics. While American party history is clearly characterized by competition between two parties, the nature of that competition has varied considerably. Samuel J. Eldersveld has noted there have been three types of party politics since 1800.[34] The first is relatively *balanced two party competition* between the two major parties, such as the period of Republican-Democratic competition that has existed since the end of World War II as the parties have traded control of the presidency. There have been ninety-eight years of such balanced two party competition. (See figure 2.1.)

Figure 2.1
PATTERNS OF PARTY POLITICS, 1800-2000

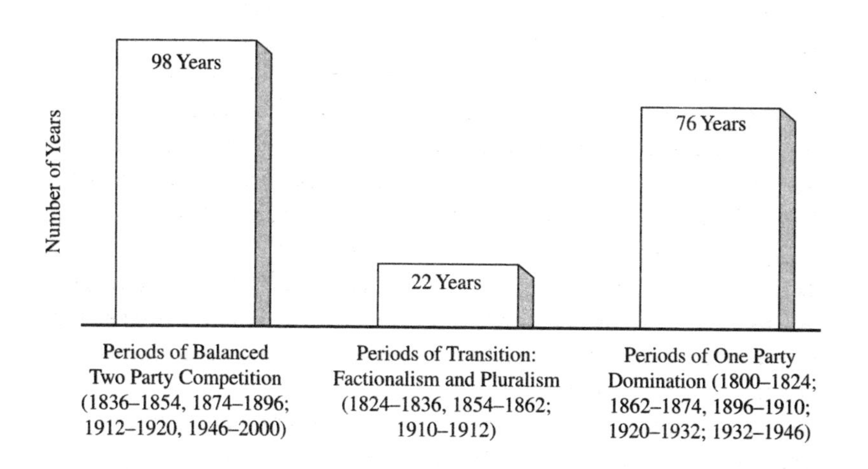

Source: Adapted from Samuel J. Eldersveld, *Political Parties in American Society* (New York: Basic Books, 1982), Table 2.2, p. 36.

While some Americans tend to think of balanced two party competition as the norm, an almost equally prevalent pattern has been *one party dominance*. There have been five periods of sustained one party dominance, the most recent being the Democratic era of 1932–1946. In addition, there have been periods of *transitional pluralism* (factionalism within the dominant party). These periods of pluralist competition within the dominant party have twice preceded the emergence of a new major party. Thus the dominant Jeffersonian coalition engaged in a series of intraparty struggles for the presidency between 1824 and 1832 before the Whig party emerged. Similarly, schisms within the Democratic and Whig parties between 1854 and 1860 occurred as the Republican party was taking its place as a major party. The split between the Progressives and Stalwart Republicans in 1910–1912 resulted in a three-way division of the vote in 1912 and permitted the minority Democrats to elect a president.

Eldersveld's analysis makes clear that the history of party competition is not the story of uninterrupted, balanced, two party competition at the national level. Three patterns of competition have existed throughout the nation's history and all three have existed during the twentieth century. The longest time span any pattern of party politics has existed uninterrupted is the period of two party competition that has existed since World War II—a more than fifty year interval from 1946 to the present. Despite the turbulence of this postwar era, the party system has shown "a capacity for absorbing and containing threats to the system."[35]

The Stability of Republican-Democratic Conflict since 1860

Since 1860, the Republicans and Democrats have confronted each other as the major combatants of the electoral arena. Each party has sustained dramatic swings of fortune—landslide wins, cliffhanger victories, and demoralizing defeats. These swings of electoral fortune, which can occur in a short time span, are captured in figure 2.2, which presents data on the two parties' percentages of the popular vote for president. For example, the Democratic percentage of the vote for president went from 61.1 percent in 1964 to only 37.5 percent eight years later in 1972; the GOP share fell from 59 to 37.4 percent between 1984 and 1992. Despite the fluidity of electoral

Figure 2.2
REPUBLICAN AND DEMOCRATIC PERCENTAGES OF THE POPULAR VOTE FOR PRESIDENT, 1896–1996

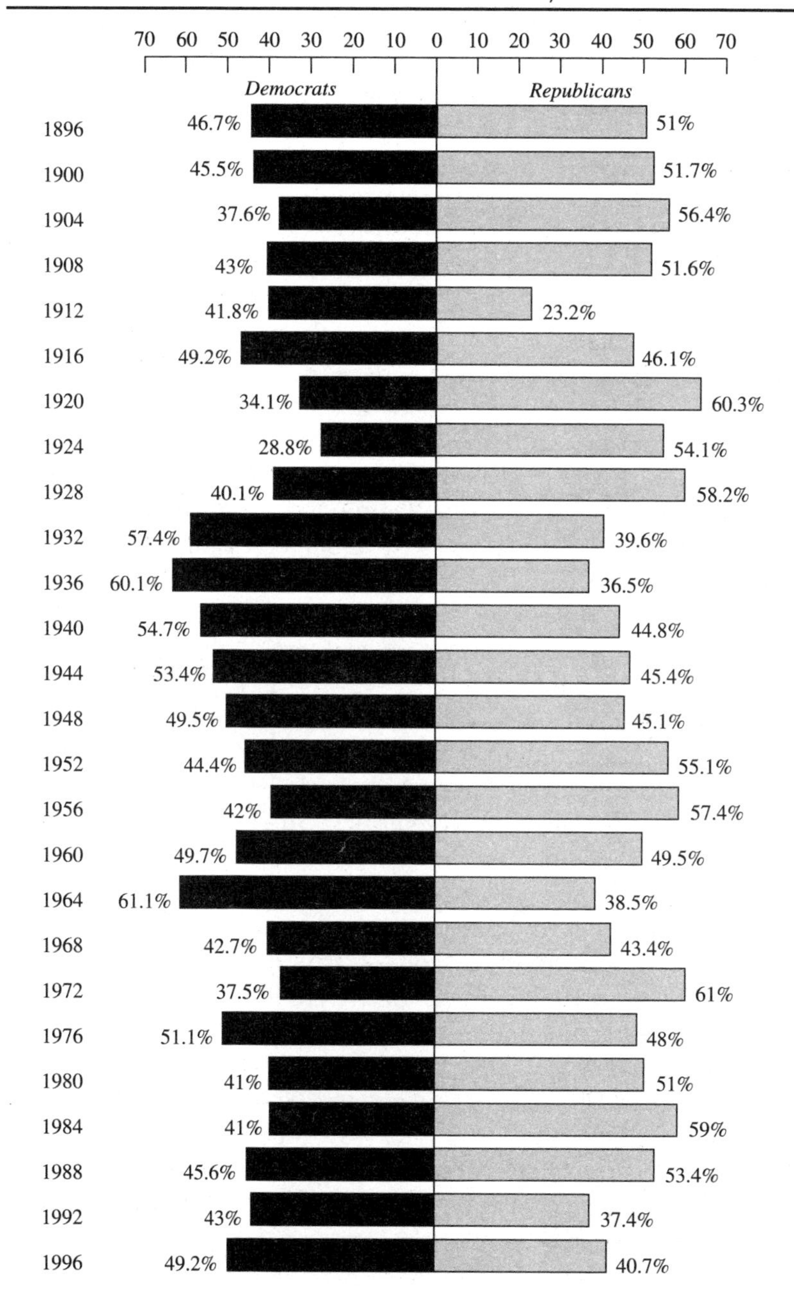

patterns both in the long run and the short term, the contest has been consistently a test of Republican-Democratic strength since 1860. The durability of this partisan division despite the potential for political dislocation caused by two World Wars, depressions, waves of new immigrants, industrialization, urbanization, and changes in lifestyle deserves probing. Why have not such dislocations caused a changed array of parties? Why have not third party movements emerged to challenge and replace one or both of the major parties the way they have in the United Kingdom, Western Europe, and Canada?

Eldersveld posits three explanations for the persistence of the equilibrium of conflict between Democrats and Republicans.[36] One reason is the parties' *capacity for absorption of protest*. Major third party protest movements have periodically arisen since 1860, but none has been able to attract a sufficient core of voters, campaign workers, and funds to sustain themselves. Each has flowered briefly and then withered as it was absorbed into one or both of the major parties. The Populists of 1892 were taken into the Democratic party in 1896 as the Democrats appropriated their platform and nominated William Jennings Bryan. Although Bryan never gained the presidency in three tries, he was brought into the government as Wilson's Secretary of State. Similarly, Theodore Roosevelt's Bull Moose Progressives of 1912 and the Robert LaFollette Progressives of 1924 were absorbed back into the GOP fold four years after their attempts to create third party movements. Most of the Dixiecrats who bolted in 1948 and almost cost Harry Truman the election were back in the Democratic party for the 1952 and 1956 elections against Eisenhower. Party insurgents and dissidents who are often dubbed extremists almost inevitably become members of the party establishment within a short period of time. The Goldwater conservatives, who challenged the eastern moderate establishment of the GOP in the 1960s, became a part of the establishment, as did the New Left liberals of the Democratic party who sought the presidential nomination for Senators Eugene McCarthy (Minn.) and George McGovern (S.D.) in 1968 and 1972. And after the 1992 elections in which Ross Perot received the highest percentage (18.9 percent) of the vote polled by a third party candidate since 1912, both the Republican and Democratic parties curried the favor of his supporters for the 1994 and 1996 elections.

Table 2.2
Major Parties Absorb Third Parties

Third Party	Year	Percent of Popular Vote	Electoral Votes	Fate in Next Election
Anti-Masonic	1832	7.8	7	endorsed Whig candidate
Free Soil	1848	10.1	0	received 4.9% of vote
Whig-American	1856	21.5	8	party dissolved
Southern Democrat	1860	18.1	72	party dissolved
Constitutional Union	1860	12.6	39	party dissolved
Liberal Republican and Democrats	1872	43.8	66[a]	Liberal Republicans dissolved
Populist	1892	8.5	22	endorsed Democratic candidate
Progressive (T. Roosevelt)	1912	27.4	88	returned to Republican party
Socialist	1912	6.0	0	received 3.2% of vote
Progressive (LaFollette)	1924	16.6	13	returned to Republican party
States' Rights Democrat	1948	2.4	39	party dissolved
Progressive (H. Wallace)	1948	2.4	0	received 0.2% of vote
American Independent	1968	13.5	46	received 1.4% of the vote
John B. Anderson	1980	7.1	0	did not run in 1984
H. Ross Perot	1992	18.9	0	received 8.4% of vote and formed the Reform party
Reform (H. Ross Perot)	1996	8.4	0	—

a.Democrats also nominated the Liberal Republican candidate Andrew Greeley, who died between the general election and the casting of the electoral votes. Sixty-three of the electoral votes he won were, therefore, cast by presidential electors for four other persons. Three were cast for Greeley, but Congress refused to count them.

Source: Congressional Quarterly, *Guide to U.S. Elections,* 3rd ed. (Washington, D.C.: Congressional Quarterly, Inc., 1994); Federal Election Commission for 1996 data.

Professor Leon D. Epstein has argued that one of the reasons that Republican and Democratic parties have been so successful in absorbing protest has been the existence of the direct primary to nominate candidates. This uniquely American institution permits insurgents outside the ranks of the established party leadership to use an intraparty route to power. By winning party nominations through the direct primary, insurgents gain access to the general election ballot without organizing third parties and thereby enhancing their chances of general election victories. Epstein also argues that the direct primary has institutionalized Republican and Democratic party electoral dominance because voters become accustomed to participating in party primaries and choosing between groups of individuals competing for their party's label. Partisan attachments are further encouraged, he believes, by the requirement in most states that primary voters publicly declare their party affiliations or even register as Republicans or Democrats in order to participate in primary elections.[37]

The Republican-Democratic party system has also been sustained by the parties' *ideological eclecticism*. The Democrats have moved from populist radicalism in 1896, to conservatism in 1904, to progressivism in 1912, to Roosevelt's New Deal in the 1930s and 1940s, to New Left foreign and economic policy in 1972, to Jimmy Carter's moderate liberalism in 1976, to Mondale/Dukakis social and economic liberalism in the 1980s, to Bill Clinton's more centrist balanced budget and "the era of big government is over" orientation. The GOP has been equally eclectic in policy orientation—from Roosevelt's progressivism in 1904, to the conservatism of normalcy in the 1920s, to the modern moderate Republicanism of Eisenhower in the 1950s, to Reagan's economic and social conservatism of the 1980s, to Bush's "kinder and gentler" conservatism of the 1990s, to the agenda of government downsizing espoused by Speaker Newt Gingrich in 1995–96. This nondoctrinaire approach to issues and changing conditions has made it possible for the two parties to respond and adapt as circumstances seemed to dictate. This ideological flexibility has enabled the parties to tolerate within their ranks a wide variety of viewpoints. It is possible for hard-core Republican conservatives like Senators Jesse Helms (N.C.) and J. Strom Thurmond (S.C.) to coexist and share power within the Senate with moderate/liberal Republicans such as John Chafee (R.I.), Olympia Snowe (Maine), and James Jeffords (Vt.). In the same way, southern moderates like Senators John Breax (La.) and Bob Graham (Fla.) coexist as Democrats with such liberals as Paul Wellstone (Minn.) and Edward Kennedy (Mass.).

The two parties have also exhibited *coalitional flexibility.* That is, they have demonstrated an ability to attract votes from virtually all elements of society, even from groups which are normally viewed as a part of the opposition. For example, the Republicans in the presidential elections of the 1980s demonstrated a capacity to win over 40 percent of the vote among labor union families, even though this group is normally Democratic. Similarly, Democrat Bill Clinton outpolled Republican George Bush among voters in the following categories, which are usually considered favorable to the GOP: professionals and semiprofessionals; and clerical, sales, and other white collar workers. The party coalitions are not static in character. They are in a constant process of "breakup, modification, and reconstruction."[38]

The Realignment Phenomenon

Throughout American party history there have been periodic electoral *realignments* at quite regular intervals. During a realignment, significant changes occur within the electorate: a minority party becomes the majority party (1860, 1932); one party achieves an infusion of strength that enables it to remain dominant (1896); changes in the partisan loyalties of voters develop (1860, 1932). In a penetrating analysis of critical elections in American history, Walter Dean Burnham noted that realignments "recur with rather remarkable regularity approximately once in a generation, or every thirty to thirty-eight years."[39] He noted realignments tend to occur as major crises intrude on the society and economy when "politics as usual" is not adequate to deal with the problems. The racial and sectional tensions of the 1850s and the Depressions of the 1890s and 1930s are examples of crises that could not be accommodated within the existing party structure. The result was highly polarized campaigns, with heightened public interest, that resulted in critical realignments of voters.

As previously noted, third party protests have been "protorealignment phenomena," which occurred before each realignment and reflected the inability of the existing major parties to meet expectations of important segments of the electorate. Prior to the realignment that constituted the beginning of the sixth party system in the mid to late 1960s, there were serious third party movements—the Dixiecrat revolt of Southern Democrats led by their presidential candidate, then Governor J. Strom Thurmond of South Carolina in 1948 and the 1968 candidacy of Governor George Wallace of Alabama, a right-wing populist who protested against the prevailing political order. The mid and late 1960s witnessed major shifts in the partisanship of blacks, who shifted overwhelmingly to the Democrats, while white southerners started their migration to the party of Lincoln. At the same time, party loyalties among the voters declined as masses of voters regularly split their tickets and made divided government an everyday feature of the political system.

Parties in Decline?

A review of American political history reveals not only frequency of change but the amazing durability and resilience of political parties. Even so, many observers see a bleak future ahead for the parties. However, the evidence is contradictory concerning the condition of parties. The signs of party decline most frequently cited include the receding impact of partisanship on voter choice; the changed nature of presidential nominating politics that has taken power from party leaders and transferred it to the media, candidate organizations, and amateur activists; the increased role played by PACs in funding campaigns; and the rise of the professional campaign and media consultants. But not all the indicators are negative concerning the state of the parties: the national party organizations have achieved unprecedented legal control over their state party affiliates in delegate selection procedures for national conventions; the national party committees have developed increasingly effective fund raising and professionalized campaign operations; state party organizations show signs of increased organizational strength over their status in the 1960s; and the parties have demonstrated that they can adapt to the growth of PACs by serving as coordinators of PAC activities. Clearly, American parties are in a state of transformation. At the same time, they demonstrate a capacity to persist. The patterns of change and persistence within various phases of party activity will be a focus of ensuing chapters.

Suggestions for Further Reading

Aldrich, John H. *Why Parties? The Origin and Transformation of Political Parties in America.* Chicago, Ill.: University of Chicago Press, 1995.

Bibby, John F., and L. Sandy Maisel. *Two Parties—Or More? The American Party System.* Boulder, Colo.: Westview, 1998.

Burnham, Walter Dean. *Critical Elections and the Mainsprings of American Politics.* New York: Norton, 1970.

Chambers, William Nesbit. *Political Parties in a New Nation: The American Experience.* New York: Oxford University Press, 1963.

Eldersveld, Samuel J. *Political Parties in American Society.* New York: Basic Books, 1982.

Epstein, Leon D. *Political Parties in the American Mold.* Madison: University of Wisconsin Press, 1986.

Hofstadter, Richard. *The Idea of a Party System: The Rise of Legitimate Opposition in the United States.* Berkeley: University of California Press, 1969.

Ladd, Everett Carll. *American Political Parties: Social Change and Political Response.* New York: Norton, 1970.

Mayhew, David R. *Placing Parties in American Politics.* Princeton, N.J.: Princeton University Press, 1986.

Reichley, A. James. *The Life of the Parties: A History of American Political Parties.* New York: Free Press, 1992.

Rutland, Robert Allen. *The Democrats: From Jefferson to Clinton.* Columbia: University of Missouri Press, 1995.

Rutland, Robert Allen. *The Republicans: From Lincoln to Bush.* Columbia: University of Missouri Press, 1996.

Shafer, Byron E., ed. *Partisan Approaches to Postwar American Politics.* Chatham, N.J.: Chatham House, 1998.

Sundquist, James L. *Dynamics of the Party System.* Washington, D.C.: Brookings Institution, 1973.

Notes

1. Richard Hofstadter, *The Idea of a Party System: The Rise of Legitimate Opposition in the United States, 1780–1840* (Berkeley: University of California Press, 1969), p. 5 3.

2. Data on the public's attitudes toward political parties are summarized in William J. Keefe, *Parties, Politics, and Public Policy in America,* 8th ed. (Washington, D.C.: CQ Press, 1998), pp. 9–17. For a more complete consideration of public support for parties, see Jack Dennis, "Trends in Public Support for the American Party System," *British Journal of Political Science* 5 (1975): 187–230.

3. Everett Carll Ladd, *American Political Parties: Social Change and Political Response* (New York: Norton, 1970), pp. 80–81.

4. Quoted by V. O. Key, Jr., *Politics, Parties, and Pressure Groups,* 5th ed. (New York: Crowell, 1964), p. 203.

5. Ladd, *American Political Parties,* p. 81.

6. Ibid., p. 87.

7. Ibid., p. 82.

8. Bureau of the Census, US. Department of Commerce, *Historical Statistics of the United States: Colonial Times to 1970* (Washington, D.C.: U.S. Government Printing Office, 1975), p. 1072.

9. Richard L. McCormick, "Political Development and the Second Party System," in William Nisbet Chambers and W D. Burnham, eds., *The American Party Systems: Stages of Political Development* (New York: Oxford University Press, 1967), p. 342.

10. Ladd, *American Political Parties,* p. 99.

11. Ibid., pp. 105–106.

12. V. O. Key, Jr., *Politics, Parties, and Pressure Groups,* 5th ed. (New York: Crowell, 1965), p. 168.

13. For a comprehensive analysis of the development of state and local party organizations, see David R. Mayhew, *Placing Parties in American Politics* (Princeton, N.J.: Princeton University Press, 1986), especially chapter 8.

14. V. O. Key, Jr., "A Theory of Critical Elections," *Journal of Politics* 17 (February 1955): 11.

15. Key, *Politics, Parties, and Pressure Groups,* p. 186; Samuel Lubell, *The Future of American Politics,* 2nd ed., rev. (Garden City, N.Y.: Doubleday, 1956), ch. 3.

16. Ladd, *American Political Parties*, pp. 175–176.

17. The impact of the direct primary on American parties is thoroughly analyzed by Leon D. Epstein, *Political Parties in the American Mold* (Madison: University of Wisconsin Press, 1986); see especially chapters 5 and 6.

18. See Mayhew, *Placing Parties in American Politics*, p. 323.

19. John H. Aldrich, *Why Parties? The Origin and Transformation of Party Politics in America* (Chicago: University of Chicago Press, 1995), pp. 241–274. For additional discussion of the changing nature of electoral politics, see Martin P. Wattenberg, *The Rise of Candidate-Centered Politics: Presidential Elections of the 1980s* (Cambridge, Mass.: Harvard University Press, 1991), and Paul R. Abramson, John H. Aldrich, and David W. Rohde, *Change and Continuity in the 1996 Elections* (Washington, D.C.: CQ Press, 1998).

20. Everett C. Ladd, "The 1996 Election and the Postindustrial Realignment," in *America at the Polls, 1996* (Storrs, Conn.: Roper Center—University of Connecticut, 1997), pp. 1, 12.

21. W. Phillips Shively, "From Differential Abstention to Conversion: A Change in Electoral Change, 1864–1986," *American Journal of Political Science* 36 (May 1992): 309–330.

22. John R. Alford and David W. Brady, "Personal and Partisan Advantage in U.S. Congressional Elections, 1946–1986," in Lawrence C. Dodd and Bruce I. Oppenheimer, eds., *Congress Reconsidered,* 4th ed. (Washington, D.C.: CQ Press, 1989), pp. 153–170.

23. Aldrich, *Why Parties?*, p. 269.

24. V. O. Key, Jr., *Politics, Parties and Pressure Groups,* p. 279.

25. Ibid., p. 255

26. Walter Dean Burnham, *Critical Elections and the Mainsprings of American Politics* (New York: Norton, 1970), pp. 27–31.

27. Paul Allen Beck, *Party Politics in America*, 8th ed. (New York: Longman, 1997), p. 49.

28. Ibid.

29. The impact of single-member plurality and various proportional representation is analyzed by Arend Lijphart, "The Political Consequences of Election Laws," *American Political Science Review* 84 (June 1990): 481–496; and Douglas W.

Rae, *The Political Consequences of Electoral Laws* (New Haven, Conn.: Yale University Press, 1967).

30. Leon D. Epstein, *Political Parties in the American Mold* (Madison: University of Wisconsin Press, 1986), pp. 244–245.

31. Ibid., p. 127.

32. Paul R. Abramson, John H. Aldrich, Phil Paolino, and David W. Rohde, "Third Party and Independent Candidates: Wallace, Anderson, and Port," *Political Science Quarterly* 110 (Fall 1995): 366–367.

33. Key, *Politics, Parties, and Pressure Groups*, p. 208.

34. Samuel J. Eldersveld, *Political Parties in American Society* (New York: Basic Books, 1982), pp. 35–36.

35. Ibid., p. 36.

36. Ibid., pp. 40–43.

37. Epstein, *Political Parties in the American Mold*, pp. 131–133, 243–245.

38. Eldersveld, *Political Parties*, p. 42.

39. Burnham, *Critical Elections and the Mainsprings of American Politics*, p. 26.

CHARACTERISTICS OF THE AMERICAN PARTY SYSTEM

CHAPTER THREE

The United States was the first nation to develop modern political parties which aligned the electorate around national issues and organized at the national, regional, and local levels to nominate candidates, contest elections, and organize governments. The early American parties stood in sharp contrast to the "capital factions" that passed for parties in Great Britain. However, as other nations followed the American example of extending the franchise to nonproperty owners, they too developed political parties capable of structuring the vote and organizing governments. Indeed, wherever elections have been conducted on a continuing basis at the national and regional levels, political parties exist. They have proved essential for organizing and mobilizing a mass electorate. As party conflict has been institutionalized in Western democracies, the party systems of these nations have come to share certain attributes: long established parties, a limited number of parties seriously contesting for office, electoral alignments focused around national issues, and class based patterns of electoral support. While the American party system shares many traits with other Western democracies, its peculiar combination of characteristics makes it distinctive.

Two Party Competition with Variations

The continuous competition between the Republicans and the Democrats for over 140 years has given the American party system a two party character. These two parties contest for control of the presidency, Congress, governorships, and state legislatures. This sets the United States apart from most other nations, which, while having a limited number of major parties, normally have more than just two. The dominant position of the two major parties is reflected in the operation of the Federal Election Campaign Act, which bestows special benefits upon major parties—defined as those parties receiving 25 percent of the popular vote for president. These benefits include federal matching funds for presidential candidates seeking party nominations, federal grants for holding national conventions, and public funding at the maximum level in general election campaigns for president. Only the Republican and Democratic parties have qualified as major parties eligible for the highest level of governmental support, which gives them a substantial advantage over minor parties.

The phrase *two party system* masks a great deal of variation in the extent and nature of interparty competition in the United States. Two party competition aptly describes competition for selected offices in some jurisdictions, but there are also offices and regions in which the norm of strong interparty competition is not met.

Party Competition at the National Level

The Presidency. Viewed from a national perspective, presidential elections are highly competitive. In the twelve presidential elections since World War II, the parties have alternated control, with the Republicans winning seven times and Democrats five times. The two party character of presidential voting is reflected in table 3.1, which presents data on the percentages of the popular vote cast for Republican and Democratic candidates in recent elections. Note that in these elections between 1948 and 1996, the Republican-Democratic share of the popular vote has dipped below 90 percent only three times (1968, 1992, and 1996) and has averaged 95.0 percent.

Table 3.1
Major Party Dominance of Presidential Voting, 1948–1996

	Candidates for President		Percentage of Popular Vote		
Year	**Republican**	**Democrat**	**Republican**	**Democrat**	**Total**
1948	Dewey	Truman	45.1	49.6	94.7
1952	Eisenhower	Stevenson	55.1	44.4	99.5
1956	Eisenhower	Stevenson	57.4	42.0	99.4
1960	Nixon	Kennedy	49.5	49.7	99.2
1964	Goldwater	Johnson	38.5	61.1	99.6
1968	Nixon	Humphrey	43.4	42.7	86.1
1972	Nixon	McGovern	60.7	37.5	98.2
1976	Ford	Carter	48.0	50.1	98.1
1980	Reagan	Carter	50.7	41.0	91.7
1984	Reagan	Mondale	58.8	40.6	99.4
1988	Bush	Dukakis	53.4	45.6	99.0
1992	Bush	Clinton	37.4	43.0	80.4
1996	Dole	Clinton	40.7	49.2	89.9

Source: Statistical Abstract of the United States, 1997, p. 271.

The Congress. The Democrats have controlled the Congress during most of the post–World War II era. Indeed, the Democrats were so dominant that until the Republican electoral sweep in the 1994 midterm elections, the GOP had not controlled both the House and Senate for forty years. Despite the frequently lopsided nature of congressional Democratic majorities, especially in the House, the national popular vote for the House, like the vote for president, shows a high level of competition and two party dominance. The combined Republican-Democratic share of the popular vote for the House of Representatives has exceeded 95 percent in every election since World War II. The minority Republican party share of the popular vote has never dipped below 40.5 percent (1974) and it has averaged 46.4 percent in twenty-five elections.

Party Competition at the State Level

A measure of state level interparty competition can be obtained by combining indicators of party voting strength: (1) percentage of votes won by each party in gubernatorial elections; (2) percentage of seats won by each party in each house of the state legislature; (3) the length of time each party controlled the governorship; and (4) the proportion of the time in which control of the governorship and the legislature has been divided between the parties.[1] When these data are combined into a single index of competitiveness for the period 1995–1998, a clear majority of the states meet the test of competitiveness (see figure 3.1) and there were no one-party Democratic or Republican states. By contrast, during the 1962–1973 period, a majority of states fell into either the one party or modified one party categories. The most notable change has occurred in the states of the Confederacy, where in the 1990s there are no longer any one party Democratic states and only three modified one party states. Evidence of the shift away from the region's heritage of one party Democratic domination was evident in 1999 when Republicans controlled seven of eleven governorships in the states of the Confederacy. The GOP has even made strides to overcome its long-term weakness in state legislatures. For example, after the 1998 elections, Republicans controlled at least one chamber in Florida, South Carolina, Texas, and Virginia. While the South has moved to two party competitiveness, there has also been a shift toward Republican control of state governments in the mountain states of the West. Thus, all eight of these states had Republican governors after the 1998 elections, and in six of the states the GOP also controlled both legislative chambers.

Research comparing social and economic conditions within the states has revealed that socioeconomic diversity contributes to interparty competitiveness. A heterogeneous population permits both parties to build up support among selected groups in society because of the inevitable conflicts, tensions, and differences that socioeconomic diversity breeds. Such indicators of socioeconomic diversity as population size, educational attainment, and home ownership are each correlated to interparty competition. In states where state legislative incumbents enjoy substantial advantages, competition is depressed; competition is enhanced as the population of legislative districts increases and makes them more diverse in their makeup. In addition, the strength of the party organizations also affects partisan competition. Strong party organizations capable of mobilizing the vote tend to encourage competitive politics.[2]

Variations in Levels of Competition for Different Offices

The index of competitiveness described in the preceding section is based exclusively upon the outcome of *state* elections and gives more weight to control of state legislatures than it does to winning the governorship. As a result, this index can obscure the extent to which interparty competition exists in contests for various offices.

Figure 3. 1

INTERPARTY COMPETITION IN THE STATES, 1962–1973 AND 1995–1998

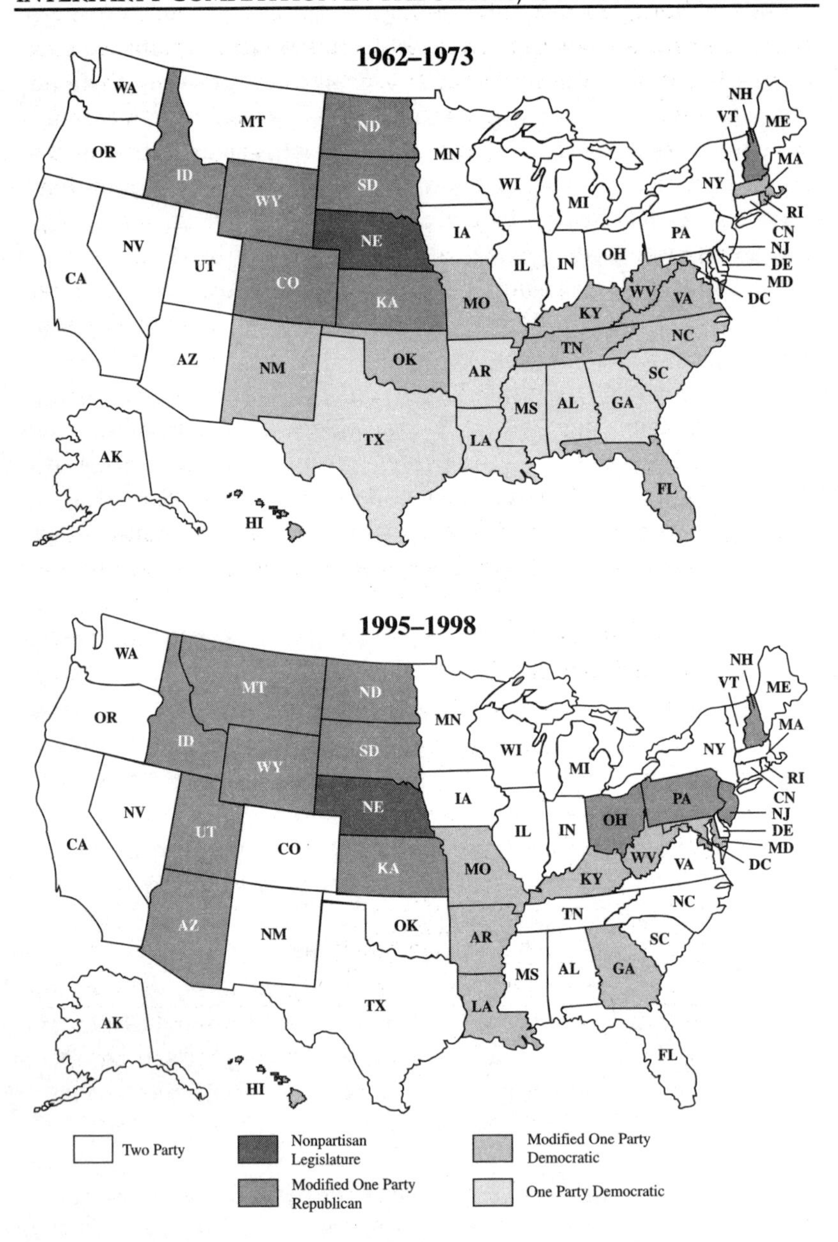

Sources: John F. Bibby and Thomas M. Holbrook, "Parties and Elections," in *Politics in the American States*, 7th ed., Virginia Gray, Russell L. Hanson, and Herbert Jacob, eds. (Washington, D.C.: CQ Press), Table 3.3; Austin Ranney, "Parties in State Politics," in *Politics in the American States*, 3rd ed., Herbert Jacob and Kenneth Vines, eds. (Boston: Little, Brown, 1976), Table 4. Reprinted by permission of Congressional Quarterly.

Statewide Elections. There is substantial evidence of a high level of interparty competition in most statewide elections. In the eight presidential elections between 1968 and 1996, twenty-three of the states have been carried by the Democratic or Republican parties at least three times, and thirty-four states have been won by each party at least twice. Every state of the old Confederacy has been won by the Republican presidential nominee at least four times since Eisenhower's penetration of the South in 1952.

Another indicator of interparty competition at the state level in presidential elections is the fact that in four of the ten elections between 1952 and 1988, two-thirds of the states were won by margins of less than 55 percent of the vote; only in the national landslides of 1964, 1972, and 1984 were a majority of the states carried by margins of 60 percent or more. In the three-way race of 1992 among George Bush, Bill Clinton, and Ross Perot, Clinton was the only candidate to carry a state—his home state of Arkansas—with more than 50 percent of the vote. In seventeen states, Clinton's winning margin was less than five percent. (See table 3.2 for the number of times the GOP has carried the states between 1968–1996.) In 1996, Perot's share of the vote fell off dramatically, and Clinton won reelection convincingly. However, even in a less competitive contest than 1992, the president's share of the vote was less than 50 percent in twelve of the thirty-one states he carried.

Table 3.2

Interparty Competition for the Presidency: Number of Times the Republican Presidential Nominee Has Carried the State, 1968–1996

0	1	2	3	4	5	6	7	8
D.C.	Minn.	Hawaii	Md.	Ark.	Conn.	Ala.	Ariz.	Alaska
		Mass.	N.Y.	Ga.	Del.	Cal.	Colo.	Idaho
		R.I.		La.	Iowa	Fla.	Mont.	Ind.
		W. Va.		Pa.	Ky.	Ill.	N.C.	Kans.
				Wash.	Maine	Miss.	S.C.	Neb.
				Wis.	Mich.	Nev.		N.D.
					Mo.	N.H.		Okla.
					Ohio	N.J.		S.D.
					Ore.	N.M.		Utah
					Tenn.	Tex.		Va.
						Vt.		Wyo.
Totals								
1	1	4	2	6	10	11	5	11

Sources: Recent volumes of the *Statistical Abstract of the United States.*

Further evidence of increasing interparty competition in statewide elections can be found in senatorial contests. This was particularly apparent in 1980 when twenty-five (76 percent) of thirty-three Senate elections were won by less than 60 percent of the vote. In elections between 1980 and 1996, 36 percent of the 306 senators elected had margins of less than 55 percent, and 78 percent had margins below 60 percent. A further indication of the generally competitive nature of senatorial elections is revealed by the fact that 75 percent of the senators serving in the 105th Congress (1997–1998) had at least one election in which they received 55 percent or less of the vote.[3]

Gubernatorial elections have also become competitive. Table 3.3 presents data on the extent of partisan change in control of governorships since 1950. During the 1950s, only 23.6 percent of gubernatorial elections resulted in a change in party control of state executive mansions. In that decade, no southern state had a switch in party control, but in the period between 1990 and 1998, 38.1 percent of the elections resulted in a change in party control of southern governorships. It is not just the states of the old Confederacy that are now characterized by frequent partisan shifts. Democrats have elected governors and alternated control since the 1950s in such traditional bastions of Republicanism as Maine, Vermont, North and South Dakota, Kansas, and Nebraska. In 1998, eight (22 percent) of the thirty-six gubernatorial contests resulted in a change in party control.

Table 3.3

Party Change in Control of Governorships, 1950–1998

Decade	Number of Gubernatorial Elections	Percent of Elections with a Party Change[a]
1950–1959	174	23.6 (41)
1960–1969	156	35.3 (55)
1970–1979	144	38.9 (56)
1980–1989	122	35.2 (43)
1990–1998	135	35.6 (48)

a. An election with a party change is defined as any election in which control of the governorship shifts from one party to another.

Sources: Adapted from Larry Sabato, *Goodbye to Goodtime Charlie,* 2nd ed. (Washington, D.C.: CQ Press, 1983), pp. 120–121: the 1980–1998 data are derived from appropriate volumes of the *Statistical Abstract of the United States; National Journal,* November 7, 1998, p. 2664.

Congressional Elections. While interparty competition is increasingly the norm in statewide competitions, it has been relatively rare in elections to the House of Representatives. On average, 69 percent of the members of Congress elected between 1980 and 1996 won with an excess of 60 percent of the vote (see figure 3.2), and, in 1998, 94 representatives (55 Republicans and 39 Democrats) were elected without major party opposition. The lack of competitiveness in these districts is reflected in the inability of most challengers to raise enough funds for meaningful campaigns against incumbents. In 1996, Democratic challengers to Republican incumbents who won by 60 percent or more averaged only $96,758 in expenditures compared to the Republican incumbents' $583,946 in average spending. Republican challengers to Democrats with 60 percent plus winning margins were as severely disadvantaged. Their average expenditure was $107,822 compared to average

Figure 3.2
PARTY COMPETITION FOR HOUSE SEATS, 1980–1996

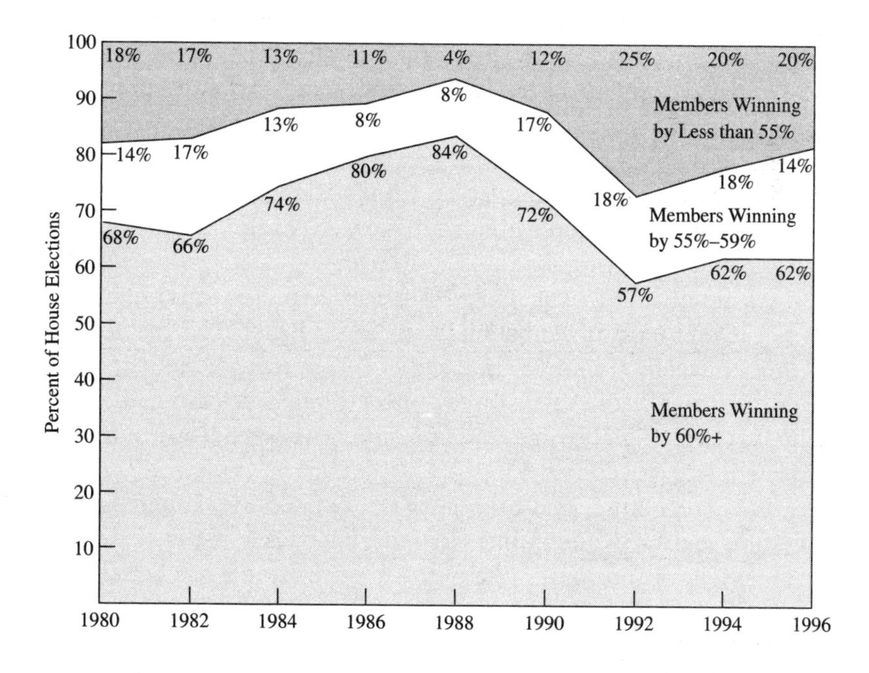

Source: Appropriate volumes of the *Statistical Abstract of the United States.*

Democratic incumbent expenditures of $477,204.[4] Such resource advantages on the side of incumbents means that in most districts the challenger's party is normally confronted with the task of recruiting a "willing loser" to run against the incumbent.

Incumbency has become a powerful advantage. Indeed, it is so strong that in any given congressional election, over 90 percent of the incumbents seeking reelection will normally win. As a result, the extent of party change in control of House seats has been extremely low. In the seven elections between 1980 and 1992, an average of only twenty-seven (6.2 percent) of the seats changed party control. It was not until the Republican sweep of 1994, when sixty-one seats (14 percent) switched party control, that the GOP achieved majority status in the House.

State Legislative Elections. The frequent absence of meaningful two party competition found in congressional elections is also present in elections to the state legislatures.[5] One party domination of legislative contests is commonplace in many of the states. The Democratic party has maintained almost total domination of state legislative elections in four southern states (Alabama, Arkansas, Louisiana, and Mississippi) where the party between 1953 and 1998 has never held less than 62 percent of the upper and lower house seats and frequently controlled in excess of 80 percent. Other states characterized by one party control of state legislatures include Maryland, Massachusetts, Rhode Island, and West Virginia for the Democrats; and Arizona, Colorado, Idaho, Kansas, South Dakota, and Wyoming for the Republicans.

As is true with the U.S. House of Representatives, incumbents' advantages are substantial in state legislative races, with incumbent reelection rates in excess of 90 percent being commonplace in many of the states, including California, Illinois, Pennsylvania, Delaware, Minnesota, Washington, Oregon, Missouri, and Wisconsin.[6]

It is clear from this brief survey of statewide, congressional, and state legislative elections that there is tremendous variability in the extent of interparty competition depending upon which type of election is being considered. The phrase "American two party system" accurately captures the totality of party competition, but it fails to capture the continuum of party competition found in the United States.

Decentralized Power Structures

It is hard to overstate the extent to which American political parties are characterized by decentralized power structures. Except for a few isolated urban machines, there is almost a total absence of hierarchical relationships within American parties. Within the party in government, presidents cannot assume that representatives and senators of their party will necessarily follow their leadership on public policy issues. Within the party organization, the national institutions of the party have a narrow range of authority over state party delegate selection procedures for national conventions, but they rarely meddle in nominations and organizational affairs of state parties. Few constraints operate upon the party in the electorate. Even incumbent presidents have found that they could not depend upon the party's voters to give them support either in bids for renomination or reelection. Power in the American parties is fragmented and scattered among many institutions, organizations, and individuals at the national, state, and local levels.

The Impact of the Constitution

Separation of Powers. The Founding Fathers purposely sought to make it difficult for any individual or faction to gain control over the national government by creating a national government composed of three branches. As a result, representatives and senators are elected separately from the president and for terms of varying length. Each has a different constituency.

The looseness of the American parties is, in part, a response to the constitutional separation of powers. Because separation of powers permits divided control of government, political parties are free to concentrate their efforts towards winning the presidency, Congress, or just one house of Congress. The minority Republicans, for example, have frequently focused their campaign drives on the White House (e.g., 1972, 1984, and 1988), or when their presidential prospects were slight, as in 1996, have targeted House races in an effort to retain control of Congress. With presidents, senators, and representatives each elected from separate constituencies for staggered terms, it is small wonder that these elected officials of the same party have only a minimal sense of interdependence. The highest prize of American politics—the presidency—can be gained without simultaneously having a partisan majority in Congress. In this system of separated governmental institutions, presidents can operate with a significant degree of independence from their party colleagues in Congress. Representatives and senators, each elected from a particular constituency, need not be supportive of their party's president for electoral survival. Indeed, it is often prudent for the national legislators to put some distance between themselves and their party's president.[7]

The incentives toward party unity and discipline are substantially stronger in countries with parliamentary regimes. In such systems, control of the legislature is the prerequisite for achieving the prime ministership or cabinet office. Control of the executive goes to the party or coalition of parties that has a legislative majority. And when that majority is lost through electoral setbacks, the cabinet must resign and make way for the opposition. Loss of the legislative majority through defections by dissident partisans or coalition members can force a cabinet either to resign or call new elections. Neither option is a pleasant one because they threaten legislators' tenure or their chances to serve in the cabinet—the most prestigious and powerful positions in public life. The parliamentary system thus creates powerful incentives toward party unity and conforming to wishes of the party leadership. But in the United States the institutional incentive to support party leadership and the president is lacking and instead independent minded behavior is encouraged.

Because the separation of powers principle is embedded not just in the national Constitution, but also in state constitutions, its party fragmenting consequences are also felt at the state level. State legislators frequently operate quite independently of their party's governor and party leadership.

Federalism. Federalism—the constitutional division of governmental power between the national government and the states—has made it difficult for political parties to develop as other than decentralized institutions. American parties did not antedate the writing of the Constitution and they, therefore, had to organize themselves to contest state elections as well as presidential races. When the American parties were developing in the nineteenth century, there were powerful incentives to organize strong state parties because "national and state political stakes were more nearly equal than they are now."[8] Although the states are less important relative to the national government in the 1990s than they were in the nineteenth century, the states continue to be potent political entities worthy of major investments by the parties to secure control. Parties organized around state as well as national elections tend to become decentralized and confederative in character. This pattern of decentralization has been strengthened by each state imposing upon its parties a unique set of statutory regulations under which the parties must operate.

Fifty semiautonomous state governments, each having a multitude of local governmental units, have created thousands of partisan elected officials, party leaders, and organizations with their own constituencies and cadres of supporters. Such localized bases of support mean that these elected officials are in a position to assert their independence from national party leaders. Often the interests of state and national party leaders and elected officials are not the same. State party leaders and candidates are likely to place a higher priority upon electing governors and state legislators than in winning control of the White House or Congress. For example, Stanley M. Friedman, the Democratic leader of the Bronx, made the following comment when asked during the 1984 presidential primary about whether he worried about presidential politics.

> It doesn't affect our life one bit. National politics—President and such—are too far removed from the bread and butter things that matter to local leaders and mayors and governor. The local leader cares about a senior citizen center, a local concern.[9]

State and national party leaders frequently come into conflict when the national and state parties compete with each other for financial contributions from party benefactors, or when national party organizations support candidates who fail to win contested primaries. Tensions are also created when state officials seek to distance themselves from national party leaders and policies that are considered political liabilities; for example, in the 1994 midterm elections some Democratic candidates, particularly in the South and Mountain West, put as much distance as practicable between themselves and President Clinton. The distinct interests, constituencies, and bases of support which federalism creates for national, state, and local party leaders and elected officials mean that party unity is always under stress. The decentralizing forces inherent in the separation of powers system are given an encouraging boost by federalism.

The Impact of Nomination and Campaign Practices

Nominations and general election campaigns are not party dominated processes in the United States. Elected officials gain nomination and election primarily through reliance on highly personalized campaign organizations, which may be supplemented by party resources. This means that parties do not control access to elective office. As a result, party leaders are not in a position to impose discipline on elected officials, who know that the party cannot assure either their electoral survival or ascent up the political ladder.

Nominations in the States. Nominations to congressional, state, and local office, with few exceptions, are made via the direct primary. This open and participatory process makes it extremely difficult for any but the most disciplined style party organization (e.g., the old Daley machine in Chicago) to control nominations and access to the general election ballot. The direct primary encourages candidates to build highly personal campaign organizations. Once a candidate is nominated in a primary, the local or national party leadership is obliged to accept that individual as a bona fide nominee of the party, whether the person was its preferred candidate or not.

The direct primary means that neither national, state, nor local party organizations are in a position to control nominations to Congress. This is in vivid contrast to most Western democracies in which parliamentary nominations are internal party decisions made by the organizational leadership. In such systems, the party organization is in a position to impose discipline on legislators because it determines which candidates will bear the party label in elections.[10] Lacking such control over nominations, American parties are not in a position to impose discipline on representatives and senators.

Presidential Nominations. Presidential nominating politics of the post-1968 era is characterized by presidential primaries that determine the candidate preferences of a majority of the delegates, open and participatory state party caucuses, and intense media coverage. Unlike the pre-1968 period, party leaders no longer exercise decisive influence over the selection of presidential nominees. Influence has shifted to candidate organizations, campaign consultants, candidate or issue oriented activists, and the mass media—

especially television. As Jimmy Carter demonstrated in 1976, it is possible for a party outsider—a person largely unknown to a party's national and state leadership and inexperienced in national government—to gain a major party nomination. Even incumbent presidents are not immune from damaging renomination challenges, as Presidents Gerald Ford (1976), Jimmy Carter (1980), and George Bush (1992) discovered. Since party organizations cannot even guarantee incumbent presidents renomination, presidents, like senators and representatives, take office with an ambiguous relationship to their party. Their sense of party obligation is often limited.

General Election Campaigns. The decentralizing forces unleashed by nomination processes are reinforced by the manner in which general election campaigns are conducted. National trends in public opinion, national media, and campaigns do influence the outcomes of congressional, state, and local elections. Candidates, however, are aware that to a significant degree elections are determined by local factors and their ability to achieve a favorable balance of campaign resources over their opponents. With such a favorable balance of resources, the skillful campaigner can overcome adverse national swings of voter sentiment and gain election.

Congressional campaigns in particular reflect this highly individualized campaign environment. Most candidates maintain highly personalized campaign organizations and raise funds from non-party sources, such as political action committees (PACs) which contributed $200.3 million to House and Senate candidates in 1997–98. The resourceful congressional incumbent normally uses the perquisites of office to project an image of electoral invincibility and will raise a substantial campaign war chest. These activities often scare off serious challengers. National or state parties customarily provide only a small percentage of the money needed to mount a reelection drive. Although national party organizations since the 1970s have become large-scale participants in congressional and senatorial campaigns through candidate recruitment, direct contributions to candidates, expenditures on behalf of candidates, and staff and technical assistance, it is not at all clear that these activities have reduced independence and fragmentation in the conduct of campaigns. This is because national party organizations are more concerned with winning elections than with restructuring electoral politics and so they have adapted their activities to a candidate-centered style of politics.[11] This campaign style encourages representatives and senators to function with considerable independence from their parties within Congress. After all, electoral survival requires cultivating trust among one's constituents and maintenance of a personal organization. Since the party cannot ensure continued congressional tenure, it is not surprising that parties often have difficulty gaining high levels of party unity on congressional roll calls. With no party to protect them, representatives and senators have created a congressional system that bestows on each member substantial resources for year around campaigning and a committee system that enables them to build support among constituencies essential for reelection.[12]

Presidential campaigns are also organized to a significant degree outside the party structure. This type of candidate oriented campaign organization is encouraged by the Federal Election Campaign Act. Candidates who agree to accept public funding of their campaigns are required under the Act to forego fund-raising activities, and the Republican and Democratic National Committees are restricted to modest levels ($11.5 million in 1996) of expenditure on behalf of their presidential and vice presidential nominees. Presidential candidates accepting public funding are also required to set up a committee to receive and expend the public funds. The law, therefore, creates an incentive for major party presidential nominees to follow their natural preference for campaign organizations which are devoted exclusively to their own candidacies and which function at some distance from their national party committees.

The tie between party organizations and candidates at all levels has also been weakened by changes in the techniques of campaigning and the resulting escalation in campaign costs. The modern campaign for major office today requires media experts, pollsters, computer specialists, direct mail consultants, accountants, lawyers, research specialists, and campaign consultants to perform get-out-the-vote activities and public relations functions that were once the province of party organizations. As candidates have relied increasingly upon these nonparty sources for essential services, the influence of the party over elected officials has diminished.

Candidates of the 1990s running for major office tend to set up shop on their own and operate as relatively independent political entrepreneurs with personalized organizations, campaign war chests, media advertising, and, once elected, a sizable staff to assist in electioneering. It is small wonder that such American politicians feel quite independent of their parties. By contrast, the British members of Parliament are heavily dependent upon their parties. The party organization controls nominations; television time is allocated to parties, not individual candidates; the parties sharply limit the amount that candidates can spend on their own campaigns; and once elected the average M.P. has few of the staff resources and other perquisites available to members of Congress. The British M.P.s are, therefore, much more dependent upon their parties and much more likely to submit to party discipline.

Some Countertrends: Nationalizing Influences

Decentralization of power pervades American parties. This attribute, however, can be overemphasized. Parties have both their national and confederative aspects. Federalism fragments the parties, but national forces have always played a significant role. Leon Epstein has observed:

> However much party organizations . . . have come to establish largely independent state and local bases, their electoral support originated in national and specifically presidential alignments. In other words, the party labels under which organizations could win (or lose) state and local offices derived electoral value from their national association.[13]

The nationalizing tendencies within American parties can be seen in (1) the impact of national forces on state voting patterns, (2) the expanded role played by national party organizations, and (3) the growth of national "presidential parties."

The Impact of National Trends on State Voting Patterns. State politics does not function in isolation from national political forces. Partisan loyalties are forged in the heat of presidential campaigns, and voters tend to support the same parties in both national and state elections. These national influences on voting make it difficult for third party movements to survive at the state level. For example, two of the strongest third parties of the pre–World War II era were the Progressives of Wisconsin and the Farmer-Labor party in Minnesota. Each was forced to merge into one of the major parties by the 1950s because the pull of national partisan alignments within the state electorates was so strong that the parties faced inevitable defeat. Even without the complications caused by third party movements, it has become increasingly difficult for a state to maintain a party alignment of voters that is significantly different from the way they align themselves in presidential elections. The strong nationalizing influences in American life make it burdensome for a state party and its candidates to adopt policy positions significantly at odds with the national image of the party. A case in point is the Democratic party of the South. The southern wing of the party has since the New Deal sought to project a more conservative image than the national Democratic party. However, the disparity between the southern Democrats and the national party has been declining since the 1960s, as fewer and fewer Democrats elected to Congress from the South can be classified as conservatives ("Boll Weevils") and Democratic governors espouse the policies of the national party. The public's tendency to perceive a link between national Democratic policy and southern Democrats, plus the changing demography and economy of the region, made possible the Republican electoral advances in the presidential elections of 1952, 1956, and 1964. These electoral beachheads were followed by Republican victories in congressional, senatorial, and gubernatorial elections during the 1980s and early 1990s. These gains were capped by the Republicans in their sweeping 1994 victory in which the party captured a majority of House and Senate seats in the states of the old Confederacy (including a majority in the House delegations from Florida, Georgia, North Carolina, South Carolina, and Tennessee). And following that election, every state of the old Confederacy but Georgia had elected at least one Republican governor between 1966 and 1998. Clearly, the electoral alignments of the South have changed dramatically and become more like those of the rest of the country. The Democratic "solid South" no longer exists.

The impact of national electoral forces on state elections is particularly noticeable in midterm elections. Reformers have sought to insulate state elections from national tides of opinion by scheduling these elections for the midterm when the president is not on the ballot. Such timing of state elections, however, has not had the anticipated effect. In midterm elections, the normal pattern of the president's party losing House seats carries over to gubernatorial elections. In all but three midterm elections between 1950 and 1998, the president's party has suffered a net loss of governorships. The exceptions were 1962 and 1998 when there was no net change; and 1986 when the Democrats were defending twenty-seven seats, an unusually large number, and the GOP was defending only nine. The average loss was five seats. Proportionally, gubernatorial elections appear more susceptible to national trends, which normally work against the president's party, than do elections for national offices such as senator and representative. (See chapter 8 for a more detailed discussion of state elections at midterm.)

Expanded Role of the National Party. Both the Republican and Democratic national party organizations have achieved increased influence since the 1960s, although the two initiated the process of party nationalization in different ways. Following the divisive Democratic Convention of 1968, the national Democratic party embarked upon major reforms of its delegate selection procedures. This reform effort took the form of an elaborate series of rules governing delegate selection procedures that the state parties were required to follow. Authority to enforce these rules was vested in the Democratic National Committee (DNC). Operating through its enforcement arm, the Compliance Review Commission, the DNC has forced state parties to comply with national party rules in delegate selection matters. Faced with this authority vested in the national party, the state parties engaged in a massive restructuring of their internal procedures to bring them into conformity with national party policy. The United States Supreme Court further strengthened the position of the national party vis-à-vis its state affiliates when it upheld the principle that national party rules take precedence over state statutes and party rules in matters pertaining to delegate selection.[14]

One of the most celebrated instances of a national party demonstrating its supremacy over state parties came in Wisconsin. National Democratic party rules banned presidential primaries in which persons other than those publicly professing a preference for the Democratic party participated (i.e., the DNC banned open primaries). Wisconsin has had an open presidential primary law since 1905, when it became the first state to enact a presidential primary statute. The open primary tradition of the state is a strong one, consistent with the state's independent and Progressive history. Despite the clear preference of the Wisconsin Democratic party and the Democratic controlled state legislature for maintaining the open primary tradition, the state was forced to abandon the open presidential primary and select 1984 delegates to the Democratic convention via a caucus system. The DNC has continued to assert its legal authority to enforce national party rules upon state parties even though it has now relented and permitted Wisconsin to operate an open presidential primary. Austin Ranney, a respected parties scholar, believes that the power conferred upon the Democratic national party organization by the rules and court decisions are so sweeping that the national party's legal authority is "at its highest peak since the 1820s."[15]

The national Republican party also gained increased influence, but in a vastly different manner than by enforcement of nationally mandated rules. By contrast, the Republicans sought to maintain the confederate character of their party by giving state parties wide latitude in matters of delegate selection and internal operation. National party power, however, has been extended through an extensive multi-million dollar program to provide financial and technical assistance to state and local party organizations and candidates. Through these activities, the Republican National Committee (RNC) has achieved an expanded role in the political system and created a relationship of interdependence between the national party and its state and local affiliates.[16] The DNC has followed the RNC example of expanding its services to its state affiliates so that it too is an increasingly significant participant in state elections. Its more limited resources have meant that it is not in a position to provide the same level of assistance as the RNC. Since the 1980s, however, the national Democratic organizations have been able to narrow the fund-raising gap between themselves and the Republicans.

Using their considerable financial resources, the Republican (RNC) and Democratic (DNC) National Committees have been able to achieve an unprecedented degree of intraparty integration, as the state parties have been used to implement national campaign strategies and avoid Federal Election Campaign Act restrictions on national party expenditures in federal elections. Massive transfers of funds were made by the national committees to their state party affiliates in the 1995–96 election cycle: the RNC transferred $66.3 million to state parties and the DNC sent $74.3 million to its state units.

These transferred funds were used to pay general party overhead, finance massive get-out-the-vote drives, and cover the cost of issue advertisements designed to support presidential candidates.[17]

The national parties allocated their funds to the state parties to implement a national campaign strategy geared toward winning key states in the presidential contest or maximizing the parties' seats in the House and Senate. This means that the national parties do not treat all of their state affiliates equally. Parties in key states such as California, Florida, and Ohio are normally showered with national party largess. But other state parties that lack national priority status can receive virtually no national party assistance. Thus, in 1995–96, the DNC did not transfer any money to its state units in New York, Rhode Island, and West Virginia, and the RNC gave a mere $6,000 to the West Virginia GOP.

A particularly dramatic example of a national party using its state organizations to carry out a national strategy occurred when the DNC transferred $32 million to state parties in twelve battleground states. These state parties in turn paid for television advertising that had been developed and placed in the media by the DNC's media production company.[18] As the national party organizations have intensified their use of state parties to achieve national campaign goals by providing technical and financial support for state parties, financing and supervising get-out-the-vote operations, and transferring funds to pay for television advertising, state parties have suffered a loss of autonomy and have become increasingly dependent upon their national parties' largess. (For a more detailed consideration of party centralization and intraparty integration, see chapter 4.)

The Growth of the "Presidential Party." Prior to the 1970s, presidential nominations were dominated by the leaders of state and local party organizations—state and county party chairmen, governors, senators, and mayors. They exercised their influence through the caucus system of delegate selection—the process by which two-thirds of the delegates were chosen. Few states used presidential primaries and it was possible to win presidential nominations without even entering a single primary. The reform era of the 1970s changed all this. As presidential nominations became dominated by presidential primaries, presidential aspirants sought the nomination through direct appeals to the primary electorate. Party leaders became less important and the personal organizations of the candidates and the media took on greater importance.

While most political scientists believe that these changes have weakened political parties, the development of candidate centered presidential politics has included one positive party development. A new "presidential party"—the national following of activists gathered about a candidate—has emerged. These activists have common bonds of shared attitudes—predominantly conservative in the GOP and mainly liberal in the Democratic party. They constitute what political scientist John Kessel has called "advocacy parties"—campaign organizations dedicated to putting their policy preferences on the public agenda. These presidential parties are more ad hoc in character than the regular party organizations, but they do have substantial continuity. A sizeable majority of the presidential activists in both parties were brought into politics years ago when they rallied to the banner of candidates such as Ronald Reagan, Barry Goldwater, Richard Nixon, Walter Mondale, Jimmy Carter, and John F. Kennedy.[19]

These networks of issue oriented activists can have an impact above and beyond presidential elections. They can also be used to mobilize support for presidential policies. President Reagan, for example, successfully used the Reagan network to mobilize grassroots lobbying for his legislative program in Congress. President Clinton and the DNC similarly sought to mobilize grassroots activists to support the president and his legislative agenda.

Broadly Based Electoral Support

In some countries, electoral alignments closely reflect social and economic cleavages—Catholics versus Protestants, rich versus poor, city versus the countryside, unions versus business, recent immigrants versus old line nativist stock. In such societies, parties have little meaning aside from the social groups they represent. When party allegiances closely reflect social and economic cleavages, political conflict is more likely to be bitter and unrestrained, as the tragic histories of Northern Ireland and Lebanon demonstrate. American parties, however, are quite different. Partisan loyalties cut across social and economic divisions. The result is parties that are broadly based coalitions of diverse and even conflicting elements. Such parties, because of the diversity of their followings, have great difficulty maintaining unity among their elected officials and in enunciating clear statements of party policy. But coalition type parties do provide a means of reconciling and compromising conflicts within society.

Evidence of the coalition nature of American political parties is revealed in the voting behavior of various socioeconomic groups in recent elections (see table 8.8, chapter 8). Clearly, the core elements of electoral support for the two parties are quite different. Persons from labor union households, blacks, manual laborers, Catholics, and Jews are more likely to support the Democrats than the Republicans; while Protestants, professional and business people, and recently members of the religious right tend to be Republican voters. These differences in the core constituencies of the two parties should not obscure the fact that both parties draw significant levels of support from virtually every major socioeconomic group in American life. The only exception to this generalization is the black voters, who have become overwhelmingly Democratic since 1964.

The extent to which electoral support for American parties cuts across various socioeconomic divisions can be seen by examining the voting patterns of groups commonly thought of as safely in the camp of one party or the other. Persons from labor union households are usually considered to be overwhelmingly pro-Democratic. However, the Republicans can normally expect to receive the votes of at least one-third of these people, and in years such as 1984, when there was a national trend toward the GOP, the Republican percentage of the union vote can reach as high as 46 percent. Similarly, in 1980, 1984, and 1988, Republican presidential nominees carried the Catholic vote. Predominantly Republican groups also give substantial support to the Democrats. Thus, as in 1996, Democratic president Bill Clinton's share of voters with incomes over $90,000 was over 40 percent.

Nonprogrammatic Parties

All parties have an interest in policy. Among the parties of Western nations, however, there is great diversity in the extent to which the parties are programmatic and the prime policymakers of the system. According to Leon D. Epstein, programmatic parties have policy positions that "are part of a settled long-range program to which the party is dedicated in definite enough terms to mark it off from rival parties."[20] The labor and social democratic parties of Western Europe are examples of parties with more strongly programmatic orientations than American parties, though these parties have recently been moderating their policies and accommodating themselves to market oriented economies. They remain, however, firmly committed to a social democratic ideology of activist government, and the process of moderating their leftist orientations has been of a lengthy duration and filled with intraparty controversies. For example, the British Labour party led by moderates such as Neil Kinnock, John Smith, and Tony Blair has been steadily moving since the early 1980s away from its traditional trade union and class conflict orientation toward a more centrist position designed to appeal to mainstream, middle-class voters.

This pragmatic approach to politics, however, was resisted by many party activists, and it was not until 1995 that Labour's leaders were finally able to get the party conference to remove a provision from the party constitution calling for public ownership of major economic enterprises. The British Conservative party, though traditionally less doctrinal than Labour, is also programmatic in the sense that it is committed to preserving capitalism and such traditional institutions as private schools and a strong military. The pursuit of its policy goals was particularly aggressive (e.g., privatization of nationalized industries and weakening trade unions) under the leadership of Prime Minister Margaret Thatcher (1979–1990). American parties are quite different. Their policy positions tend to be more ad hoc in character and adopted to meet immediate problems or electoral circumstances and not based upon long range programs to which the parties are committed.

Neither the Democrats nor the Republicans have a clear image of the type of society they wish to foster. Neither party is committed to socialism or unfettered capitalism. Both have modified their positions frequently on such issues as governmental regulation of business, foreign policy, and the extent of government support for social welfare programs. It is even common for prominent leaders of seemingly divergent viewpoints to combine forces in the Congress. Thus liberal Democratic Senator Tom Harkin (Iowa) and conservative Republican Orrin Hatch (Utah) were key advocates of the Americans with Disabilities Act of 1990, which prohibited discrimination against persons with disabilities; liberal Edward Kennedy (D-Mass.) worked with conservative Dan Quayle (R-Ind.) to pass job training legislation; in 1993 House Republican Whip Newt Gingrich worked cooperatively with President Clinton to pass the North American Free Trade Agreement, which was opposed by a majority of House Democrats including Majority Leader Richard Gebhardt (D-Mo.) and Chief Whip David Bonior (D-Mich.). After a period of intense partisan confrontation between the Republican controlled Congress and President

Clinton that led to a partial shutdown of the government in 1995, the GOP leadership and the president compromised their differences and agreed upon plans to balance the budget and reform the welfare system.

The broad coalition nature of the parties' electoral support makes it extremely difficult for them to make ideological, consistent, and coherent policy appeals to the voters representing such a wide spectrum of interests and viewpoints. Even if the parties were inclined toward programmatic politics, their decentralized character would make enforcing party unity next to impossible.

The substantial policy diversity that exists *within* each party is shown in table 3.4, which portrays the extent of liberalism among Democratic senators and the extent of conservatism among Republicans on scales developed by the *National Journal*.[21] The basic policy orientation of the two parties is divergent, with the most conservative senators found within the GOP and the most liberal senators residing in the Democratic party. Within that basic pattern, however, the two parties are far from monolithic in their approach to public policy issues. Liberals, moderates, and conservatives cohabit within both parties. Given this lack of internal policy agreement, the parties are less than reliable instruments of governmental policy making. The various constituencies of party officeholders pull them in different directions. The problem of relying upon party loyalty to implement government policies is shown in table 3.5, which presents data on congressional support for the president's legislative program. Presidents are not able to count upon the loyalty of their party's members in the Congress. The levels of defection can be significant. Even with the Congress controlled by his own party, President Clinton's position on legislation during 1997 was supported by House Democrats on average only 71 percent of the time. The North American Free Trade Agreement (NAFTA), a major Clinton priority, passed the House in 1993 only because Republicans gave it strong support, as a majority of House Democrats actually voted against the measure (156 opposed; 102 in favor). In addition, key items on Clinton's legislative agenda, most notably health care reform, were killed not only due to GOP opposition but because they lacked sufficient Democratic support. The internal unity problems of the congressional parties are illustrated by table 3.6, which lists Democratic senators who most frequently opposed the positions of their president, as well as Republican senators who gave President Clinton support over 50 percent of the time in 1994.

Table 3.4

Ideological Diversity within the Republican and Democratic Parties in the U.S. Senate, 105th Congress, 1st Session, 1997

Democratic Liberalism Scores
The Democratic senators' liberalism scores shown below are stated as percentiles and are based on their average scores on economic, social, and foreign policy issues. For example, a score of 90 on the liberalism scale means that the senator was more liberal than 90 percent of the total Senate membership.

	Percentile
Liberal Democrats	
Boxer (Cal.)	91.5
Wellstone (Minn.)	91.5
Sarbanes (Md.)	91.5
Reed (R. I.)	90.2
Kennedy (Mass.)	89.0
Bumpers (Ark.)	88.8
Feingold (Wis.)	88.8
Durbin (Ill.)	87.3
Akaka (Hi.)	86.8
Harkin (Iowa)	85.7
Mainstream Democrats	
Daschle (S.D.)	79.7
Rockefeller (W. Va.)	78.2
Inouye (Hi.)	77.5
Mikulski (Md.)	77.3
Glenn (Ohio)	77.0
Dodd (Conn.)	75.5
Johnson (S.D.)	75.2
Bacus (Mont.)	74.8
Dorgan (N.D.)	73.0
Feinstein (Cal.)	72.8
Moderate Democrats	
Kohl (Wis.)	65.5
Robb (Va.)	65.2
Cleland (Ga.)	64.8
Graham (Fla.)	63.5
Moynihan (N.Y.)	60.8
Biden (Del.)	60.8
Landrieu (La.)	59.8
Lieberman (Conn.)	57.5
Ford (Kent.)	56.8
Breaux (La.)	53.8

Republican Conservatism Scores
The Republican senators' conservatism scores shown below are stated as percentiles and are based upon averages of their scores on economic, social, and foreign policy issues. For example, a score of 90 on the conservatism scale means that the senator was more conservative than 90 percent of the total Senate membership.

	Percentile
Conservative Republicans	
Ashcroft (Mo.)	91.5
Brownback (Kans.)	91.5
Gramm (Tex.)	91.5
Hutchinson (Ark.)	91.5
Kyl (Ariz.)	91.5
Sessions (Ala.)	91.5
Thurmond (S.C.)	91.5
Allard (Colo.)	87.5
Grams (Minn.)	87.5
Helms (N.C.)	87.5
Mainstream Republicans	
Kempthorne (Ida.)	79.3
Santorum (Pa.)	76.5
Hutchinson (Tex.)	75.5
Coverdell (Ga.)	75.3
Hagel (Neb.)	74.7
Bennett (Utah)	70.7
McCain (Ariz.)	69.8
Murkowski (Alaska)	69.0
Coats (Ind.)	68.5
Moderate Republicans	
Cochran (Miss.)	56.5
Lugar (Ind.)	55.5
Roth (Del.)	55.0
Stevens (Alaska)	50.3
D'Amato (N.Y.)	49.7
Collins (Me.)	47.7
Snowe (Me.)	47.2
Specter (Pa.)	45.1
Jeffords (Vt.)	35.3
Chafee (R. I.)	29.0

Source: National Journal, Special Supplement: *Annual Congressional Vote Ratings,* March 7, 1998, pp. 7, 12–14. Reprinted by permission.

Table 3.5
Support for President's Position on Roll Call Votes by Members of the President's Party in Congress, 1954–1998

			Average Percent of Members of President's Party Supporting His Position	
Years	**President**	**Party**	**Representatives**	**Senators**
1993–1998	Clinton	Democrat	78	81
1989–1992	Bush	Republican	69	77
1981–1988	Reagan	Republican	68	79
1977–1980	Carter	Democrat	69	69
1974–1976	Ford	Republican	72	65
1969–1974	Nixon	Republican	73	63
1964–1968	Johnson	Democrat	71	81
1961–1963	Kennedy	Democrat	75	83
1954–1960	Eisenhower	Republican	80	68

Sources: Norman J. Ornstein, Thomas E. Mann, and Michael J. Malbin, *Vital Statistics on Congress, 1997–1998* (Washington, D.C.: Congressional Quarterly, Inc., 1998), pp. 208–209; *Congressional Quarterly Weekly Report,* Jan. 3, 1998, p. 27.

Table 3.6
Democratic Senators Voting Most Frequently in Opposition to the President's Position on Senate Roll Calls, and Republican Senators Most Frequently Voting in Support of the President, 1997

Democratic Senators	Percent of Votes Opposed to the President's Position	Republican Senators	Percent of Votes in Support of the President's Position
Hollings (S.C.)	25 %	Jeffords (Vt.)	78%
Ford (Kent.)	21	Snowe (Me.)	78
Breaux (La.)	19	Collins (Me.)	76
Byrd (W. Va.)	19	Chaffee (R.I.)	75
Conrad (N.D.)	19	Specter (Pa.)	71
Dorgan (N.D.)	19	Stevens (Alaska)	71
Moynihan (N.Y.)	18	McCain (Ariz.)	70
Wellstone (Minn.)	17	Cochran (Miss.)	68

Source: *Congressional Quarterly Weekly Report,* Jan. 3, 1998, p. 35; Jan. 9, 1999, p. 86.

Given the lack of party unity that often exists in Congress, it is frequently necessary to form cross-party alliances to pass legislation, for example, the previously noted bipartisan coalition required to pass NAFTA as well as welfare reform (1996) and a balanced budget agreement (1997). Similarly, President Ronald Reagan relied upon a coalition of Republicans and conservative/moderate Democrats to pass major budget and tax changes early in his administration. This alliance of Republicans and southern Democrats, dubbed the Conservative Coalition, has had a major impact upon congressional decision making. The coalition formed on average in 20 percent of the House and Senate roll call votes between 1965 and 1988, and it gained legislative victories 74 percent of the time. However, as conservative and moderate Democrats from the South have been replaced by conservative Republicans, both parties have become more homogeneous in terms of policy orientation. This has led to heightened internal party unity, intensified partisan conflict, and a decline in the importance of the Conservative Coalition (Republicans and southern Democrats), which appeared on only 6 percent of congressional roll calls in 1998.[22]

While it is clear that American parties are relatively nonprogrammatic and contain substantial policy differences within their ranks, this line of argument must not be carried too far. It should not be inferred that there are no significant differences in the policy orientations of the Republican and Democratic parties. As noted in chapter 1, shifts in party control of the national government—as during the Reagan and Johnson administrations—have resulted in major changes in public policy. It does make a difference whether Republicans or Democrats are in control of Congress and the presidency. Thus, upon taking control of Congress in 1995, the Republicans, particularly in the House, moved with unusual unity and aggressiveness to implement a policy agenda of dramatically reducing the role of government; and in the highly polarized political environment of the 1990s, the congressional Democrats have strongly resisted this policy shift. Table 3.4, while demonstrating the policy diversity within the parties, also points up the differences in policy orientation between the two parties. The Democratic members of Congress are substantially more liberal, on the whole, than are the Republicans.

Though much maligned by cynical reporters, party platforms also show substantial differences between the parties.

Analyses of recent party platforms reveal significant differences between the two parties and consistent efforts by the officeholders of the two parties to implement those platforms. In 1996, there were sharp differences between the Democratic and Republican platforms on such issues as taxes, balanced budget amendments, health care, the environment, abortion, and immigration reform. The platform is important, Gerald Pomper has observed, because

> it summarizes, crystallizes, and presents to the voters the characteristics of the party coalition. . . . The stands taken in the platform clarify the parties' positions on . . . controversies and reveal the nature of their support and appeal.[23]

Not only are the policy positions of the parties' platforms and their elected officials different, but so are their rank and file voters and activist participants. Although both Republican and Democratic rank and file voters tend to be moderate in ideology, Democrats are more liberal than Republicans. The ideological orientations of party activists (national convention delegates) show even greater differences between the parties. Party activists in both parties tend to be much more extreme in ideological positions, with Republican activists considering themselves much more conservative than GOP rank and file voters, and Democratic activists ranked more liberal than Democratic voters. For example, in a *New York Times* poll of 1996 national convention delegates and rank and file party voters, 43 percent of Democratic delegates considered themselves liberal, while only 27 percent of Democratic voters thought of themselves as liberals; among Republicans, 66 percent of the delegates said they were conservatives compared to 53 percent of the GOP voters.[24]

Party activists, who are highly influential in nomination contests and in providing campaign support, are an important force that pulls the two parties apart on policy. Candidates must have the support of these party workers. The fact that in the Republican party they are more conservative and in the Democratic party more liberal than the parties' rank and file voters means that there are strong pressures within the system maintaining differences in policy between the parties. But even with these differences, American parties remain relatively nonprogrammatic and pragmatic in their approach to issues.

Quasi-Public Institutions with Ambiguous Membership

In most democracies other than the United States, political parties are considered private organizations like the Elks, American Legion, Rotary, or American Bar Association. They make and enforce their own rules concerning qualifications for membership, organizational structure, and activities. There are few laws governing their internal decision making processes. Membership normally involves a process of application and approval. Members are then expected to assume obligations such as paying annual dues. In return, party members are permitted to take part in party activities such as the selection of candidates.

By contrast, American parties are quasi-public institutions that are heavily regulated by statute, especially state laws. The very existence of American parties is almost mandated by state statutes that legally define parties and prescribe their organizational structure, membership criteria, leadership selection methods, and the procedures for nominating candidates. By controlling who may vote in party primaries, for example, state statutes set the qualifications for membership in American parties. In closed primary states, voters are required to state publicly their party preference before being allowed to participate in the preferred party's primary. Party membership in these circumstances is essentially a matter of self-designation. In open primary states, it is possible to vote without ever publicly professing a preference for one party over another. The voters decide in the secrecy of the voting booth in which party's primary they will vote. Austin Ranney has observed that such statutory regulation of party membership has made the Republican and Democratic parties

> unique among the world's parties in that neither has effective control of its own legal membership and there is no formal distinction between member and supporter.[25]

In some jurisdictions, including Wisconsin and Minnesota, the party organizations do have modest sized dues-paying memberships. But these formal members have few privileges that are not extended to non–dues-paying supporters of the party. Both are entitled to participate in primary elections to select the party's nominees. Party membership in the United States is, therefore, an ambiguous phenomenon and largely a matter of self-designation.

The extensive regulation of parties by state statutes in such matters as membership, organization, leadership selection, nominations, and campaign finance has meant that parties are not free to run their own internal affairs as they see fit. Not unlike public utilities that provide public services in a manner prescribed by law, parties also perform essential public functions under government regulations.[26] They are, therefore, quasi-public institutions with relatively open membership qualifications.

Weak Parties, But Substantial Partisan Influence

While sharing many features in common with the parties of other Western democracies, American political parties have a distinguishing set of characteristics—two-partyism, decentralized power structures, broadly based electoral coalitions, moderate policy orientations, and quasi-public status. Taken as a whole, these are features which limit party influence on governmental policymaking. At the same time, party influences pervade the political system—in electoral politics, in organizing governmental institutions, and in influencing policy making. This seeming contradiction of parties being relatively weak, decentralized, and frequently lacking in unity, while at the same time being an important—but not necessarily dominant—influence on electoral and governmental politics is one of the distinguishing aspects of the American political system.

Suggestions for Further Reading

Beck, Paul Allen. *Party Politics in America.* 8th ed. New York: Longman, 1996.

Eldersveld, Samuel J. *Political Parties in American Society.* New York: Basic Books, 1982.

Epstein, Leon D. *Political Parties in the American Mold.* Madison: University of Wisconsin Press, 1986.

__________. *Political Parties in Western Democracies.* New York: Praeger, 1967.

Gillespie, J. David. *Politics at the Periphery: Third Parties in Two-Party America.* Columbia, S.C.: University of South Carolina Press, 1993.

Keefe, William J. *Parties, Politics, and Public Policy in America.* 8th ed. (Washington, D.C.: CQ Press, 1998).

Rae, Nicol C. *The Decline and Fall of the Liberal Republicans.* New York: Oxford University Press, 1989.

_________. *Southern Democrats.* New York: Oxford University Press, 1994.

Rosenstone, Steven J., Behr, Roy L., and Lazarus, Edward H. *Third Parties in America: Citizen Responses to Major Party Failure.* 2nd ed. Princeton, N.J.: Princeton University Press, 1996.

Shafer, Byron E., ed. *Partisan Approaches to Postwar American Politics.* Chatham, N.J.: Chatham House, 1998.

Notes

1. The index of competitiveness was developed by Austin Ranney, "Parties in State Politics," in Herbert Jacob and Kenneth Vines, eds., *Politics in the American States,* 3rd ed. (Boston: Little, Brown, 1976), pp. 59–61.

2. Samuel C. Patterson and Gregory A. Caldeira, "The Etiology of Partisan Competition," *American Political Science Review* 78 (September 1984): 691–707. See also John F. Bibby and Thomas M. Holbrook, "Parties and Elections," in Virginia Gray and Herbert Jacob, eds., *Politics in the American States,* 6th ed. (Washington, D.C.: CQ Press, 1996), ch. 3.

3. Norman J. Ornstein, Thomas E. Mann, and Michael J. Malbin, *Vital Statistics on Congress, 1997–1998* (Washington, D.C.: Congressional Quarterly, 1998), p. 69.

4. Ibid, p. 88.

5. Ronald E. Weber, Harvey J. Tucker, and Paul Brace, "Vanishing Marginals in State Legislative Elections," *Legislative Studies Quarterly* 26 (February 1991): 29–47.

6. William E. Cassie and David A. Breaux, "Expenditures and Election Results," in *Campaign Finance in State Legislative Elections,* Joel A. Thompson and Gary E. Moncrief, eds. (Washington, D.C.: Congressional Quarterly, 1998), p. 103; see also Gary W. Cox and Scott Morgenstern, "The Increasing Advantage of Incumbency in the U.S. States," *Legislative Studies Quarterly* 26 (November 1991): 495–514.

7. On America's system of separated institutions, see Charles 0. Jones, *The Presidency in a Separated System* (Washington, D.C.: Brookings, 1994).

8. Leon D. Epstein, *Political Parties in Western Democracies* (New York: Praeger, 1967), p. 33.

9. Maurice Carroll, "For Once, a Primary Unites a Party," *New York Times,* March 25, 1984, p. 6E.

10. For a fascinating account of how British parties can control parliamentary nominations to enforce party discipline, see Leon D. Epstein, "British M.P.s and Their Local Parties: The Suez Cases," *American Political Science Review* 54 (June 1960): 627–639; see also Anthony King, ed., *New Labor Triumphs: Britain at the Polls* (Chatham, N.J.: Chatham House, 1998), pp. 66–68.

11. Gary C. Jacobson, *The Politics of Congressional Elections*, 3rd ed. (New York: HarperCollins, 1992), p. 77.

12. David Mayhew, *Congress: The Electoral Connection* (New Haven, Conn.: Yale University Press, 1974).

13. Leon D. Epstein, "Party Confederations and Political Nationalization," *Publius* 12 (Fall 1982), p. 71.

14. *Democratic Party of the United States of America v. Bronson C. LaFollette*, 449 U.S. 897 (1981).

15. Austin Ranney, "The Political Parties: Reform and Decline," in Anthony King, ed., *The New American Political System* (Washington, D.C.: American Enterprise Institute, 1978), p. 230.

16. John F. Bibby, "Party Renewal in the National Republican Party," in Gerald Pomper, ed., *Party Renewal in America* (New York: Praeger, 1981), pp. 102–115.

17. On the expanded role of the national party organizations and the growth of intraparty integration, see Paul S. Herrnson, "The Revitalization of National Party Organizations," in L. Sandy Maisel, ed., *The Parties Respond* (Boulder, Colo.: Westview Press, 1998), ch 3; and John F. Bibby, "Party Networks: National-State Intergration, Allied Groups, and Issue Activists," in John C. Green and Daniel M. Shea, eds., *The State of the Parties* (Lanham, Md.: Roman and Littlefield, 1999), ch. 5.

18. Jill Abramson and Leslie Wayne, "Democrats Used State Parties to Bypass Limits," *New York Times* (national edition), October 2, 1997, pp. A1, A8.

19. John H. Kessel, *Presidential Campaign Politics*, 4th ed. (Pacific Grove, Cal.: Brooks/Cole, 1992), pp. 113–114.

20. Epstein, *Political Parties in Western Democracies*, p. 262.

21. Richard E. Cohen, "Business as Usual," *National Journal*, March 7, 1998, pp. 4–16.

22. *Congressional Quarterly, Weekly Report*, January 1999, p. 38

23. Gerald M. Pomper and Susan S. Lederman, *Elections in America* (New York: Longman, 1980), p. 173.

24. *New York Times* (national edition), August 26, 1996, p. A12.

25. Austin Ranney, *The Governing of Men*, 4th ed. (Hinsdale, Ill.: Dryden Press, 1975), p. 199.

26. Leon D. Epstein, *Political Parties in the American Mold* (Madison: University of Wisconsin Press, 1986), ch. 6.

PARTY ORGANIZATIONS

CHAPTER FOUR

Party organization in the United States conjures up a variety of strikingly different images, depending upon one's perspective.

To a ward committeeman in Chicago, or a party functionary in Nassau County (Long Island), the party organization is a hierarchically run machine that dispenses jobs, social services, and help with the governmental bureaucracy in return for electoral support.

To a Minnesota Democrat, the party organization is a group of issue oriented liberals who take party platforms seriously, seek to control primary election outcomes through party endorsements of candidates, and work as campaign volunteers.

To a rural southern Democrat, the party organization is a group of courthouse politicians who perfunctorily fill formal positions, but whose activity is limited.

To most California activists, the real party organization is the candidate's personal following and his or her professional campaign consultants.

To many state legislators, the party organization that really matters is the state legislative campaign committee chaired by the party leader in the legislature, which provides money and technical assistance to candidates.

To the staff member of the Republican National Committee, the party organization is a large bureaucracy consisting of hundreds of paid professionals using the most sophisticated techniques and operating with receipts in excess of $100 million.

As these illustrations suggest, party organization in the United States exists in an almost infinite variety of forms. The type of organization operating in any political jurisdiction depends upon a variety of factors: the level of government involved (e.g., local, state, or national), the type of governmental regulations under which it must operate, the extent of interparty competition that exists, the clientele or bases of party support, regional and local traditions, and the nature of the electorate. Generally, however, American political party organizations are *cadre* type rather than *mass membership* parties. Cadre parties are characterized by a small number of leaders and activists who maintain the organization, recruit candidates, seek to influence nominations, and campaign for the party's nominees. The party organization is active mainly during the election season and the party in the electorate has little impact on the organization or control over its elected officials. By contrast, a mass membership party is characterized by a large dues-paying membership that plays an active role in selecting party leadership and in developing policy positions. The mass membership party tends to be active the year around and exerts substantial influence over the party's governmental officeholders.

The American cadre type of party structure is based upon a complex set of interlocking national party rules, state and federal statutes, and state and local party rules. It is organized to carry out its primary task—the winning of elections. Party organization, therefore, is built around geographic election districts, starting with the basic unit of election administration, the precinct. Above that in ascending order are city/village/town committees, county or township committees, legislative district committees, congressional district committees, state central committees, and at the national level the national committee (see figure 4.1). Although the party organization builds from the local precinct to the national committee, this structure should not be viewed as a hierarchy. As V. O. Key, Jr., observed, party organization "may be more accurately described as a system of layers of organization."[1] Each separate layer focuses its efforts on the elections within its particular jurisdiction. Thus county parties are concerned first with control of the courthouse offices, state committees with the governorship, and the national committees with control of the presidency. At the same time, each level of party organization normally needs to obtain the collaboration of other layers of organization to achieve their objectives. But as Key has noted, "that collaboration comes about, to the extent that it does come about, through a sense of common cause rather than by the exercise of command."[2]

This layered organizational structure which characterizes American parties is called *stratarchy*, "an organization with layers, or strata, of control rather than centralized leadership from the top down."[3] Each stratum has its own organization and functions to perform and each is quite autonomous within its own sphere, while maintaining contact with party units above and below. Samuel

Figure 4.1
LAYERS OF PARTY ORGANIZATIONS IN THE UNITED STATES

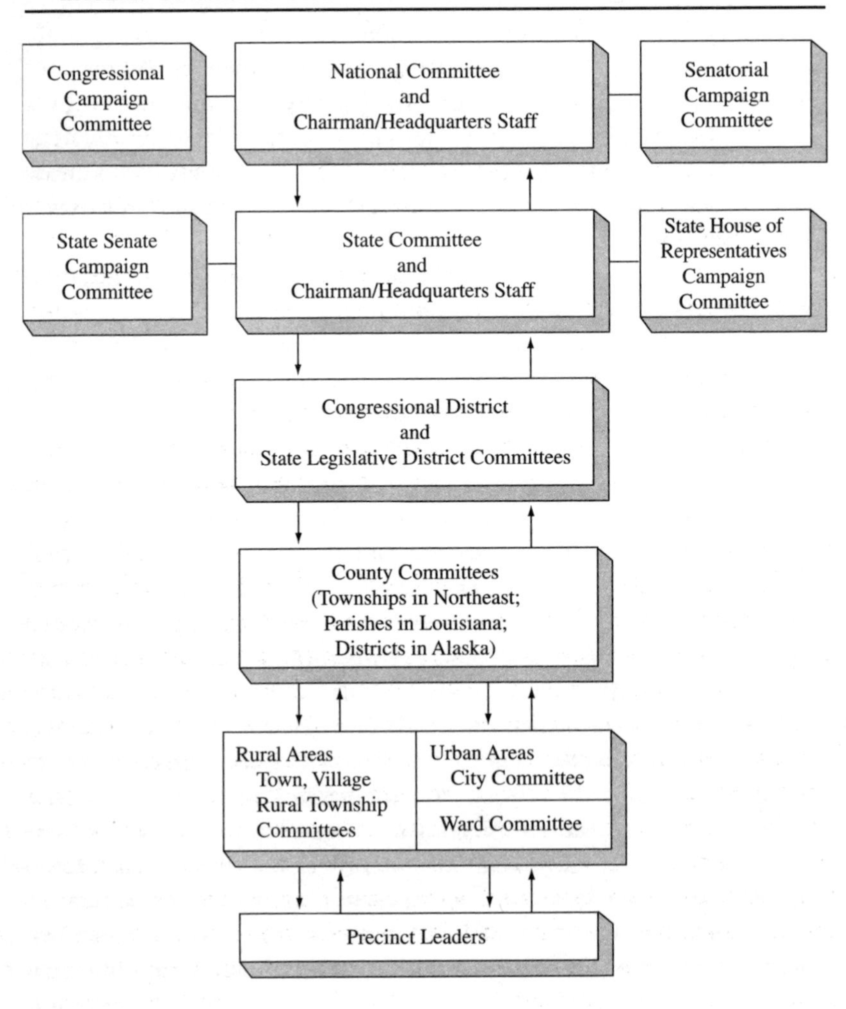

Eldersveld has noted that a special component of stratarchy is *reciprocal deference*. That is, between the layers of organization "there is a tolerance of autonomy, of each layer's status and its right to initiative, as well as tolerance of inertia."[4] This tolerance stems from the lack of effective sanctions which higher levels of the party may exercise over lower level units and the fact that each stratum needs the assistance of the other for such activities as fund-raising and mobilizing the vote. The spirit of tolerance for autonomy was captured by a midwestern state party chairman who commented about his relationship with the county party organizations in his state.

> At best we are a loose confederation. I have no jurisdiction over county chairmen. I'd have resented a state chairman telling me what to do when I was county chairman.

The party organizational structure suffers further fragmentation due to the existence at the national level of congressional and senatorial campaign committees in each party, which operate with substantial autonomy from the national committees. There is similar organizational structure at the state level, where state legislative campaign committees function independently of the state committees of the party.

Supplementing and at times dominating the loosely structured system of formal party organization are thousands of organizations formed by individual candidates seeking both their party's nomination and general election victory. These personal candidate organizations are focused upon winning elections for a single individual for one office. Often, especially in the case of presidential candidate organizations, they command greater financial resources, professional staff, and volunteer workers than regular party organizations. They are, however, less permanent and less encompassing in their electioneering activities.[5]

Also operating within the orbit of party organizations are party-allied groups that assist the parties and their candidates with fund raising, voter mobilization, and issue development. While legally autonomous from the parties, these groups' activities are often crucial to Republican and Democratic candidates, for example, organized labor's massive get-out-the-vote activities and advertising campaigns on behalf of Democrats and the voter guides distributed by the Christian Coalition for the benefit of Republicans.

Another element in party organizations is professional campaign consultants, political "hired guns" whose skills are now deemed absolutely essential for any major campaign. These specialists in the various campaign arts—media advertising, direct mail, polling, campaign management, fund raising—tend to work exclusively for one party or the other and hence must be considered a part of each parties' resource base. The party organization, therefore, is in reality a *network* that extends beyond the regular and legally constituted party structure to include candidate organizations, party-allied groups, and campaign consultants.[6]

The National Parties

The National Committees

Traditionally the national party committees have been cited as classic examples of the decentralized character of American parties. These bodies composed of delegates from the respective state parties were created in the mid-1800s to serve as the interim agents of the party conventions. Since their principal function during the post-Civil War era was managing the presidential campaign, the committees were active for only a few months during a four year period. It was not until the chairmanship of Will Hayes (1918–1921) that the Republican National Committee (RNC) established a year round headquarters with full time paid staff; and the Democratic National Committee (DNC) did not do so until 1928. The ad hoc character of national committee staffing extended well into this century, with the campaigns of 1928 and 1932 conducted largely by congressmen, senators, governors, and other party notables with the assistance of borrowed professionals.

Gradually the national committees became more institutionalized with expanded full time staff, elaborate division of labor, heightened professionalism, and larger budgets.[7] Thus since 1950, the size of the DNC staff has never dipped below forty persons, and the RNC has exceeded eighty. These personnel perform fund raising, public relations, voter mobilization, national convention management, campaign management and training, research, and policy development functions. Although the budgets and staff increased and the functions of the committees have been extended from an exclusive concern with presidential elections, the committees traditionally exercised little power. The leading study of the RNC and DNC published in 1964 characterized national committee politics as "politics without power."[8] While this was something of an exaggeration, the phrase did aptly capture the inability of the national committees to exert significant influence upon the behavior of state and local party leaders and elected officials. National committees are the most inclusive organization within the parties. Only the national committee represents the party organizations of the fifty states plus ex officio representation for important elected officials and organized interests. Active and aggressive leadership of the national committee is capable of generating publicity for the party, raising campaign funds, mobilizing voters, and providing financial and technical assistance to candidates and state and local party units. The national committee can be an effective catalyst for stimulating the party organization, even though its formal powers are limited. This has been especially true for the party which does not hold the White House. For the out-party, the national committee is normally a major arena of party activity and struggles for power.[9]

National Committee Membership. For most of their history, the RNC and the DNC had roughly comparable bases for committee membership. Each state party organization selected a national committeeman and woman to serve on the committee. State party chairmen were made members of the RNC in the 1960s and the Democrats adopted this policy in the 1970s. The committees' membership reflected the confederate nature of the national parties with each state having equal representation and its national committee members serving essentially as party ambassadors from their states.

As a part of a series of major party reforms, the Democrats significantly changed the basis for representation on the DNC in 1974. These changes involved a major expansion of the size of the committee, representation for elected officials and various party auxiliaries, and equal representation of the sexes. The principle of state equality was abandoned in favor of a formula which took into account the population of the state and its record of support for Democratic candidates. The Republicans have not moved to change their representational scheme and maintain the principle of state equality and a confederate party system. The composition of the

The Institutionalization of the National Party Committees

Staff Growth

Committee	1972	1976	1980	1984	1988	1992	1996
Republican National Committee	200 *	200	350	600	425	300	271
National Republican Congressional Committee	5	8	40	130	80	89	64
National Republican Senatorial Committee	4	6	30	90	88	135	150
Total	209	214	420	820	593	524	485
Democratic National Committee	30	30	40	130	160	270	264
Democratic Congressional Campaign Committee	6	6	26	45	80	64	64
Democratic Senatorial Campaign Committee	4	5	20	22	50	35	38
Total	40	41	86	197	290	369	366

*Estimate based upon staffing data for 1960s and 1970s.

Sources: Paul S. Herrnson, *Party Campaigning in the 1980s* (Cambridge, Mass.: Harvard University Press, 1988), p. 39; Paul S. Herrnson "Resurgent National Organizations," in L. Sandy Maisel, ed., *The Parties Respond: Changes in the American Party System* (Boulder, Colo.: Westview Press, 1990), pp. 41–66, and 2nd ed. (1994), pp. 45–66;Paul S. Herrnson, "National Party Organizations at the Century's End," in L. Sandy Maisel, ed., *The Parties Respond: Changes in the American Party System* (Boulder, Colo.: Westview Press, 1998), p. 61; (facing page) Federal Election Commission.

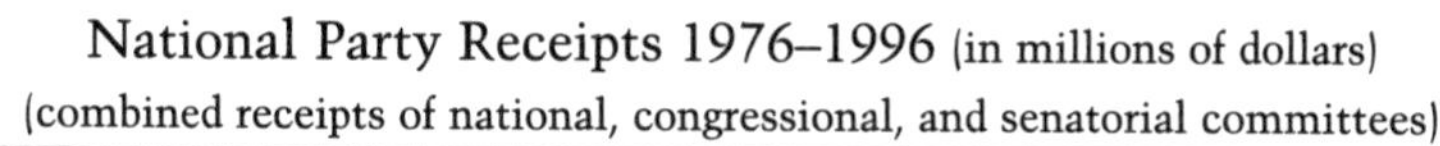
National Party Receipts 1976–1996 (in millions of dollars)
(combined receipts of national, congressional, and senatorial committees)

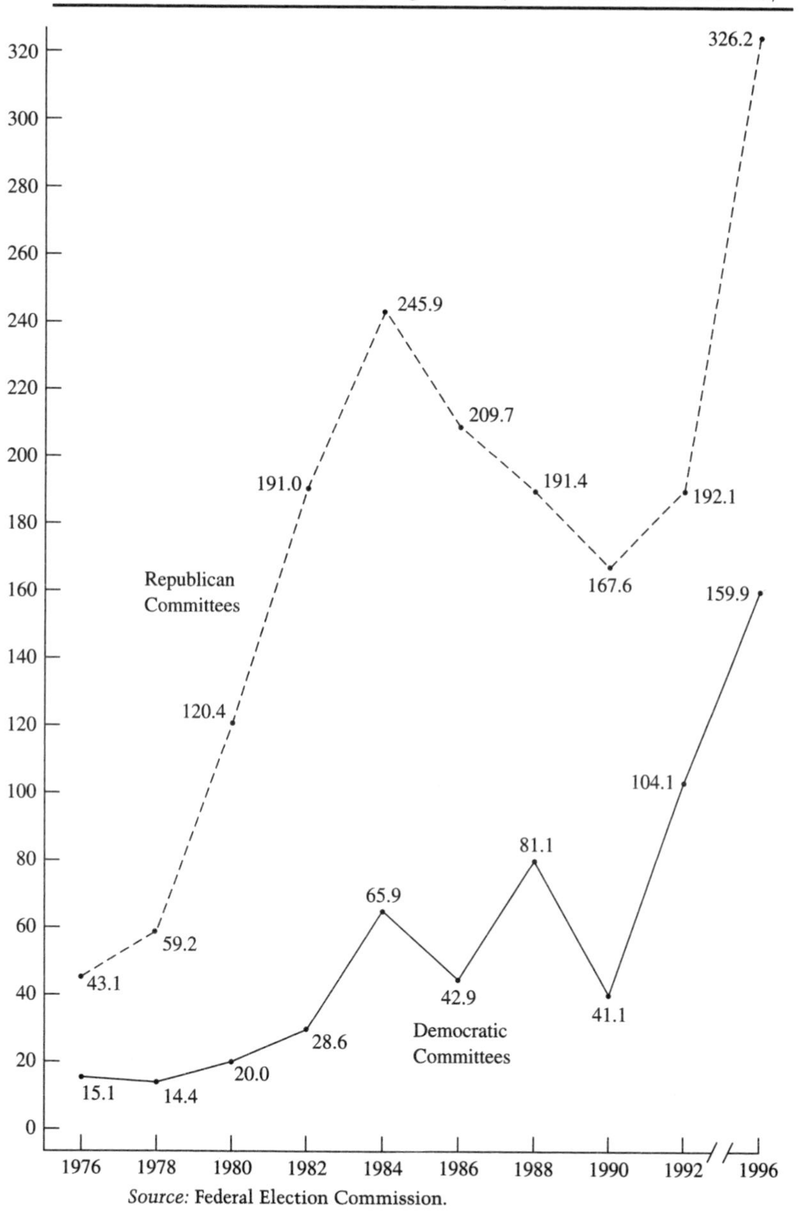

Source: Federal Election Commission.

DNC and RNC is described in figure 4.2. The large number of people serving on the national committees, especially the DNC, has meant that deliberative action is almost impossible at national committee meetings. Instead, the locus for decision making is with the national chairman and the executive committee, who meet prior to national committee meetings. The full national committees normally ratify the recommendations of the chairman and executive committee.

The observer of DNC and RNC meetings is immediately struck by the fact that the differences between the two committees go well beyond their respective sizes. Differences in style of operation and party constituencies are apparent.[10] Republican National Committee meetings are extremely well organized, structured, and professionally staffed. There is an air of formality and relative order about the conduct of the meetings. DNC meetings are less well organized, informal, and have a rather ad hoc character. Orderliness prevails in RNC sessions, while confusion is common at DNC meetings. The major subunits of RNC gatherings are meetings of the state chairmen and regional associations. There are also informal meetings of various ideological and candidate factions. The DNC has all of these types of subunits and factions, but in addition has active caucuses for blacks, Hispanics, and women which have played a major role in DNC meetings. Through the efforts of Chairman Paul Kirk (1985–1989), these caucuses lost official recognition in 1985. Kirk believed that the prominence of the caucuses was conveying an image of the party as a collection of special interests. The caucuses continue to exist on an informal basis, however, and the black, women's, and Hispanic caucuses retained ex officio representation on the DNC Executive Committee.[11] There is no comparable specialized representational structure—formal or informal—within the RNC. This no doubt reflects the important role which organized groups have traditionally played within the Democratic coalition. By contrast, the Republicans, with their more homogeneous constituency and middle-class orientation, have had a less extensive and explicit relationship with organized groups.

The National Chairman. Because the national committees are unwieldy in size and meet but twice a year, the national chairman plays a key role in determining how the committee will operate.

Figure 4.2
COMPOSITION OF THE REPUBLICAN AND DEMOCRATIC NATIONAL COMMITTEES

Republican National Committee	Number	Democratic National Committee	Number
1 national committeeman for each state, D.C., Guam, Puerto Rico, American Samoa, and Virgin Islands	55	National committee members—apportioned among the states on the same basis as national convention delegates (at least 2 per state)	212
1 national committee-woman for each state, D.C., and territory	55		
State chairman from each state, D.C., and territory	55	State party chair and next highest official of the opposite sex from each state, D.C., Puerto Rico, American Samoa, Guam, Virgin Islands, and Democrats abroad	112
(Republican rules provide ex officio membership on the RNC executive committee for representatives of the following: Republican Finance Committee, National Federation of Republican Women, Republican State Chairmen's Advisory Committee, Budget Committee, and other Republican groups that may be granted membership by the Executive Committee.)		Chair of Democratic Governors Association, plus 2 additional governors	3
		Two Democratic leaders from the House and Senate	4
		Chair of Democratic Mayors Conference, plus 2 additional mayors	3
		Chair of National Conference of Democratic Lieutenant Governors, plus one additional lieutenant governor	2
		Chair of National Conference of Democratic Secretaries of State, plus one additional secretary of state	2
		Chair of National Association of Democratic State Treasurers, plus one additional state treasurer	2
		Chair of Democratic County Officials Conference, plus 2 additional officials	3
		Chair of Democratic State Legislative Leaders Association, plus 2 legislators	3
		Chair of National Democratic Municipal Officials Conference, plus 2 officials	3
		President of Young Democrats and 2 members	3
		Chair of College Democrats of America, plus one additional member	2
		President of National Federation of Democratic Women, plus 2 members	3
		DNC officers	11
		Not more than 75 additional members	75
Total	165		443

The chairman's policies and programs, in turn, are implemented by the headquarters staff. Republican and Democratic rules now require that the chairman serve on a full time basis. This prevents elected officials like United States senators and representatives from becoming national chairmen. Incumbent presidents are accorded the power to designate who will serve as their party's chairman. Up until the 1980s, it was customary at national conventions for the presidential nominee to designate a national chairman for the upcoming campaign. This designation was then ratified by the national committee. In the interest of party unity, recent presidential nominees have allowed national chairmen to serve out their terms, which run until the January after presidential elections. The presidential nominees, however, do install their own campaign personnel in key national committee positions to make certain that the national committee and presidential campaign are working in harness.

For the party which does not control the presidency—the out-party—control of the national chairmanship is an important element in the struggle for intraparty ascendancy. Losing presidential campaigns inevitably breed struggles for control of the national committee. Often this takes the form of attempts to depose the national chairman. For example, Senator Barry Goldwater's choice for chairman, Dean Burch (1964–65), was forced to resign after the disastrous 1964 Republican campaign; Jean Westwood (1972), Senator George McGovern's pick for DNC chair in 1972, found it necessary to relinquish her post after the Nixon landslide; and following the GOP defeat in 1996, eight candidates engaged in an expensive, hard fought, and often ideologically divisive campaign for the RNC chairmanship, which was won on the third ballot by James Nicholson.

Traditionally there have been two basic styles of national committee leadership. One was the speaking chairman, who saw the role as one of acting as spokesperson on behalf of the party, generating publicity, and criticizing the opposition. Senator Robert Dole (Kan.) during his tenure (1971–73) as RNC chairman played this role, using his often caustic wit to defend the Nixon administration and attack the Democrats. Similarly, President Bush in 1990 selected Secretary of Agriculture Clayton Yeutter, a man with little campaign or day-to-day party management experience, to be RNC chairman because he wanted a spokesman for broad party themes.

The growing institutionalization of the national committees, with their enlarged staffs and budgets, and the rules requirement that chairmen serve on a full time basis, has meant that increasingly national chairmen have tended to emphasize not their role as party spokespersons, but their role as organizational leaders. Their job is to create a headquarters capable of providing the services needed to win elections. The classic example of a chairman who emphasized building an effective party organization (a "nuts and bolts" chairman) was Ray C. Bliss (1965–1969), who headed the RNC after the 1964 electoral disaster. Bliss seldom spoke in public and devoted his energies toward rebuilding the GOP organizations—especially in metropolitan areas.[12] Although recent national chairmen have generally been effective party spokespersons, their principal qualification for the job has been extensive experience as party organizational and campaign leaders. Thus George Bush's first RNC chairman, Lee Atwater (1989–1990), had served as a political consultant and Bush's campaign strategist in 1988; and Haley Barbour, who was elected to head the RNC in 1993, previously had been a state party official, senatorial candidate, White House political aide, and political consultant. Similarly, DNC chairmen have come out of the ranks of experienced party and campaign leaders. For example, Ron Brown, who chaired the DNC from 1989 to 1993 (the first African-American to lead a national committee), had previously served as chief counsel and deputy chairman of the DNC and was a proven fund-raiser and well-connected Washington attorney and lobbyist. Stephen Grossman, whom President Clinton picked in 1997 when the DNC was mired in debt from the 1996 campaign, was one of the party's most skillful fund raisers; his successor, Joseph Andrew, had been an effective state chair in Indiana.

Frequently, a major responsibility of the national chairman is maintaining or restoring a sense of party unity. The national chairman, therefore, must give recognition to the various factions (congressional, gubernatorial, candidate, racial, ideological, and regional), mediate disputes, and negotiate compromises on party rules and policy positions. One of the most skilled mediators of intraparty squabbles was DNC chairman Robert Straus (1972–1977), who guided the party after the internal divisiveness of the McGovern nomination and defeat. Similarly, after the 1992 GOP loss of the White House, RNC Chairman Haley Barbour sought to unite the

GOP by focusing upon disagreements with Clinton administration policies, downplaying divisive social issues such as abortion, and emphasizing grassroots organizational efforts in preparation for the 1994 midterm elections and the 1996 presidential election.

The national chairmen who have been considered the most effective have generally been those leading the out-party. Out-party chairmen have considerable flexibility and can exert an independent influence on their party because they normally have personally campaigned for the post and developed a core of supporters among party leaders. For example, out-party DNC Chairman Ron Brown (1989–1992) helped put the party in position to regain the White House by strengthening its finances and instituting "coordinated campaign" structures within the states that combined the resources of the party organizations, candidates' personal organizations, and party-allied interest groups. Similarly, the RNC's Haley Barbour (1993–1996) played a critical role in the GOP winning control of Congress for the first time in forty years by borrowing large sums and providing unprecedented national committee support for the 1994 congressional campaigns.

By contrast, the chairman of the party that controls the White House—the in-party—has little flexibility or independence. Such a chairman serves at the pleasure of the president and tends to be dominated by the political operatives at the White House. Senator Bob Dole (R-Kans.), who served as head of the RNC during President Nixon's reelection campaign, has even gone so far as to assert "When your party's in power, the chairman doesn't have any decision-making role."[13] Similarly, Senator Robert Kerrey (D-Neb.) complained in 1998 that the DNC was a "wholly owned subsidiary of the [Clinton] White House,"[14] and in testimony before a Senate committee DNC chair Donald Fowler provided a vivid portrait of White House Deputy Chief of Staff Harold Ickes "operating from his White House office, calling crucial shots at the Democratic National Committee as it sought to raise tens of millions of dollars for the President's reelection" in 1996.[15]

Presidential influence over the national committee is so pervasive that chairmen can have their role usurped by White House decree. For example, dissatisfaction with DNC performance caused the Clinton White House to insert former House Democratic Whip Tony Coelho (Cal.) into the DNC as overseer of the 1994 midterm elections. DNC chairman David Wilhelm, who was left as only a figurehead leader of the committee, then announced plans to resign after the elections and return to Chicago.[16] Then after suffering major setbacks in the 1994 elections and while seeking a spirited and articulate party spokesperson, Clinton installed Senator Christopher Dodd (Conn.) as the party's general chairman (a part-time position) and Donald L. Fowler, a former South Carolina party chair, as national chairman, responsible for the day to day management of the DNC.

As David Wilhelm's fate illustrates, the White House staff and its Office of Political Affairs has characteristically emerged since the 1960s as the central institution for presidential party management. In the current era of candidate centered politics, national committees no longer manage presidential campaigns. Nor do the national committees any longer dispense federal patronage. That role is now performed by the White House Personnel Office. In terms of its relations with the president, the in-party national committee provides backup political support and implements the political strategies of the president. Thus, during the Clinton administration, the DNC paid the retainer fees of professional campaign consultants who advise the president, including multimillion dollar fees annually to presidential pollsters.[17]

Although Presidents Reagan, Bush, and Clinton have been supportive of their national committees and worked closely with them, particularly on fundraising, some recent presidents have quite literally sought to dismantle the national committee because they wished to concentrate party leadership in the hands of White House staffers. The Nixon administration tended to downplay the role of the RNC as a campaign mechanism to help all GOP candidates and instead emphasized the chairman's role as a publicist for the president. Another notable example of White House neglect of the national party machinery occurred during the Carter administration, when the president and his staff through inattention to the party organization left the DNC unprepared for the 1978 midterm elections.[18] Then, as the 1980 elections approached, the Carter White House used the meager financial resources of the DNC to fund presidential polls by the president's pollster, Pat Caddell. Even President Clinton, who has been an assiduous fund-raiser for his party, came in for criticism because Clinton and White House consultants diverted DNC efforts away from electoral support activities into television campaigns for the President's embattled legislative program during 1993–1994.[19]

Committee Activities. The actual work of the national committees is done by their professional staffs (1996: 271 at the DNC and 264 at the RNC), which operate out of permanent party headquarters buildings on Capitol Hill. These facilities are jammed with hi-tech equipment, including state-of-the-art television studios. While the titles of the administrative divisions of the RNC and DNC vary slightly, both have staff specialists for fund-raising, political operations (assistance to candidates and party organizations), communications, voter mobilization, liaison with voter groups, convention and meeting arrangements, and administration. The in-party also has an office that handles liaison with the White House and the administration.

Because the RNC developed the capacity to raise large sums of money in the 1960s, through its direct-mail solicitations as well as its large giver programs, it was able to initiate a broad array of party support programs before the DNC was able to do so. The RNC has continued to retain its financial resource advantage over the DNC during the 1990s and to operate a more extensive party/candidate support operation than the DNC. However, the DNC has been rapidly narrowing the fund-raising gap and it, too, is now engaged in an expanding array of activities patterned after those initially developed by the RNC.[20]

Fund Raising. Both national committees have the capacity to raise large sums of "hard money"—funds raised in accordance with Federal Election Campaign Act (FECA) restrictions, for example, the RNC's $187 million and the DNC's $108 million during the 1995–1996 election cycle. Most of this money is raised from individual donors often in contributions of less than $100 in response to direct-mail solicitations. Both committees also operate extensive large-giver programs (e.g., fund-raising dinners and receptions). Amassing "soft money" has become an increasingly significant aspect of the RNC and DNC fund-raising operations. "Soft money" is money raised outside the restrictions of the FECA and is collected in large denominations from individuals, corporations, unions, and other interest groups. It may not be used for direct support of federal candidates. However, both parties have discovered ways to use this money in ways that technically have not been interpreted as direct support for federal candidates but do in fact provide significant aid to these candidates. For example, soft money has been used extensively in recent years to fund major get-out-the-vote drives and "issue advocacy" advertising—media advertising that portrays a party's candidates favorably while not explicitly calling for their election or the defeat of opponents. In the 1995–1996 election cycle the RNC raised $100 million in soft money and the DNC collected $99 million.

Assistance to State and Local Party Organizations. Under the leadership of Chairman Bill Brock after the 1976 elections, the RNC initiated a massive effort to strengthen its state and local parties and assist state level candidates. Among the programs which Brock developed that have been continued and expanded by his successors are (a) assistance in developing a professionalized fund-raising operation; (b) grants to hire professional staff members; (c) computer/data processing assistance; (d) campaign schools for candidates and their managers; (e) financial and technical assistance to state legislative candidates; (f) issues research; (g) assistance with redistricting; (h) campaign management training; and (i) national committee field staff to provide on-the-spot counseling and assistance to party leaders. Because the DNC has lagged behind the RNC in fund raising, it was not until the mid-1980s that it was able to follow the Republican example and implement programs of assistance to state and local party units. The DNC's major effort is assisting state parties in operating "coordinated campaign" organizations which are jointly funded by the DNC, state parties, allied interest groups such as organized labor, and Democratic candidates. These organizations are geared to provide a broad range of services to candidates, including voter registration, voter list development, get-out-the-vote drives, polling, targeting, press relations, scheduling, and media purchases.

Campaign Activities. Federal law permits the national committees to spend a fixed amount, which is adjusted for inflation every four years, to support their presidential nominees' campaigns ($11.5 million in 1996). Another major presidential campaign activity is financing state level get-out-the-vote drives and other party-building activities in accordance with the strategies of the presidential candidates. These activities are funded with "soft money"—money raised outside the restrictions of the Federal Election Campaign Act which may be used for so-called general "party building" activities, in contrast to activities designed to help specific candidates. In non-presidential election years, the RNC and DNC support the campaigns of congressional, senatorial, and state level candidates with funds and technical assistance.

Communications. Each national committee has a series of specialized publications for state leaders, county leaders, and party rank and file. There are also major campaign advertising efforts. Notable examples include the party focused commercials developed by the RNC for the 1980 campaign and the DNC's $2 million effort attacking the GOP's campaign manifesto, "Contract with America," in 1994. In addition, the RNC in particular has taken advantage of technological advances to broadcast satellite television programs from its state-of-the-art studio.[21]

Conventions. The national committees are responsible for planning, arrangements, and management of the national conventions.

Research. The research operations of the committees provide issue material to candidates and party leaders and engage in opposition research designed to expose the weaknesses of opposition party candidates.

Revitalization and Party Centralization. Until the 1970s, national committees had been viewed as so weak and lacking in political clout that a landmark study in 1964 characterized them as "political without power."[22] They were largely the creatures of and financed by state party organizations. Today, no informed observer would describe the national committees with a phrase like "politics without power." Indeed, the entire relationship between the national committees and their state affiliates has been transformed. The traditional emphasis on the decentralized character of American parties is still quite appropriate, but power and influence have increasingly been flowing toward the national party organizations. This process of power centralization has occurred through national party rules enforcement and providing funds and services to state parties.

The DNC has achieved increased power within the Democratic party through its role as the initiator and enforcer of national party rules governing delegate selection to the national convention. This power was gained through a series of party reform commissions starting with the McGovern-Fraser Commission appointed after the divisive 1968 convention. This commission and its successor commissions recommended to the DNC a detailed and codified set of party rules governing delegate selection.

The DNC has used this newfound legal authority to compel state Democratic parties to bring their delegate selection procedures into compliance with national party rules. Failure to comply can result in a state's national convention delegation not being seated at the convention. Faced with this type of national party sanction, the state parties embarked upon a massive restructuring of their internal procedures. This impressive display of national party legal authority over party organizations culminated in a series of United States Supreme Court decisions upholding the principle that national party rules take precedence over state party rules and state statutes in matters of delegate selection.[23]

Although these Supreme Court decisions confer similar authority upon the national Republican party, it has not followed the Democratic route of imposing restrictions on state parties. Indeed, it has followed a conscious policy of refraining from exercising this authority and has sought to maintain the confederate character of the party organization. This GOP reluctance to extend its rule enforcement authority should not be interpreted as indicative of an absence of centralizing tendencies within the party. Within the Republican party, centralization has moved forward since the 1960s through a series of RNC programs designed to strengthen state and local organizations and to assist federal, state, and local candidates. Through its extensive programs of assistance to party organizations and candidates, the RNC has significantly increased its influence over state parties because most are anxious to participate in RNC initiated programs and share in their benefits. As one midwestern Republican state chairman commented, "I figure that I should go along with the National Committee as much as possible because I want as much of their money as I can get." By using their ample financial resources to aid state parties and candidates, the RNC has achieved an enlarged role in the political process and increased the functional interdependence of the national and state Republican parties.[24]

As the DNC has followed the Republican example of extending significant amounts of aid to its state affiliates, it, too, has achieved enhanced influence. For example, in 1986 when the DNC initiated its first major program of providing professional staff to state party organizations—a $1.2 million operation in sixteen states—state Democratic parties in exchange for this aid were required to sign an agreement committing them to continue DNC sponsored party-building programs and to cooperate with the DNC in presidential nominating procedures and national campaigns. Similarly, in 1992 before a state party could participate in a "coordinated campaign" operation it had to have its organization approved by the DNC and the Clinton campaign organization. And in those instances where the state party organization was found to be incapable of operating an effective "coordinated campaign," the DNC brought in staff on a temporary basis to run the operation.

Because of programs of support for state parties and candidates that were initiated on a large scale first by the RNC and recently on a more limited scale by the DNC, the direction in the flow of intraparty funds has been reversed. Since the 1980s, the flow in both parties has been from the national party to the state party organizations instead of in the more traditional state to national party direction. The national committees are, therefore, no longer dependent upon their state organizations and have achieved substantial autonomy as well as enhanced leverage over their state party organizations because of their superior financial and technical resources. A by-product of this revolution in intraparty patterns has been an unprecedented level of party integration.[25]

Party Integration in Federal Election Campaigns. Large-scale transfers of party funds from the national committees to state parties are encouraged by provisions of the Federal Election Campaign Act (FECA). The act imposes strict limits on the amount of money national parties can contribute or expend on behalf of candidates for the presidency and Congress. The FECA does, however, permit state and local parties to spend without limit on "party building" activities such as voter registration and get-out-the-vote drives. As a result, both national parties collect large sums of money and then transfer a substantial share of these funds to state and local party organizations to support "party building" activities and issue advocacy advertising that assist candidates for the presidency and Congress (see table 4.1). In those cases where the state parties are deemed to be organizationally too weak to manage get-out-the-vote

Table 4.1
National Party Disbursements from Nonfederal Accounts ("Soft Money"), 1995–1996

	Transfers to State Parties	Contributions to State/Local Candidates	Share of Joint Activity*
RNC	$47,819,748	$ 654,671	$39,112,386
Rep. Sen. Comm.	1,644,300	565,571	5,626,708
Rep. Cong. Comm.	385,000	834,500	7,402,086
Rep. Total	$49,849,048	$2,054,742	$52,141,180
DNC	$53,908,259	$ 176,901	$27,367,256
Dem. Sen. Comm.	5,514,620	1,708,694	2,174,696
Dem. Cong. Comm.	4,013,613	970,250	3,159,557
Dem. Total	$63,436,492	$2,855,845	$32,701,509

*Joint activity includes such party building activities as voter registration drives, voter-list development, and get-out-the-vote drives.

Source: Federal Election Commission.

programs effectively, it is not unusual for the national party to use the state parties as the legal entity (often as check writing vehicles to pay vendors) through which they operate in pursuit of national party electoral goals.

With the FECA encouraging the national party organizations to channel funds and campaign activities through the state parties in an effort to influence the outcome of federal elections, the state parties have become an integral part of presidential, Senate, and House campaigns. Fund transfers from the national party organizations to state parties, joint national-state party campaign activities, and national party technical assistance to state affiliates have all resulted in a nationalizing of party campaign efforts and substantially heightened levels of integration between the two strata of party organization. Thanks to the assistance provided by the national party committees, many state parties have been strengthened. But in the process, they have grown increasingly dependent upon the national party organization and lost some of their traditional autonomy.

The Hill Committees

Increasingly important elements of the national party are the congressional and senatorial campaign committees. These organizations—whose official names are Democratic Congressional Campaign

National-State Party Integration: Using State Parties to Implement National Campaign Strategies, 1996

The Democratic National Committee transferred $76.6 million in hard and soft money to its state parties, while the Republican National Committee made transfers totaling $65.2 million. These funds were allocated to the state parties in a manner designed to implement national strategies geared to winning critical states in the presidential race and maximizing the parties' seats in the House and Senate. Thus, state parties in the battleground state of Ohio were favored with national party largess ($4.7 million from the RNC and $5.5 from the DNC), while state parties in West Virginia, where the electorate is overwhelmingly Democratic, got only token transfers from their national parties ($6,000 from the RNC and $50,313 from the DNC).

* * *

To avoid Federal Election Campaign Act restrictions, the DNC transferred $32 million to state parties in twelve key battleground states. These state parties then paid for television ads that had been developed and placed by the DNC's media production company. The Republicans also funneled national party money to state affiliates to purchase advertising developed under national party auspices.

* * *

Both parties operated massive voter mobilization programs through joint national-state parties operations. The RNC's Victory '96 voter contact program—involving 84 million pieces of targeted mail, absentee ballots, voter identification and turnout phone calls (14.5 million calls to Republican households), volunteer phone centers, and collateral materials—was funded with $15.3 million in RNC money and $48.3 million in state party funds.

* * *

Both the RNC and DNC channeled money to state parties by getting donors to contribute directly to state organizations that were important in the national campaign strategy. In the case of the DNC, these contributions amounted to $3.6 million. By diverting the checks to state parties the DNC was able to avoid criticism that they were accepting contributions from controversial interests (e.g., gambling, tobacco) and help donors who did not want either the fact or the amount of their contributions to be known.

* * *

To get hard money into crucial congressional races, national party committees swapped soft money for hard money with their state parties. For example, the Michigan Republican party sent $100,000 in hard money to the RNC and received in return $150,000 in soft money from the RNC. And when the DNC was mired in debt and short of hard money for the 1998 congressional campaign, it engineered a much more extensive ($1 million) soft-for-hard money swap with twelve state parties, which received a soft money commission of 10 to 15 percent for the hard money dollars they sent to the DNC.

* * *

With Bob Dole assured of the Republican presidential nomination but his campaign strapped for cash in May 1996, the Wisconsin GOP picked up the tab for his expenses while making a campaign appearance in the state.

Sources: Washington Post, July 1, 1996; February 18, 1997; October 2, 1997; April 24, 1998; *Milwaukee Journal Sentinel,* May 30, 1996; Republican National Committee; Federal Election Committee.

Committee (DCCC), National Republican Congressional Committee (NRCC), Democratic Senatorial Campaign Committee (DSCC), and the National Republican Senatorial Committee (NRSC)—are organizationally autonomous from the national committees and operate quite independently. The members of these Capitol Hill committees are members of the House and Senate. These committees concentrate their efforts on holding their parties' marginal seats and on assisting challengers and open seat candidates with a reasonable chance of success against opposition party members. As a result, safe incumbents as well as challengers and open seat candidates with no realistic likelihood of winning receive little in the way of party assistance (see table 4.2).

Table 4.2

Allocation of National Party Funds in U.S. House and Senate Elections, 1996: Concentrating on Competitive Races Where There Is a Chance to Win

	House		Senate	
	Republicans	**Democrats**	**Republicans**	**Democrats**
Vulnerable Incumbents	37% (75)	17% (44)	34% (9)	16% (5)
Strong Challengers	26 (44)	40 (75)	19 (5)	27 (9)
Strong Open Seat Candidates	23 (32)	20 (32)	41 (12)	52 (12)
Totals	86% (151)	77% (151)	94% (26)	95% (26)
Safe Incumbents	2% (125)	6% (112)	3% (4)	— (2)
Challengers with Little Chance	6 (112)	13 (125)	1 (2)	1 (4)
Open Seat Candidates with Little Chance	6 (18)	4 (18)	2 (2)	4 (2)
Totals	14% (255)	23% (255)	6% (8)	5% (8)
Total Funds Allocated (in millions of dollars)	$9.987	$7.860	$11.513	$9.246

Source: Adapted from Federal Election Commission data analyzed by Paul S. Herrnson, *Congressional Elections: Campaigning at Home and in Washington*, 2nd ed. (Washington, D.C.: CQ Press, 1998), p. 82.

The Federal Election Campaign Act (FECA) imposes severe restrictions on the amount of money party committees can contribute to congressional and senatorial candidates ($5,000 per election to House candidates or $10,000 for the primary and general election combined, and $17,500 for senatorial candidates). Such restrictions mean that national party committees can have only minimal impact on congressional campaigns through direct contributions to candidates.

In addition to being authorized to make limited contributions directly to candidates, the party organizations are also permitted by the FECA to make expenditures in support of their parties' candidates. These monies are called *coordinated expenditures* and are normally used for polls, producing campaign advertising, and buying media time—major expenses that involve technical expertise. The limits on coordinated expenditures, unlike the direct contribution limits, are adjusted at each election for inflation. In 1998, the coordinated expenditure limit for party committees was $32,550 for each House race. The congressional campaign committees also engage in candidate recruitment and training. Because of its significantly superior financial resources, the NRCC has been a much more important source of campaign support for its candidates than has the DCCC, though since 1982 the Democratic committee has become substantially more active.

The senatorial campaign committees are in a position to play a substantially more prominent role than the congressional committees. The FECA permits coordinated expenditures on behalf of senatorial candidates at a level of two cents times the voting age population of the state, with the amount adjusted for inflation since 1974. Under this formula, the amount of money that a party committee may spend in populous states can be significant. For example, the coordinated expenditures limit in 1998 for a Senate race in California was $1.5 million. This limit can be doubled by a device first developed by the Republicans and approved by the courts. Through a technique called an agency agreement, the NRSC has assumed the spending quota of state party committees and thus been able to double the national party spending limit in selected states. As a result of this device, both the Republican and Democratic senatorial campaign committees have been able to pump large sums into key races. In most states, the NRSC's greater financial resources enabled it to engage in a higher level of coordinated expenditures than was possible for the DSCC.

In addition to making direct contributions and coordinated expenditures, the Hill committees also encourage *"party-connected"* funds to flow to their candidates. These are contributions from the political action committees (PACs) operated by House and Senate party leaders as well as individual members and former members.

In 1996, $8.6 million in these "party-connected" funds were contributed to House and Senate candidates. Among the more prominent leadership PACs there are those of Speaker Newt Gingrich (R-Ga.), who contributed $771,500 to his fellow GOP candidates, and Minority Leader Richard Gephardt (D-Mo.) who gave $461,095. As with regular party money, "party-connected" money is allocated strategically, that is, it goes into competitive races where there is a real opportunity to win.[26]

Not only do the Hill committees make contributions and steer "party-connected" funds to their candidates, they also assist candidates with fund raising, for example, by providing lists of contributors, having party leaders attend candidates' fund-raising events, and steering contributions from wealthy individuals and PACs to deserving candidates.

Despite the substantial role that the congressional and senatorial campaigns committees play in helping to fund candidates, it is important to keep in mind that the party-based money constitutes a relatively small proportion of candidates' total receipts—5 percent of House candidates' total receipts in 1996 and 9 percent of senatorial candidates' receipts.[27] The bulk of campaign money comes from nonparty sources (individuals are the largest source, followed by PACs). As a result, the ability of the party leadership to affect their colleagues' roll call voting behavior and increase party unity by either granting or withholding party funds is extremely limited. And as long as party funds are allocated strategically rather than on the basis of candidates' ideology, Hill committee resources are not likely to be an effective tool for congressional leaders to use in trying to impose discipline upon their colleagues.

There is evidence, however, that the national party committees are affecting the way House and Senate campaigns are run. Party favored candidates have found that there is no "free lunch" in politics. In exchange for national party funds, candidates are often required to agree to certain conditions, for example, to conduct polls, to air their television ads at a predetermined stage of the campaign, and to surrender contributor lists in return for party fund-raising help.

Although it has been traditional for congressional campaigns to be fought primarily on local issues, Republican and Democratic congressional leaders have been increasingly active since the 1980s in seeking to set a national campaign agenda. A particularly notable example of party leadership trying to nationalize congressional campaigns occurred in 1994 as GOP House leaders focused upon their ten-point Contract with America (a policy agenda for the next Congress) and what they viewed as the ethical and policy failures of the Clinton administration and the House Democrats. This effort to nationalize the campaign helped the Republicans win control of both chambers of Congress for the first time in forty years.

Democrats sought to nationalize the 1996 campaign by portraying the Republicans as "extremists" who would gut Medicare, Medicaid, and education, while giving tax breaks to the rich and allowing corporations to pollute the environment at will. The task of nationalizing the campaign was made difficult, however, by the fact of divided party control of the government. With a Democratic president and a Republican Congress, it was difficult for voters to affix blame or credit for the state of the union on one party.[28]

Party-Allied Groups

A party's organizational resources, in their totality, involve more than the formal, legally constituted party organizations such as the national or the Senate and House campaign committees. The organizational resource base of the parties also includes other organizations on which the parties rely for electoral services. One of the earliest manifestations of allied groups being integrated into the party structure was the emergence during the 1940s of labor unions as a source of support upon which the Democratic party came to rely. Led by the CIO, unions provided campaign funds to candidates, mobilized voters, and sought to influence public opinion. Unions were such an integral part of the Democratic party that Yale political scientist David R. Mayhew concluded after an exhaustive analysis that the "Democratic party in the 1940s and 1950s [was] made up largely of machines and unions."[29] At the same time, most corporations had GOP leanings.

Although close ties between organized interests and parties are hardly a new phenomenon, there has been in recent elections a dramatic increase in the involvement of party-allied groups. Indeed, allied group support for party candidates and interaction between these groups and the party organizations has become so heavy that the concept of party organization requires a broad definition.

The 1996 election was replete with evidence of extensive involvement by allied groups in partisan campaigns and of close

Party-Allied Groups Were Heavily Involved in the 1996 Elections

The 1996 campaign was unprecedented for the level of party-allied group involvement and integration of these groups into the party structure. The following are prominent examples of the close linkages that have developed between parties and allied groups.

* * *

The AFL-CIO carried out a $35 million issue advocacy and voter mobilization campaign intended to help the Democrats regain control of the House. This was in addition to the $1.2 million spent by COPE, its political action committee, and $49 million spent by affiliated union PACs.

* * *

In the final weeks of the campaign, Americans for Tax Reform flooded 150 House districts with 17 million pieces of literature and 4 million phone calls designed to counter Democratic and AFL-CIO ads claiming the Republicans would cripple Medicare. This operation was funded by $4.6 million from the RNC.

* * *

Worried by the AFL-CIO drive to help the Democrats regain control of the House, the U.S. Chamber of Commerce mounted a $7 million advertising campaign to counter the AFL-CIO.

* * *

The Christian Coalition distributed 45 million voter guides and operated phone banks in several races to the benefit of the GOP.

* * *

The RNC solicited and collected contributions of over $1 million for the Right to Life Committee, Americans for Tax Reform, and the American Defense Institute, then bundled the checks and turned them over to these organizations, which engaged in voter mobilization and issue advertising to help Republican candidates.

* * *

The DNC solicited and referred large donors to Vote Now '96, a group that registers voters among groups traditionally loyal to the Democrats. Vote Now '96 spent $3 million.

* * *

Citizen Action, a liberal consumer group, spent $7 million on ads, mailings, and telephone calls blasting the Republican record on Medicare, the environment, and education.

* * *

The Sierra Club, an environment group, spent $3.5 million on advertising and $3 million on voter guides distributed by tens of thousands of volunteers, in addition to $750,000 in direct contributions to candidates.

Sources: Elizabeth Drew, *Whatever It Takes: The Real Struggle for Political Power in America* (New York: Viking, 1997); *Washington Post,* October 23, November 22, 1996, February 9, 1997; *National Journal,* February 22, 1997.

linkages between the parties and these groups. For example, RNC and Republican House and Senate campaign committee personnel worked closely with the leaders of Americans for Tax Reform, the Christian Coalition, the National Federation of Independent Business, the National Rifle Association, and the National Beer Wholesalers on electoral strategy and campaign activities. The chairman of the GOP congressional campaign committee even went so far as to state that these groups and their leaders were the most important people behind the Republicans retaining control of the House in 1996.[30]

A similar pattern was evident between the Democrats and their allied groups. Pro-Democratic groups—AFL-CIO, EMILY's List, National Education Association (NEA), Sierra Club, National Abortion Rights Action League, National Committee for an Effective Congress, and the League of Conservation Voters—worked together and with Democratic leaders on the campaign. The Clinton-Gore Committee even went so far as to integrate Democratic allied groups into the campaign and created a national steering committee that included representatives of the president's campaign committee, the DNC, AFL-CIO, NEA, and EMILY's List. This group met periodically at DNC headquarters to discuss which states should be given priority and which of the coalition's partners were actively organizing and doing direct mail and get-out-the-vote drives in various states.[31]

Even though party allied groups have become an increasingly important campaign resource of the parties and their candidates, it must be kept in mind that these partisan allies have their own agendas and maintain an autonomous organizational structure. And although the ties between parties and allied groups may be close, these groups do not necessarily coordinate all their activities with either candidates or parties. In addition, they are not above voicing loud, public criticisms of their preferred party's actions on occasion.

Additional Components of the Party Network: "Think Tanks" and Consultants

In addition to prominent party allied groups such as the AFL-CIO or Citizens for Tax Reform, the party organizational networks extend to the proliferation of Washington public policy research organizations (dubbed "think tanks"). A prime example is the

Progressive Policy Institute, an affiliate of an unofficial Democratic group with centrist leanings, the Democratic Policy Council. The Progressive Policy Institute has been a source of policy proposals used by Democratic candidates, including Bill Clinton. Republicans also have research institutes to assist them, notably the conservative Heritage Foundation and the American Enterprise Institute.

Political consultants have also become a prominent element in the infrastructure of candidates' campaigns for major offices and the parties' organizational networks. A substantial share (41 percent in a recent survey) of campaign consultants serve an apprenticeship within party organizations before moving out into the private sector. And once out on their own, they normally reinvent a relationship with the party that helped to train them.[32] Because trust and loyalty are important to politicians, consultants normally work exclusively for only one party. It is a rare consultant, indeed, who can pull off the feat of working both sides of the political street in the manner of Senator Majority Leader Trent Lott (R-Miss.) and President Clinton's former consultant, Dick Morris.

To win elections, party organizations need the technical/professional skills and the personalized and comprehensive candidate services that consultants can provide. The parties, therefore, seek to retain the talents of their former employees, who are familiar with the party organizations and its network. National and Hill committees of both Republicans and Democrats regularly purchase the services of consultants for polling, research, and candidate consulting. Not only do the party committees hire consultants for specialized work, they (especially the Hill committees) also provide their candidates with lists of approved and reliable consultants. Hiring a consultant off of the approved list can at times be a requirement for the candidate to receive party funding. Clearly, consultants add essential resources to the parties' organizational infrastructure.

State Parties

State Parties and the Law

As noted in chapter 3, there is a tendency in the United States for extensive statutory regulation of parties by the states. These regulations take an almost infinite variety of forms. Some states engage in only a minimal amount of regulation, while others have extensive party regulatory statutes. Most states regulate party membership (which voters may participate in primary elections), organizational structure, access to the general election ballot, methods of nomination, and campaign finance. There is, however, a great deal of variation among the states in the extent and manner of regulation.

Data collected by the Advisory Commission on Intergovernmental Relations demonstrate both the pervasiveness and the variety of state regulation: thirty-six states regulate the procedures used to select state committee members; thirty-two states stipulate the composition of state committees; twenty-two states specify when these committees must meet; twenty-seven states regulate their internal rules and procedures. Only five states (Alaska, Delaware, Hawaii, Kentucky, and North Carolina) do not specify some aspect of the parties' organizational structure, procedures, and composition.[33]

A major factor in the proliferation of party regulatory statutes in the United States was the spread of the direct primary as the principal nominating device for state and congressional office. Requiring parties to nominate candidates via the primary meant that the states had to enact laws which defined parties, fixed eligibility to vote in party primaries, regulated the conduct of primary elections, and assured general election ballot access to primary winners. Regulations such as these almost mandate the existence of political parties and have made state parties quasi-public agencies. Their legal position has much in common with that of public utilities. Both the party and the utilities perform essential public functions under the protection of the law.[34] Both, however, must submit to extensive statutory regulation.

While most state parties have a status similar to that of public utilities, the legal position of the parties is in the process of modification as a result of a series of recent Supreme Court decisions holding that political parties have First and Fourteenth Amendment rights of free political association. In the case of *Tashjian* v. *Connecticut* (1986), the Court ruled that Connecticut could not constitutionally ban voters who registered as independents from voting in the Republican primary after the state GOP had authorized both registered Republicans and independents to vote in a Republican primary. The Court also struck down (*Eu, Secretary of State of California* v. *San Francisco County Democratic Central Committee*, 1989) a series of unusually restrictive provisions in the California statutes that had banned party endorsements in primary elections, limited state chairmen's terms to two years, and required the state chairmanship to be rotated between residents of northern and southern regions of the state. The *Eu* and *Tashjian* decisions caused some to speculate about the possibility of state parties being "privatized" and freed from being treated as quasistate agencies. However, such an outcome is highly unlikely, as it would require the abandonment by the states of primary elections as the principal means of nominating partisan candidates for public office. Since the states are not likely to take such an unpopular step and the Supreme Court is not apt to require it, continued extensive state regulation of parties will probably continue into the foreseeable future.

Although the Court has been willing to relieve state parties of excessively burdensome regulations, it has also demonstrated that it will allow states considerable leeway in determining the nature of their electoral and party systems. Thus, in 1997, it held in *Timmons* v. *Twin Cities New Party* that while parties have an unquestioned right to nominate their own candidates, the states also have a constitutional right to regulate elections and prevent manipulations of the ballot and factionalism among the voters. The Court ruled that Minnesota had the power to prevent the left-leaning New Party from engaging in the practice of "*cross filing*" or "*fusion*" by nominating a candidate for the state legislature who had already accepted the Democratic nomination. This decision was a severe blow to a struggling minor party and, in effect, gave the Court's blessing to state efforts to promote a two-party system.

The State Committees

In each of the states there is a Republican and Democratic state committee. The actual title varies, but a common title is Republican or Democratic State Central Committee. State statutes and party by-laws determine the basis for membership on the state committee. Committee members may be elected to represent counties, congressional districts, legislative districts, major municipalities, or party auxiliary groups like the Federation of Republican Women, Young Republicans, and Young Democrats. The size of these bodies varies from about twenty persons in Iowa to over a thousand in California. Because the size of state committees is frequently unwieldy and their meetings infrequent, many state parties rely heavily upon an executive committee to carry out state committee functions between meetings. The responsibilities of the state committees include overseeing the work of the state chairman and the headquarters staff, calling of state conventions, adoption of party policies, supervision of platform drafting, fund raising, and assisting candidates and local organizations.

The State Chairman

With state committees composed of part-time volunteers, the person responsible for directing the activities of the state party is the state chairman. Most state chairmen are elected by the state committee (73 percent) although 27 percent are chosen by state party conventions. Approximately three quarters of the state chairmen are elected to two year terms with the balance chosen for four years. The turnover, however, is high, with tenure averaging less than three years. State parties, therefore, are plagued with lack of continuity in their leadership. Each chairman faces a unique set of circumstances, but the main duties of the chairman include supervising the headquarters staff, fund raising, candidate recruitment, serving as a party spokesperson, liaison with elected officials, and strengthening local organizations. In addition, state chairmen serve as members of their parties' national committees.

The Role of the Governor

It is an unusual governor who actively seeks to direct the affairs of the state central committee. In a nationwide study, less than 50 percent of the state party chairs reported that they believed it necessary to have the governor's approval before taking action. Most considered the governor's role in party affairs to be advisory rather than controlling.[35] And just as governors do not exert day-by-day control over their state party organizations, such organizations play only a supportive or supplementary role in gubernatorial campaigns. In this era of candidate-centered politics, governors rely primarily upon their own personal campaign organizations. Even governors such as Tommy Thompson (R-Wis.), who have been particularly supportive of their parties, carefully cultivate a personal following that transcends partisanship, and engage in the extensive fund raising required to maintain a sophisticated personal campaign apparatus.

Governors do normally seek to influence and can even control the selection of their party's state chair, lest the party machinery fall into unfriendly hands. New York and New Jersey, for example, have long traditions of governors handpicking the party chairs and expecting the designatees to follow the governors' instructions.

Since the interests of the governor and the state party are seldom identical, conflicts are not uncommon. Thus in Virginia, Governor Douglas Wilder's appointee as state chair was forced in 1992 to share power with the state Democratic party's steering committee when he was accused of placing the governor's national political ambitions ahead of the state party's electoral interests.

The actual pattern of governor-state party relations varies from those in which the state party organization is dominated by the governor and closely tied to his or her political fortunes to those exhibiting the type of outright hostility described above. A New England Democratic chair described a tightly linked governor-state party relationship as follows.

> I'm the governor's agent. My job is to work with him. If I look good, he looks good, because I'm his man. I don't bother him with messy stuff. He expects me to handle it my way. I meet with the [local] leaders on his behalf. I'm liaison to city and town leaders. (Personal interview)

There are also some governors who rely upon their state party chairs to assist them in influencing state legislators in support of the governor's legislative agenda. There are also those rare state chairs whose intraparty power base is so strong that they can operate with considerable independence from their governor. New York State GOP Chair William Powers has been this type of chair. His independence derives from his rebuilding the party structure while the Democrats still controlled the governorship, promoting an obscure state senator, George Pataki, to be the party's gubernatorial nominee, and playing a major role in Pataki's victory in 1994.[36]

More common, however, is a relationship of coordinate responsibility: the governor and state chair consult on appointments, candidate recruitments, fund raising, and other major party activities. The governor assists the party with fund raising and candidate recruitment, but neither the governor nor his/her staff run the state central committee and headquarters. Likewise, the state party chair does not seek to manage the governor's campaign organization or determine gubernatorial policy. A Republican chair in a Midwestern state with a long tradition of professionalized party leadership summarized his relationship with a governor of his party as follows: "I don't go to his office and he doesn't come over here. . . . A lot of people think he isn't interested in the party. But that's just not true. He cares and he helps me. His attitude is 'What can I do to help?'" The governor corroborated these comments by saying that his state party chair "doesn't want to be governor and I don't want to be party chairman" (personal interviews).

The Demise of the Traditional State Organization

Although state parties went through a revitalization in the 1970s and 1980s, they bear scant similarity to the old-style organizations that dominated politics in the Middle Atlantic, New England, and lower Great Lakes states at the turn of the century. These patronage based organizations, which controlled nominations and ran their candidates' campaigns, had largely passed from the scene by the mid-1980s. Unlike their predecessor organizations, the modern day state parties do not control nominations nor run campaigns. In the candidate-centered environment of the 1990s, state parties are instead service agencies for candidates and local parties, as well as the vehicles through which national parties pursue their campaign strategies.

Patronage as a basis for party organizations has been severely weakened by civil service laws, strengthened public employee unions, and a critical public. These anti-patronage forces have been augmented by a series of Supreme Court decisions which have undermined large-scale patronage operations in both parties. In *Eldrod* v. *Burns* (1976), the Court ruled that the Cook County Democrats could no longer fire people on the basis of their party affiliation. This decision was followed by one declaring that the Illinois GOP could not use "party affiliation and support" as the basis for filling state jobs unless party affiliation was an "appropriate requirement" for the positions (*Rutan* v. *Republican Party*, 1990). In once patronage rich Illinois, the Democratic state chair has lamented that "the party no longer functions as an employment agency. More and more, we must rely on a spirit of volunteerism."[37]

Even though patronage jobs no longer provide a basis for building a strong organization, there are other forms of patronage which can be utilized. Gubernatorial appointments to state boards and commissions controlling gambling, licensing, hospitals, state investments, higher education, environmental and recreation policy, and cultural activities are much sought after by persons seeking policy influence, recognition, and material gain. Partisan considerations can affect state decisions regarding state contracts, bank deposits, economic development, and the purchase of professional services. These types of preferments, however, are useful to the party primarily for fund raising, and do not provide campaign workers the way large-scale patronage operations did.[38]

The Service-Oriented State Organization of the 1990s

To survive and perform a meaningful role in current state politics, the parties have had to adapt to an environment characterized by not only an absence of large-scale patronage, but also (1) candidate-centered campaigns often staffed by professional consultants and funded in significant degree by PACs, (2) heightened interparty competition for statewide offices, and (3) strengthened national party organizations. In adapting to these conditions, the state party organizations have become service agencies to their candidates and local affiliates. The institutionalization of state parties as campaign service organizations parallels the resurgence of party organizations at the national level, where a massive fund-raising capacity has transformed the once weak RNC and DNC into major service agencies to candidates and state/local parties. There are also parallels between the major campaign roles played at the national level by the senatorial and congressional campaign committees and state legislative campaign committees, which have emerged as the principal party campaign resource for state legislative candidates.

Among the indicators of the evolution of most state parties into organizations capable of providing significant services to candidates and local parties are (1) permanent headquarters, (2) professional leadership and staffing, and (3) adequate budgets and programs to maintain the organization, support candidates and office-holders, and assist local party units.[39]

Permanent Headquarters. As late as the 1970s, state parties frequently were ad hoc operations run out of the offices or homes of the state chairs. This type of operation has now largely ceased to exist as the parties have established permanent headquarters in the state capital. These headquarters are increasingly located in modern office buildings stocked with hi-tech equipment for data processing, fund raising, communications, and printing.

Professional Staffing. In the 1960s, most state party headquarters operated with a minimal staff—often only an executive director, a secretary, and a few volunteers. Today professional leadership is the norm. Over 30 percent of the state chairs work full time at the jobs and nearly every state party has either a full-time chair or executive director.[40] Headquarters staffs have also grown in size and there is increased specialization among the personnel. Staff turnover, however, is high. State chairs normally serve only two or three years and professional operatives tend to be transients who move about the country from job to job with party organizations, candidates, and campaign consultants.[41]

Finances. Operating a professionalized headquarters, of course, requires an ability to raise significant amounts of money on a continuing basis. Table 4.3 demonstrates that state party organizations have for the most part developed substantial financial resources. In the 1995–1996 election cycle, a majority of state parties reported to the Federal Election Commission that they had raised in excess of $2 million. Although the Republican organizations in the past have generally had more substantial budgets than their Democratic counterparts, the data in table 4.3 show the two parties having remarkably equal access to financial resources. There are, however, differences between the parties in terms of funding sources. The Republican state parties are more dependent upon contributions from individuals and less dependent upon national party organizations or other organizations (e.g., unions and PACs) than are Democratic state units.[42]

Organizational Building and Maintenance Activities. Since the 1960s, state parties have become involved in programs aimed at building and maintaining the organization. An expanded number of state parties now have multifaceted fund raising operations,

Table 4.3
State Party Receipts Reported to the Federal Election Commission, 1997–1998[a]

Receipts	Number of State Party Organizations		Totals	
	Democratic	Republican	Number	Percent
Less than $500,000	5	4	9	9
$500,000–$999,999	6	9	15	15
$1,000,000–$1,999,999	10	13	23	23
$2,000,000–$3,999,999	12	9	21	21
$4,000,000–$5,999,999	7	7	14	14
$6,000,000–$7,999,999	4	3	7	7
$8,000,000–$9,999,999	5	2	7	7
$10,000,000–$11,999,999	0	1[b]	1	1
$12,000,000–$13,999,999	0	1[c]	1	1
$14,000,000–$19,999,999	1[d]	0	1	1
$20,000,000–$39,999,999	0	0	0	0
$40,000,000 and over	0	1[e]	1	1
Totals	50	50	100	100%

a. The dollar amounts shown are state party receipts reported to the Federal Election Commission, include funds transferred to state parties by national party committees, and do not include funds used exclusively in state elections.

b. Ohio Republican Party

c. Florida Republican Party

d. California Democratic Party

e. California Republican Party

Source: Data provided by the Federal Election Commission.

run voter identification and mobilization operations, publish newsletters, engage in public opinion polling and issue development, and assist local party units.

Candidate Support Activities. The state parties' role in providing services to candidates is revealed in table 4.4. In these candidate support activities, Republican state organizations tend to be more active than their Democratic counterparts.

Most state parties are either unable or unwilling to take sides in primary elections. A recent survey of ninety-two state chairs revealed that only sixteen said that their organizations normally support candidates before the primaries—a form of involvement that old-style state leaders would have considered both normal and essential for maintaining the organization. Some state chairs do attempt to avoid primary fights by seeking to persuade aspiring candidates not to run, but many leaders abstain even from this type of intervention.[43] With the state parties in the main sitting out the primaries, candidates are forced to rely upon their own personal organizations to contest the primaries.

The personalized nature of primary election campaigns carries over to the general election, where even the most professionalized state parties are capable of providing only selected professional services to candidates. Again, it is the candidates' personal organizations which actually manage campaigns. The state party's campaign role, while often significant, especially in such areas as candidate training, voter identification, and get-out-the vote drives (e.g., the Florida GOP operates a program to contact over one million potential absentee voters), is supplementary in character and one that is consistent with the candidate-centered nature of 1990s politics.

Table 4.4

Assistance to Candidates by State Parties (in percents)

Type of Assistance Provided to Candidates	Republican State Parties	Democratic State Parties
Financial contributions to		
gubernatorial candidates	81%	54%
congressional candidates	71	55
state legislative candidates	95	52
local candidates	39	23
Fund raising assistance to		
state candidates	96	63
congressional candidates	63	30
Voter registration drives	73	81
Public opinion polling	78	50
Media consulting	75	46
Campaign seminars/ training	100	76
Coordinating PAC contributions	52	31
Advertising in newspapers	36	40

Sources: Advisory Commission on Intergovernmental Relations, *The Transformation of American Politics: Implications for Federalism* (Washington, D.C.: A.C.I.R., 1986), 115; and A. James Reichley, *The Life of the Parties: A History of American Political Parties* (New York: Free Press, 1992), p. 390.

Party Differences. Although both Democratic and Republican state parties have grown increasingly capable of providing services to candidates and local affiliates, there are important interparty differences. As is true at the national level, Republican state organizations tend to be stronger than those of the Democrats.[44] The existence of stronger Republican organizations at the national and state levels reveals one of the differences between Republican and Democratic politics. For Republican candidates, the party organization tends to be a more important resource in the electoral process than it is for Democrats.

The interparty differences in the strength and role of party organizations are probably explained in part by the greater reliance of Democratic candidates on support from allied organizations such as labor unions, teachers, and social action groups. These differences between the parties in their reliance upon allied groups point up again the need to view parties from a broadened perspective. Parties encompass more than the formal and legally constituted organizations. Because certain non-party groups are major participants in electoral politics and part of the parties' network of supporters, these groups and their activities should be factored into any assessment of state party organizational strength.

State Legislative Campaign Committees

Increasingly important elements of the state party organizational structure are the legislative campaign committees. These organizations are fashioned after the congressional and senatorial campaign committees at the national level. They are composed of incumbent legislators who raise funds and hire staff to assist their parties' legislative candidates. In some states these committees have become substantially more important than the regular state party as a source of support for legislative candidates. Indeed, in most states legislative campaign committees have emerged as the principal party support mechanism for legislative candidates.[45] The most active legislative campaign committees are found in states with high levels of interparty competition, high campaign costs, and weak state central committees. The development of strong legislative campaign committees is also associated with high levels of legislative professionalism—full-time legislators who are paid a reasonable salary and supported by ample staff. As legislative service increases in value and competition for control of legislative chambers intensifies, legislative leaders have created campaign committees to protect their own interests as well as those of the party and individual legislators.

Unlike the state central committee in which the Republicans tend to be organizationally stronger, Democratic legislative campaign committees do not labor under a disadvantage. This reflects the fact that in recent decades Democrats have controlled the bulk of legislative chambers. With the power that chamber control provides, Democratic (and Republican committees in states where the GOP is in the majority) legislative campaign committees have been able to tap into lucrative sources of funds—such as PACs which are concerned about maintaining access to powerful legislators—and thereby raise large war chests of money to support their candidates with cash and services. Democratic committees' effectiveness has also been enhanced through alliances with activist unions, especially teachers' unions.

Candidate recruitment is one of the critical roles performed by campaign committees, since quality candidates tend to have success in raising money, attracting volunteer workers, and making a competitive run for legislative seats. As state politics expert Alan Ehrenhalt has observed, "Legislative elections are . . . really . . . a competition to attract candidates who have the skills and energy to win and the desire and resourcefulness to stay in office."[46]

Legislative campaign committees in many of the states have become full service campaign organizations which closely resemble regular party organizations in that they provide candidates with money, campaign staff, and technical services (media consulting and in some instances polls), and in some states they even get involved in voter mobilization activities. In Ohio and Illinois, for example, legislative campaign committees operate with budgets in excess of $2 million.

Legislative campaign committees follow a strategy of concentrating their resources on close races in an effort to either maintain or win control of legislative chambers. Minority parties, therefore, tend to support challengers to a greater extent than do majority parties. As is true of the national House and Senate campaign committees, their state level counterparts target their resources on competitive races—those of vulnerable incumbents, strong challengers, and open seat candidates. A recent survey of party funding of legislative candidates found that 80 percent of Republican funds and 50 percent of Democratic money went to nonincumbents. This interparty difference reflects the fact that the Democrats have been the majority party and the Republicans the minority party in most state legislatures in recent decades.[47]

Although shared goals, party loyalty, and personal associations encourage an element of cooperation and coordination between legislative campaign committees and state central committees, legislative campaign committees tend to operate independently. They are run by legislative leaders and they service primarily the agendas and priorities of legislative partisans. This gives them autonomy and freedom from the agendas of state central committees and both presidential and gubernatorial campaign organizations.[48]

County and Local Parties

The most frequently cited type of local party organization is the big city machine best exemplified by the Cook County Democratic organization during the era of Mayor Richard J. Daley.[49] This organization was run as a hierarchy by the mayor who worked through his ward leaders and their precinct captains. The organization was sustained by patronage. Ten thousand city jobs were distributed on the basis of patronage. A single ward leader could have as many as five hundred jobs to distribute to his followers. The organization's ward and precinct leaders also served as ombudsmen, assisting residents with their problems in dealing with governmental agencies. Loyalty to the organization and its candidates was achieved through the material or tangible rewards that the organization provided.

This style of politics is not unique to Chicago or the Democratic party. Traditional organizations still function in a few places such as Philadelphia and Albany. One of the most professional and effective party organizations is the Republican party of Nassau County (Long Island), New York. Most members of the party executive committee hold patronage positions in county government; the county chairman is a full-time salaried leader; the party raises more money than the GOP state committee, owns a three story headquarters building, operates its own printing plant and artist's studio, and makes extensive use of pollsters.[50] Indeed, this organization has emerged as the strongest force in New York state Republican politics.

There are also well-funded and professionalized local parties based upon volunteers rather than patronage. One of the most effective is the GOP of Santa Clara County, California. It has a paid executive director, a headquarters complete with computerized volunteer and voter lists, and a sophisticated targeting system for reaching voters.[51]

Such organizations, however, are not the norm of American local politics. Most county parties are not bureaucratic or hierarchically run organizations. Their leaders and workers are part-time volunteers; there is no permanent headquarters or paid staff; activity is not a year round phenomenon, but rather cyclical, and concentrated around campaign season. Although it has been commonplace to assert that parties are in a state of decline and may even be dying, case studies of local parties and national surveys reveal substantial party activity at the county level. Table 4.5 reports the findings of nationwide surveys of county leaders. It demonstrates that the lack of a bureaucratic structure does not necessarily imply a low level of party activity. It should also be noted that there are virtually no important party differences in the level of campaign activity engaged in by Republican and Democratic county parties. While Republican organizations are stronger at the national and state levels, they do not appear to be more active at the county level. Comparisons between the results of surveys of county party activity in the mid-1960s, 1980, and the 1990s do not support the thesis that parties are in decline. Rather, the direction of change is toward more active county parties.[52] Such national level studies, however, tend to obscure the tremendous diversity that exists among county and precinct party organizations. The range runs from counties which literally have no party organization to those with paid staff, permanent headquarters, and computer facilities. Even parties with full organizational structures, however, may be characterized by organizational slack. For example, Eldersveld's study of Wayne County (Detroit) led him to conclude there is a "tendency for local activists to perform at a minimal level of efficiency, without too much system, in a rather hit-and-miss mode of operation."[53] He found, for example, that canvassing of voters and election day work frequently went undone. Although Eldersveld's studies do not support the proposition that parties are becoming weaker, they do point up the tremendous diversity among local party organizations and the difficulty these organizations have in realizing their full potential.

A force that may cause county parties to become more effective is the increased interest in local parties being demonstrated by the national party committees. As their fund raising capacity has increased, the Republicans, in particular, have been providing financial and technical assistance to county parties.

Table 4.5

Campaign Activity Levels of Local Party Organizations, 1980 and 1996

Direct Campaign Activity	Percent Republicans 1980	Percent Democrats 1980	Percent Republicans 1996	Percent Democrats 1996
Distributes campaign literature	79	79	87	86
Organizes campaign events	65	68	82	81
Contributes money to candidates	70	62	63	59
Organizes telephone campaigns	65	61	63	59
Buys newspaper ads for party and candidates	62	62	68	63
Distributes posters or lawn signs	62	59	93	93
Coordinates county-level campaigns	56	57	54	58
Prepares press releases for party and candidates	55	55	68	69
Sends mailings to voters	59	47	60	58
Conducts registration drives	45	56	34	45
Organizes door-to-door canvassing	48	49	57	55
Buys radio/TV time for party and candidates	33	33	28	25
Utilizes public opinion surveys	16	11	15	13
Conducts get-out-the-vote effort	n/a	n/a	72	70
Maximum N	1,872	1,984	335	340

Source: John Frendreis and Alan R. Gitelson, "Continuity and Change in the Electoral Roles of Local Parties," a paper prepared for delivery at the State of the Parties: 1996 conference, Ray C. Bliss Institute of Applied Politics, University of Akron, October 9–10, 1997. Used by permission.

Does Party Organization Make a Difference?

A key question concerning party organizations is whether or not they can make a difference in determining election outcomes. Journalistic reports and scholarly case studies provide evidence that the party organization can have a critical impact. A dramatic example occurred in the 1996 House elections in Washington state, which has permitted permanent absentee voting since 1993. With a growing proportion of the state's voters using absentee ballots rather than going to the polls, the state's Republican party has followed a strategy of focusing upon absentee voters. This strategy paid off in 1996 with victories in two congressional districts in which Democratic candidates ran ahead of their GOP opponents based upon ballots cast at the polls.[54]

Recent studies by political scientists also document the impact of party organizational strength and electoral activity. Thus analyses of gubernatorial elections show that the party with an organizational strength advantage gains increments of voters over the opposition party.[55] However, development of a sophisticated party organization does not guarantee victories at the polls, as the history of the organizationally strong and innovative Republican congressional campaign committee demonstrates. The relationship between party organizational strength and electoral success is complex and the organization's impact is often indirect in character. A strong party organization can provide the infrastructure for candidates and activists (1) to continue the battle in the face of short-term defeats and enduring minority status, and (2) to take advantage of favorable circumstances when they arise (e.g., the retirement of a popular opposition party incumbent, divisiveness within the dominant party, or low approval ratings for an incumbent president).

In spite of commentaries in the media about the decline of parties, political science research reveals vibrant campaign activity at the local grass roots. Party canvassing of voters reaches approximately one quarter of the electorate in election years and increases voter turnout.[56] A study of the 1992 presidential campaign found local parties extensively engaged in distributing yard signs and literature, telephoning, transporting voters to the polls, registration, and arranging campaign events, with the local Democratic parties more active than their GOP counterparts. The extent to which local parties were active depended upon the following factors: the extent of the party's electoral support in the local area, the organizational capacity of the local party, the extent of campaign competition from the opposition, and the degree to which the local party was integrated into the national campaign apparatus.[57] In addition to these voter mobilization activities, the local parties can also have an indirect impact upon electoral fortunes when they recruit a full slate of candidates for local offices. These local candidates can have a "trickle up" effect by adding increments of voters to the party's total vote for offices higher up on the ballot.[58]

The Party Activists

Party organizations require officers, workers, and volunteers—political activists willing to give their time, talents, and treasure for the success of the party and its candidates. There are a variety of incentives that cause people to become actively involved in political activity.

Incentives to Participate

Patronage and Preferments. Some people become involved in politics because of direct material rewards. Patronage, awarding government jobs to the supporters of the winning candidate, has a long tradition in American politics dating at least to the era of Jacksonian democracy. Andrew Jackson believed that "to the victor belongs the spoils" and that the average citizen was qualified to hold appointive governmental office. Patronage appointees traditionally have been a major source of party workers. Civil service laws (appointment on the basis of merit, using competitive examinations), reform movements, and court decisions have reduced the number of patronage positions available for the parties to fill. At the federal level, for example, the number of positions available for distribution to presidential supporters is extremely limited due to civil service laws. Out of a total federal civilian workforce of 2.9 million persons, only about 3,000 full-time federal jobs are open to political appointees. Even in Chicago, the once vast patronage army (10,000 jobs were once at the disposal of the mayor, aldermen, ward committeemen, and the heads of various agencies) that maintained Mayor Richard J. Daley's Democratic machine is now only a shadow of its former self. Daley's son, who became mayor in 1989, has not sought to base his power on a revival of the old patronage system. Today Chicago's patronage is primarily of the "pinstripe" variety. That is, city business is funneled to firms that assist candidates in raising the big money that is needed for advertising and computerized mailings that have, to a large degree, replaced the armies of patronage workers. For example, in the year after Richard M. Daley's election, over half of the legal business of the city was channeled to a firm which had raised more money for Daley than any other city law firm. Other businesses which aided the mayor's campaign also were rewarded with city contracts.[59]

There remain state governments (e.g., New Jersey, Pennsylvania, Illinois, and Indiana) in which patronage continues to thrive. For example, in New Jersey the governor appoints all department heads, plus state judges, state and county prosecutors, tax officials, and many salaried and unsalaried commission, board, and authority members. However, even in states with long traditions of patronage based policies, patronage is on the decline. Thus, Indiana discontinued the practice of giving lucrative franchises for dispensing auto and drivers licenses to county party leaders, who in turn were expected to kick back part of the proceeds to the state party.

Not all patronage is dispensed by governmental executives. Members of Congress, state legislators, and city council members normally hire their staffs on the basis of political loyalty. These officials may also exert heavy influence on the appointments made by the executive branch. Some executive appointments are actually controlled by legislators, as in the case of senatorial influence over the appointment of federal judges, marshals, and attorneys. In spite of its organization building potential, patronage poses problems for party leaders. As noted above, the pool of available patronage jobs is shrinking due to civil service laws, strong public employee unions, tight budgets, privatization of governmental functions, and court decisions. A further problem for the parties in making patronage appointments is that governmental jobs may carry with them qualifications that deserving party workers cannot meet—such as legal training or skill in operating sophisticated equipment. In addition, most available patronage positions have little appeal to the educated, middle-class persons that the parties are seeking to enlist in their ranks. Traditionally, patronage has been most appealing to the disadvantaged. A final problem for party leaders is the fact that elected officials may seek to use their appointing power to build a personal following rather than to strengthen the more inclusive party organization.

Patronage jobs are not the only material incentive available to political leaders. Governmental officials can give preferential treatment ("preferments") to persons they are seeking to recruit into party service or reward for past service. Preference in the awarding of government contracts has been a traditional way of rewarding business leaders who supported the winning candidate. The importance of government contracts to the construction industry has been a major reason for the industry's involvement in campaign finance. Preference can also be extended through administrative decisions and leniency in the enforcement of governmental regulations. Heavily regulated businesses (e.g., liquor, transportation) are normally involved in politics in a major way.

Elected Office. Holding major elected office carries with it prestige and power not found in most patronage positions. Party involvement can provide a stepping-stone to elective office. There are today few party organizations that are so strong that they can guarantee a party nomination to a preferred candidate. At the same time, party involvement and the support derived from party workers can be an essential ingredient in securing the nomination to a key office. The allure of public office, for example, is quite strong among state party chairs, who frequently run for high status offices such as governor or senator.

Because parties play a significant role in nominations and have control over important campaign resources, incumbent officeholders frequently play an active part in party affairs. This involvement helps them hold their existing positions secure and provides a basis for moving up the ladder of elected positions.

Social Benefits. Not all the benefits of political participation are based upon material rewards. There are also solidarity or social benefits. The friendships and camaraderie of the organization can be a strong force that binds individuals to the party. Similarly, the sense of recognition that an individual feels when a prominent elected official calls one by name in a crowd, personally acknowledges letters or phone calls, or extends an invitation to a social gathering can cause individuals to engage in political work on a continuing basis.

Studies of party activists in a number of cities such as Houston, Los Angeles, and Chicago have consistently shown that important reasons for participation in party politics include "social contacts and friendships," "personal recognition," and the "fun and excitement of campaigns." And the longer people participate in party work, the more important such personal motivations become. Although many first engaged in political activity out of concern for issues or ideology, the longer they participated the less important these concerns became as group solidarity incentives took a greater prominence.[60]

Issues and Ideology. Politics ultimately involves the direction which governmental policy will take. It is not, therefore, surprising that an important motivational force for participation is concern for issues and ideology. Concern for public policy is especially important in creating a stimulus for entry into party work. Persons anxious about health care, schools, abortion, civil rights, women's rights, the environment, and the scope of government activity can be stimulated to take part in politics. Issue oriented concerns are, however, difficult to sustain as a basis for continuing participation because of their transitory nature and the frustrations they frequently cause. Social or solidarity motivations for participation are easier to maintain in most communities.

A variety of studies focusing upon party activists operating in different settings—local party organizations to national conventions—indicate that issue oriented incentives have become more common in American politics. The importance of issue oriented motivations was presented in bold relief by the conservative fervor of Barry Goldwater's delegates at the 1964 Republican convention, and the intense liberalism of George McGovern supporters at the 1972 Democratic convention. The trend toward advocacy parties has also been revealed in studies of county level leaders of presidential campaigns as well as Republican and Democratic county chairs. These party leadership corps tend to contain a large proportion of "true believers"—persons driven by a commitment to enact specific policies or ideology. These activists may also be viewed as "purists" in that while they want to win elections, they are prepared to lose if unable to convince the electorate to endorse their policies.[61]

The Distinctiveness of Activists

Most Americans' political involvement seldom extends beyond the minimal act of periodically voting. Political activists are, therefore, set apart from the average citizen by their high levels of political participation. They also have other distinctive characteristics. First, activists tend to come from families that are active and interested in politics. Second, party activists are generally of relatively high socioeconomic status. Politics takes time, knowledge, and financial resources. These commodities tend to be concentrated among the middle and upper middle classes. The party leadership corps are not, therefore, necessarily representative demographically of their party's voters. Analysis of the social backgrounds of state party chairmen demonstrates this tendency of political leaders to come from upper middle-class backgrounds. Over 76 percent of the state party chairs come from either professional, business, or managerial occupations.[62] Similarly, 56 percent of Republican national convention delegates had incomes in excess of $75,000 compared to 18 percent of Republican voters, while 46 percent of Democratic delegates had that level of income compared to only 10 percent of Democratic voters.[63]

Party activists are also distinguishable from ordinary voters in terms of ideological orientation. Activists are much more likely to view the world from an ideological perspective and adopt a liberal or conservative position on issues. As would be expected, Democratic and Republican activists tend to see politics from differing ideological vantage points, with Democrats being significantly more liberal than Republicans. Studies of national convention delegates have consistently documented the substantial ideological differences between Republicans and Democrats. As can be seen in table 4.6, Democratic and Republican delegates are further apart ideologically than are rank and file voters of the two parties. There is also an ideology gap between each party's activists and its party voters. Table 4.6 also illustrates this pattern by comparing the ideology of national convention delegates and party voters. Republican activists are much more conservative than GOP voters, while Democratic leaders are significantly more liberal than their party's voters.

Table 4.6
The Ideology of National Convention Delegates, Party Voters, and All Voters: A Comparison, 1996 (in percent)

Political Views	Republican Delegates	Republican Voters	All Voters	Democratic Voters	Democratic Delegates
Very liberal	0%	1%	4%	7%	15%
Somewhat liberal	0	6	12	20	28
Moderate	27	39	47	54	48
Somewhat conservative	31	36	24	14	4
Very conservative	35	17	8	3	1

Source: New York Times, national edition, August 26, 1996, p. A12. Copyright © 1996, *The New York Times*. Reprinted by permission.

Party Organizations as Networks of Issue-Oriented Activists

Issue and ideological concerns have become so important as a motivation for participation that party organizations are increasingly becoming networks of "issue-based participatory activists."[64] The influence of the Christian Right within the Republican party is one manifestation of this pattern; the influence of pro-choice, gay rights, environmental, and affirmative action supporters in the Democratic party is another. The source of this trend toward party organizations based upon issue-oriented activists can be traced to a series of complex interacting forces: the emergence of a range of culture/social issues such as abortion, school prayer, women's rights, law and order, gay rights, and environmentalism; broad socioeconomic trends, such as rising levels of educational attainment, a shrinking blue-collar workforce, and increased white-collar employment; plus, the decline in the availability of patronage as an incentive to participate in politics.[65]

Evidence of the degree to which party organizations are becoming networks of issue activists abounds. There is a gap between the policy positions and ideology of delegates to national conventions and rank and file party voters, with GOP delegates being more conservative than their party's voters and Democratic delegates being more liberal than their voters (see table 4.6). Similarly, surveys of individuals participating in the presidential nominating politics through state party caucuses and conventions reveal that the bulk of these party activists "have a pronounced ideological tilt to them" that is more pronounced than that of primary voters or party identifiers.[66] Liberals and moderates are an increasing rare breed among GOP convention goers, while liberals dominate Democratic caucuses and conventions. State party conventions also show a pattern of interest group involvement among the delegates, with Democrats showing higher levels of participation in educational, social-issue, and environmental organizations than their Republican counterparts.[67]

Issue-based groups are also becoming ensconced in the party organizational structure. *Campaigns and Elections* magazine reported in 1994 that the Christian Right was the dominant faction in eighteen state Republican organizations and that it had substantial influence in thirteen others.[68] Evidence of this faction's influence was demonstrated at the 1997 meeting of the RNC when the Christian Coalition's executive director, Ralph Reed, helped engineer a third ballot switch of votes by thirty religious right committee members, a switch that enabled James Nicholson to win the RNC chairmanship.[69] The Democrats, too, have seen issue-oriented activists achieve substantial influence within their structure. This led to significant defections by moderate Democratic voters in the 1960s through the 1980s and defeats for the party's presidential candidates.[70]

The increasing involvement and influence of issue-oriented activists within the parties is not just creating conflicts between rank-and-file party voters and organizational activists. It is causing conflicts between officeholders and party organizations as well. In some jurisdictions, an almost schizophrenic party structure is emerging. That is, elected officials who need broad public support in order to win elections exist side-by-side with a growing body of party organizational activists who are concerned mainly about ideology and principles. The potential for intraparty conflict in this mix was on display within the Kansas GOP in 1998 as well as among Virginia Republicans in 1996 and the Minnesota Republican party in 1994. In Kansas the incumbent governor, Bill Graves, was given a primary scare by the state Republican chairman, who accused Graves of not being conservative enough. Two years earlier, in Virginia, moderate Republican Senator John Warner declined to speak at his party's state convention because conservative party leaders did not want him at the meeting, thereby leaving his primary opponent to speak unrebutted to 3,000 delegates. And in Minnesota, the 1994 GOP party convention dominated by the religious right endorsed one of its own for governor over the incumbent governor, moderate Republican Arne Carlson. In spite of party organizational opposition to their candidacies, Graves, Warner, and Carlson went on to win their parties' primaries and the general election by substantial margins.

As these struggles within the GOP illustrate, the ideological orientations of party activists have profound implications for the functioning of the American political system, because these are the individuals who have influence over nominations, party policy positions, and campaign strategy. While there is an overall tendency for Republican activists to be conservative and Democratic leaders to be liberal, neither party's activists constitute a monolithic bloc. As a result, there is constant tension within each party between the "true believers" who reject compromise and want party policy to reflect their policy views and those activists of a more moderate persuasion who are willing to compromise on ideology in order to attract a wider spectrum of voters and win elections. Nowhere is this tension more apparent than in presidential nominating politics, where ideologically committed activists exert a powerful influence over the delegate selection process and the national conventions. For example, the 1992 Republican convention was characterized by the hard edged conservatism of television commentator Pat Buchanan, who led a damaging challenge from the right flank to George Bush's renomination, and of religious broadcaster Pat Robertson; and in 1996, conservative activists foiled presidential nominee Bob Dole's attempts to moderate the party's platform. At the 1992 and 1996 Democrat conventions, with Bill Clinton assured of the nomination, the party was able to contain the liberal passions of the delegates and project a more centrist party image (after having failed to do so in the 1980s), as the Clinton team carefully managed every detail of the convention.

The parties are also pushed apart because candidates are normally recruited from the ranks of the activists. In addition, activists are an important constituency of candidates. Candidates need campaign workers and financial contributors, and they need them before they make their appeals to the mass electorate in the general election. Winning elections first requires putting together a campaign organization, adequate financing, and securing a party nomination. In these endeavors party activists are especially important. But these middle-class activists are not apt to be attracted by material rewards like patronage. It is, therefore, necessary to motivate them through intangible rewards—such as participation in a just cause. Because of the need to appeal to an activist constituency that is more liberal in the Democratic party and more conservative in the Republican party than rank and file party voters, it is often difficult for centrist candidates to secure their parties' presidential nomination. A candidate for the Republican presidential nomination needs strong conservative credentials to appeal to the activist constituency that plays a dominant role in nominations, while Democratic presidential aspirants need to demonstrate their liberal credentials.

Party Organizations: Adaptable and Durable

As voters during the 1960s and 1970s were shown to be less influenced by partisan considerations and as competing types of organizations like PACs, campaign/media consulting firms, and candidate organizations gained heightened prominence, there were dire predictions about the future of party organizations. One prominent journalist, who espoused the thesis of party decline, even wrote *The Party's Over.*[71] This chapter's survey of party organizations in America demonstrates that parties have shown qualities of adaptiveness and durability in a changing and frequently hostile political environment. There is even evidence of increased organizational strength, especially among national party organizations. It has also been shown that party organizations can have an impact on a party's capacity to win elections. American parties, however, are characterized by a diffusion of power and stratarchial power relationships. They function under unusually restrictive statutory regulations and they exist in a wide variety of forms with differing levels of effectiveness.

Suggestions for Further Reading

Cotter, Cornelius P.; Gibson, James L.; Bibby, John E; and Huckshorn, Robert J. *Party Organizations in American Politics*. New York: Praeger, 1984.

Epstein, Leon D. *Political Parties in the American Mold*. Madison: University of Wisconsin Press, 1986.

Gierzynski, Anthony. *Legislative Party Campaign Committees in the American States.* Lexington: University of Kentucky Press, 1992.

Herrnson, Paul S. *Party Campaigning in the 1980s.* Cambridge: Harvard University Press, 1988.

Klinkner, Philip A. *The Losing Parties: Out-Party National Committees, 1956-1993.* New Haven: Yale University Press, 1994.

Kolodny, Robin. *Pursuing Majorities: Congressional Campaign Committees in American Politics.* Norman: University of Oklahoma Press, 1988.

Maisel, L. Sandy, ed. The Parties Respond: Changes in American Parties and Campaigns. 3rd ed. Boulder: Westview Press, 1998.

Mayhew, David R. *Placing Parties in American Politics.* Princeton, N.J.: Princeton University Press, 1986.

Reichley, A. James. *The Life of the Parties: A History of American Political Parties.* New York: Free Press, 1992.

Schwartz, Mildred A. *The Party Network: The Robust Organization of Illinois Republicans.* Madison: University of Wisconsin Press, 1990.

Shafer, Byron E., ed. *Partisan Approaches to Postwar American Politics.* Chatham, N.J.: Chatham House, 1998.

Shea, Daniel M. *Transforming Democracy: Legislative Campaign Committees and Political Parties.* Albany: State University of New York Press, 1995.

Notes

1. V. O. Key, Jr., *Politics, Parties, and Pressure Groups.* 5th ed. (New York: Crowell, 1964), p. 316.

2. Ibid.

3. Samuel J. Eldersveld, *Political Parties in American Society* (New York: Basic Books, 1982), p. 99.

4. Ibid.

5. Joseph S. Schlesinger argues that these candidate organizations are basic units of the party. See his "The New American Political Party," *American Political Science Review* 79 (Dec. 1985): 1152–1169.

6. Mildred A. Schwartz, *The Party Network: The Robust Organizations of Illinois Republicans* (Madison: University of Wisconsin Press, 1990).

7. The development of the national committees into institutionalized bureaucracies is described in Cornelius P. Cotter and John F. Bibby, "Institutional Development of Parties and the Thesis of Party Decline," *Political Science Quarterly* 95 (Spring 1980): 1–27.

8. Cornelius P. Cotter and Bernard C. Hennessy, *Politics without Power: The National Party Committees* (New York: Atherton, 1964).

9. For an in-depth analysis of out-party national committees, see Philip A. Klinkner, *The Losing Parties: Out-Party National Committee, 1956–1993* (New Haven, Conn.: Yale University Press, 1994).

10. For an insightful analysis of the differing political cultures of the Republican and Democratic parties, see Jo Freeman, "The Political Culture of the Democrats and Republicans," *Political Science Quarterly* 101, no. 3 (1986): 327–356; see also Klinkner, *The Losing Parties*, ch. 10.

11. James R. Dickenson, "DNC Withdraws Recognition of 7 Caucuses," *Washington Post*, May 18, 1985, p. A7; Peter Bragdon, "DNC Approves Kirk's Plan To Alter Democrats' Image," *Congressional Quarterly Weekly Report* (June 29, 1985), p. 1287.

12. John F. Bibby and Robert J. Huckshorn, "Out-Party Strategy: Republican National Committee Rebuilding Politics, 1964–66," in Bernard Cosman and Robert J. Huckshorn, eds., *Republican Politics: The 1964 Campaign and Its Aftermath for the Party* (New York: Praeger, 1968), pp. 205-233.

13. David S. Broder, "At White House Order," *Washington Post*, January 23, 1991, p. A17.

14. *Wall Street Journal*, May 1, 1998, p. A1.

15. Francis X. Clines, "Still Offstage, Ickes Has Star Billing at Hearings," *New York Times* (national edition), September 11, 1997, p. A12.

16. Dan Balz, "Party's Top Soldier Keeps Marching Even as White House Sounds Taps," *Washington Post*, August 11, 1994, p. A18.

17. "The Vote Processor," *The Economist*, August 13, 1994, p. 30. On DNC payments to Clinton's consultants, see Elizabeth Drew, *On the Edge: The Clinton Presidency* (New York: Simon and Schuster, 1994), p. 124.

18. David S. Broder, "A Neglected Democratic Party," *Washington Post*, June 14, 1978; David S. Broder, "A.K.A. Difficult Circumstances," *Washington Post*, March 4, 1981; David Adamany, "Political Parties in the 1980s," in Michael J. Malbin, ed., *Money and Politics in the United States* (Chatham, N.J.: Chatham House, 1984), p. 86. For an historical account of White House–national committee relations, see James W. Davis, *The President as Party Leader* (New York: Greenwood Press, 1993), ch. 5.

19. David S. Broder, "The Road Back," *The Washington Post*, January 20, 1994, C7.

20. For accounts of national committee activities in the 1990s, see Paul S. Herrnson, "National Party Organizations at the Century's End," in L. Sandy Maisel, ed., *The Parties Respond: Changes in American Parties and Campaigns*, 3rd ed. (Boulder, Colo.: Westview Press, 1998), ch. 3; and Anthony Corrado, "The Politics of Cohesion: The Role of the National Party Committees in the 1992 Elections," in Daniel M. Shea and John C. Green, eds., *The Changing Role of Contemporary*

American Parties (Lanham, Md.: Rowman and Littlefield, 1995), ch. 5.

21. James A. Barnes, "Haley's Comet," *National Journal*, February 25, 1995, pp. 474–478.

22. Cornelius P. Cotter and Bernard Hennessy, *Politics without Power* (New York: Atherton, 1964).

23. *Democratic Party of the United States of America v. Bronson C. LaFollette*, 449 U.S. 897 (1981), and *Cousins v. Wigoda*, 419 U.S. 477 (1975).

24. The contrasting patterns of party centralization are discussed more fully in John F. Bibby, "Party Renewal in the National Republican Party," in Gerald Pomper, ed., *Party Renewal in America: Theory and Practice* (New York: Praeger, 1981), pp. 102–115.

25. See John F. Bibby, "State Party Organizations: Coping and Adapting to Candidate-Centered Politics and Nationalization," in Maisel, *The Parties Respond*, pp. 41–46.

26. Paul S. Herrnson, *Congressional Elections: Campaigning at Home and in Washington* (Washington, D.C.: CQ Press, 1998), pp. 83–84.

27. Thomas E. Mann, Norman J. Ornstein, and Michael J. Malbin, eds., *Vital Statistics on Congress, 1997–1998* (Washington, D.C.: Congressional Quarterly, 1998), pp. 103–104.

28. Herrnson, *Congressional Elections*, pp. 73–74.

29. David R. Mayhew, *Placing Parties in American Politics* (Princeton, N.J.: Princeton University Press, 1986), p. 324.

30. Elizabeth Drew, *Whatever It Takes: The Real Struggle of Political Power in America* (New York: Viking, 1997), pp. 14, 85, 207.

31. Ibid., pp. 74–77.

32. Robin Kolodny and Angela Logan, "Political Consultants and the Extension of Party Goals," *P.S.*, 31 (June 1998): 156.

33. For a detailed analysis of state regulation of parties, see *The Transformation of American Politics: Implications for Federalism* (Washington, D.C.: Advisory Commission in Intergovernmental Relations, 1986), pp. 123–160.

34. For an insightful consideration of political parties as public utilities, see Leon D. Epstein, *Political Parties in the American Mold* (Madison: University of Wisconsin Press, 1986), ch. 6.

35. Cornelius P. Cotter, James L. Gibson, John F. Bibby, and Robert J. Huckshorn, *Party Organizations in American Politics* (New York: Praeger, 1984), pp. 111–112.

36. James Dao, "A Political Kingmaker Takes No Prisoner," *New York Times* (national edition), January 18, 1998, p.23.

37. A. James Reichley, *The Life of the Parties: A History of American Political Parties* (New York: Free Press, 1992), p. 385.

38. Ibid.; for a thorough analysis of the current status of patronage, see Anne Freedman, *Patronage: An American Tradition* (Chicago: Nelson-Hall, 1994).

39. Cotter et al., *Party Organizations in American Politics,* pp. 13–40; Reichley, *The Life of the Parties*, pp. 386–391; and Advisory Commission on Intergovernmental Relations (ACIR), *The Transformation in American Politics: Implications for the Future* (Washington, D.C.: ACIR, 1986).

40. Cotter et al., *Party Organizations in American Politics*, pp. 416–419; Reichley, *The Life of the Parties*, p. 389.

41. Reichley, *The Life of the Parties*, pp. 391-392.

42. Robert Biersack, "Hard Facts and Soft Money: State Party Finance in the 1992 Federal Elections," in *The State of the Parties: The Changing Role of Contemporary Parties*, Daniel M. Shea and John C. Green, eds. (Lanham, Md.: Rowman and Littlefield, 1994), pp. 105–132.

43. Reichley, *The Life of the Parties*, p. 390.

44. Cotter et al., *Party Organizations in American Politics*, pp. 26–30; Malcolm E. Jewell and David M. Olson, *Political Parties and Elections in American States*, 3rd ed. (Chicago: Dorsey Press, 1988), pp. 63–70; and Reichley, *The Life of the Parties*, pp. 386–390.

45. For a detailed analysis of legislative campaign committees, see Anthony Gierzynski, *Legislative Party Campaign Committees in the American States* (Lexington: University of Kentucky Press, 1992); and Daniel M. Shea, *Transforming Democracy: Legislative Campaign Committees and Political Parties* (Albany, N.Y.: State University Press of New York, 1995).

46. Alan Ehrenhalt, "How a Party of Enthusiasts Keeps Its Hammerlock on a State Legislature," *Governing*, June 1989, pp. 29–30.

47. Anthony Gierzynski and David A. Breaux, "The Financing Role of Parties," in Joel A. Thompson and Gary F. Moncrief, eds., *Campaign Finance in State Legislative Elections* (Washington, D.C.: CQ Press, 1998), pp. 195–196.

48. Frank J. Sorauf, *Inside Campaign Finance: Myths and Realities* (New Haven: Yale University Press, 1992), p. 120. See also Daniel M. Shea, "The Development of Legislative Campaign Committees: A Second Look," *American Review of Politics* 15 (Summer 1994): 213–234.

49. For a complete survey of traditional party organizations, see David R. Mayhew, *Placing Parties in American Politics* (Princeton, N.J.: Princeton University Press, 1986).

50. Tom Watson, "All Powerful Machine of Yore Endures in New York's Nassau," *Congressional Quarterly Weekly Report*, Aug. 17, 1985, pp. 1623–1625.

51. David S. Broder, "Ground War Heating Up in California," *Washington Post*, Sept. 18, 1988, p. A16.

52. James L. Gibson, Cornelius P. Cotter, John F. Bibby, and Robert J.

Huckshorn, "Whither the Local Parties?: A Cross-Sectional and Longitudinal Analysis of the Strength of Party Organizations," *American Journal of Political Science* 29 (Feb. 1985): 139–159; James L. Gibson, John P. Frendreis, and Laura Vertz, "Party Dynamics in the 1980s: Change in Party Organizational Strength 1980–1984," *American Journal of Political Science* 33 (Feb. 1989): 139–160; and John Frendreis and Alan R. Gitelson, "Continuity and Change in the Electoral Roles of Local Parties," a paper prepared for delivery at the "State of the Parties: 1996" Conference, Ray C. Bliss Institute of Applied Politics, University of Akron, October 9–10, 1997.

53. Eldersveld, *Political Parties in American Society*, p. 145.

54. "GOP Retains Hold on Washington State," *Washington Post,* November 29, 1996, p. A16.

55. Cotter et al., *Party Organizations in American Politics*, ch. 5.

56. Peter W. Wielhouwer and Brad Lockerbie, "Party Contacting and Political Participation, 1952–1990," *American Journal of Political Science* 38 (February 1989): 226.

57. Paul Allen Beck, Audrey Haynes, Russell J. Dalton, and Robert Huckfeldt, "Party Effort at the Grass Roots: Local Presidential Campaigning in 1992" (paper delivered at the annual meeting of the Midwest Political Science Association, Chicago, April 1994). On local party activities acting as a catalyst to stimulate political activists, see Robert Huckfeldt and John Sprague, "Political Parties and Electoral Mobilization: Political Structure, Social Structure, and the Party Canvass," *American Political Science Review* 84 (March 1992): 70–86.

58. John P. Frendreis, James L. Gibson, and Laura L. Vertz, "The Electoral Relevance of Local Party Organizations," *American Political Science Review* 84 (March 1990): 226–235.

59. Freedman, *Patronage,* p. 70.

60. See the four-city study, William Crotty, ed., *Political Parties in Local Areas* (Knoxville: University of Tennessee Press, 1986); and Eldersveld, *Political Parties in American Society*, p. 178.

61. See John M. Bruce, John A. Clark, and John H. Kessel, "Advocacy Politics in Presidential Parties," *American Political Science Review* 85 (December 1991): 1089–1106. On the ideology of national convention delegates, see Herbert McCluskey, Paul J. Hoffman, and Rosemary O'Hara, "Issue Conflicts and Consensus among Party Leaders and Followers," *American Political Science Review* 54 (June 1960): 406–427; Aaron Wildavsky, "The Goldwater Phenomenon: Purists, Politicians, and the Two Party System," *Review of Politics* 27 (July 1965): 386–413; and Warren E. Miller and M. Kent Jennings, *Without Consent: Mass-Elite Linkages in Presidential Politics* (Lexington: University of Kentucky Press, 1988).

62. Robert J. Huckshorn, "The Social Backgrounds and Career Patterns of

State Party Chairpersons" (unpublished manuscript, 1982).

63. Delegate surveys, *Washington Post*, August 12, 1992, p. A23, and August 16, 1992, p. A18. Delegate surveys, *Washington Post*, August 11, 1996, p. M8, and August 25, 1996, p. M4.

64. Byron E. Shafer, ed., *Postwar Politics in the G-7: Order and Eras in Comparative Perspective* (Madison: University of Wisconsin Press, 1996), p. 36.

65. Ibid., p. 34.

66. William G. Mayer, ed., *In Pursuit of the White House: How We Choose Our Presidential Nominees* (Chatham, N.J.: Chatham House, 1996), p. 133.

67. John F. Francis and Robert Benedict, "Issue Group Activists at Conventions," in Ronald B. Rapoport, Alan I. Abramowitz, and John McGlennon, eds., *The Life of the Parties: Activists in Presidential Politics* (Lexington: University of Kentucky Press, 1986), pp. 105–110.

68. Clyde Wilcox, *Onward Christian Soldiers: The Religious Right in American Politics* (Boulder, Colo.: Westview Pres, 1996), pp. 75–77.

69. David S. Broder, "Two Called to Serve," *Washington Post*, January 29, 1997, p. A21.

70. David G. Lawrence, *The Collapse of the Democratic Presidential Majority* (Boulder, Colo.: Westview Press, 1997), pp. 102–103.

71. David S. Broder, *The Party's Over: The Failure of Politics in America* (New York: Harper and Row, 1971); for a scholarly discussion of the possibility of partyless politics, see Walter Dean Burnham, *Critical Elections and the Mainsprings of American Politics* (New York: Norton, 1970).

NOMINATIONS FOR STATE AND CONGRESSIONAL OFFICES

CHAPTER FIVE

Although Americans pride themselves on having operated with free elections for over two hundred years, the voter's choice in general elections is severely limited. In most elections, citizens are faced with choosing between Republican and Democratic nominees, or "wasting" their vote on a third party candidate who has only the remotest chance of winning. The functioning of American democracy, therefore, is affected in critical ways by the decisions the two major parties make in selecting persons to bear their labels in the general election. For the party, the nomination process is a crucial part of its activities. It is this activity more than any other which distinguishes the political party from other political organizations such as the AFL-CIO, Americans for Democratic Action, Common Cause, Chamber of Commerce, or Farm Bureau. Only political parties nominate candidates on their own labels and present them to the voters as their official representatives. The nomination is also critical for the parties because selecting the "right" candidate can determine whether a party will win or lose the general election. A candidate lacking in appeal to the party's traditional voters and independents, or one who divides rather than unites the party's electorate and workers, is not likely to gain public office. Finally, the nomination process is important to the party because control of the party is at stake. Influence over the selection of party nominees goes a long way toward determining which party factions will gain ascendancy in terms of the policy direction of the party and the rewards which elected officials bestow upon their supporters. The critical character of the nomination process for the parties was aptly summarized by the late E. E. Schattschneider.

> Unless the party makes authoritative and effective nominations, it cannot stay in business. . . . The nature of the nomination procedure determines the nature of the party; he who can make nominations is the owner of the party. . . . [1]

In most Western democracies, the selection of candidates rests in the hands of the party organization—the party officers and activists. Operating largely without government regulation, these leaders designate the party's candidates and there is no appeal to the party-in-the-electorate of their decisions. The average voter participates only in the general election—a contest between the parties—and not in the intraparty contest to select nominees. Nominating processes in the United States, by contrast, not only involve party activists, but also permit extensive participation by rank and file voters. Indeed, a persistent trend in the evolution of nominating practices in the United States has been toward increasing the opportunities for popular participation and weakening the capacity of party organizational hierarchies to control candidate selection for local, state, and national offices. The American nomination process is not only unique for the amount of popular participation that it permits, but also for the wide variety and high level of statutory regulation that governs it.

The Evolution of the Direct Primary

From Legislative Caucus to Party Convention

After the American Revolution, the legislative caucus evolved as the principal means of making nominations for state offices. The legislative caucus was a meeting of all the party's elected members of the state senate and house of representatives. A similar method of nomination—the congressional caucus—was used to select presidential candidates. The legislative caucus was not a particularly representative institution, because it left unrepresented those districts which had elected opposition party legislators. To correct this problem, some of the states used a "mixed caucus" system, which permitted special delegates, representing districts held by the opposition party, to participate in the caucus to nominate candidates.

Andrew Jackson's failure to gain the presidential nomination from the oligarchs of the congressional caucus in 1824 and the subsequent defeat of the caucus nominee, William H. Crawford, contributed in a significant way to the demise of the caucus system. Jackson was a popular figure—the hero of the Battle of New Orleans and a symbol of democracy and egalitarianism. His backers sought to discredit the caucus system. It was replaced by a convention system of nomination.

The convention process normally started with local or precinct caucuses that selected delegates to attend county conventions. The county conventions then selected delegates to a state party convention. The state conventions nominated the party's candidate for statewide office such as governor, attorney general, and secretary of state. Courthouse candidates were nominated by the county conventions and there were also congressional district conventions to select candidates for the United States House. Its supporters considered the convention system to be a democratic reform designed to permit greater popular participation and improved representation for party rank and file voters. Like the legislative caucus, the convention nominating process fell into disrepute. The convention process was susceptible to manipulation and domination by party leaders and "bosses," who were often under the influence of well-financed interests anxious to gain favorable concessions from state governments. It was charged that conventions too often selected candidates who were not the popular choice of party voters. There was a further problem of convention nominations being tantamount to election in one party areas so that, in effect, the actual choice of public officials was being made at party conventions and not by the voters at the general election.

The Direct Primary: "Escape from One-Partyism"

Early in the twentieth century, the convention system was replaced in most states by the direct primary—nomination of party candidates by the voters directly. The primary permitted direct expression of voter preferences and struck down "the intermediate links between rank and file of the party and would-be candidates."[2]

While there was a great deal of oratory about democracy, citizen participation, corrupt party machines, and special interests during the time when the direct primary was being adopted, V. O. Key has concluded that the primary was "at bottom an escape from one-partyism."[3] The Civil War and Reconstruction made the South a one party Democratic area. The direct primary, therefore, evolved in the South as a means to permit popular government where interparty competition of a meaningful nature had ceased. The importance of a lack of interparty competition as an impetus to adoption of the direct primary is illustrated in Virginia and North Carolina, the southern states that held out the longest against instituting primaries. These were also the southern states with the highest level of interparty competition during the 1880s and 1890s, the decades preceding widespread adoption of the primary.[4]

The electoral realignments of the 1890s solidified Democratic one party dominance of the South, but also created one party Republican areas in the Northeast, Midwest, and West. The primary, therefore, spread through these states as interparty competition diminished and GOP state convention nominations became tantamount to election. In 1903, Wisconsin was the first state to enact a comprehensive direct primary law. In states with more established party systems and real two party competition, such as New York, Delaware, Connecticut, and Rhode Island, the primary was adopted more slowly.

Although one of the reasons for instituting the direct primary was to deal with the problems created by one-partyism, there is evidence that the introduction of the direct primary frustrated and delayed the development of two party competition. The primary weakened the minority party because it focused public attention upon contests within the dominant party. Voters were channeled into the primary of the dominant party because that was where the election was actually being decided. Persons with political ambitions also gravitated into the majority party because they saw little future in the minority party. These patterns of behavior caused V. O. Key to conclude that "primary competition tended to be substituted for general election competition; competition within parties for competition between parties."[5] He believed that without the direct primary, interparty competition would have come sooner to one party areas of the North and South.

The Direct Primary and Progressivism

The direct primary embodied an essential element of faith of the reformist progressive movement of the early twentieth century. The Progressives believed intermediaries between the people and their government should be removed and that the voters should be able to choose nominees for office without encroachments on their sovereignty by party leaders. Robert M. La Follette, Sr., the leader of the Wisconsin Progressives, stated the case for the direct primary.

> Under our form of government the entire structure rests upon the nomination of candidates for office. This is the foundation of representative government. If bad men control nominations we cannot have good government. . . .
>
> [We] must abolish the caucus and convention by law, place nominations in the hands of the people, and make all nominations by direct vote at a primary election.
>
> With nominations of all candidates absolutely in the control of the people . . . the public official who desires re-nomination will not dare to seek it, if he has served the machine and the lobby and betrayed the public trust.[6]

The Progressives fought for the direct primary not only because it was consistent with their democratic faith, but because it provided a means of challenging the power of established party leaders, achieving political power, and fulfilling personal ambition. La Follette in Wisconsin, Hiram Johnson in California, and other Progressive leaders used the primary to strengthen their faction's influence within the dominant Republican party of their states.

The Direct Primary in the South

While the direct primary in the North was designed to provide a forum for electoral competition and advance the fortunes of the progressive faction of the GOP, in the South the movement supporting the direct primary had a different mix of motives. The direct primary was designed to unify the Democratic party under conservative leadership, weaken the Republican opposition, and prevent black voters from having electoral influence. Use of the primary to select Democratic candidates, it was thought, would give greater legitimacy to the nominee than would selection by party conventions, and the party might thereby be unified. It was hoped that settling intraparty differences in the primary and presenting a united front in the general election would reduce the influence of the opposition parties and their voters—mainly blacks, who up until the Depression of the 1930s were overwhelmingly Republican. Southern Democratic parties also adopted rules barring blacks from voting in party primaries, in order to prevent any candidate or faction from making appeals to black voters in order to gain a party nomination.[7]

The advocates of the primary in the South were largely successful in achieving their goals. The Democratic primary became the only significant election; only in states with concentrations of Republicans in mountain areas was the GOP a force of modest significance (e.g., Tennessee, Kentucky, Virginia, North Carolina); and the white primary effectively excluded blacks from the electoral process.

Post–World War II Trends

During the years after World War II, the primary was instituted in those states which had been holdouts. In 1976, Indiana adopted the primary for nominating statewide candidates and became the last of the holdout states to accept the primary. Other states which became primary states were Rhode Island (1947), Connecticut (1955), and New York (statewide offices, 1967). In enacting the primary laws, Rhode Island, Connecticut, and New York also made provision for preprimary endorsement of candidates by the party organizations.[8]

The nature of southern primaries has also changed with the demise of the whites only primary, the enfranchisement of blacks, and the emergence of strong Republican parties. Blacks are now an increasingly larger proportion of the southern Democratic party's supporters and active participants in the primaries as both voters and candidates. While it was only a minor force in southern state politics, the Republican party frequently opted to take advantage of a provision in state law which permitted nominations via conventions. As the party has gained electoral strength in the region, it has increasingly used the primary to nominate its candidates.[9]

State Regulation of the Direct Primary

There is tremendous diversity among the states in the operation of the direct primary. The constitutional principle of federalism permits the states wide latitude in tailoring their election laws to fit state traditions, political conditions, and the preferences of state leaders and voters.

Nomination by Convention

Although the direct primary is the predominant method of nominating candidates, thirteen states either permit or require conventions. In Connecticut, for example, the winner of the party's endorsement at the state convention automatically becomes the nominee unless challenged in the primary by a candidate who received at least 15 percent of the convention votes. Several of the southern states (Alabama, Georgia, South Carolina, and Virginia) permit the parties to nominate either by primary or convention. This option permits state parties to determine which method of nomination they wish to use based upon strategic considerations. In 1993, for example, the Virginia Republicans opted for the convention method after the party's primary-nominated candidate of 1989 lost the gubernatorial election. And Virginia Democrats have used the convention system since divisive primaries played a role in the party's losing gubernatorial elections in the late 1960s and 1970s. The convention method of nomination, of course, enhances the influence which party leaders have over the nominating process because candidates cannot appeal effectively over the heads of party leaders to rank and file voters, as in a primary.

Party Affiliation Requirements for Voting

There is wide variation among the states in terms of the party affiliation requirements imposed in order for a voter to participate in primaries. The states array themselves along a continuum regarding the severity of their party affiliation requirements from those which restrict participation to registered partisans to others with no restrictions (see table 5.1).

Closed Primaries. Sixteen states have closed primaries. In these states, voters must register as party affiliates in order to vote in a party primary. Participation is thus restricted to those who are willing to register publicly as partisans; those who register as independents are barred from voting. A voter who wishes to switch party registration must do so in advance of the primary, normally twenty to thirty days prior to the primary.

Table 5.1

Party Affiliation Requirements for Voting in Direct Primaries

Closed: Party Registration Required; changes permitted in fixed time period before primary	Semiclosed: Voters may register or change party registration on election day	Semiopen: Voters required to publicly request party ballot	Open: Voter decides in which primary to vote in privacy of voting booth	Blanket: Voter may vote in more than one party's primary, but one candidate per office	"Nonpartisan": Top two primary vote-getters, regardless of party, are nominated for the general election
Arizona	Colorado[e]	Alabama	Hawaii	Alaska	Louisiana
Connecticut[a]	Iowa	Arkansas	Idaho	California	
Delaware	Kansas[e]	Georgia	Michigan	Washington[f]	
Florida	Maine[e]	Illinois	Minnesota		
Kentucky	Massachusetts[d]	Indiana	Montana		
Maryland	New Hampshire[d]	Mississippi	North Dakota		
Nebraska[b]	New Jersey[e]	Missouri	Utah		
Nevada	Ohio	South Carolina	Vermont		
New Mexico	Rhode Island[e]	Tennessee	Wisconsin		
New York	Wyoming	Texas			
North Carolina[c]		Virginia			
Oklahoma					
Oregon[c]					
Pennsylvania					
South Dakota					
West Virginia[c]					

a. Unaffiliated voters may vote in some Republican primaries but not in Democratic primaries.
b. Unaffiliated voters may vote in either party's primary for U.S. Senator or Representative
c. Unaffiliated voters may vote in Republican primaries.
d. Independents may change registration on election day.
e. Persons who have not previously voted in a primary may change registration on election day.
f. State Republican party rules restrict participation in the Republicans primary to registered Republicans and voters without party affiliation.

Source: The author is indebted to Professor Malcolm E. Jewell for providing information on voter qualification to participate in primaries of the states.

Ten states have created *semi-closed* primary systems. These states have loopholes in their closed primary laws that permit voters to register or change party registration on election day. However, only Iowa, Ohio, and Wyoming give voters an unrestricted right to register or change party registration on election day. Two states, Massachusetts and New Hampshire, grant this privilege only to independents; and five other states grant it only to persons who have not previously voted in a primary.

There are also several state Republican parties that permit unaffiliated voters (voters not designating party affiliations at the time of registration) to vote in their primaries. As a result of the *Tashjian* decision (see chapter 4), in which the Supreme Court held that a state could not prevent a party from opening its primary elections to unaffiliated voters, the Republican parties of Connecticut, North Carolina, Oregon, and West Virginia have opened their parties to unaffiliated voters. In each of these states, Republicans constituted a minority of the registered voters. The GOP state organizations therefore sought to take advantage of the *Tashjian* decision in an effort to encourage greater public interest in their party's affairs. In addition, Nebraska permits unaffiliated voters to vote in either party's primary for United States senator or representative (but not for governor).[10]

The justification for the closed primary is that since primaries are the process through which party nominees are chosen, only party affiliates with a reasonably stable commitment to the party should be permitted to vote. It is argued that the selection of a nominee is one of the most important decisions that a party makes and it should not be turned over to nonparty members or made vulnerable to "raiding" from outsiders, who lack a long-term commitment to the party. Party organization leaders have traditionally preferred the closed primary system because it prevents "cross-overs" by voters from the opposition party, creates a known constituency to whom appeals for support can be made, and makes control of the nomination process somewhat easier to achieve.

Public Statement of Party Preference Required. Eleven states (mainly in the South) operate *semi-open* primary systems, in which voters are not required to register as party affiliates, but they are required to declare publicly in which party's primary they wish to participate. No official record is kept of the voters' publicly stated preference, and voters are free to change their party preference at each primary. Some states require voters to submit their preference in writing and a few states require a voter to swear that they support the party, if their participation in a primary is challenged. By requiring voters to publicly declare a party preference, the semi-open primary system denies voters the anonymity of their party preference that is provided by open primary systems.

Open Primary. Nine states provide for the open primary in which no requirements concerning party affiliations are imposed upon persons voting in the primary. In open primary states, the voters decide in the privacy of the voting booth in which party's primary they wish to vote. As in the previously described types of primaries, voters in open primary states are restricted to voting in only one party's primary. Particularly open primaries occur in states such as Wisconsin and Minnesota which combine open primary laws with election day registration at the polls. In these states, a voter need not be registered prior to the primary in order to vote, since registration is permitted at the polls on primary election day.

The basic rationale for the open primary is that all voters should be permitted to participate in the crucial decisional process of selecting nominees for public office and that such participation should not be restricted to those who publicly acknowledge a partisan preference. In addition, the advocates of the open primary stress that it protects the privacy of party preference and electoral choice.

Blanket Primary. Washington, Alaska and California operate under the most "open" primary procedures. The blanket primary permits the voter to take part in more than one party's primary by switching back and forth between parties from office to office. In Washington state, for example, it is possible for an elector to vote in the Republican primary for governor, the Democratic primary for United States senator, the Republican primary for United States representative, and Democratic state legislative primaries. Although Alaska statutes provide for a blanket primary, the Alaska Republican party has taken advantage of its power under the *Tashjian* decision, which gives state parties the power to determine who may vote in their primaries, to restrict participation in GOP primaries to registered Republicans and voters without a partisan affiliation.[11]

"Nonpartisan" Primary. An unusual variation on the open primary was instituted in Louisiana in 1975. Under this system all candidates, irrespective of party affiliation, are listed alphabetically within office blocks on the ballot. If a candidate receives a majority of the votes cast in the open primary, then that candidate is elected and no general election is held for that office. If, however, no candidate receives a majority of the votes cast in the open primary, then the two candidates with the highest number of votes, irrespective of party, will face each other in the general election.

Louisiana's unique "nonpartisan" primary was a project of the state's roguish Democratic governor, Edwin Edwards, and was intended to benefit his party. In 1975, at the time of its adoption, the Republican party was relatively weak, and its candidates were not assured of making it into the general election run-off. Malcolm E. Jewell, a distinguished student of state politics, has concluded that "the major consequence of the nonpartisan primary has been to blur differences between the parties." Thus, in 1991, the losing Republican gubernatorial candidate had been elected to the post four years previously as a Democrat, and the Republican governor elected in 1995 had been a Democrat until six weeks before the election.[12]

Regulation of Candidacies and Cross-Filing

In addition to regulating which persons may vote in a party primary, states decide the qualifications a candidate must meet in order to run. Most of the states permit a person to run in only one party's primary and only the most minimal tests of party membership are required. However, nine states permit candidates to be endorsed by more than one party. Up until 1959, California was the most notable example of this practice, which is called cross-filing. Under California's cross-filing system, a candidate could run in both the Republican and Democratic primaries and if this candidate won both parties' primaries, then the individual's name would go on the general election ballot as both the Democratic and Republican nominee. This was a system that tended to favor the long dominant Republican party, whose candidates were apt to be better known. They, therefore, benefited greatly from the generally lower turnout and lower levels of voter knowledge of candidates that exists in primaries. In a number of instances, prominent Republicans won both parties' nominations for state constitutional offices and the United

States Senate. One consequence of cross-filing in California was to delay a build up in strength by the minority Democratic party, because the majority party could bore from within by capturing the nominations of the weaker party. V. O. Key has observed that "the rule limiting entry to candidacy in the party primary is . . . a rule of critical importance in maintenance of party competition."[13]

An interesting variation of cross-filing exists in New York, where it operates to encourage minor parties and facilitate coalitions of the Democratic party with the Liberal party and the Republicans with the Conservative party. New York permits parties that nominate candidates by convention—the Liberals and Conservatives—to nominate the same candidate as the major parties. It is, therefore, common for Democratic nominees to appear on the general election ballot in both the Democratic and Liberal party columns, and for GOP nominees also to be listed as Conservative party candidates. Thus, in 1994, Republican George Pataki upset Democratic Governor Mario Cuomo, even though Cuomo received more votes on the Democratic line than Pataki did on the GOP line. However, Pataki's 328,000 votes on the Conservative party line and 54,000 on the Freedom party line gave him a narrow 173,798 margin of victory.

The provision for cross-filing or fusion tickets in New York has created a powerful incentive for the creation and maintenance of minor parties and made them a critical element of the state's electoral politics. At the same time, the possibility of these parties refusing to nominate their coalition partner's candidate and instead running their own candidate, or even nominating the other major party's nominee, can pose a serious threat to their coalition partner's electoral prospects. The Liberal and Conservative parties are, therefore, in a position to exert leverage on the major parties to nominate candidates acceptable to the third parties. The results of these maneuverings frequently have a major impact on the outcome of general elections.[14] For example, the 1980 Senate race was a three-way contest because the Liberal party declined to nominate the Democratic nominee, Elizabeth Holtzman, and instead ran the incumbent Jacob Javits, who had lost the Republican primary to Alfonse D'Amato. Running as the Republican-Conservative nominee, D'Amato eked out a narrow win while receiving 45 percent of the vote compared to 44 percent for Holtzman and 11 percent for Javits. Clearly, the split Democratic-Liberal vote contributed to

D'Amato's victory, as did the contribution to his vote total made by voters who cast their ballots for him as the Conservative party nominee.

Regulation of the Proportion of the Vote Required for Nomination: The Runoff Primary

The normal practice in the states is for the nomination to go to the candidate who receives the most votes (a plurality) in the primary, even if that individual receives less than a majority of the votes cast. In nine southern and border states, a majority of the vote in the primary is required for nomination, and in North Carolina 40 percent of the primary vote is required for nomination. If no candidate receives a majority, then a second or runoff primary is held between the top two finishers in the first primary. This system was instituted in the South during an era when the Democratic party was dominant and its nomination was tantamount to election. To assure that the person nominated in the Democratic primary, and therefore "elected," had the support of a majority of Democratic voters, the run-off primary was instituted.

The potential for a second primary diminishes the internal party pressures for preprimary coalition formation and, therefore, tends to increase the number of candidates in the initial primary. The run-off can also result in a different candidate winning the nomination than led in the first primary, for example, Senator Phil Gramm (R-Tex.) first entered Congress as a Democratic member of the House after coming in second in the first primary and then winning the run-off in 1978 (he later switched to the Republican party).

The rise of the Republican party in the South has dramatically altered the importance of the Democratic primaries. Democratic nominees are no longer assured of general election victory. As Republican strength in general elections has increased, voter participation in Democratic primaries has waned as voters have delayed their balloting participation until the general election, "when it really matters."[15] For example, in Texas, turnout in the Democratic gubernatorial primary dropped from 1.8 million in 1978 to 1.03 million in 1994, and in 1998, the party had an uncontested primary, which drew even less interest.

Even though general elections have become increasingly important in the South, the second primary system has been a major point of contention within the Democratic party. The enfranchisement of black voters in the South and their overwhelming allegiance to the Democratic party have meant that blacks are now a major factor in Democratic nominating politics, both as voters and as candidates. Their impact has been enhanced by the growing support which Republicans are gaining from the white urban and suburban middle class and young voters. As a result of this combination of factors, black candidates periodically gain a plurality of the vote in the initial primary. Some have then failed to win a majority in the run-off as the white vote coalesced around a white candidate. In his 1984 presidential campaign, Jesse Jackson lobbied to put an anti-runoff plank in the Democratic party platform on the grounds that it disadvantaged black candidates. Democratic leaders resisted Jackson's plea because they were fearful that such a course would cause further erosion of support among white voters should the Democrats nominate a black to face a white Republican in the general election.

Analyses of election results have shown that in those states having runoff primaries, it was necessary to hold a runoff primary only in approximately 10 percent of statewide and congressional elections between 1970 and 1986. In 70 percent of the run-offs, the leader in the first primary went on to win. However, the success rate for African-American candidates who led in the first primary fell to 50 percent in the second primary.[16]

Regulation of Access to the General Election Ballot: "Sore Loser" Laws

The importance of a party nomination is enhanced if a candidate who loses a primary is not permitted to run in the general election as an independent. In twenty-seven of the states, the legislatures have enacted "sore loser" statutes that prevent independent candidacies by persons who lost a primary nomination. Such statutes are party-protective measures in that they limit the extent to which intraparty factional struggles can be carried over into the general election. Critics charge that these laws unduly limit candidacy. This was the claim of John B. Anderson as he sought to gain access to the presidential ballot in 1980 after his abortive campaign for the Republican nomination. The Supreme Court, however, has upheld the constitutionality of "sore loser" statutes (*Storer v. Brown*, 1974).

Preprimary Endorsements

Clearly the intent of the progressive reformers and one of the consequences of the direct primary has been to reduce party organization control over nominations. Party organizational influence has not, however, been totally removed from the process and this is especially true in those states which utilize preprimary endorsements by the party organizational leadership. Endorsements can be statutory mandates, informal practices of the party organization, or a practice of party affiliated organizations.

State Statutory Requirements for Endorsement

In seven states (Colorado, Connecticut, New Mexico, New York, North Dakota, Rhode Island, and Utah) state law provides for preprimary endorsement by party conventions. The existence of these statutory requirements for endorsing conventions reflects the ability of the party organizations in these states to retain a significant role in the nomination process even while the state legislatures were succumbing to the pressures for the direct primary. Endorsement frequently carries with it the right to have one's name placed on the primary ballot or to be listed first on the ballot. In Rhode Island, for example, endorsed candidates have an automatic right to a place on the primary ballot, but other candidates must qualify by circulating petitions. Access to the ballot may also be restricted by requiring that a candidate receive a fixed percentage of the convention delegate votes in order to enter the primary. The minimum convention vote required for getting one's name on the primary ballot is 25 percent in New York, 20 percent in New Mexico, and 15 percent in Connecticut. These requirements have frequently prevented challenges to the party organizations' preferred candidates. New Mexico's endorsing conventions have been used to achieve slates balanced between Hispanic and Anglo candidates.[17] In Utah, the convention designates for each office two candidates whose names are placed on the primary ballot. However, if one candidate receives 70 percent of the convention vote, that individual is automatically declared the party nominee. A candidate in Colorado can avoid a primary and become the party's nominee if he or she receives the support of 50 percent of the convention delegates. It is possible in several of the states with statutory requirements for preprimary endorsement for candidates to get on the primary ballot by securing the requisite number of signatures on a petition.

Extralegal Endorsements

In ten states, endorsements by one or both parties are provided for by party rules, with the endorsing done either by party conventions or by committees. For example, both parties in Illinois, Massachusetts, and Minnesota regularly endorse candidates, and California recently joined the list of states with endorsement permitted under state party rules. Other states that use party endorsement include Delaware, Michigan, Pennsylvania, Ohio, and Virginia.[18] In New Jersey, county party organizations frequently endorse candidates in an effort to influence who will enter and win the primary. Behind the scenes, it is not unusual for party leaders to assist a favored candidate while discouraging others from getting into the race. There are also unofficial party endorsements by party affiliated groups in California. These unofficial party affiliates, including the Republican Assembly and the California Democratic Council, seek to influence nominations through their group endorsements.

Extralegal endorsement practices often reflect a desire on the part of party activists to select candidates committed to a particular political faith or faction. In Minnesota, for example, ideological concerns have played a major role in endorsement politics, as the Democratic Farmer-Labor party has utilized endorsement to maintain a liberal policy orientation. While the state Republicans, in their efforts to further a conservative agenda, even went so far as to deny endorsement in 1994 to its moderate, pro-choice incumbent governor, Arne Carlson. Not all endorsement activities are motivated, however, solely out of ideological concerns. An interest in maintaining political control, not ideology, has been a major motivation of the Illinois Democratic State Central Committee in its slate-making. Other party interests that can be advanced through endorsement are selecting the strongest candidate and avoiding a divisive primary that could split the party for the general election.

The various methods used by state and local party organizations to influence primary elections demonstrate that parties can be a critical factor in the nomination process. However, since 1980, the trend has been one of declining primary wins for party-endorsed gubernatorial candidates. Thus, in 1994, six of eleven endorsed gubernatorial candidates lost their parties' primaries.[19] This occurred even in Connecticut, a state with a long tradition of party organizational control over nominations.

Consequences of Preprimary Endorsements

Reduced Primary Competition. Preprimary endorsement reduces the amount of competition in primaries. Candidates who fail to gain endorsements often withdraw from the race and do not enter the primary. While there is frequently competition in gubernatorial primaries, it is much less common in states requiring statutory endorsements. In states having statutory endorsement there was competition in 45 percent of the gubernatorial primaries between 1982 and 1994, whereas there was competition in 80 percent of the primaries in states with nonstatutory endorsement procedures.[20] When considering these data it should be noted that several of the states with statutory endorsement have traditionally been strong organization states, while the states using extralegal techniques frequently have weak party structures in the Progressive tradition. Strong organizations can more effectively discourage candidates from entering primaries if they fail to gain endorsement. Preprimary endorsements have their greatest impact in reducing primary competition through the elimination of minor candidates. Major challengers, however, can normally mount effective primary campaigns even without endorsements.

Incumbent governors normally face little or no opposition in their drives for renomination. Thus between 1982 and 1992, there were nineteen incumbent governors seeking renomination in states with endorsement systems and eighteen were successful in winning both endorsement and renomination. Of the eighteen, twelve were unopposed in both the party convention and primary.

From 1960 to 1980, endorsed gubernatorial candidates were victorious in 82 percent of the primaries that were contested. However, between 1982 and 1994 this figure plummeted to only 46 percent, with only negligible differences between statutory and nonstatutory endorsement systems.[21] The change in the fortunes of endorsed candidates has been particularly striking for both parties in Minnesota and Rhode Island.

The most common reason for endorsed gubernatorial candidates failing to win their party's primary has been that the endorsee had strong support among activists within the state party organization, while the primary winner could appeal to a broader constituency. Thus in 1994, the strongly conservative and pro-life GOP convention in Minnesota denied its moderate and pro-choice governor, Arne Carlson, the party's endorsement. The popular governor, however, went on to crush his endorsed opponent in the primary. Strong backing from organized groups allied with the party provided the basis for overcoming the failure to win a state party's preprimary endorsement. For example, liberal labor unions, environmental, consumer, and women's groups formed a coalition that enabled Connecticut State Comptroller William E. Curry to win the 1994 Democratic gubernatorial primary over an endorsed candidate. Nonendorsed candidates may also be successful when they have a high degree of name recognition, as Democrat Bruce Sundlin of Rhode Island did in 1990 after twice having run in gubernatorial primaries.

A potential disadvantage of being the endorsed candidate is getting tagged with the label of being the candidate of the "bosses" or "kingmakers." This tactic was used successfully by John Silber to defeat an endorsed candidate in the 1990 Democratic gubernatorial primary in Massachusetts.

Although the impact of preprimary endorsements on primary outcomes appears to have declined in recent years, a comprehensive study conducted by Sarah McCally Morehouse found that preprimary endorsements do tend to lessen the impact of campaign spending. Endorsed candidates usually succeed in getting themselves as well known as their challengers because the endorsement process requires them to engage in extensive face-to-face meetings with at least a thousand party activist delegates from across the state. The public visibility gained through the endorsement process thus helps to compensate for any campaign spending advantage their challengers may have. Further offsetting the impact of challenger spending in gubernatorial primaries are the resources of time and effort ploughed into the race by the party organizations on behalf of their endorsed candidates. By contrast, in states that do not use preprimary endorsing conventions, the candidates spending the most money normally have the best chance of winning the primary.[22]

Competition in Primaries

It was the expectation of the reformers that the direct primary would stimulate competition among candidates for party nominations. This hope has not been fulfilled, however. In a substantial percentage of the primaries, nominations either go uncontested or involve only nominal challenges to the front runner. The two key determinants of intraparty competition in the primaries are the extent of the interparty competition and incumbency.

The Impact of Interparty Competition

V. O. Key first demonstrated that competition in primaries is significantly influenced by the pattern of two party competition that exists within a state or district. Competition in primaries is greatest where a party's prospects in the general election are the highest.[23] Recent research has confirmed Key's earlier findings of the relationship between the level of interparty competition in a state and the extent of primary competition. Analyses of gubernatorial and senatorial primaries have demonstrated that competition is greatest when the opposition party is weak and has little chance of winning the general elections.[24] In Kentucky, where Democratic nominees are heavily favored to win general elections for governor, no winner of the Democratic gubernatorial primary from 1959 to 1995 has received in excess of 53.8 percent of the vote; and in the four primaries between 1979–1991 at least three major candidates contested for the nomination, and the winner never received more than 45 percent of the vote.

The impact of general election prospects on primary competition is also evident in nominations for the U.S. House. In districts that are generally considered safe for one party, the dominant party normally has a contested primary—often with more than two candidates—when the incumbent is not seeking reelection. Of course, when the prospects of victory in the general election are dismal, there is little or no competition for party nominations. Indeed, in congressional districts that heavily favor the incumbent's party, it is frequently impossible for the minority party to induce anyone to enter the primaries. For example, in 1998 there was no major party challenger for ninety-four House incumbents. Incumbency is a distinct advantage in nominating contests and the presence of an incumbent in a primary is usually enough to ward off serious opposition. Since incumbents tend to scare off strong competitors in the primaries, they, of course, win renomination in overwhelming proportions. Between 1977 and 1998, 177 incumbent governors sought renomination and 169 (95 percent) were successful. When no incumbent is running, however, the competition in the primary can be intense. For example, in Kansas in 1994, when the incumbent Republican governor did not seek reelection, there was a six-candidate race for the GOP nomination. It was won by Bill Graves with 41 percent of the vote and a five-way race on the Democratic side. Graves went on to win the general election with 64 percent of the vote.

The advantages of incumbency are particularly striking in nominations for the United States House of Representatives. Between 1980 and 1996, the percentage of incumbent representatives renominated never dipped below 95 percent. The incidence of primary victories for incumbent senators was also high—consistently above 90 percent (see table 5.2). The tendency of incumbents to discourage strong primary opposition and win renomination is also prevalent in state legislative elections. Thus for most members of Congress and state legislators, the primary is not unlike the common cold. It is a nuisance, but seldom fatal.

The Impact of Nominating Procedures

The type of nominating procedures used within a state also affects the extent of primary competition. As noted previously, states which use preprimary endorsement procedures have lower levels of competition because of the ability of party organizations to restrict candidacies in these states. Runoff primaries tend to multiply the number of candidates in the initial primary, as do blanket primaries.[25] Interestingly, studies of competition for nominations for governor and senator have not demonstrated that open primaries encourage a higher level of competition than closed primary systems. Apparently, the absence of a requirement for party registration by voters is not a sufficient condition to produce intraparty nominating contests.

Voter Turnout in Primaries

Just as the reformers' high hopes for competition in primaries have been largely unfulfilled, so too have their expectations concerning voter participation. An average of only about 30 percent of the voting age population votes in gubernatorial primaries in years when both parties have contested primaries. If only one party has a major primary contest, voter participation is often substantially lower. When turnout is measured as a percentage of the voting age population in all the states holding primaries, the

Table 5.2

Renomination Rates of Incumbent United Sates Representatives and Senators, 1980–1998

	Incumbent Representatives					Incumbent Senators				
	Seeking	Renominated		Defeated		Seeking	Renominated		Defeated	
Year	Renomination	N	Percent	N	Percent	Renomination	N	Percent	N	Percent
1998	403	402	99.8	1	0.2	30	30	100.0	0	0.0
1996	384	382	99.5	2	0.5	21	20	95.2	1	4.8
1994	386	382	99.0	4	1.0	26	26	100.0	0	0.0
1992	368	349	94.8	19	5.2	28	27	96.4	1	3.6
1990	406	405	99.8	1	0.2	31	31	100.0	0	0.0
1988	408	407	99.8	1	0.2	27	27	100.0	0	0.0
1986	393	391	99.5	2	0.5	28	28	100.0	0	0.0
1984	395	392	99.2	3	0.8	26	26	100.0	0	0.0
1982	393	383	97.5	10	2.5	31	30	96.8	1	3.2
1980	398	392	98.5	6	1.5	27	25	92.6	2	7.4
Totals	3,934	3,885	98.7 (Mean)	49	1.3 (Mean)	275	270	98.6 (Mean)	5	1.9 (Mean)

Sources: Thomas E. Mann, Norman J. Ornstein, and Michael J. Malbin, *Vital Statistics on Congress, 1997–1998* (Washington, D.C.: Congressional Quarterly, Inc., 1998), pp. 61–62. *Congressional Quarterly Weekly Report,* July 11, 1998, p. 1864. Reprinted by permission.

turnout rate is often quite low—an average of 24 percent in midterm elections from 1962 to 1994. It was only 18.22 percent in 1994 and 17 percent in 1998.[26]

There are regional variations in turnout rates with several of the western states (e.g., Montana and Wyoming) having some of the highest levels of voter participation. These are states that also have high turnout rates in general elections. Traditionally, the primary turnout has been high in southern Democratic primaries. Indeed, because historically the Democratic primary was the real election in the South, there was a pattern of higher turnout in primaries than in the general election. However, as general elections have become increasingly competitive between the Democrats and Republicans, the pattern of participation in southern primaries has changed dramatically. Overall, the percentage of the electorate participating in gubernatorial primaries has declined; the Democratic share of the popular vote in primaries has gone down; and the level of participation in Republican primaries has increased (see the example of Texas in table 5.3). With the frequently low level of turnout that prevails in primary elections, questions naturally arise about the representativeness of primary voters.

Personal Characteristics and Turnout

The same sorts of personal characteristics that are associated with voting in general elections are operative in primaries. Primary voters tend to be better educated and older than nonvoters. They are also more knowledgeable concerning politics, more interested in campaigns, and have a greater sense of civic duty. Primary voters rank even higher in these characteristics that distinguish voters from nonvoters than do voters in general elections. Primary turnout is also strongly affected by the strength of a person's party identification (i.e., one's psychological attachment to a political party). Political scientists have consistently demonstrated that the stronger an individual's party identification (e.g., being a strong Republican versus a weak Republican) the more likely that person is to vote. Jewell's study of primary voting has shown that party identification has an even stronger and more consistent impact on primary turnout than it does in general elections. He also found that party identification was especially important in determining which younger and less interested voters will vote in primaries.[27]

Table 5.3
The Changing Patterns of Participation in Southern Primaries: The Case of Texas

Popular Vote in Texas Gubernatorial Primaries, 1978–1994

Year	Republican	Democrat	Total	Percent of Voting Age Population	Percent of Total Vote	
					Rep.	Dem.
1978	153,614	1,777,731	1,931,345	21	8%	92%
1982	265,851	1,256,717	1,522,568	15	17	83
1986	544,719	1,118,321	1,633,040	14	22	78
1990	850,452	1,412,455	2,262,907	19	37	63
1994	557,340	1,036,944	1,594,284	12	34	66

Note: In 1998, there were no competitive races for statewide office, and voter turnout fell to 11 percent of registered voters. The Democratic gubernatorial nomination was uncontested, and 597,011 votes were cast in the Republican primary, which was won by Governor George W. Bush, who received 97 percent of the vote.

Sources: Congressional Quarterly, *Guide to U.S. Elections*, 3rd ed. (Washington, D.C. Congressional Quarterly, Inc., 1994), pp. 766–767; Committee for the Study of the American Electorate, press release, September 23, 1994. Reprinted by permission.

The tendency of party activists to have higher rates of turnout in primaries and also to have stronger ideological orientations than rank and file voters has caused political scientists to consider whether patterns of voter turnout bias the outcomes of a primary.[28] That is, do the patterns of primary turnout introduce a bias into the results of primaries, which in the Republican party favors conservative candidates and in the Democratic party helps liberal candidates? Some studies of presidential primaries have indicated that such biases do operate, and there have been a number of cases in the 1990s when social conservatives have mobilized their followers to help conservative Republican candidates win primaries over more moderate and arguably more electable Republicans. These highly conservative Republican nominees then went on to lose in the general election, for example, Al Salvi's loss in 1996 to Richard Durbin in the Illinois Senate race. However, there have been few thorough analyses of the representatives of state-level primary electorates. As Jewell and Olson have pointed out, there is probably little reason to expect that there would be a consistent pattern of unrepresentativeness in turnout across the states.[29] Turnout is likely to be affected by the particular mix of candidates on the ballot in any given state's primary. If a liberal Democratic incumbent is running against token opposition, moderate and conservative partisans may have little incentive to vote, whereas a contest for an open seat between clearly identified liberal and conservative candidates could stimulate these people to vote in larger numbers.

Political/Institutional Influences on Turnout

There are a variety of political/institutional variables that affect turnout. These variables relate to the statutory regulations surrounding the primary, the nature of the party system, and the levels of competition that exist in primary contests.[30]

Majority versus Minority Party Status. Turnout tends to be highest in the primary of the party which has the greatest likelihood of winning the general election, precisely because that party's contest is more likely to determine which person will eventually hold public office.

Competition. Competition for a party's nomination spurs voters to participate in primaries. In the absence of a real contest for a nomination, voter turnout diminishes. A party's share of the primary electorate may vary dramatically depending upon whether or not it has a red hot contest in a given year. For example, in the 1992 Wisconsin primary for United States senator, there was a hotly contested three-way race for the Democratic nomination to take on a vulnerable GOP incumbent, Senator Robert Kasten, that attracted 68 percent of the voters. The GOP primary, in which Kasten had only token opposition, drew only 32.3 percent of the vote. Two years later the situation was reversed as four Republicans ran spirited primary campaigns for their party's nomination and the right to face the incumbent Democratic Senator Herb Kohl in the general election. With media and public interest focused on the only primary in which there was a meaningful contest, it was the Republican primary this time that attracted more than two-thirds of the voters. The extent of competition is influenced by such factors as *endorsement* and *incumbency,* both of which operate to depress competition and thus indirectly reduce turnout, Traditions of competition in state primaries, as in the one party South, can have the effect of stimulating turnout.

Closed versus Open Primaries. Because open primaries do not require voters to disclose publicly a partisan preference, open primaries tend to have higher levels of turnout than do closed primaries. Independents can be precluded from participation in closed primary states.

The National Party Organizations and Nominations in the States

The traditional recruitment and nomination processes within the states illustrated the decentralized character of the American party system. Despite the importance of congressional and senatorial nominations for the functioning of the national level parties, the national party organizations traditionally played only a minor role in candidate recruitment and nomination. Recruitment was a matter of self-selection, with aspiring members of Congress determining on their own when the time was ripe for them to move from careers in statehouses, city halls, courthouses, or the private sector to the Congress. Aspiring representatives and senators put together personal organizations to contest first the primary and then the general election. Party leaders in Congress and occasionally the president sometimes gave informal encouragement to promising candidates, but it was traditional for the national party leadership to stay aloof from state nomination contests.

A classic example of national party weakness in influencing congressional nominations occurred in 1938, when President Franklin D. Roosevelt sought to purge dissident conservatives in the primaries. Despite the fact that Roosevelt was at the zenith of his popularity during this period, his intervention in the primaries against incumbent senators in Oklahoma, Georgia, South Carolina, and Maryland failed, His inability to influence primary election outcomes paralleled the experience of President William Howard Taft and Senate Republican Leader Nelson Aldrich (R.I.), who sought to oust western Progressives in the Republican primaries of 1910. Usually, the president and national party leaders remained silent, even when their loyal supporters had been challenged in the primaries.

The traditional hands-off policy of national parties toward congressional and senatorial nominations changed in the late 1970s and early 1980s because of the realization that candidate quality is a major determinant of electoral success. The national party committees now aggressively recruit candidates to enter primaries, and just as aggressively discourage others. These candidate recruitment efforts are concentrated in competitive constituencies. However, there are also attempts to find candidates in districts considered safe for the opposition party, in order to prevent the general election from going uncontested and to build a base of support for future elections when conditions may be more favorable (e.g., after an incumbent retires).[31]

National and regional party staff meet with state and local party officials to identify and encourage candidates to run. To entice potentially attractive candidates into the primaries, polls, promises of campaign money and services, and the persuasive talents of party leaders, House and Senate members, and even presidents are utilized. The parties' staffs also serve as liaison persons with PACs and campaign consultants who have the financial resources and skills needed to run effective congressional campaigns. The intensity of the recruiting efforts and the importance of finding quality candidates for competitive constituencies was apparent in 1998 as the "spin doctors" of both parties' campaign committees sought to publicize their own recruiting successes and their opponents' failures to lure strong candidates into the race.

It is, of course, difficult to determine whether the activities of national party organizations were decisive in the decisions of candidates to seek party nominations in target constituencies. However, as one staffer of the Democratic Congressional Campaign Committee (DCCC) observed:

> A telephone call from one's county or state party chairman may not be quite enough to encourage someone to subject him or herself to the hard work and personal sacrifice associated with running for Congress, but a call from . . . [the Chairman of the DCCC], promising party assistance in fundraising and campaign advertising . . . and a few calls from some other well-known party leaders might be just enough to get a person to commit him or herself.[32]

National party candidate recruitment activity is not without its risks. Conflicts can arise between national and state party leaders and bitter resentments can build up among supporters of a candidate not favored by national party officials. These problems can damage the chances of the eventual nominee. As a result, the national party tends to stay neutral if there is more than one candidate in the primary. The major exceptions to the rule of neutrality in primaries tend to occur when an incumbent representative or senator is being seriously challenged. Thus, in 1998, the national Republican party poured resources into the primary campaign of a twenty-eight-year incumbent and committee chairman, Representative Bill Goodling (Pa.), and helped him fend off a major challenge.

The heavy involvement of the national parties in candidate recruitment in recent years is clearly a departure from past practices, but it has not done away with the dominant pattern of self-selected candidacies. However, the national parties' continuing involvement in recruitment and high levels of candidate support in general elections may create a pool of successful candidates with strong ties to national party and congressional leaders. To the extent that these officeholders perceive national party support to have been a critical factor in their nomination and election, they may feel a sense of obligation to the leaders who helped them in their hour of need. That sense of obligation is a potential lever of influence for the congressional leaders in seeking to affect the voting of representatives and senators in the halls of Congress. To date, however, the new activism of the congressional and senatorial campaign committees has not been used by party leaders in Congress to enforce discipline and unity. An aggressive future leader, however, could seek to expand influence over colleagues on the basis of campaign support that has been provided. Such a leader might also threaten to withhold it from dissident members.

The Direct Primary and the General Election

The primary, of course, has significant implications for the general election. It narrows the field of candidates and choice available to the voter. The outcome of a primary may also affect a party's general election prospects—enhancing those prospects if a strong candidate wins and diminishing the chances of winning if a weak candidate is nominated. Party leaders are frequently concerned about the potential divisiveness of a contested primary. They fear that a hotly contested primary will leave the party disunited for the general election. Preprimary endorsements are one method of seeking to prevent divisive primaries. Others include channeling financial and campaign support to a preferred candidate in an effort to discourage opposition. There are many frequently cited examples of divisive primaries which have resulted in the party's nominee going down to defeat. For example, in 1986, Guy Hunt was successful in his bid to become the first Republican governor of Alabama since Reconstruction because of a protracted dispute within the Democratic party over which candidate had won a hotly contested runoff primary; and in 1998 it was the Republican incumbent governor, Fob James, who lost his reelection bid after a bitter and well-financed primary challenge.

Despite these and other examples of a party going down to defeat after a divisive primary, there is no consistent pattern which demonstrates that contested primaries are necessarily damaging. Of course, one reason that primary contests do not consistently result in general election losses is that primary competition is most frequent within the stronger of a state's two parties.[33] There are also circumstances when a contested primary may help the nominee. Battling for a party nomination normally generates substantial publicity for the candidates and keeps their names before the public. A tough primary fight may even enhance the image of the winning candidate as an attractive personality, skilled campaigner, and person who is knowledgeable about critical issues. The absence of a primary fight can push a candidate off the evening news programs and front pages of the papers in the crucial months of the spring and summer before an election. Such lack of publicity and testing of the candidate in a primary can be a serious liability in the general election.

Furthermore, candidates who have been tested in tough primary battles are apt to be improved campaigners, more able fund raisers, and generally stronger candidates for the experience. Their organizations are more likely to be well-established and ready to contest the general election than those of the candidates who ran unopposed in the primaries. Candidates learn valuable lessons about what works and what does not work in the course of campaigning, and candidates who have survived intense primary fights are likely to have learned more than those who had no significant primary opposition.

The Direct Primary and Political Parties

The institutionalization of the direct primary as the principal method of nominating state and congressional candidates in the United States is part of a long-term trend toward shifting power away from party leaders to rank and file voters. In their effort to weaken the capacity of parties to control the selection of candidates for major elective office, the reformers of the progressive era have been largely successful. In only a handful of jurisdictions are party organizations sufficiently strong that they can bestow their endorsement upon a candidate and assure the individual's nomination in a primary. Even the much vaunted Cook County (Illinois) Democratic organization can no longer control even mayoral nominations in Chicago.

As the impact of preprimary endorsements and the national congressional campaign committees illustrate, however, party support can be helpful to a candidate in gaining a nomination. Party organizational support is not irrelevant in the primary process, but it is seldom sufficient to secure a nomination. Rather, the candidate must build a personal organization and following among the voters if the hurdle of the primary is to be cleared successfully. The direct primary has, therefore, contributed to a candidate-centered type of politics in America, in contrast to the more party-centered politics of most Western style democracies that do not utilize the primaries for nominations.

Although the direct primary has contributed to a weakening of political parties organizationally, Leon D. Epstein believes that the primary helps to account for the extraordinary and continued *electoral dominance* of the Republican and Democratic parties. He believes that the direct primary institutionalized the Republican and Democratic labels in electoral politics. The primary provides unusual opportunities for insurgents to win major party nominations and thereby forego the normally self-defeating process of running as third party candidates. Challengers to established party organizational leadership are thus encouraged to seek intraparty avenues to power and voters become accustomed to choosing from among individuals and factions that are competing for a party label.

Epstein's argument, of course, is paradoxical. It asserts that while strengthening the parties electorally, the primary has weakened the party organization and the party in the government. The primary has thus by statute institutionalized the electoral looseness of American parties, but in the process also has acted as a party preservative. But as preservatives in food processing change the nature and quality of what is being preserved, the direct primary has left the parties as persistent electoral labels whose importance is frequently questioned after election day.[34]

Suggestions for Further Reading

Epstein, Leon D. *Political Parties in the American Mold.* Madison: University of Wisconsin Press, 1986. Chapters 6 and 8.

Jewell, Malcolm E. *Parties and Primaries: Nominating State Governors.* New York: Praeger, 1984.

Jewell, Malcolm E., and Olson, David M. *American State Political Parties and Elections*, 3rd ed. Chicago, Ill.: Dorsey Press, 1988. Chapter 4.

Key, V. O., Jr. *American State Politics: An Introduction.* New York: Knopf, 1956.

Morehouse, Sarah McCally. *The Governor as Party Leader: Campaigning and Governing.* Ann Arbor: University of Michigan Press, 1998.

Notes

1. E.E. Schattschneider, *Party Government* (New York: Farrar and Rinehart, 1942), p. 64.

2. V.O. Key, Jr., *American State Politics: An Introduction* (New York: Knopf, 1956), pp. 87–88.

3. Ibid., p. 88.

4. Ibid., p. 91.

5. Ibid., p. 117.

6. Ellen Torelle, ed., *The Political Philosophy of Robert M. La Follette* (Madison, Wis.: Robert M. La Follette Co., 1920), 29–31.

7. Malcolm E. Jewell, *Parties and Primaries: Nominating State Governors* (New York: Praeger, 1984), pp. 9–11.

8. Ibid., pp. 11–12.

9. Malcolm E. Jewell and David M. Olson, *American State Political Parties and Elections*, rev. ed. (Homewood, Ill.: Dorsey Press, 1982), p. 107.

10. The impact of the *Tashjian* decision is analyzed in Leon D. Epstein, "Will American Political Parties Be Privatized?" *The Journal of Law and Politics* 4 (Winter 1989): 239–274.

11. Gerald A. McBeath, "Transformation of the Alaska Blanket Primary System," *Comparative State Politics* 15 (August 1994): 25–41.

12. Personal correspondence with the author.

13. V. O. Key, Jr., *Politics, Parties and Pressure Groups*, 5th ed. (New York: Knopf, 1964), p. 393.

14. For an analysis of the operation of New York's cross-filing system, see Howard A. Scarrow, *Parties, Elections, and Representation in the State of New York* (New York: New York University Press, 1983), pp. 55–80; and Robert J. Spitzer, "Multiparty Politics in New York," in Paul S. Herrnson and John C. Green, eds., *Multiparty Politics in America* (Lanham, Md.: Rowman and Littlefield, 1997), pp. 125–137.

15. Larry Sabato, *Goodbye to Good-Time Charlie: The American Governorship Transformed* (Washington, D.C.: CQ Press, 1983), pp. 119, 124.

16. Charles S. Bullock, III, and Loch K. Johnson, *Runoff Elections in the United States* (Chapel Hill: University of North Carolina Press, 1992).

17. Sarah McCally Morehouse, *The Governor as Party Leader: Campaigning and Governing* (Ann Arbor, University of Michigan Press, 1998) pp. 22–23.

18. Ibid.

19. Malcolm E. Jewell and Sarah McCally Morehouse, "What Are Party Endorsements Worth? A Study of Preprimary Endorsements in Ten States in 1994," a paper presented at the Annual Meeting of the Midwest Political Science Association, Chicago, April 5-8, 1995. For evidence of endorsements helping candidates with primaries, see James P. Melcher, "The Party's Still Lively: New Findings about Statewide Preprimary Endorsements," *American Review of Politics* 19 (Spring 1998): 53–56. See also Andrew D. McNitt, "The Effect of Endorsement on Competition for Nominations: An Explanation of Different Nominating Systems," *Journal of Politics* 42 (Feb. 1980): 257–266, and Tom W. Rice, "Gubernatorial and Senatorial Primary Elections: Determinants and Consequences," *American Politics Quarterly* 13 (Oct. 1985): 434–435.

20. Morehouse, *The Governor as Party Leader*, p. 255.

21. Ibid.

22. Ibid., pp. 121, 181–200.

23. Key, *Politics, Parties and Pressure Groups*, pp. 379–380; Key, *American State Politics*, pp. 107–111.

24. William D. Berry and Bradley C. Canon, "Explaining Competitiveness of Gubernatorial Primaries," *Journal of Politics* 55 (May 1993): 454–471; Rice, "Gubernatorial and Senatorial Primary Elections," pp. 433–434. See also David M. Olson, *Political Parties and Elections in America*, 3rd ed. (Chicago: Dorsey Press, 1988), p. 105.

25. Rice, "Gubernatorial and Senatorial Primary Elections," pp. 435–437; and Berry and Canon, "Explaining Competitiveness . . .", pp. 459–471.

26. Committee for the Study of the American Electorate, press release, September 23, 1995; Terry M. Neal, "Primary Turnout Continues to Decline," *Washington Post*, September 29, 1998, p. A4.

27. Jewell, *Parties and Primaries*, p. 176.

28. V. O. Key considered the consequences of unrepresentative primary electorates in his *American State Politics*, pp. 153–165.

29. Jewell and Olson, *American State Political Parties and Elections*, p. 136

30. Jewell, *Parties and Primaries*, p. 176.

31. On national party recruitment activities, see the publications of Paul S. Herrnson: *Congressional Elections: Campaigns at Home and in Washington*, 2nd

edition (Washington, D.C.: CQ Press, 1998), pp. 39–40; and *Party Campaigning in the 1980s* (Cambridge: Harvard University Press, 1988), pp. 48–54.

32. Herrnson, *Party Campaigning in the 1980s*, p. 54.

33. Jewell and Olson, *American State Political Parties*, p. 149; see also Patrick J. Kenney, "Sorting Out the Effects of Primary Divisiveness in Congressional and Senatorial Elections," *Western Political Quarterly*, 41 (1988): 756–777; and Mark C. Westlye, *Senate Elections and Campaign Intensity* (Baltimore, Md.: Johns Hopkins University Press, 1991).

34. For a full exposition of Epstein's intriguing argument concerning the electoral impact of the direct primary on parties, see Leon D. Epstein, *Political Parties in the American Mold* (Madison: University of Wisconsin Press, 1986), pp. 244–245.

Presidential Nominating Politics

Methods of Delegate Selection
- State Delegate Selection Procedures Must Conform to National Party Rules
- Presidential Primaries
- State Party Caucuses and Conventions
- Combination Presidential Primary and Convention Systems
- Automatic Unpledged Delegates

Phases of the Nomination Process
- Phase I: Laying the Groundwork and Preliminary Skirmishing
- Phase II: Delegate Selection—The Early Contests and the Consequences of Front Loading
- Phase III: Delegate Selection—The Later Primaries and Caucuses
- Phase IV: The Convention—Ratifying the Decision of the Primaries and Kicking Off the General Election Campaign

The Ongoing Process of Party Reform
- The Reformed Democrats
- The Unreformed Republicans
- Campaign Finance: The Federal Election Campaign Act

Participation in Presidential Nominating Politics
- Voter Turnout in Presidential Primaries
- Participation in Caucuses/Conventions
- National Convention Delegates

Media Politics in Presidential Nominations

A Lengthy, Candidate-Centered, Primary-Focused, Participatory, and Media-Oriented Process

CHAPTER SIX

Vice President Hubert H. Humphrey, while winning the 1968 Democratic presidential nomination, did not open his campaign until March of that year and did not enter a single presidential primary. Instead he depended upon his support among party leaders. By contrast, Senator Bob Dole campaigned actively for over two years and contested forth-three primaries on his way to the 1996 Republican presidential nomination. President Bill Clinton ran in thirty-five primaries and his White House political office for four years ran a sophisticated operation designed to discourage any opposition to his renomination. Humphrey's campaign was funded with contributions from private individuals and organizations; Dole's and Clinton's campaigns were fueled by a combination of private contributions and funds assigned to them under the national government's policy of providing matching grants to candidates.

The differing paths to presidential nominations taken by Humphrey versus those of Dole and Clinton, all three holders of major public office and prominent party leaders, reflect the fundamental changes that have occurred in presidential nominating politics since 1968. A process once dominated by party leaders, who heavily influenced the selection of national convention delegates, is now a process which is candidate-centered. A process that once relied upon internal party procedures to select delegates through caucuses and conventions now relies primarily upon presidential primaries to determine the allocation of delegates among contenders for a party's nomination. Participation was once restricted to party regulars in the caucus and convention states and to primary voters in a few primary states. Now presidential nominating politics is an open and participatory process characterized by mass citizen involvement in primaries and open access to party caucuses. Now that the presidential primaries and some caucuses receive saturation media coverage, the media has far reaching influence concerning who ultimately wins a nomination. Presidential nominating politics of the 1990s is candidate-centered, primary focused, participatory, and media intensive.

Methods of Delegate Selection

The national nominating conventions held in the summer of presidential election years are the culmination of a long season of campaigning to select national convention delegates. The delegates, meeting in convention, nominate the party's candidates for president and vice president, adopt a platform, and approve rules that will govern the party. The composition of the convention, of course, determines the nature of the decisions the convention will make on the nominations, platform and rules. The processes of delegate selection, therefore, are critical to the outcomes of the convention.

There are three principal methods of delegate selection: (1) the presidential primary; (2) the party caucus/convention process; and (3) automatic selection by virtue of the party or elected position an individual holds. Both parties use the presidential primary and caucus/convention selection processes, but only the Democrats have automatic delegates (see figure 6.1). The various states are free to devise their own methods of delegate selection as long as those methods conform to guidelines contained in the rules of the national Republican and Democratic parties. The procedures for selection of delegates are frequently set forth in state statutes, which may be supplemented by state party rules. In the absence of state statutes governing delegate selection, state parties may adopt rules to determine how delegates will be chosen. Because each state legislature and/or state party organization is involved in devising the procedures for delegate selection, there are a wide variety of practices followed within the states.

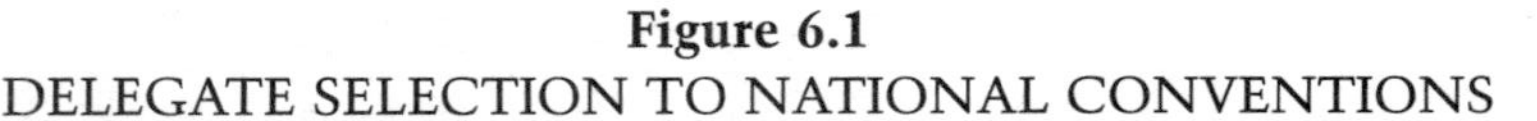

Figure 6.1
DELEGATE SELECTION TO NATIONAL CONVENTIONS

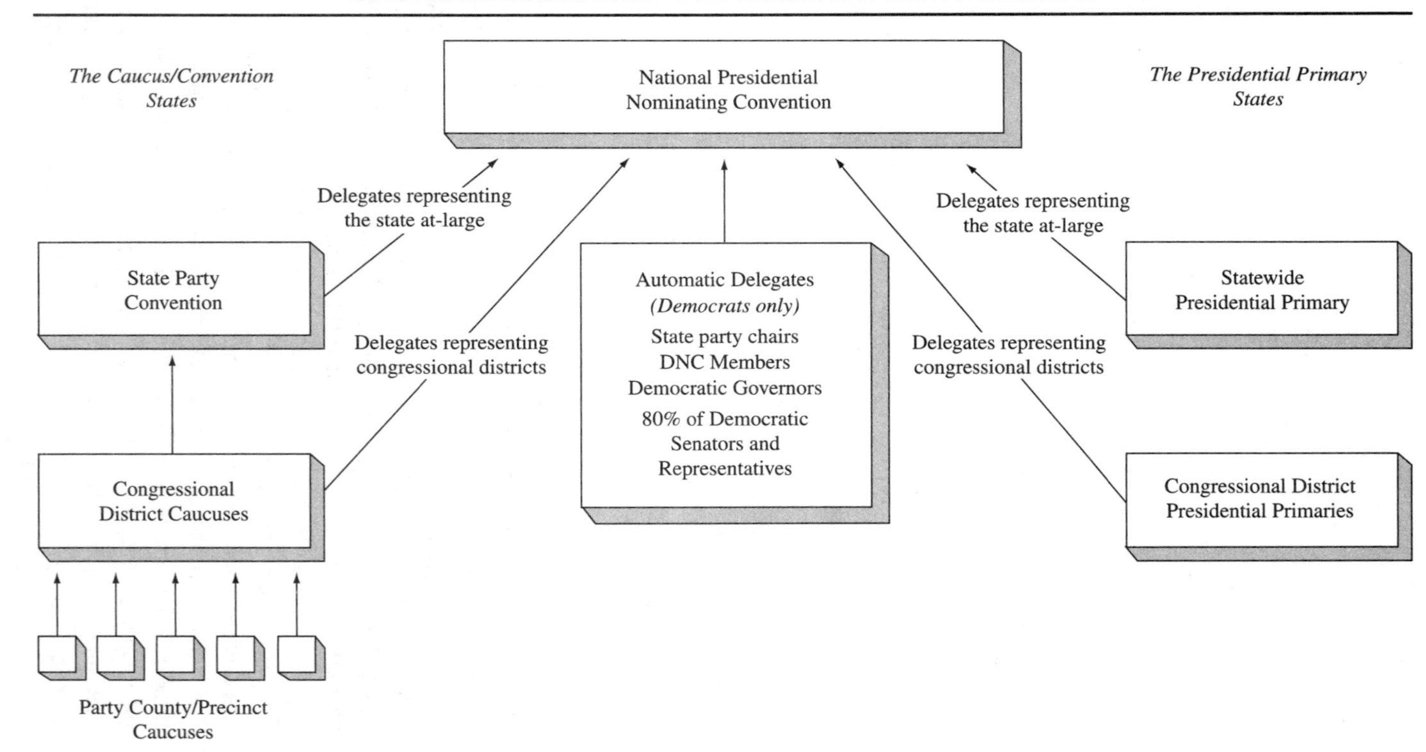

State Delegate Selection Procedures Must Conform to National Party Rules

Although the states have some latitude in determining how their delegates to national conventions will be chosen, the procedures they devise must be in strict conformity with national party rules. In other words, national party rules take precedence over state statutes and state party rules in matters of delegate selection. A state delegation that is not chosen in conformity with national party rules runs the risk of not having its delegation seated at the national convention—a severe sanction, which the national party can impose.

The most celebrated instance of conflict between a state party and its national organization over the delegate selection procedures took place in Wisconsin. In 1903 Wisconsin was the first state to adopt a presidential primary law, but it was a law which also provided for conducting the presidential primary under open primary procedures. After 1974, national Democratic party rules forbad selecting delegates through open primary procedures and thus Wisconsin's law was out of conformity with national party rules. Wisconsin sought to maintain its open primary, but the United States Supreme Court upheld the right of a national party organization to determine delegate selection procedures.[1] Wisconsin Democrats, therefore, were forced in 1984 to abandon the open presidential primary for selecting their convention delegates and adopt caucus procedures that satisfied the national Democratic party. In an effort to put this often bitter controversy behind it and prepare for the 1988 elections, the Democratic National Committee in 1986 agreed to permit states with open primary traditions (Wisconsin and Montana) to utilize open presidential primaries. While making this accommodation to Wisconsin, the DNC continued to assert its power to regulate delegate selection procedures. Thus Wisconsin conceded the principle of the national party's legal supremacy, but the national party conceded the substance of the open primary issue.

Presidential Primaries

The largest share of convention delegates is chosen through procedures which involve presidential primaries. In 1996, there were thirty-five Democratic and forty-three Republican presidential primaries that were used to allocate delegates among presidential candidates. These primaries determined the allocation of 75 percent of the delegates to the Democratic convention and 85 percent of the

Figure 6.2

PRIMARIES DECIDE PRESIDENTIAL NOMINATIONS: THE PROLIFERATION OF PRESIDENTIAL PRIMARIES AND PERCENT OF DELEGATES SELECTED BY PRESIDENTIAL PRIMARIES, 1968–1996

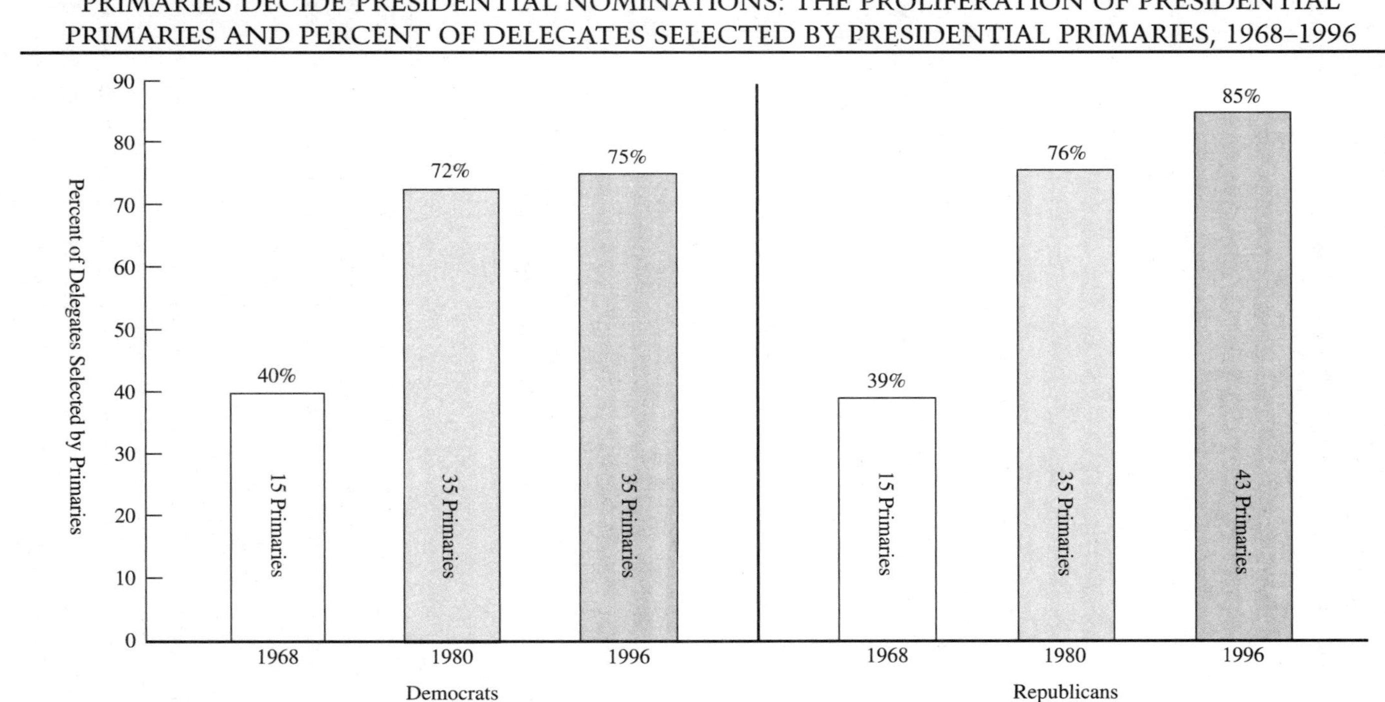

Sources: Federal Election Commission, *Federal Elections 96* (Washington, DC: Federal Election Commission, 1997), pp. 31–49; Congressional Quarterly, *Guide to U.S. Elections*, 3rd ed. (Washington, DC: Congressional Quarterly, 1994), p. 481; *Congressional Quarterly Weekly Report*, August 3, 1996, p.63, and August 17, 1996, p. 79. Reprinted by permission.

total GOP delegates. In addition, there were three Democratic primaries and one Republican primary which were so-called "beauty contests"—they tested the popularity of the candidates, but were not used to allocate delegates to the national conventions.[2] The number of states and territories using the presidential primaries has increased significantly since 1968, when fifteen Republican and Democratic primaries were used in the selection of 39.1 percent of the delegates (see figure 6.2).

However, the number of primaries held in any given presidential election year has been subject to considerable variation depending on political conditions. Thus, in 1984, there were only twenty-five primaries used to select Republican delegates due to the fact that Ronald Reagan was unopposed for his party's nomination, and, similarly, in 1996, the number of Democratic primaries declined when President Clinton had no significant opposition for renomination.

With the largest share of the delegates selected through procedures that involve presidential primaries, it has become imperative for presidential candidates to enter virtually all of the primaries in order to win sufficient delegates to gain a convention majority. The importance of the primaries, however, goes beyond the number of delegates which are at stake in these contests. The results of primaries constitute an ostensibly objective indicator of a candidate's ability to win the election. Primaries, therefore, are particularly important because of the image of candidate popularity, electability, and momentum they can convey.

The mechanics of the presidential primaries vary from state to state depending upon applicable state laws and party rules. For example, in some states the names of individuals who are running for delegate positions are on the ballot and voters vote directly for delegates. In other states, the names of the presidential candidates are on the ballot, but the names of persons seeking to be delegates are not. There is normally a contest for delegates in each congressional district and an additional contest to determine how the delegates who will represent the state at-large will be allocated among the presidential candidates. A presidential candidate, therefore, can lose the statewide vote and fail to win any at-large delegates and still pick up delegates by making a strong showing in the primaries of individual congressional districts within a state.

State Party Caucuses and Conventions

Until the 1972 conventions, a majority of the states used state party caucuses and conventions to select delegates. For example, in 1968 almost two-thirds of the delegates to national conventions were chosen via party caucuses and conventions. This is a procedure which involves a relatively small proportion of the electorate. It is party members and activists who normally have the interest, motivation, and knowledge to participate in the series of party meetings that culminate in congressional district and state party meetings to choose delegates.

In caucus/convention states, the process of delegate selection involves a progression of party meetings starting at the local level, running through the congressional district, and culminating in a state party convention. The process normally begins with local caucuses at either the precinct or county level. Party members and activists attend these meetings, often after having been mobilized by presidential candidate organizations or interest groups. Local caucus participants register their candidate preferences and also elect representatives to the next level of party organizational meeting in the process—the congressional district caucus. At the congressional district caucus, representatives chosen by the various local caucuses meet to (1) register their preference for the party's presidential nominee; (2) elect delegates to the national convention to represent the congressional district; and (3) elect delegates to the state party convention. The national convention delegates selected to represent the congressional district at the national convention are chosen to reflect the extent of support candidates for the presidency have among the congressional district caucus participants. Delegates from the various congressional districts in a state then meet in a state party convention to elect national convention delegates to represent the state-at-large.

Because the caucus system is an internal party process, it places a premium on a candidate having dedicated supporters—the type of people who are willing to spend evenings and weekends taking part in lengthy party meetings. It also requires an effective organization to mobilize people to turn out and support the candidate at each stage in the process. It is essential that a presidential candidate's organization have intimate knowledge of the state laws and party rules for delegate selection and of intraparty politics. Whereas presidential primaries are media oriented in order to appeal to a mass electorate, the caucus/ convention process is more of an intraparty affair which requires an efficient organization.

Combination Presidential Primary and Convention Systems

Some states use a combination of the presidential primary and party convention to choose their national convention delegates. Illinois, for example, uses a presidential primary to elect national convention delegates to represent the state's congressional districts. However, it uses a state party convention to choose the delegates that will represent the state-at-large. There are also states in which presidential primaries are purely popularity contests that have no binding effect on delegate selection, because the delegates are actually chosen in party caucuses and conventions (e.g., Vermont).

Automatic Unpledged Delegates

In an effort to increase convention participation by party leaders and elected officials, the Democrats for their 1984 convention made provision in their rules for granting automatic delegate status to major party leaders and elected officials. These delegates would not be officially pledged to any presidential candidate. Under Democratic rules, national committee members, state party chairs and vice chairs, and Democratic governors are automatically convention delegates as are Democratic members of the United States House and Senate. Designation of the congressional delegates is made by the House and Senate Democratic caucuses. In 1996, approximately 20 percent of the 4,289 Democratic delegates were "super delegates." There are no automatic delegates to Republican national conventions. Republican party leaders and elected officials must go through the regular primary and caucus procedures in order to become delegates.

Phases of the Nomination Process

Achieving a presidential nomination has become a fulltime, often four year endeavor. Indeed, the task is so demanding that individuals holding a major public office frequently conclude that they cannot pursue the presidency and also discharge their public duties. As a result, a substantial share of the major party nominees, excluding incumbent presidents and vice presidents, in recent years have been politicians out of office: Democrats Jimmy Carter (1976) and Walter Mondale (1984); Republican Ronald Reagan (1980). Similarly, major contenders such as Ronald Reagan (1976), George Bush (1980), Jesse Jackson (1984 and 1988), Paul Tsongas (1992), and Pat Buchanan (1992 and 1996) held no public office during their quests for the presidency, and other strong candidates, like Democratic Senators Edward Kennedy (D-Mass.) in 1980, Gary Hart (D-Colo.) in 1984, and Albert Gore (D-Tenn.) in 1988 did not hold party leadership positions in the Senate. Indeed, the process of gaining a major party nomination is so demanding that it is widely believed that Senator Howard Baker (R-Tenn.) retired from the Senate and his post as majority leader in 1984 because he did not believe that he could pursue the presidency in 1988 while simultaneously serving as his party's leader in the Senate. Similarly, Senator Gary Hart, an early front runner for the 1988 Democratic nomination, decided not to seek reelection to the Senate in 1986 so that he might concentrate on the presidential contest. Exceptions to the tendency of individuals with major governing responsibilities not to seek presidential nominations occurred in 1988, when Massachusetts Governor Michael Dukakis won the Democratic nomination and Senate Republican leader Bob Dole (Kansas) mounted major drives for the GOP nomination in 1988 and 1996. The lengthy and often intense schedule of the presidential nominating process can be broken down into a series of phases that culminate with the national convention.[3]

Phase I: Laying the Groundwork and Preliminary Skirmishing

During the period following a presidential election, prospective candidates for a presidential nomination four years hence begin the planning and preparations for their campaigns. This frequently involves recruiting a professional staff experienced in national politics, creating a political action committee (PAC) and tax exempt foundation to fund candidate activities, and developing a campaign plan. Candidates crisscross the nation making appearances before the state party conventions, civic groups, trade associations, unions, and candidates' fund raisers in an attempt to gain media attention and make contacts with party leaders. Iowa and New Hampshire are inevitable and frequent stops on the campaign itinerary of presidential candidates, because these states hold critical early events in the national convention delegate selection process. Thus, in 1998, eight Republican presidential hopefuls spent a June weekend in Iowa at a GOP gala seeking media exposure and support from grassroots activists in anticipation of the Iowa caucuses in 2000. Trips abroad are also scheduled so that the candidate can be pictured with world leaders and an image of experience in foreign affairs can be conveyed.

The extent of early campaign preparations and maneuvering can be seen in the activities of prospective candidates during 1993 — three years in advance of the 1996 presidential election. Political action committees (PACs) or tax exempt foundations, set up to avoid the restrictions of the Federal Election Campaign Act, were already operating on behalf of Republicans Bob Dole, Dick Cheney, Phil Gramm, and Lamar Alexander, while at the same time other potential contenders for the nomination stimulated speculation by appearing on the talk show circuit, discussing controversial issues, and publishing books (e.g., Dan Quayle and William Bennett). Dole was particularly geared up for the grueling trail of 1996 presidential primaries and caucuses. His PAC had seven field operatives and conducted a training school for eighty-five supporters from around the country who would serve as advance staff for Dole when he visited their states; his Better America Foundation, a GOP think tank to develop policy proposals, was up and running; and his PAC had $2.9 million in the bank for distribution to candidates in the 1994 midterm elections. Dole was constantly on the road during the first year of the Clinton presidency, visiting thirty-nine states to meet state party leaders, to help raise campaign war chests for state and congressional candidates, and to fire up the party faithful, while building a following for himself.[4]

The pace of presidential campaigning intensifies during the year of the midterm elections as the candidates seek to play a prominent role in assisting their parties in congressional, senatorial, and state elections. There are appearances at fund raisers for party candidates from Maine to California. Most of the major contenders have their own personal PACs which fund their campaign forays and provide contributions to state and congressional candidates. The strategy is to create a sense of obligation among officeholders that can be converted later into commitments of support for the presidential nomination.

During the year preceding the presidential election, the pace of campaigning accelerates with frequent visits to key primary states. One of the staples of this phase of the campaign has been appearances at state party conventions, which occasionally conduct straw polls of candidate popularity among the delegates. These tests of popularity among party activists are used by the candidates to demonstrate support for the nomination. Straw polls, however, carry special risks for the early front-runner candidate, who may be upset by a well-organized campaign conducted by a less well-known candidate.

It is also essential in the year before the presidential primaries begin for candidates to raise serious money for their nomination campaigns. There are two types of candidates that have special advantages in raising campaign war chests—candidates with national stature and those who can compensate for a lack of national stature through access to well-heeled constituencies. For example, Dole's visibility and stature as a recognized national party leader gave him a major fund-raising advantage in the run-up to the 1996 Republican nomination battle, and of course President Clinton took full advantage of his position to harvest early money for his renomination and reelection campaigns. Senator Phil Gramm (R-Tex.) was also highly successful in tapping financial sources within Texas. At a single fund-raising dinner in Dallas in February 1995, he raised over $4 million. He then made a candid declaration: "I have the most reliable friend you can have in American politics, and that is ready money"—a comment that did little to enhance his public image.[5]

Although Gramm's bid for the nomination failed, it is difficult to overstate the importance of early fund raising: from 1980 through 1996, the candidates in both parties that had led their competitors in fund raising on December 31 of the year before the presidential election have gone on to win the nomination. As former Tennessee Governor Lamar Alexander, another unsuccessful GOP aspirant, noted during the year before the 1996 campaign, "The 1995 primary is the fund-raising primary."[6]

It is not just the party regulars and financial contributors that are courted. Candidates also woo interest groups that can provide their campaigns with organizational muscle and grassroots workers. Democratic candidates in recent years have sought the support of the AFL-CIO, the National Education Association (NEA), the National Organization of Women (NOW), and other liberal organizations. Republican presidential aspirants have tried to line up support among conservative interest groups.

Although organized interests can play critical roles in mobilizing people to turn out and support a favored candidate at primaries and caucuses, too close an identification with interest groups does have its downside. For example, the support of the AFL-CIO, NEA, and NOW was extremely helpful to Walter Mondale's 1984 campaign in the early primaries and caucuses. However, the endorsements of these organizations also left him vulnerable to charges by his opponents that he was the candidate of the "special interests." As a result of the Mondale experience, Democratic candidates were more subtle in 1988 and 1992. They solicited help from the interest groups, but avoided heavy pressure for endorsements.[7]

Even incumbent presidents find it necessary to engage in extensive planning and organizing to assure their nomination and to avoid damaging challenges in the primaries. President Clinton was particularly effective in achieving these goals in 1996. To ensure support from key Democratic electoral constituencies and head off any potential rivals for the nomination, his administration adopted a number of policy positions. For organized labor, it called for raising the minimum wage, issued an executive order banning replacement workers by federal contractors, and promised to veto three GOP sponsored bills opposed by the AFL-CIO. For women's groups and abortion rights advocates, the Clinton administration strongly endorsed Henry Forster for surgeon general. For minorities, Clinton gave strong support to affirmative action programs. Potential challengers to Clinton's renomination were also thwarted by the president's opposition to the policies of Speaker Newt Gingrich and the new Republican congressional majority elected in 1994. Democrats came to see the president as their last line of defense against the GOP Congress and its policies. The White House also worked intensely to be certain that state and local Democratic organizations did not hold any straw polls regarding prospective Democratic nominees, since these polls held the potential for embarrassing the president. Skilled political operatives were recruited for the White House, the president's campaign committee, and the Democratic National Committee. In addition, the White House–dominated DNC ran a $16 million advertising campaign in 1995 in over twenty key states, burnishing Clinton's image as a protector of Medicare and Medicaid.[8] Clinton's strategy proved successful as he became the first Democratic president to secure renomination without any meaningful opposition since Franklin Roosevelt accomplished that feat in 1936.

In contrast to President Clinton's success in avoiding a primary opponent, his Republican predecessor, George Bush, was confronted with a damaging challenge from television commentator Pat Buchanan in 1992. The significance of this challenge to Bush's renomination was noted by his pollster and strategist, Robert

Teeter, who compared Bush's situation in 1992 with Clinton's having foreclosed any chance of a challenge in 1996.

> One of the most damaging things to us in 1992 was Pat Buchanan's [challenge] taking away three or four months we could have used to set our message and strategy before the Democrats had their candidate. . . . Clinton has the advantage . . . of being able to decide on his own plan, looking ahead to November and executing it. And he also has $37 million he can use during the primary period to strengthen himself for the general election.[9]

Phase II: Delegate Selection—The Early Contests and the Consequences of Front Loading

The early contests for delegates are important not only because of the number of delegates at stake, but also because of the benefits that attach to doing well in these events. Events of critical importance are the Iowa caucuses, the first major delegate selection event of the season, and New Hampshire's first in the nation primary. Each normally receives saturation TV coverage. The results of these early contests establish front runners for the nomination and begin the process of narrowing the field of candidates. Those who do well in these events gain publicity, standing in the polls, increased fund-raising capacity, and support from influential party leaders. Those who falter in the early contests find that their poll ratings, fund-raising, and support from prominent leaders all diminish, and many are forced to drop out of the race.

The early stage of the primary and caucus season has been described as the "media fishbowl" phase of the presidential nominating campaign.[10] It is a time when the electronic and print media have their greatest impact through their allocation of coverage to the candidates and their assessments of who won and who lost delegate selection contests. These assessments help to winnow the field of candidates. What matters most in the early contests is how the results of the primaries and caucuses are interpreted. One need not come in first in the primaries and caucuses to achieve a major publicity victory. Indeed, a candidate can come in first in an early primary and still be considered a loser. For example, in 1972 Senator Edmund Muskie (D-Me.) received 46 percent of the New Hampshire Democratic primary vote in a multicandidate field. Senator George McGovern (D-S.D.) came in second with 37 percent. McGovern, however, was viewed as the winner because he did better than expected, while Muskie did less well than the anticipated 50 percent he was supposed to receive in a state bordering on his native Maine.

The Iowa Caucuses and New Hampshire Primary. The importance of the early contests was vividly demonstrated in 1988 and 1992. George Bush, the front runner for the 1988 GOP nomination, sustained a near fatal blow with his third place finish in the Iowa caucuses behind Bob Dole and Pat Robertson, each of whom gained reams of favorable publicity for their strong showings. Dole's campaign in particular gained momentum (dubbed the "Iowa bounce" by journalists) as the battleground for the GOP nomination shifted to the New Hampshire primary. Dole's Iowa bounce, however, was quickly deflated by Bush's come-from-behind 38 to 28 percent victory in New Hampshire, where Robertson finished a weak third with 9 percent of the vote. As a result of the New Hampshire primary, Bush was back in front; the Dole and Robertson campaigns were severely weakened; and the other candidates (Jack Kemp, Alexander Haig, and Pierre DuPont) were effectively out of the race.

On the Democratic side, in 1988, the Iowa caucuses and New Hampshire primary established Michael Dukakis as a major contender for the nomination. He gained a third place finish in Iowa, trailing the first and second place finishers from the neighboring states of Missouri and Illinois, Representative Richard Gephardt and Senator Paul Simon. Dukakis then scored an impressive victory (36 percent) over Gephardt (20 percent) and Simon (17 percent) in New Hampshire. As was the case with Dole, failure to capitalize on the "Iowa bounce" severely slowed the campaign momentum of both Gephardt and Simon and left Dukakis the front runner.

In 1992, the Iowa caucuses lost their usual importance because in the Republican case, President Bush was unchallenged, while for the Democrats, Senator Harkin's victory was discounted because it was his home state. New Hampshire's primary, however, again had a major impact.

President Bush's campaign received a severe jolt when conservative columnist and talk show participant Pat Buchanan attacked the President in a bitter and derisive manner (referring to Bush as "King George"), received 37 percent of the vote, and held Bush to only 53 percent. This was correctly interpreted as a forbidding sign of weakness for Bush, even though Buchanan was not seen as a serious contender for the GOP nomination.

A strong second-place finish to native New Englander Paul Tsongas's win in the Democratic primary revived Clinton's campaign, which had been thrown seriously off track by well-publicized allegations of his womanizing and draft dodging. At the same time, the weak showings of Harkin and Kerrey foreshadowed their rapid demise as serious contenders for the nomination.

Front Loading the Presidential Primaries. In 1996, more and more states engaged in a competition to move ahead the dates of their primaries in an effort to give their states' electorates greater influence over the selection of presidential nominees. This process of bunching the primaries early in a presidential year has been dubbed *front loading*. Thus, in 1996, following fast after New Hampshire's first in the nation primary on February 20, a series of single state and multistate primaries followed in quick succession, so that three weeks after the New Hampshire primary 50 percent of the delegates had been selected. By the end of March, over 70 percent were chosen (table 6.1 shows the high level of front loading in 1996). The extent to which the front loading process has intensified can be seen in data compiled by the *New York Times*. In 1996, half of the Republican delegates had been chosen by the ninth week of the primary season and three-quarters by the twelfth week, whereas, in 1988, it took thirteen weeks to pick 50 percent of the delegates and nineteen weeks to select 75 percent.[11]

Front loading of the primary process has the effect of favoring candidates who have the following characteristics: (1) they have public visibility and name recognition; (2) they are well organized on a nationwide basis and thus are capable of mounting primary campaigns in a number of states simultaneously and in quick succession; and (3) they have ample financial resources. The one candidate for the GOP nomination with these characteristics in 1996 was Bob Dole. It was these advantages that enabled him to wrap up the nomination before the end of March, following the California primary.

Early setbacks in 1996 for the Dole campaign gave temporary encouragement to his challengers. Thus, when Dole, as the Republican front-runner, won the Iowa caucuses by only a narrow margin over Pat Buchanan, this was interpreted by the media as something of a defeat. Dole then suffered further humiliations, first at the hands of Buchanan in the New Hampshire primary and then from wealthy publisher Malcolm (Steve) Forbes in the Arizona and

Table 6.1
Front Loading the Presidential Primaries, 1996

Date	State Primary	Number of Delegates at Stake	
		Republican	Democratic
February 20	New Hampshire	16	26
February 24	Delaware	12	21
February 27	Arizona	39	52
	North Dakota	18	22
	South Dakota	18	22
March 2	South Carolina	37	a
March 3	Puerto Rico	14	58
March 5	"Junior Super Tuesday"		
	Colorado	27	58
	Connecticut	27	67
	Georgia	42	91
	Maine	15	32
	Maryland	32	88
	Massachusetts	37	114
	Rhode Island	16	32
	Vermont	12	22
March 7	New York	102	b
March 12	"Super Tuesday"		
	Florida	98	178
	Louisiana	30	71
	Mississippi	33	47
	Oklahoma	38	52
	Oregon	23	57
	Tennessee	38	83
	Texas	123	229
March 19	"Big Ten Primary"		
	Illinois	52	193
	Michigan	57	156
	Ohio	67	172
	Wisconsin	36	93
March 26	California	165	424
	Nevada	14	26
	Washington	36	90
Total	30	1274	2576

a. South Carolina Democrats did not hold a primary to select delegates.
b. New York Democrats did not hold a primary, since Clinton was the only candidate to qualify for the ballot.

Note: Total delegates selected by the end of March in presidential primaries and caucuses exceeded 70 percent in both parties.

Delaware primaries. These wins by Dole's less-experienced and less-well-known rivals made it appear that Dole's march to the nomination was in jeopardy. Yet, as the schedule of primaries intensified, Dole's inherent advantages of visibility, organization, and money enabled him to win primaries in bunches and lock up the nomination by the end of March.

The Iowa caucuses and the New Hampshire primary feature "retail politics"—direct selling of candidates through extensive personal contact with voters. But after New Hampshire's primary, the nominating terrain changes dramatically, and the style of campaigning becomes "wholesale politics"—reaching the mass electorate through heavy reliance on media advertising in a number of states simultaneously as groups of states hold their primaries in rapid succession. Candidates with limited resources who focus their efforts on a single early primary such as New Hampshire's can at times achieve victories (e.g., Democrat Paul Tsongas in 1992 and Republican Pat Buchanan in 1996). But in a heavily front loaded system, these victories can seldom be sustained, because the candidates are not equipped to compete on a nationwide basis against their better organized and well-heeled opponents.

In addition to accentuating the importance of candidate visibility, organization, and money, front loading of the primaries also has had the effect of diminishing the importance of the Iowa caucuses and the New Hampshire primary. Thus, Dole in 1996 and Clinton in 1992 demonstrated that it was not necessary to win the New Hampshire primary in order to become the nominee, for, long after losing the New Hampshire primary, they had the resources to mount major campaigns in the series of multistate primaries that occurred in the weeks immediately after the New Hampshire primary.

The 1996 Republican nomination battle illustrated another consequence of front loading: intense and costly primary battles in February and March can leave the winner's treasury depleted and hamper his ability to gain needed public exposure and media advertising in the months prior to the national convention. This was clearly Dole's problem in 1996. With the nomination battle won, he ceased to receive as much media attention as he had when there was still a real contest for the nomination; and his campaign was so low on funds that it could not continue to engage in a level of media advertising sufficient to counter the advertising of the Clinton campaign and the DNC.

Republican leaders were so concerned about the adverse impact of front loading on Dole's campaign that they persuaded the 1996 GOP convention to approve a series of rules changes designed to discourage front loading in 2000. These rules changes "required all states to submit final delegate selection plans by July 1, 1999, in order to prevent late jockeying for a high profile date at the beginning of the delegate selection calendar" and "gave states extra delegate bonuses for moving their primaries or caucuses to a later date in 2000."[12] In spite of efforts such as these by the Republicans to halt the trend toward front loading, the pressure to front load the presidential primary schedule coming from states anxious to play a crucial role in presidential nominations is not expected to abate.

Phase III: Delegate Selection—The Later Primaries and Caucuses

The early primaries and caucuses traditionally establish who is the front runner, which candidates are still serious contenders, and even indicate who is going to be the nominee. In John Kessel's phrase, there is a "mist clearing" that occurs after the initial contests.[13] In 1992, for example, it was clear after the March primaries in Illinois and Michigan that no opponent could deny George Bush's renomination; and after Bill Clinton dispatched Paul Tsongas in the southern primaries on Super Tuesday, he clearly established himself as the candidate to beat.

As noted previously, the intensified front loading that occurred in 1996 rendered the later primaries (i.e., those held after the end of March) little more than formalities, since Dole and Clinton had already amassed enough delegates to be assured of winning their parties' nominations. Therefore, if heavy front loading continues to characterize the delegate selection process, the later primaries are not likely to attract much attention *unless* the results of the early primaries are inconclusive and do not produce a candidate who has won a majority of the delegates.

Even if the front runner does not wrap up the nomination during the early primaries, past experience has demonstrated that front runners do not need to win all the later primaries in order to capture nominations. This has been particularly true for the Democrats because they use a proportional system to allocate delegates to competing candidates. Under this proportional system, delegates are awarded to candidates based upon their share of the vote in a state's primary. As a result, all that is required for a front runner to cinch the nomination is to win a sufficient share of the vote in primaries to continue piling up delegates until he or she has a majority. As Democratic rules experts Elaine Kamark and Kenneth Goldstein have observed:

> The . . . effect of a nomination system dominated by proportional representation is . . . to reinforce the importance of the earliest contests. In a proportional system an early winner can withstand losses later on in the season because he can continue to win delegates even while losing primaries. There are no late bloomers in proportional systems.[14]

A clear example of this pattern occurred in 1976, when Jimmy Carter suffered a string of primary defeats in May and June, but still was able to accumulate delegates because proportional rules allowed him to claim his share. These delegates, when added to those he won in the early primaries, gave him a majority at the convention.

The Republican delegate selection process does not require the use of proportional representation and as a result in some of the states a winner-take-all system is used to allocate delegates. As a result, losses in the later primaries are potentially more damaging to Republican front runners than they are to Democratic leaders. In 1976, President Gerald Ford came close to losing the GOP because he lost a series of winner-take-all primaries to Ronald Reagan during May.

Normally by the end of the caucus and primary season it becomes clear who the eventual nominee will be, because the candidate organizations and news media keep a running count on the candidate preferences of the delegates as they are chosen. George Bush, Ronald Reagan's main competition for the 1980 Republican nomination, bowed to the inevitability of Reagan's nomination when he withdrew from the race over a month before the convention. He commented, "I am an optimist. But I also know how to count to 998," the number of delegates needed for the GOP nomination. The winners of the 1984, 1988, 1992, and 1996 Republican and Democratic nominations were also known in advance of the conventions. In 1984 and 1992 Democratic nominees Walter Mondale and Bill Clinton even went so far as to announce their selections for vice-presidential running mates before the conventions convened.

Although it usually becomes clear who the presidential nominees will be during the later primaries and caucuses, this stage in the nominating process can have crucial and long term implications for the outcome of the general election. Lengthy, contentious, acrimonious primary campaigns cost the eventual nominee valuable time needed for intraparty fence mending and planning of general election campaign strategy. However, the theory that divisive presidential primaries cause general election defeats is open to serious doubt. For example, vulnerable incumbents (e.g., Ford in 1976, Carter in 1980, Bush in 1992) almost inevitably engender serious challengers for renomination. But these vulnerable incumbents were in serious electoral trouble even before they faced intraparty challenges for the nomination. By contrast, strong incumbents (e.g., Reagan in 1984 and Clinton in 1996) normally face no serious opposition in the primaries and have a relatively easy time in the general election.[15] Still, there is evidence that if there is prolonged divisiveness that continues into the convention and the selection of a vice presidential nominee, it can adversely affect a party's chances in November.[16]

Presidential Primary Results, 1996

	Number of Primaries on Ballot	Number of Primaries Won	Total Vote	Percent	Best Showing
Republicans					
Bob Dole	42	39	8,337,069	59.1	N.J., 82.3%
Patrick Buchanan	41	1	3,002,673	21.3	Mich., 33.9%
Malcolm Forbes	36	36	1,423,679	10.1	Ariz., 33.4%
Lamar Alexander	34	0	495,728	3.5	N.H., 22.6%
Alan Keyes	37	0	447,000	3.2	N.J., 6.7%
Others	39	0	408,899	2.9	—
Democrats					
Bill Clinton	33	33	9,573,832	88.5	Wash., 98.5%
Lyndon LaRouche, Jr.	27	1	598,129	5.5	N.D., 34.7% [a]
Uncommitted	12	1	395,323	3.7	Mich., 86.6% [b]

a. Clinton was not entered in the North Dakota primary.
b. Clinton was not entered in the Michigan primary.

Sources: Federal Election Commission, *Federal Elections 96* (Washington, DC: Federal Election Commission, 1997), pp. 31–49: *Congressional Quarterly Weekly Report,* August 3, 1996, pp. 63–64, and August 17, 1996, pp. 79–80. Used by permission.

Phase IV: The Convention—Ratifying the Decision of the Primaries and Kicking Off the General Election Campaign

National conventions are no longer deliberative bodies whose delegates weigh the competing claims of rival candidates for the nomination. Conventions ratify the decisions of the preconvention campaign fought out in presidential primaries and caucuses. The principal significance of the modern day national convention, therefore, is that it is the kickoff of the general election campaign. It is an opportunity for the party and its nominee to set the themes of the campaign and project a favorable candidate image during a period when the party will have a virtual monopoly on television news coverage. The *Washington Post*'s respected national politics reporter, Dave Broder, summarized the significance of conventions as follows.

> Convention week is important, not because it marks the end of the nominating period, but because it is the start of the general election. It is the time when most voters take their first serious look at the candidates and their parties and begin to focus on the choice they will make in November.[17]

The nominations now are made on the first ballot. No convention has gone beyond the first ballot in selecting a nominee since the 1952 Democratic convention, which chose Adlai Stevenson on the third ballot. Even though the actual nomination may have been decided well in advance of the convention, what happens at the convention and how it is presented in the news media can have important implications for the campaign.

During the first two days of a convention, the major items on the agenda are the reports of the convention committees—Credentials, Permanent Organization, Rules, and Resolutions (Platform). The full convention must consider these reports and then adopt or amend them before the convention can proceed to the nomination stage of its schedule. The Credentials Committee makes recommendations to the full convention concerning which delegates from a given state should be seated in those instances where there is a dispute about who are the bona fide and properly chosen delegates. The Committee on Permanent Organization, now largely a pro forma group, nominates persons to serve as the permanent officers (e.g., permanent chairman, secretary, parliamentarian, sergeant at arms). The Rules Committee recommends the procedures under which the convention will operate and the Resolutions Committee drafts the party platform.

The tone of any convention is heavily influenced by the strength of the coalitions supporting the various candidates for the nomination. A convention where the candidates are relatively close in delegate strength is apt to be contentious and potentially divisive (e.g., Republicans in 1976). By contrast, in those instances where one candidate is the overwhelming choice of the delegates (e.g., Republicans in 1980, 1984, 1988, and 1996; Democrats in 1976, 1992, and 1996) the convention is frequently harmonious and serves to unify the party. A leading candidate with only a narrow majority of the delegates is apt to be confronted with a series of tests on credentials, rules, or platform issues in the early days of the convention. In challenging the front runner on these issues, rival candidates hope to make a strong showing on a test vote, thereby casting doubt in the minds of weakly committed delegates about the ability of the front runner to actually gain a convention majority for the nomination.

The Ted Kennedy forces in 1980, for example, mounted a campaign for what they dubbed an "open convention." This was an effort to change the convention rules to permit delegates to vote for their preferred candidate irrespective of the candidate to whom they were pledged by virtue of the outcome of primaries and caucuses in their home states. The Kennedy campaign hoped to free delegates from their commitments to President Carter so that some of them might switch to Kennedy, who was viewed as being ideologically closer to the delegates than Carter. The Carter organization naturally opposed this move to weaken potentially its base of delegate support. When Carter won this key test of strength by over five hundred votes, Kennedy announced that he would not allow his name to be put in nomination. Thus the critical vote in the convention was not the roll call on the nomination, but the test of Carter strength on the rules.

The critical test votes may also come on credentials or platform issues. For example, there was a major credentials dispute at the 1972 Democratic convention, which resulted in the seating of McGovern rather than Humphrey delegates from California and Illinois. The outcome of these credentials fights assured McGovern of the nomination. Sensing the risk inherent in these test votes, the front runner may decline to be drawn into a confrontation. The Reagan organization in 1976 sought a confrontation with President Gerald Ford's forces over the wording of foreign policy planks in the Republican platform. The proposed Reagan amendment to the Resolutions Committee draft was thought to be embarrassing to the Administration and its secretary of state, Henry Kissinger. Ford's strategists understood that Reagan's foreign policy plank had substantial appeal to the generally conservative delegates. Ford's spokesmen, therefore, endorsed the Reagan platform language on foreign policy, and avoided any chance of losing a critical test vote. President Carter's strategists made a similar decision at the 1980 Democratic convention when they accepted a series of Kennedy platform amendments rather than risk losing an open Carter-Kennedy fight on the floor of the convention. Carter, like Ford, through this maneuver was able to avoid the appearance of weakness in an early test of convention strength.

A candidate with overwhelming delegate support, such as President Reagan in 1984 or Bill Clinton in 1992, does not need to worry about crucial test votes because any opposition is too weak to mount a serious challenge. In these circumstances, the convention takes on something of the atmosphere of a coronation—a celebration of the nominee. With the eventual nominee's organization in full control of every facet of the convention, the emphasis is on presenting the best possible image of the party and candidate for the viewing audience on television. The 1984 and 1988 Republican conventions, which renominated President Reagan and nominated vice president Bush as well as Clinton's Democratic nominations in 1992 and 1996 are classic examples of conventions designed for television and in which there were virtually no visible disagreements. The conventions were planned to convey the image of a party united behind a popular and experienced leader.

The convention provides the nominee with an opportunity to unify the party by making overtures to the various factions of the party, especially those which lost the presidential nomination. Concessions are frequently made on the platform or rules. In 1988, for example, it became clear before the Democratic Convention that Michael Dukakis, the prospective presidential nominee, would have to reach an accommodation with Jesse Jackson. Jackson commanded substantial delegate strength and was pressing to have his issue concerns addressed in the party platform and rules. He also indicated that as the runner-up in the nominating contest, he deserved to be offered the position of Dukakis's vice presidential running mate. In the interest of party harmony, the Dukakis forces made nine platform concessions to Jackson and agreed to two rules changes for the 1992 nomination. These rules changes were (1) a requirement that each state's delegates be allocated in accordance with the proportion of the vote received by the candidates in primaries or caucuses, and (2) a reduction in the number of super or automatic delegates (rescinded by the Democratic National Committee in 1990). The party unifying function of these concessions was marred somewhat when Jackson was not offered the vice presidential nomination and then learned about the selection of Senator Lloyd Bentsen (Texas) from a reporter rather than from Dukakis.

The vice presidential nomination is, however, often used to unify the party and broaden the presidential nominee's electoral support. Dukakis's selection of Senator Bentsen was an attempt to appeal to moderate and conservative Democrats, especially southerners, who had deserted the party in the Reagan elections. Bob Dole's choice of former congressman and cabinet officer Jack Kemp in 1996 was designed to reassure conservatives (because of Kemp's pro-life and supply-side economic views) and also to broaden the ticket's appeal (because of Kemp's advocacy of social programs, which while conservative included minorities and the disadvantaged).

The vice-presidential choice can also be used to reinforce campaign themes of the presidential nominee. For example, Clinton's selection of fellow southern moderate Senator Al Gore (Tenn.) in 1992, for example, was designed to emphasize the campaign themes of a new generation of leadership and a more centrist ("New Democrat") approach to public policy, while also enhancing the party's prospects in the South."[18]

The climax of the convention is the nominee's acceptance speech, a major media event which provides an opportunity to bind up wounds within the party, portray the candidate in a highly favorable manner, and present the themes of the campaign. Most nominees receive a postconvention "bounce" in the polls. The Gallup Poll, for example, reported that Clinton's support in the polls went up a whopping 16 percentage points following the 1992 Democratic convention, whereas the average "bounce" for nominees had been 5.7 percentage points in the previous eight Democratic conventions. The more divisive GOP convention provided only a 5 percentage point bump in the polls for its President Bush (see table 6.2). A healthy postconvention "bounce" and lead in the polls, however, are no assurance of a general election victory in November; for example, in 1988 Dukakis's eleven point postconvention lead in the polls over Bush evaporated quickly early in the campaign. Even so, the image of the candidate and party created at the convention can be extremely important. A divisive convention can be severely damaging since between 1980–1992 anywhere from 53 to 70 percent of the voters made up their minds about how to vote by the end of the conventions.[19]

The Ongoing Process of Party Reform

Political rules are never neutral. They benefit some and are hurtful to others. Nowhere are these truisms more apparent than in the rules governing presidential nomination politics. These rules, therefore, have been and continue to be points of contention among

Table 6.2
Presidential Nominees' Postconvention "Bounce"
in the Gallup Poll of Voters' Candidate Preferences
(percent of points gained in the Gallup Poll)

	Candidate's Party	
Year/Candidates	**Dem.**	**Rep.**
1996 Clinton vs. Dole	+5	+11
1992 Clinton vs. Bush	+16	+5
1988 Dukakis vs. Bush	+7	+6
1984 Mondale vs. Reagan	+9	+4
1980 Carter vs. Reagan	+10	+8
1976 Carter vs. Ford	+9	+5
1972 McGovern vs. Nixon	±0	+7
1968 Humphrey vs. Nixon	+2	+5
1964 Johnson vs. Goldwater	+3	+5
1960 Kennedy vs. Nixon	+6	+14
Average, 1960–1996:	+6	+7

Source: Gallup Poll Monthly, August 1992, p. 25; Stephen J. Wayne, *The Road to the White House 1996, post-election ed.* (New York: St. Martin's, 1997), p. 193.

the various party factions struggling to control presidential nominations. The immediate causes of the latest surge of nomination reforms were the divisive 1968 and 1972 Democratic conventions and the Watergate scandals of the early 1970s. These events, plus attempts to remedy problems in the nominating process that were perceived to have contributed to the party losing five of six presidential elections between 1968 and 1988 created a powerful impetus for an ongoing process of reform within the Democratic party.

The Reformed Democrats

There was widespread belief within the Democratic party in 1968 that the convention of that year had been unrepresentative of the sentiments of Democratic voters and that party leaders had used unfair tactics in securing the nomination for Hubert Humphrey. In an effort to placate the dissidents and confident that a mainline Democrat, Senator Edmund Muskie (Maine), would be the nominee in 1972, party regulars readily agreed to the reformers' demand for a commission to overhaul Democratic rules of delegate selection. This commission came to be known as the McGovern-Fraser Commission for the men who served as its chairmen, Senator George McGovern and Representative Donald Fraser (Minn.). The Commission proceeded to propose a series of major changes in the Democrats' nomination process that were put into effect for 1972. Successive reform commissions and the DNC continued to reformulate and refine the rules governing the party's nominating process so that today they constitute an elaborate and codified set of procedures that are rigorously enforced by the DNC.[20] Among the most salient features of these reformed rules are the following.

- *Openness.* Required that state parties have written rules of delegate selection, give public notice of all meetings, and have uniform statewide times and dates for meetings; mandatory assessments of delegates are banned; and requirements that a state party can impose in order for a person to become a candidate (e.g., the number of signatures on a petition) for delegate have been eased.
- *Proportional Representation.* Required that delegates chosen through presidential primaries and party caucuses be allocated among the candidates based upon their share of the vote. A minimum threshold of 15 percent of the vote in a primary or

caucus is required before a candidate can be awarded delegates. All types of winner-take-all primaries are banned.

- *Ban on Open Primaries.* Banned open presidential primaries, with special exemptions granted to Wisconsin and Montana because of their open primary traditions.
- *Automatic (Super) Delegates.* Granted automatic, unpledged (uncommitted) delegate status to the following Democratic party officials and public office holders: the president and vice president; members of the House and Senate; members of the Democratic National Committee; Democratic governors; and former presidents, vice presidents, speakers of the House, Senate majority leaders, and former DNC chairs.
- *Affirmative Action.* Required state parties to encourage participation and representation of minorities and traditionally under-represented groups.
- *Equal Division.* Required state delegations to be composed of an equal number of men and women.
- *Three-fourths of a state's delegates must be selected through either primaries or caucuses at the congressional district level,* that is, all of a state's delegates cannot be selected on the basis of a state-wide primary.

These rules changes have transformed the nomination process most significantly by reducing the ability of party leaders to influence or control the delegate selection process. Traditional party-dominated systems of delegate selection were abolished. Caucus systems which involved party officials coming together to start the process of delegate selection were banned or replaced by participatory caucuses in which any professed Democrat could participate. Also prohibited were the "delegate primaries" used in Pennsylvania and New York. In these primaries, party notables ran for delegate under their own names without indicating on the ballot their preferred presidential candidate. Both the party official dominated caucuses and delegate primaries had assured party leaders of a dominant voice in delegate selection within their states. Byron Shafer, a leading analyst of Democratic reforms, has noted that these changes put party officeholders at "an active disadvantage" and meant that "the guaranteed role of the regular party has been discarded.[21]

The Democratic reforms also encouraged the proliferation of presidential primaries and thereby made the nomination process highly participatory, candidate-centered, and media oriented. Rather than risk using caucus/convention procedures that might run afoul of vigorously enforced national Democratic party rules and result in a state's delegates not being seated at the convention, many of the states opted for the presidential primary as a safe alternative. The presidential primary also had widespread appeal because of its participatory nature and seemingly representative character. Thus between 1968 md 1976 the number of Democratic primaries jumped from fifteen to twenty-seven.

While the immediate impetus for changes in delegate selection procedures occurred within the Democratic party, the Democratic reforms had a spill-over effect on the GOP. State legislatures in revising their statutes to make them conform to national Democratic rules frequently adopted the same or similar rules for both the Democrats and Republicans. The number of Republican primaries, therefore, also increased after 1968.

In addition to making the nomination process more open and participatory, less party-centered and more candidate centered, and more media oriented, Kamark and Goldstein argue that the reform process has had the following disadvantageous consequences for the Democratic party.[22] First, proportional, representation encourages a "predisposition of the Democratic party to break down into factions" because various elements of the party can be assured of winning delegates for their standard bearer under a proportional system.

Second, proportional representation is apt to prolong the divisiveness of the nomination battle and make achieving party unity more difficult. That is, second- and third-place finishers in the primaries—some of whom may be leaders of the more ideologically extreme elements in the party—may be encouraged to stay in the race because proportional representation enables them to keep on acquiring delegates in the primaries. This is less of a problem for the Republican party which relies primarily upon winner-take-all primaries rather than proportional representation. In 1992, Jerry Brown and Pat Buchanan both garnered approximately 20 percent of their respective parties' total primary vote. This gave Brown 608 delegates under the Democrats' proportional system, while Buchanan won only 78 delegates under the GOP winner-take-all rules. Had the GOP used proportional representation, Buchanan would have won over 600 delegates and been in a position to play an even more disruptive role in 1992 Republican nominating politics.

The Unreformed Republicans

Reform of party rules has been an almost quadrennial activity and frequent source of intense controversy within the Democratic party as contending interests, factions, and candidates seek to shape the rules for the next nominating contest to their advantage. The Republicans have followed a quite different strategy and have sought to maintain the basic party structure and rules which evolved prior to the era of the McGovern-Fraser Commission.[23] Party rules of delegate selection have not been a major source of controversy within the GOP the way they have been for the Democrats. The element of the Democratic party that supported Senators Eugene McCarthy (Minn.) and Robert Kennedy (N.Y.) in 1968 and which thought that the rules had prevented their side from winning the nomination demanded reform. By contrast, the intense ideological element of the Republican party has not found the rules a barrier to party influence and ascendancy. As far back as 1964, the conservative wing of the party demonstrated the permeability of the party structure and succeeded in nominating its candidate, Senator Barry Goldwater (Ariz.). In 1976, it almost upset an incumbent president when Ronald Reagan nearly gained the nomination over President Gerald Ford. The conservatives succeeded in nominating Reagan in 1980 and 1984 and were generally satisfied with George Bush in 1988. From the Republican perspective, its nominating procedures have worked quite well. It has produced nominees capable of garnering broad electoral support, including four electoral college victories and one near miss since 1972.

Republican Rules Are Harder to Change.[24] It is not possible under Republican rules for the Republican National Committee (RNC) to promulgate rules changes affecting an upcoming national convention in the way the DNC can. The normal method of rules change in the GOP is for the RNC Rules Committee to recommend changes to the full national committee, which in turn makes recommendations to the national convention rules committee. The committee then makes a report to the convention which must give final approval to a proposed rules change. This lengthy procedure imposes major obstacles to any major revisions of GOP rules and prevents tampering with the rules between conventions. There are also significant substantive differences between the rules of the two parties.

Delegate Apportionment. The GOP uses a significantly different formula to apportion delegates among the states. The Republican formula is weighted to reflect the electoral votes and the extent of Republican voting strength in the state. It does not reflect population to the extent that the Democratic formula does. Republican conventions are also somewhat smaller in terms of total delegates than Democratic conventions. In 1996 there were 4,289 Democratic delegates and 1,990 Republican delegates (see figure 6.3).

Figure 6.3
REPUBLICAN AND DEMOCRATIC CONVENTION DELEGATES, 1932–1996

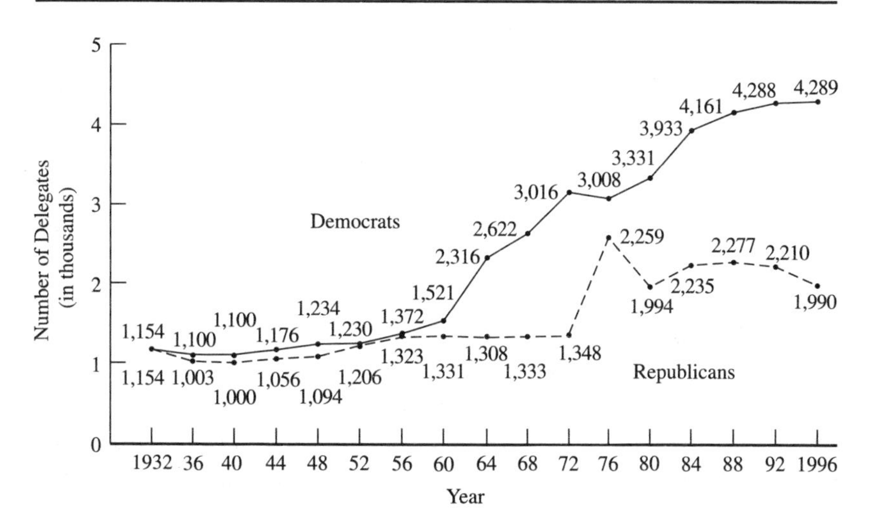

Source: Congressional Quarterly, *Guide to U.S. Elections,* 3rd ed. (Washington, D.C.: Congressional Quarterly, Inc., 1994), p. 15; *Congressional Quarterly Weekly Report,* August 3, 1996, p. 74, and August 17, 1996, p. 90. Used by permission.

Maintaining the Confederate Character of the Party. The Democratic rules changes that culminated with the adoption of the party charter in 1974 significantly strengthened the national party organization at the expense of the state parties in matters of delegate selection. The national Democratic party has an elaborate set of rules governing these matters which it vigorously enforces upon the state parties. By contrast, the Republican rules give the state parties wide latitude in matters of delegate selection and the RNC has adopted a permissive attitude toward its state parties.

Republican rules contain no mandates banning open primaries, requiring affirmative action programs or equal division of the sexes in state delegations, setting threshold requirements or provisions for proportional representation, or stipulating the percentage of state delegations that must be selected at the congressional district level. Further evidence of the party's commitment to maintenance of its confederate character is the requirement of equal state representation on all convention committees. One man and one woman delegate from each state, regardless of state size, is required for each convention committee. The Democrats, by contrast, allocate committee seats in accordance with a more complicated formula that takes into account state population and support for the Democratic ticket.

No Automatic Delegates. The Democrats have sought to increase the participation in their conventions by party and elected officials by granting them automatic delegate status, but the Republicans have consistently resisted such proposals. The provision for automatic delegates by the Democrats was believed to be necessary because the reforms caused the number of party and elected official delegates to fall off dramatically. The highly structured Democratic rules frequently required such officials to run against their own constituents, if they wished to become delegates. This was an undertaking in which few wished to engage. The less restrictive GOP rules governing delegate selection by state parties have meant that it has been easier within the Republican party to designate party leaders as delegates. As a result, there is no strong pressure in the GOP for giving party leaders automatic delegate status.

These differences between the parties are sufficiently important that some scholars believe that a partial explanation for the Democrats' recent difficulties in presidential politics lies in their continuing process of rules reform.[25] The differences between the largely unreformed GOP and the reformed Democratic party, however, should not obscure the basic similarities in the nomination process as it operates within both parties. In both parties the bulk of the delegates are selected through presidential primaries and it is the early primaries for both Republicans and Democrats that have disproportionate influence upon the choice of a nominee. The process is highly participatory, even in caucus/convention states because party rules and state laws permit participation by even the most nominal of partisans. The media play a major role in screening the candidates and in interpreting the results of caucuses and primaries. Party organizations and leaders are no longer the dominant players. Their place has been taken by the organizations of the candidates and the media.

Campaign Finance: The Federal Election Campaign Act

The Watergate revelations of campaign finance irregularities in 1972 led the Congress to enact campaign finance reforms, the Federal Election Campaign Act (FECA) Amendments of 1974. The key provision of the act, as it pertains to presidential nominating campaigns, is that relating to public funding. Candidates for major party nominations are eligible to receive federal matching funds for their campaigns, provided they comply with the following conditions.

- Raise at least $5,000 in individual contributions of $250 or less in each of 20 states. Only individual contributions of up to $1,000 can be accepted and only the first $250 counts toward the federal match.
- Abide by an overall expenditure limit which is adjusted prior to each election to account for inflation. In 1996 the overall expenditure limit is $30.1 million, plus an additional 20 percent to cover fund-raising costs.
- Abide by individual state expenditure limits based upon a formula of $0.16 cents per voter, plus an inflation adjustment.
- Disclose all contributions and expenditures of $200 or more.

Candidates for presidential nominations are not required to accept federal matching funds for their campaigns, and candidates who decline public funding need not abide by FECA expenditures limits. Between 1976 and 1996, however, only two serious candidates, former Governor John Connally of Texas in 1980, and multimillionaire publisher Malcolm (Steve) Forbes in 1996, have declined federal funding. The reasons for candidate reluctance to forego federal matching funds include: (1) candidates who rely exclusively on private contributions or their own personal bank accounts are likely to be put on the defensive and be accused of seeking to buy the presidency; (2) matching funds provide an efficient way of supplementing private contributions to fund a campaign, and (3) it is extremely difficult to raise adequate amounts of money without federal matching funds because contribution limits ($1,000 for individuals and $5,000 for PACs) apply even to candidates not accepting matching funds. Forbes' reason for not taking matching money was that he believed that FECA state spending limits put him at a disadvantage against the front runner, Bob Dole. Forbes, therefore, sought to concentrate his campaign on the Iowa caucuses and a few early primaries and spent heavily in those states (i.e., he spent at higher levels than the FECA state expenditure limits would have permitted if he had accepted matching funds). His heavy spending from a personal fortune, however, proved ineffective. He had won only seventy delegates after an expenditure of over $41 million.

The FECA has not made money less important than it was prior to 1974. The FECA changed the rules of the game but the role of campaign funding remained crucial. As Nelson Polsby and Aaron Wildavsky have pointed out, the provision in the law for matching funds can have the effect of magnifying the disparity of funds which various candidates have available. The following example demonstrates how matching funds can accentuate financial disparities among candidates.[26]

Candidate	Amount Raised from Private Sources	+	Federal Matching Funds	=	Total
A	$2 million	+	$2 million	=	$4 million
B	$4 million	+	$4 million	=	$8 million
C	$8 million	+	$8 million	=	$16 million

Longer Campaigns. With the severe limits that the FECA imposes on the amount of money an individual or group can contribute and the stipulation that only individual contributions of $250 or less count toward the federal match, it is necessary to start campaigns for the presidency early. Fund raising is now more difficult and it takes longer to set up a viable fund-raising organization, since much of the money must be obtained through direct mail solicitation.

Centralization of Campaigns. Because the FECA contains both a national expenditure limit and individual state expenditure limits for candidates accepting federal matching funds, it is necessary for each candidate's organization to impose stringent expenditure controls in order to prevent violations of the law. Therefore, presidential contenders must plan their campaigns carefully when allocating expenditures among the states.

Highly Public Fund Raising. Not only has the FECA forced candidates to start their fund raising earlier, the law has also transformed the search for money from a largely private to a highly public activity. In the prereform system, a small number of rich people could and did bankroll nominating campaigns and public awareness of the sources of money was minimal. Once the law limited individual contributions to $1,000, it was necessary to hold countless events—receptions, luncheons, and dinners—across the country in order to amass the millions needed for a viable campaign. And with federal matching funds available only for contributions of $250 or less, each small contributor literally doubled in value. Candidates, therefore, adopted the strategy of making mass direct mail appeals for funds usually at least a full year prior to the beginnings of the primaries and caucuses.

The FECA also required presidential candidates to make quarterly reports of their receipts and expenditures. These reports, which are made public, stimulate a flurry of news reports and only candidates who are raising serious money are accorded viable candidate status in the media.

Advantage for Well-Known Candidates. In order to utilize direct mail effectively, the candidate signing the appeal needs ready name identification and well-known positions on issues that can stimulate people to open their wallets. A candidate lacking these attributes begins the quest for funds and a presidential nomination at a great disadvantage.

Spending Limits Dictate Strategy. Candidate organizations have always had to make strategic decisions concerning which primaries and caucuses to contest and the extent to which campaign resources will be committed to a particular state. With the enactment of the FECA, the task became more complicated because it involved more than weighing of political factors. It also became necessary to consider national and state spending limits. State spending limits make no distinction between caucus/convention states and primary states or between early and late primaries. The state spending limits are based on the voting age population of the state, not the state's political significance. The 1996 spending limits for New Hampshire, a key early primary, and for the convention in Guam are the same. The state expenditure limits mean that candidates can no longer spend in a state in accordance with their perceptions of the state's importance in their campaigns. Candidates have, of course, sought ways to skirt the low FECA expenditure limits for strategically important states. Among the devices used to evade the spending limits in the crucial New Hampshire primary are renting autos in neighboring states for use in New Hampshire, allocating a large share of television time purchased on Boston stations (the main media outlets for New Hampshire) to the Massachusetts spending limit, having candidates and staff stay in motels in neighboring states, and adding a request for funds to television ads and then allocating half of the ad cost to fund raising rather than the New Hampshire campaign.

The extreme difficulty of making allocations of funds to specific state campaigns is made even more difficult because the individual state limits add up to nearly three times the overall national spending limit. The candidates, of course, spend most heavily in states they consider crucial to their nomination prospects. With the highly front-loaded schedule of primaries and caucuses, this means that candidates normally expend the bulk of their funds early in the delegate selection season.

Participation in Presidential Nominating Politics

The extent of participation in candidate selection has been a continuing concern of those who have shaped the rules governing presidential nominating politics. A basic tenet of the progressives, who developed the presidential primary early in this century, was a belief that the citizenry should make presidential nominating decisions, not party leaders. The presidential primary was, therefore, an element in the progressive reform agenda. Latter day reformers, who pushed for the McGovern-Fraser Commission reforms and for greater use of the presidential primary, were also committed to participatory democracy. These reformers believed that more participation in the process would result in more representative conventions, nominees who would have a higher level of legitimacy with the public, and more public support for the political system.[27] In practice, however, participation rates in presidential nominating politics are quite low.

Ross Perot Nominates Himself: Running as an Independent

As Ross Perot demonstrated in 1992, it is possible to become a serious contender for the presidency without securing either the Republican or Democratic party nominations. A person can run as an independent.

Getting on the ballot as an independent candidate is, however, an arduous, labor-intensive, and expensive enterprise. Unlike the GOP and Democratic nominees, independent candidates are not automatically placed on the November general election day ballots of the fifty states and the District of Columbia. To get on the ballot, independent candidates must meet the often demanding requirements of state ballot access laws. At a minimum this means that they must secure the signatures of thousands of voters on a petition. This daunting task can drain off scarce financial and personnel resources from campaign activities and thereby cripple an independent candidacy—as was demonstrated by the underfunded and understaffed campaign of John Anderson in 1980.

Ross Perot, however, did not suffer from a shortage of campaign resources. The Texas billionaire had spent $17.5 million of his own money by August 1992 on petition drives to get his name on the general election ballot of the states, even though he announced during the Democratic convention in July that he was withdrawing from the race. In New York state alone, Perot spent $1 million on his petition drive which involved over eighty paid employees (mainly imported from his Dallas headquarters) plus temporary workers from employment agencies.

As a vehicle for his 1996 run for the presidency, Perot created a "party"— the Reform party—which used a complicated nationwide vote process conducted by telephone, mail, and Internet to select its nominee. The party, however, turned out to be a personal vehicle for Perot, who easily defeated a former Colorado governor, Richard Lamm, a maverick Democrat, for the Reform party nomination, amid complaints that party members' votes were never counted.

Winning major party nominations costs approximately $40 million, but as Perot's two campaigns show, running as an independent or starting a new third party also requires financial and organizational resources of major proportions. Only when a candidate has these resources are independent and third-party candidacies viable options.

Sources: Steven A. Holmes, "Perot Ponders Reentering Presidential Campaign," *New York Times*, National Edition, September 24, 1992, p. A12; William G. Mayer, "The Presidential Nominations," in Gerald Pomper, ed., *The Election of 1996* (Chatham, N.J.: Chatham House, 1997), pp. 68–70.

Voter Turnout in Presidential Primaries

Voter turnout in primaries has consistently lagged substantially below that in general elections. The research of Austin Ranney has shown that between 1948 and 1968, presidential primary turnout averaged 27 percent of the voting age population (VAP), compared to 62 percent in the general elections.[28] He noted, however, that many of these primaries were uncontested, i.e., no serious national candidate was competing or only one candidate was on the ballot. In the eleven instances between 1948 and 1968 when a state did have contested elections in both parties' primaries, the turnout averaged 39 percent. In spite of the contests for the GOP and Democratic nominations in 1992, voter turnout was low—an average of 19.6 percent of the VAP.[29]

The proliferation of primaries since 1968 has meant that in absolute terms the number of people voting in presidential primaries has increased significantly. In 1968 there were fifteen Republican and Democratic primaries in which 12 million voters participated. With forty-three Republican and thirty-five Democratic primaries in 1996, total turnout was 24.5 million people, compared to an all-time high of 35.1 million in 1988. The number of persons voting in presidential primaries is subject to considerable variation from one election year to another depending upon the number of primaries being held and whether one or both parties' nominations are hotly contested.[30] Thus, in 1996, with President Clinton's renomination uncontested on the Democratic side, and a spirited contest among the Republicans, voter turnout fell to approximately 13 percent of the voting-age population, with the GOP primaries attracting 58 percent of the primary voters—3.3 million more voters than did the Democratic primaries.

A major point of contention among proponents and opponents of presidential primaries relates to the representativeness of the primary voters. That is, do they distort the choice of nominees because they are not representative of party rank and file voters? All studies of primary turnout demonstrate that the actual voting electorate in presidential primaries tends to be weighted in favor of those who are older, better educated, and more well-to-do. These findings respecting the demographic unrepresentativeness of presidential primary voters are similar to those for general elections and gubernatorial and congressional primaries.

There are significant demographic differences in the composition of the Republican and Democratic parties' presidential primary electorates. The Democratic presidential primary voters are much more heterogeneous. Thus on Super Tuesday in 1988, 17 percent of Democratic voters were black, 3 percent were Hispanic, and 14 percent were union members. By contrast, there were negligible numbers of blacks and Hispanics among the Republican Super Tuesday voters and union members constituted only 8 percent of the total.[31]

Those who do participate in presidential primaries tend to be more partisan (i.e., have a strong commitment to their party) than nonvoters, irrespective of their party preferences.[32] Regarding the ideological representativeness of presidential primary voters, political scientists have produced conflicting conclusions depending upon the methodology employed. When primary voters were compared to all eligible voters[33] or general election voters,[34] they were shown to be ideologically unrepresentative; that is, Republican primary voters were more conservative and Democratic primary voters were more liberal. However, when voters in Democratic and Republican primaries were compared to their respective party followings (general election voters who identified with the party or voted for its nominee), primary voters were not shown to be unrepresentative.[35] Nonetheless, the distinctive partisan and ideological orientations of Republican and Democratic primary voters do have a profound impact upon presidential nominating politics. With Republican primary voters tending to be conservative and Democratic primary voters weighted on the liberal side, candidates' strategies are affected. Indeed, all successful Republican nominees since 1964 have sought to demonstrate that they had strong conservative credentials and no candidate who has campaigned openly as a moderate or liberal has been successful. The Democratic picture is almost a mirror image of the Republicans. Successful Democrats in the modern era have generally sought to demonstrate their liberal credentials.

Participation in Caucuses/Conventions

Because caucuses require participants to attend meetings that are often lengthy and contentious and, in many states, held in the midst of winter, citizen participation in caucuses is substantially low—commonly around 2 percent of the eligible voters.[36] However, because of their special importance as the major presidential nominating event prior to the New Hampshire primary, the Iowa caucuses do normally attract higher levels of turnout—14 to 20 percent of the registered voters between 1976 and 1988.[37] However, turnout was off dramatically in 1992 and 1996. The drop in participation in 1992 was because neither party's caucuses were seriously contested. A popular favorite son candidate, Senator Tom Harkin, was running on the Democratic side, and Vice President George Bush had strong support among the Republicans. In 1996, only the Republicans had a contested nomination.

Like primary voters, caucus participants tend to be middle- and upper-middle class, better educated than average, and older. They also tend to be strongly partisan and often have intense ideological commitments. More ideologically extreme candidates, therefore, normally do better in caucuses than in primaries. For example, in 1988, television evangelist Pat Robertson with his loyal following of fundamentalist Christians flooded the 1988 Iowa caucuses to beat out an embarrassed George Bush for second place behind Senator Bob Dole; Jesse Jackson's committed followers enabled him to finish first in the 1988 Michigan caucuses and make strong showings in five other caucus states; and in 1992 former California governor Jerry Brown defeated Bill Clinton in the Maine, Utah, Washington, Nevada, Vermont, and Alaska caucuses. In 1996, the hard-core committed followers of Pat Buchanan, the most conservative candidate in the GOP field, carried him to victory in the Louisiana caucuses and thereby thwarted Senator Phil Gramm, who had staked his campaign on winning in Louisiana. Buchanan then went on to embarrass front runner Bob Dole by finishing a strong second in the Iowa caucuses and, in the process, denied Dole a convincing victory.

Candidates with strong organizations capable of mobilizing their supporters to turn out at the caucuses also tend to do well. In the 1984 Democratic nominating contest, it was party insider Walter Mondale who did best in the caucus states because he had the backing of party organizations and labor unions that were capable of turning out their followers on the day of the caucuses. Similarly, George Bush benefited from his superior organization in the 1992 caucuses.

National Convention Delegates

National convention delegates are not a representative cross-section of either their parties' rank and file voters or the adult population. Status as a convention delegate is a reward that is given to only the most intensely involved supporters of the candidates and party workers. As table 6.3 demonstrates, convention delegates are not a representative cross section of the adult population. Reflecting the general American patterns of participation in party politics, national convention delegates are drawn primarily from generally well educated, middle- and upper-middle-class strata of society. It is these people who have the time, leisure, money, and interest to participate actively in politics. There are, however, differences in the composition of Republican and Democratic conventions, with the Democrats having higher proportions of blacks, Hispanics, Catholics, and union members.

The most striking differences between Republican and Democratic delegates are not in their socioeconomic characteristics, but in their political philosophies and positions on public policy issues (see table 6.3 and figure 4.6). Republican delegates are strongly conservative in their orientation, while the Democrats tend toward a liberal position. It is also clear that the delegates from both parties are unrepresentative ideologically of both their own party's rank and file voters and the total adult population. Democratic delegates are substantially more liberal than their party rank and file and the general public, while Republican delegates are more conservative than their party's voters and the general public. These are the inevitable consequences of the tendency of party activists to be drawn from the most politically committed elements of society and the processes through which delegates are chosen. Participation is skewed toward the extreme ends of each party's dominant ideological tendency and the convention delegates reflect this bias. The generally liberal character of Democratic delegates and conservative orientation of Republican delegates have implications for the conduct of the conventions and the image that these conventions convey to the public through the news media. For example, as the Bush campaign sought to use the 1992 Republican convention to shore up its political base on the right, an unusually harsh conservative image was conveyed to television viewers when prime time speaking slots were accorded Pat Buchanan and Pat Robertson; and recent Democratic conventions have had a definite liberal tone as presidential nominees (Carter, Mondale, and Dukakis) were forced to accord a prominent place on the convention program to their more liberal opponents (Senator Ted Kennedy in 1980; Jesse Jackson in 1984 and 1988), while also making concessions to them regarding platform and rules. To combat these noncentrist party images that have been so damaging in the past, the Clinton and Dole convention managers strove to convey more moderate images of their parties at the 1996 conventions.

Table 6.3
1996 Democratic and Republican National Convention Delegates and Voters Compared
(Percentage)

	Democratic Delegates	Democratic Voters	All Voters	G.O.P. Voters	G.O.P. Delegates
Men	47	37	46	53	64
Women	53	63	54	47	36
White	71	71	84	95	91
Black	17	20	11	2	3
Age					
18 to 29 years old	6	18	17	19	2
30 to 44 years old	27	29	32	33	26
45 to 64 years old	55	30	30	25	53
65 and older	11	23	21	22	17
Political ideology					
Very liberal	15	7	4	1	0
Somewhat liberal	28	20	12	6	0
Moderate	48	54	47	39	27
Somewhat conservative	4	14	24	36	31
Very conservative	1	3	8	17	35
Member of a labor union	34	13	11	7	4
College graduate	69	17	23	30	73
Family income					
Under $50,000	29	78	71	60	23
$50,000 to $75,000	22	10	14	19	18
Over $75,000	46	8	11	17	47

Note: Age, political ideology, and family income may not add up to 100 percent, because people who did not respond are not shown.

Source: New York Times/CBS Poll, *New York Times*, National Edition, August 26, 1996, p. A12. Copyright © 1996 by The New York Times. Reprinted by permission.

Media Politics in Presidential Nominations

The media have always played a significant role in presidential nominating politics because reporters and commentators are inevitably forced to make decisions about which candidates deserve extensive coverage, which candidates did well or poorly in the primaries and caucuses, which candidates are the front runners, and which candidates are surging or fading. The decisions that the media make on such issues have significant effects on the nominating campaign and can influence how the field of candidates is narrowed to a small number of serious contenders. With the opening up of the caucuses and the proliferation of the primaries, the role of party leaders as the arbitrators of presidential nominations has declined, while the role of the media has been expanded.

The impact of the media on presidential nominating politics is illustrated by TV coverage of the Democratic race during the early contests of 1984.[38] Based upon polls which showed Walter Mondale and Senator John Glenn as the leading candidates, the networks accorded the largest share of their coverage to these two candidates during the days prior to the Iowa caucuses. Such an allocation of coverage worked to the advantage of Mondale and Glenn and to the disadvantage of the other candidates—Gary Hart, Ernest Hollings, Reuben Askew, George McGovern, Alan Cranston, and Jesse Jackson. Mondale did well in the Iowa caucuses, as was expected, and, therefore, continued to get substantial media coverage. Hart unexpectedly won second place and immediately was on a media roll. His surprising finish catapulted him into national prominence with a wave of essentially favorable news stories about his against-the-odds rise to serious contender status. Hart was accorded this status on the basis of receiving just 15 percent (15,000) of the votes (Mondale received 45 percent).

During the period between the Iowa caucuses and the New Hampshire primary, Hart received approximately equal television coverage to the front runner, Walter Mondale. This gave Hart's campaign a tremendous boost. Media decisions about whom to cover and who had done well in Iowa, therefore, helped to determine the future course of the nomination contest. Instead of an eight person race, it was essentially a two person race after Iowa.

It was not just the decisions the media made on whom to cover that were important. Equally critical were the decisions that were made concerning the tone of the coverage. In the period between the Iowa and New Hampshire contests, coverage of Hart was essentially positive. Tough investigative reporting on the candidate was postponed—to Hart's great advantage. The extensive and favorable publicity given the Hart campaign as it moved on to New Hampshire gave him significant aid in staging a defeat of the front running Walter Mondale in the snows of New Hampshire. But in the three weeks between New Hampshire's primary and "Super Tuesday" (when, on March 13, five states held primaries), the tenor of coverage for Hart changed from soft background pieces about the young candidate with "new ideas" to tough investigative reporting. Questions were raised constantly by the media about such things as whether Hart had been forthright in disclosing information about his name change and age. There was also a questioning in the media about whether or not he was really a candidate with new ideas and whether he had the requisite experience to be president. After this barrage of less than favorable coverage, Hart's fortunes began to fade. On Super Tuesday he won two New England primaries and one in Florida, but lost to Mondale in Georgia and Alabama.

Interestingly, those voters who made up their minds about how to vote between New Hampshire and Super Tuesday were much less likely to favor Hart than those who made up their minds before New Hampshire, when the Hart coverage was essentially favorable. Clearly, media coverage had an impact on the outcome of the Democratic nomination in 1984. It was not the only important factor, but the early phases of the Hart-Mondale contest demonstrate that presidential nominating politics is media centered and that the media personnel are major participants in the process.

The media's crucial role in influencing the public's perception of the candidates was again evident in the 1992 Democratic nominating contest. The front runner going into the New Hampshire primary was Bill Clinton. However, following a barrage of media coverage on Clinton's alleged marital infidelity and avoidance of the draft, his standing in the polls plummeted. To deal with the infidelity issue, Clinton and his wife made a dramatic joint appearance just before the Super Bowl on "60 Minutes"; and in an attempt to defuse the draft question, Clinton himself went on "Nightline" with host Ted Koppel. Although he finished second to former Senator Paul Tsongas in the New Hampshire primary, Clinton used the media to preempt Tsongas's victory by beating Tsongas to the television cameras on election night to proclaim himself the "comeback kid." The perception that Clinton had done better than expected, had made a strong showing in Tsongas's backyard, and had skillfully defended himself revived Clinton's campaign and gave him the momentum to move on to the Super Tuesday primaries in the South, where he would have home-court advantage.[39]

A Lengthy, Candidate-Centered, Primary-Focused, Participatory, and Media-Oriented Process

The American system for nominating presidents is primary focused, open and participatory, candidate centered, and media oriented. It is a process that confounds most European observers who are accustomed to a leadership selection process which is dominated by party leaders. The leaders of political parties in most Western style democracies, except the United States, are chosen by their parties' members in the lower house of the national legislature. British political scientist Anthony King noted the contrasting patterns of American and British leadership selection processes when he made the following observations. He characterized the British system in this way[40]:

1. Party leaders entered politics at an early age and served a considerable number of years in Parliament before being elected leader.
2. Party leaders had served in a number of different national offices prior to their selection.
3. The leaders were assessed and voted upon exclusively by their fellow politicians.
4. The campaigns for the leadership were short, with little wear and tear on the candidates.
5. The cost of the leadership campaigns was low.
6. The process of selecting the leaders was entirely a party process.

By contrast, the American selection process has had these characteristics:

1. Candidates and even nominees frequently have never served in any capacity within the national government (e.g., Carter, Reagan, and Clinton). Some have entered politics in late mid-

dle age (e.g., Eisenhower and Reagan). There have even been nominees who at the time of their nomination held no public office (Eisenhower in 1952, Nixon in 1968, Reagan in 1980, Mondale in 1984).
2. The candidates are voted upon and assessed mainly by voters in primaries, rather than party leaders.
3. The nominating campaigns are exceedingly long and involve enormous wear and tear on the candidates.
4. The cost of the campaigns is high.
5. The process is by no means an exclusively party process.

The post-1968 reforms of the nominating process have served to widen the difference between American and British leadership selection processes. Prior to 1968, the American nomination process involved a more extensive role for party leaders than the current system. The party leader dominated process has been praised because the candidates were assessed by politicians who had worked closely with them and knew their abilities and liabilities. This system, however, was criticized by reformers for its alleged exclusiveness which restricted participation. As controversy rages every four years over the nominating process, note that no selection process is foolproof. The party dominated process that produced Franklin Roosevelt and Dwight Eisenhower as presidential nominees also produced John W. Davis and Warren G. Harding. Granting that no set of procedures guarantees success, it is important that the presidential nominating process continue to be critically evaluated because structure and procedure do have an impact.[41]

Suggestions for Further Reading

Abramson, Paul R.; Aldrich, John H.; and Rohde, David W. *Change and Continuity in the 1996 Elections.* Washington, D.C.: CQ Press, 1998. Chapter 1.

Bartels, Larry M. *Presidential Primaries and the Dynamics of Public Choice.* Princeton: Princeton University Press, 1988.

Busch, Andrew E. *Outsiders and Openness in the Presidential Nominating System.* Pittsburgh, Penn.: University of Pittsburgh Press, 1997.

Kessel, John H. *Presidential Campaign Politics*, 4th ed. Pacific Grove, Calif.: Brooks/Cole, 1992. Part I.

Mayer, William G., ed. *In Pursuit of the White House: How We Choose Our Presidential Nominees.* Chatham, N.J.: Chatham House, 1996.

Norrander, Barbara. *Super Tuesday: Regional Politics and Presidential Primaries.* Lexington: University of Kentucky Press, 1992.

Polsby, Nelson W., and Wildavsky, Aaron. *The Consequences of Party Reform.* New York: Oxford University Press, 1983.

______.*Presidential Elections: Contemporary Strategies of American Electoral Politics*, 9th ed. New York: Free Press, 1996.

Shafer, Byron E., Quiet Revolution: *The Struggle for the Democratic Party and the Shaping of Post-Reform Politics.* New York: Russell Sage Foundation, 1983.

______.*Bifurcated Politics: Evolution and Reform in the National Party Convention.* Cambridge, Mass.: Harvard University Press, 1988.

Wayne, Stephen J. *The Road to the White House 1996*, post-election ed. New York: St. Martin's, 1997, Chs. 4–5.

Notes

1. *Democratic Party of the United States of America v. Bronson C. LaFollette*, 449 U.S. 897 (1981). For a detailed account of the efforts of the national Democratic party to close the Wisconsin primary, see Gary D. Wekkin, *Democrat versus Democrat* (Columbia: University of Missouri Press, 1984).

2. Nonbinding presidential primaries for the Democrats were held in Vermont, Idaho, and North Dakota and for the Republicans in Vermont.

3. For a detailed analysis of presidential nominating politics, see Stephen J. Wayne, *The Road to the White House, 1996*, Post-Election Edition (New York: St. Matin's, 1997), pp. 97–199.

4. James A. Barnes, "Ready or Not?" *National Journal*, June 25, 1994, pp. 1494–1499.

5. *Congressional Quarterly Weekly Report*, February 25, 1995, p. 630, and August 19, 1995, p. 1124.

6. Ruth Marcus, "Before the Campaign Trail, the Money Chase," *Washington Post*, March 5, 1995, p. A6.

7. Rhodes Cook, "The Nomination Process," in Michael Nelson, ed., *The Elections of 1988* (Washington, D.C.: CQ Press, 1989), p. 33

8. Ann Devroy and Frank Swoboda, "Clinton Woos Traditional Allies," *Washington Post*, February 22, 1995, pp. A1, A12; David S. Broder, "Early Clinton Tactics Avoid 1996 Party Fight," *Washington Post*, December 15, 1995, pp. A1, A12–A13; Ruth Marcus and David S. Broder, "Dole Reaches for Prize after 10 State Sweep," *Washington Post*, March 7, 1996, p. A14.

9. Quoted by David S. Broder, "Early Clinton Tactics Avoid 1996 Party Fight," *Washington Post*, December 15, 1995, p. A12.

10. Cook, "The Nomination Process," p. 34.

11. *New York Times*, national edition, January 5, 1996, p.A8.

12. "Nominating Process Rules Change," *Congressional Quarterly Weekly Report*, August 17, 1996, p. 2299.

13. John Kessel, *Presidential Campaign Politics*, 4th ed. (Pacific Grove, Calif.: Brooks/Cole, 1992), p. 34.

14. Elaine Ciulla Kamark and Kenneth M. Goldstein, "The Rules Do Matter: Post-Reform Presidential Nominating Politics," in L. Sandy Maisel, ed., *The Parties Respond: Changes in the American Party System* (Boulder, Colo.: Westview, 1990), p. 188.

15. Lonna Rae Atkeson, "Divisive Primaries and General Election Outcomes: Another Look at Presidential Campaigns," *American Journal of Political Science* 42 (January 1998): 256–271.

16. Martin P. Wattenberg, *Candidate-Centered Politics: Presidential Elections of the 1980s* (Cambridge: Harvard University Press, 1991), pp. 45–65; see also James I Lengle, Diana Owen, and Molly Sonner, "Divisive Nominating Mechanisms and Democratic Party Electoral Prospects," *Journal of Politics* 59 (May 1995): 370–383.

17. David Broder, "A Chance to Be 'Presidential,' " *Washington Post*, July 15, 1984, p. 8.

18. Rhodes Cook, "Clinton Aims for New Image, Young Moderate, Southern," *Congressional Quarterly, Weekly Report*, July 11, 1992, pp. 2017–2020.

19. William H. Flanigan and Nancy H. Zingale, *The Political Behavior of the American Electorate*, 9th ed. (Washington, D.C.: CQ Press, 1998), p. 150.

20. On Democratic reforms, see David E. Price, *Bringing Back the Parties* (Washington, D.C.: CQ Press, 1984), chs. 6–7. On the post-reform nomination process, see Leon D. Epstein, "Presidential Nominations Since Party Reform," *American Review of Politics* 14 (Summer, 1993): 149–162.

21. Byron E. Shafer, Quiet Revolution: *The Struggle for the Democratic Party and the Shaping of Post-Reform Politics* (Russell Sage, 1983), p. 526.

22. Kamark and Goldstein, "The Rules Matter," pp. 186–189.

23. The differing approaches of the Republican and Democratic parties to party reform are described in John F. Bibby, "Party Renewal in the National Republican Party," in Gerald Pomper, ed., *Party Renewal in America: Theory and Practice* (New York: Praeger, 1980), pp. 102–115.

24. The differences between Republican and Democratic party rules are described in more detail in Robert J. Huckshorn and John F. Bibby, "National Party Rules and Delegate Selection in the Republican Party," *P.S.* 16 (Fall 1983): 656–666.

25. For a critical evaluation of the Democratic reforms, see Nelson W. Polsby, *Consequences of Party Reform* (New York: Oxford University Press, 1983). A sympathetic consideration of the Democratic reforms is found in William Crotty, *Party Reform* (New York: Longman, 1983).

26. Nelson W. Polsby and Aaron Wildavsky, *Presidential Elections: Strategies of American Electoral Politics*, 7th ed. (New York: Scribners, 1988).

27. Austin Ranney, *Participation in American Presidential Nominations* (Washington, D.C.: American Enterprise Institute, 1977), p. 14.

28. Ibid., pp. 24–25.

29. Committee for the Study of the American Electorate data reported in the *New York Times*, July 2, 1992, p. A8, National Edition.

30. For an analysis of the factors affecting voter turnout in presidential primaries, see Barbara Norrander and Greg Smith, "Type of Contest, Candidate Strategy, and Turnout in Presidential Primaries," *American Politics Quarterly* 13 (Jan. 1985): 28–50; and Barbara Norrander, "Selective Participation: Presidential Primary Voters as a Subset of General Election Voters," *American Politics Quarterly* 14 (Jan. 1986): 35–53.

31. Barbara Norrander, *Super Tuesday: Regional Politics and Presidential Primaries* (Lexington: University of Kentucky Press, 1992), p. 130.

32. William Crotty and John S. Jackson, *Presidential Primaries and Nominations* (Washington, D.C.: CQ Press, 1985), pp. 91–92.

33. Ibid., p. 93.

34. Kamark and Goldstein, "The Rules Matter," p. 184.

35. John C. Geer, "Assessing the Representativeness of Electorates in Primary Elections," *American Journal of Political Science* 32 (November 1988): 929–945; see also Barbara Norrander, "Ideological Representativeness of Presidential Primary Voters," *American Journal of Political Science* 33 (August 1989): 570–587; and Larry M. Bartels, *Presidential Primaries and the Dynamics of Public Choice* (Princeton: Princeton University Press, 1988), pp. 140–148.

36. Ranney, *Participation in American Presidential Nominations*, 1976, p. 15.

37. Walter J. Stone, Alan I. Abramowitz, and Ronald B. Rapoport, "How Representative Are the Iowa Caucuses?" in Peverill Squire, ed., *The Iowa Caucuses and the Presidential Nominating Process* (Boulder, Colo.: Westview Press, 1989), pp. 11–12.

38. For an analysis of network coverage of the 1984 convention, see William C. Adams, "Convention Coverage," *Public Opinion* 7 (Dec./Jan. 1985): 43–48. The most complete consideration of the impact of television coverage upon national conventions and public perceptions of the parties is found in Byron E. Shafer, *Bifurcated Politics: Evolution and Reform in the National Party Convention* (Cambridge, Mass.: Harvard University Press, 1988), especially chapters 7 and 8.

39. Ross K. Baker, "Sorting Out and Suiting Up: The Presidential Nominations," in Gerald M. Pomper, ed., *The Election of 1992: Reports and Interpretations* (Chatham, N.J.: Chatham House, 1993), pp. 47–51.

40. Anthony King, "How Not to Select Presidential Candidates: A View from

Europe," in Austin Ranney, ed., *American Elections of 1980* (Washington, D.C.: American Enterprise Institute, 1981), pp. 310–313.

41. For an insightful analysis of the impact of proposed changes in the nominating process, as well as discussion of the advantages of maintaining a system that permits incremental change and experimentation, see Epstein, "Presidential Nominations since Party Reform," *American Review of Politics* 14 (Summer 1993): 149–162.

THE GENERAL ELECTION: REGULATION AND CAMPAIGN STRATEGY

CHAPTER SEVEN

Once the field of candidates has been narrowed through the nomination process, the scene of the party battle shifts to the general election. Nominations are intraparty struggles, while the general election is an interparty struggle which operates in a different type of political environment. In the general election competition, there is normally a higher level of citizen interest, an expanded electorate, larger campaign expenditures, and greater media exposure. The nomination is an interim stage in the process of selection of government officials. In the general election, all decisions are final.

A critical factor in influencing the nature of campaigns and the outcome of elections is the set of rules under which the election is conducted. In the American federal system, the rules of the election game are a combination of federal and state regulations. As originally written, the Constitution contained few provisions regulating elections. Article II provided for the election of the president by an electoral college, with the state legislatures free to determine the manner in which their states' electors would be chosen. Article I mandated that senators should be elected by state legislatures and that the House should be chosen by "the people of several states" and that the voters "in each state shall have the qualifications requisite for electors of the most numerous branch of the state legislature." Congress was also empowered to make laws and alter regulations of the states regarding the "Times, Places, and Manner of holding Elections for Senators and Representatives."

As a result of the dearth of constitutional provisions relating to elections, most regulation of elections was left to the states. With each state making its own election rules, there was naturally substantial diversity in state regulations of federal elections. Some states elected members of the House from districts, while other states used at-large electoral systems; some states held elections in even numbered years and others did so in odd numbered years; and some states required only a plurality for election while others required a majority. The diversity of election practices and state prerogatives in these matters has been gradually reduced through federal statutes and constitutional amendments. For example, starting in 1842, federal law required the states to elect representatives from districts in even numbered years on the Tuesday following the first Monday in November. Among the most significant changes in the law regulating elections have been those actions by the federal government to extend the suffrage to blacks, women, and eighteen year olds and to make the Senate a popularly elected body.

Extending the Suffrage

When the Constitution was ratified, exercise of the franchise was commonly limited to those males who could meet property owning or tax-paying qualifications. As a result, it is estimated that one-half to three-quarters of adult males could not vote. By the Jacksonian era, however, the states had removed most of these economic restrictions on voting so that virtually all adult white males could vote.

Voting Rights for Blacks

The first major step toward enfranchising black citizens was ratification of the Civil War amendments, the Fourteenth Amendment guaranteeing all persons the equal protection of the laws, and the Fifteenth Amendment banning denials of voting rights on the basis of "race, color or previous condition of servitude." However, the southern states, where the black population was concentrated, circumvented these amendments through such devices as the poll tax, literacy tests, and white primaries. Requiring payment of a poll tax prior to election day and administering literacy tests in a discriminatory manner meant that blacks had great difficulty having their names entered on the official voting rolls. The white primary further disenfranchised black citizens by excluding them from participation in Democratic primary elections, the real elections in most of the South until well into the 1960s. Physical force and intimidation were also all too frequent techniques used to prevent southern blacks from voting.

Through judicial decisions (e.g., the Supreme Court banned the white primary in 1944)[1] and the federal Civil Rights Acts of 1957, 1960, 1964, and 1965, racial barriers to voting have been largely removed. Particularly important was the Voting Rights Act of 1965. It suspended literacy tests in all states and counties in which less than 50 percent of the voting age population was registered to vote in 1964. It also provided for federal registrars to register votes and supervise the electoral process in these areas. The act further required officials in these states to submit to the federal Justice Department any changes in election law so that the Attorney General could review the change and veto those which he deemed discriminatory. Black registration in the South increased dramatically in the decades after passage of this legislation so that it approximated that of whites (see table 7.1). While blacks were not an important voting bloc prior to the 1960s, they are now a major electoral force overwhelmingly supportive of Democratic candidates in all of the southern states. The number of black elected officials in the region is also on the rise. As of 1993, there were over 4,900 black elected officials in the South.

Table 7.1

Voter Registration in Eleven Southern States, 1960–1986[a]

	1960	1970	1980	1986
Whites				
Number[a]	12,276	16,985	24,981	27,028
Percent of Voting Age Population	61.1	69.2	71.9	69.9
Blacks				
Number[a]	1,463	3,357	4,254	5,450
Percent of Voting Age Population	29.1	62.0	55.8	60.8

a. Reported in thousands

Sources: Statistical Abstract of the United States, 1990, p. 264; *Statistical Abstract of the United States, 1972,* p. 374.

Women's Suffrage

The movement for women's suffrage began at approximately the same time as that for blacks, but its progress was much more rapid. Although eleven states had given women the right to vote by 1918, it was not until the ratification of the Nineteenth Amendment in 1920 that women generally were permitted to vote. This amendment almost doubled the voting age population in a single stroke. It did not, however, result in any significant changes in the conduct of elections, which party won, or the direction of national policy. Women's voting patterns have tended to be quite similar to those of men. However, beginning in the 1980s, noticeable differences in the way men and women cast their ballots developed and the phrase "gender gap" entered the vocabulary of election analysts (see chapter 8).

Eighteen-Year-Old Voting

Until 1971, every state but Alaska, Georgia, and Kentucky required that individuals be twenty-one years of age in order to vote. The Twenty-Sixth Amendment lowered that requirement to eighteen and thereby expanded the electorate by some 25 million voters. The young voters' impact, however, has not been great because of their low rates of turnout in elections. Nor have young people tended to line up in overwhelming support of any particular candidate or party. During the 1972 election, the first election when eighteen-year-olds were eligible to vote, Democratic nominee George McGovern and some analysts anticipated that young voters would support McGovern overwhelmingly. McGovern, however, was disappointed in the vote he received from this age group, which did not behave in a monolithic pattern. In the presidential elections of the 1980s and 1990s, younger voters tended to favor the winning candidate in roughly the same proportions as middle-aged voters.

Nationalization of Voting Rights and State Administration of Elections

Eligibility to vote is now governed largely by the Constitution and federal law, so that voting is a right of national citizenship. Within the structures of federal law, however, the states continue to play a major role in the electoral process. They set the residency (maximum of thirty days) and registration requirements for voting. These regulations are designed to insure that only the residents of a state participate in its elections and to preserve the integrity of elections by preventing people from voting more than once and in various locations. State statutes governing residency and registration vary widely (see chapter 8) and can operate in a manner that facilitates or hinders citizen participation in elections. In addition, states may restrict voting by convicted felons and resident aliens. State and local governments are also largely responsible for the administration of elections—printing ballots, providing polling places and poll workers, fixing the hours that the polls are open, counting the ballots, certifying outcomes, and regulating campaign practices on election day (e.g., the extent and nature of campaigning permitted near polling places).

Direct Election of the Senate

Senators were originally selected by the state legislatures in conformity with the Constitution. Senators elected under these circumstances were often considered as ambassadors from their states to the national government, and some state legislatures carried the ambassadorial aspects of a senator's duties so far as to instruct senators on how to vote. Occasionally, senators resigned their offices rather than submit to the instructions of their legislatures. More severe problems, however, were caused by the frequent deadlocks that occurred within state legislatures when they sought to elect senators. When such deadlocks happened, Senate seats were left vacant until the impasse could be resolved. A notable example of deadlock took place in Delaware, when an intraparty feud between Republican factions in the legislature left the state without any senatorial representative between 1901 and 1903. In addition to the problems of legislative deadlock, there were charges of corruption in the legislative maneuvering to elect senators and the belief that legislative elections distorted and even blocked the will of the people from being expressed in the Senate. A movement, therefore, developed for direct election of senators by the people, and six states followed Oregon's example of holding nonbinding popular elections for the Senate. The state legislature was then expected to officially confirm the voters' choice. In 1913, the Seventeenth Amendment was adopted requiring the states to select their senators through popular election.

Party Column versus Office Bloc Ballot Forms

The type of ballot that voters use can have an influence on how they vote. There are two common ballot forms in use in the United States. *The party column ballot* is used in twenty-six states. It is arranged so that all the candidates of one party are listed in one column (or row on a voting machine). By marking or punching a single box or pulling a party lever, in twenty of the party column states, voters can cast a straight party vote for all the candidates of their preferred party. Thus, the party column ballot encourages straight ticket voting. The other major ballot form is the *office bloc ballot*, which organizes the names of the candidates according to the office they are seeking. This type of ballot, which is used in twenty-four states, does not permit a voter to cast a straight party vote by making a single mark or pulling a party lever on a voting machine. Therefore, the office bloc ballot tends to discourage party line voting and encourages candidates to attract attention to themselves and only incidentally to their party.[2] The increased use of the office bloc ballot is consistent with a trend in campaign practices and voting behavior which emphasizes voting for individual candidates rather than for a political party.

Financing Elections

Without substantial funds, it is rarely possible to run a credible campaign. Money is not the only critical campaign resource—name identification, charisma, incumbency, volunteers, party organizational support, interest group backing, and a favorable balance within the constituency of party voters are also important. But without money, the basics of a campaign are impossible to obtain. Money purchases a headquarters, staff, polls, media advertising, and travel. As the technology of campaigning has become more advanced and the electronic media has become an indispensable part of major campaigns, campaign costs have escalated dramatically. Professional campaign consultants to advise on the use of the modern campaign technology have become a standard feature of most campaigns for major office. These experts frequently demand large fees for their services. For example, a top campaign consulting firm can collect fees of approximately $60,000 to $100,000 for consulting on senatorial and gubernatorial races, plus commission fees of 15 percent on media booking and production costs. These fees can net consultants an additional $250,000 to $500,000 or more.[3] With the saturation media advertising that characterized the 1996 presidential campaign, the fees collected by professional media consultants were even more substantial. Clinton-Gore consultant, Dick Morris, for example, collected $1.2 million in media commissions plus a $15,000 monthly retainer; and Squire Knapp Ochs agency netted $2.5 million in fees.[4]

The escalating cost of campaigns for the House and Senate is demonstrated in table 7.2, which shows the average expenditures between 1986 and 1996 for incumbents, challengers, and open seat candidates. Table 7.2 also reveals that $600,000-plus House campaigns are now commonplace. Even $1 million House campaigns (102 in 1996) are no longer unusual. Campaigns for state office have also become costly. For example, in the 1998 Illinois gubernatorial race, Republican George Ryan spent $13 million in a winning effort.[5] Even state legislative races can be extremely expensive, with some candidates spending approximately half a million dollars in states where a switch in party control of a few seats could result in the change of party control of a legislative chamber.

Table 7.2

Average Expenditures of House and Senate Candidates, 1986–1996

Election Cycle	Average Expenditure	Incumbent Average	Challenger Average	Open Seat Average
		House of Representatives		
1986	$259,544	$334,386	$124,815	$431,213
1988	273,380	378,544	119,621	465,466
1990	325,145	422,124	134,465	543,129
1992	409,836	594,729	167,891	439,795
1994	420,132	590,746	225,503	543,464
1996	516,219	678,556	286,582	647,336
		Senate		
1986	$2,789,360	$3,307,430	$1,976,286	$3,358,295
1988	2,802,690	3,748,126	1,820,058	2,886,383
1990	2,592,163	3,582,136	1,705,098	1,599,792
1992	2,891,488	3,850,323	1,826,251	3,004,464
1994	3,868,298	4,581,199	3,803,230	2,932,537
1996	3,550,866	4,236,694	3,139,479	3,310,759

Source: Federal Election Commission data.

The level of campaign spending is related to the candidates' chances of winning and the closeness of the contest. For example, in House elections, incumbents and open seat (where no incumbent is running) candidates have the best chance of victory and they normally spend at higher than average levels (see table 7.3). Closely fought races also cause high spending by both incumbents and challengers. The eighteen Democrats who defeated Republican incumbents in 1996 spent on average almost $1.06 million, while the incumbents they defeated, on average spent $1.2 million.

Analyses of campaign spending and election outcomes have shown that the level of expenditure by a candidate can affect the result, but the individual who spends the most does not necessarily win. Sufficient funds to run an adequate campaign are absolutely essential and large disparities in financial resources can be hurtful to the disadvantaged candidate. Research on House elections demonstrates that campaign spending is particularly important for candidates challenging incumbents. The more challengers spend, the better known they become to the voters and the better able voters are to make an evaluation of them (as well as more critical evaluations of the incumbents). Large-scale spending by a challenger can cut the incumbent's advantage in voter recall and recognition in half. Spending by incumbents, however, has less impact. As campaign finance expert Gary Jacobson has observed, for incumbents

Table 7.3

Mean Expenditures in U.S. House of Representatives Elections, 1996

	Amount	Difference from Mean
All Candidates	$ 516,219	——
All Incumbents	678,556	+162,337
All Challengers	286,582	-229,637
Open Seat Candidates	647,336	+131,117
Republican Incumbents Who Won by Less than 60%	1,045,710	+529,491
Democratic Incumbents Who Won by Less than 60%	975,666	+459,447
Defeated Republican Incumbents	1,171,514	+655,295
Defeated Democratic Incumbents	710,406	+194,187
Republican Challengers Who Defeated Democratic Incumbents	1,231,615	+715,396
Democratic Challengers Who Defeated Republican Incumbents	1,063,039	+546,820

Sources: Federal Election Commission data; Thomas E. Mann, Norman J. Ornstein, and Michael J. Malbin, *Vital Statistics on Congress, 1995–1996* (Washington, D.C.: Congressional Quarterly, 1998), pp. 81, 88–89. Used by permission.

"the campaign adds little to the prominence and affection they have gained prior to the campaign by cultivating the district and using the many perquisites of office."[6]

Because of the escalating cost of campaigns, the inevitable differences among candidates in their financial resources, and the recurring

Major Provisions of the Federal Election Campaign Act

Public Disclosure: All contributions of $200 or more must be identified and all expenditures of $200 or more must be reported.

Contribution Limits: In any election (primary or general election) the following limits apply.

Individuals: $1000 per election (primary and general election are considered separate elections)
$20,000 to a national party committee per calendar year
$5000 to other political committees per calendar year
Total not to exceed $25,000 per year

Candidates: not limited in the amounts they can contribute to their *own* campaigns. However, if a presidential candidate accepts public funding, the following limits apply: $50,000 in the prenomination stage; $50,000 in the general election

Multicandidate Committees (e.g., PACs): $5000 per election;
$15,000 per calendar year to national party committees

Party Committees: $5000 per election to U.S. House candidates;
Republican and Democratic senatorial campaign committees or RNC and DNC, or combination of both may give $17,500 to U.S. Senate candidates.

Coordinated Expenditures in House and Senate Contests

Party committees (national and state) can spend $32,550 (1998) to support House candidates.

Party committees (national and state) can spend 2¢ per voter (adjusted for inflation) to support Senate candidates.

Matching Funds for Candidates for Presidential Nominations

Major party presidential nomination candidates are eligible for federal matching funds charges of improprieties, there have been periodic demands for regulation of campaign finance. The resulting statutes at the national and state levels have used the following methods to regulate campaign finance: (1) public disclosure of contributions and expenditures; (2) contribution and expenditure limits, and (3) public funding of campaigns.

To receive federal matching funds, a candidate must:

1. Raise at least $5000 in individual contributions of $250 or less in each of 20 states. Individual contributions of up to $1000 can be accepted, but only the first $250 counts toward the federal match.
2. Abide by an overall expenditure limit ($37.2 million in 1996), plus fund-raising expenses. (Overall expenditure limit is adjusted for inflation for each presidential election year.)
3. Abide by state expenditure limits based upon a formula of 16¢ per voter, plus an inflation adjustment.

Public Funding of the General Election Campaign for President

Major party candidates may elect to receive public funding for their general election campaigns ($61.8 million in 1996). Such funding is conditional upon the candidate's agreeing not to accept or spend other funds in the campaign.

Candidates who do not accept public funds are not limited in the amount they can spend.

(There is no public funding of congressional and senatorial campaigns.)

State and Local Party Spending in Presidential Elections

State and local party organizations are authorized to engage in get out the vote campaigns (signs, handbills, posters, bumper stickers, yard signs, registration drives, etc.) and there are no limits on the amounts they may spend.

National Party Committees

National party committees are authorized to spend $11.6 million in support of their parties' presidential tickets. (1996).

Public Disclosure

The Federal Election Campaign Act (FECA) requires that all contributions of $200 or more must be identified and all expenditures of $200 or more must be reported. Candidate committees and parties must also file periodic preelection reports and a final postelection report with the Federal Election Commission (FEC). All of the states also have disclosure laws, which vary widely in their provisions.

Contribution and Expenditure Limits

In federal elections individuals may contribute no more than $1000 to any one candidate per campaign (primaries and general elections are considered separate) up to a total of $25,000 in an election year. Nonparty political action committees may give no more than $5000 to any one candidate per campaign. In House elections, party committees are restricted to direct contributions of $5000 per candidate per election. This means that party committees can contribute up to a total of $10,000 to House candidates ($5000 for the nomination campaign and $5000 for the general election). Both the national committees and the congressional campaign committees are permitted to make contributions at this level. As a result, national level party committee contributions to House candidates may total $20,000. State party organizations may also contribute directly to congressional candidates. In addition to direct contributions, *party* committees are also authorized to make *coordinated expenditures* on behalf of the party and its candidates. Coordinated expenditures involve spending by the parties to support candidates (e.g., for polls, media production, campaign consultants) which benefits specific candidates, but does not entail direct financial contributions to a candidate's campaign committee. In 1998, the amount of coordinated expenditures authorized by law to assist a particular House candidate was $32,550.

National party committees are permitted to spend more extensively in Senate races. Direct party contributions to senatorial candidates are restricted to $17,500. Party coordinated expenditures are based upon a formula of two cents per eligible voter in the state (adjusted for inflation since 1974). The two cents per voter formula when applied to large states like California or Texas means that party committees are in a position to be of major assistance to their party's nominee for the Senate ($1.518 million for California; $883,863 for New York in 1998). State party committees are also permitted to spend two cents per voter in coordinated expenditures to support senatorial candidates. However, most state parties are not in a position financially to take full advantage of this provision in the law. To compensate for the inability of most state parties to spend to the legal limit in support of senatorial candidates, the Republicans pioneered the development of the "agency agreement" technique. Under this procedure, state parties assign their quota of coordinated expenditures to the national party to act as their agent. As a result of this procedure, the Republican and Democratic senatorial campaign committees have been able to double the level of their coordinated expenditures in key races.

Republican party committees play a more significant role in funding congressional and senatorial campaigns than do Democratic party organizations, especially in the campaigns of nonincumbent House and Senate candidates (see figure 7.1). Although Democratic national committees continue to lag behind the GOP in the level of their support for candidates (e.g., in 1996 Democratic committees spent $17.9 million and Republican committees spent $22.6 million in support of congressional candidates), the party has not only increased its overall level of support, but has also narrowed the gap between the parties since the mid-1980s. In addition, the Democratic Congressional Campaign Committee has been particularly effective in channeling PAC contributions to candidates involved in close races.

Because of the gap between the party fund-raising capacities of the Democrats and Republicans, the two parties have adopted different approaches to the perennial issue of campaign finance reform. Not surprisingly, the Republicans have sought to lift the limits on party expenditures in support of candidates; the Democrats, with a party structure less capable of raising campaign dollars, have opposed lifting the party expenditure limits of FECA. As the traditional majority party in the Congress (until after the 1994 elections), the Democrats had superior access to PAC funds. They were, therefore, reluctant to cut off PAC contributions, while the Republicans (at least while they were in the minority) advocated severe limits on PAC contributions. Incumbents of both parties, however, have become addicted to PAC money.

Although political parties are restricted in terms of how much they may spend to support congressional and senatorial candidates, there are no overall limits on the amount the candidates'

Figure 7.1

POLITICAL PARTY SUPPORT OF HOUSE AND SENATE CANDIDATES

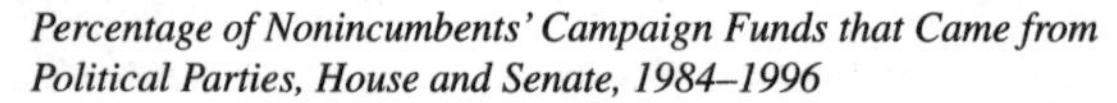

Percentage of Nonincumbents' Campaign Funds that Came from Political Parties, House and Senate, 1984–1996

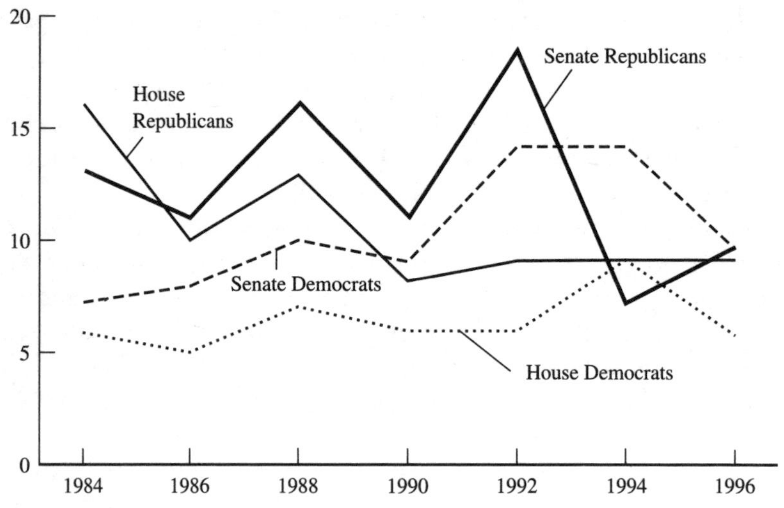

e: Nonincumbents include challengers and open-seat candidates who ran in the general election.

Political Party Contributions and Coordinated Expenditures for Congress, 1976–1996

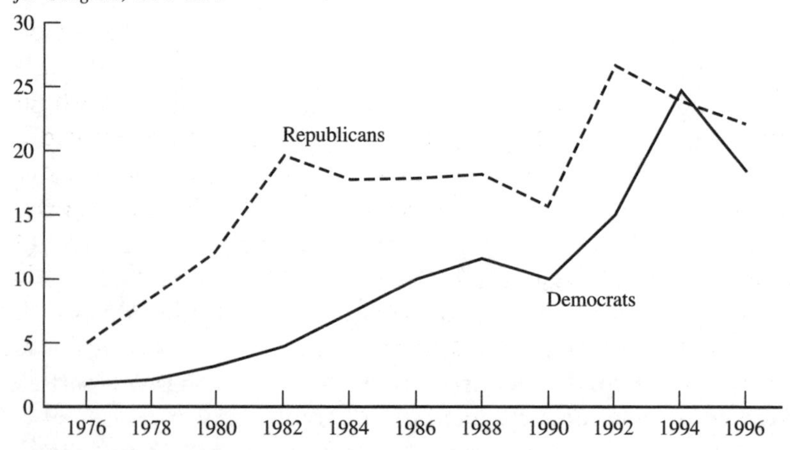

Source: Thomas E. Mann, Norman J. Ornstein, and Michael J. Malbin, *Vital Statistics on Congress, 1997-1998* (Washington, D.C.: Congressional Quarterly, 1998), pp. 96, 105. Used by permission.

organizations may spend. The outer range of expenditures in races for positions on Capitol Hill, therefore, can be extremely high. For example, in 1996, Speaker Newt Gingrich (R-Ga.) spent $5.6 million for his reelection bid and Democrat Mark Warner spent $11.5 million in his unsuccessful bid for the Senate in Virginia.

Nor are there limits on how much of their own money candidates may spend in pursuit of public office. The Supreme Court has ruled that the limit on candidate contributions to their own campaigns which was contained in the Federal Election Campaign Act of 1974 was unconstitutional. As a result, some wealthy candidates have lavishly funded their own campaigns. Michael Huffington holds the record for candidate-funding of a campaign. In 1994, he spent $27.9 million of his own money. Whereas Huffington's wealth failed to gain him a seat in the Senate, Senator Herbert Kohl (D-Wis.), is an example of how personal funding of campaigns has paid off handsomely. While declining PAC contributions and using the slogan "nobody's senator but yours," he spent $6.9 million of his own money to win an open seat in 1988 and $6.4 million gaining reelection in 1994.

Independent Expenditures

The Supreme Court also struck down as a violation of the First Amendment rights to freedom of speech and association a provision in the FECA which restricted to $1000 the amount that groups could spend to support candidates. This FECA provision limited so-called "independent expenditures" by political action committees and individuals in support of candidates. These are expenditures made by organized groups or individuals without consultation or coordination with the candidate's organization. In senatorial and presidential elections, the magnitude of these expenditures can be great. In 1996, Senator Phil Gramm (R-Tex.) was the beneficiary of $1.2 million in independent expenditures in support of candidacy, while Mary Landrieu, the Democratic senatorial nominee in Louisiana, had to contend with over a million dollars in negative advertising funded with independent expenditures. Independent expenditures are a campaign activity that is mainly the domain of large well-funded groups such as the National Rifle Association, American Medical Association, AFL-CIO, Sierra Club, the National Association of Realtors, and U.S. Chamber of Commerce.

In 1996, a dramatic upsurge occurred in independent expenditures by interest groups seeking to avoid the contribution limits of the FECA. Whereas independent expenditures for congressional races totaled $4.9 million in 1994, the FEC reported that the total jumped to almost $21 million in 1996. As these expenditures have escalated, the candidates' control over the issue agendas of campaigns has been substantially weakened. For example, the *Washington Post* reported that in the Twenty-First District of Pennsylvania during one twenty hour period in 1996 there was a barrage of 500 television ads mainly by such interest groups such as the American Hospital Association, AFL-CIO, U.S. Chamber of Commerce, the liberal Citizen Action, and the conservative Citizens for Republican Education Fund. Most of this advertising came without the advance knowledge or involvement of the candidates.[7]

Another type of campaign expenditure that is constitutionally protected by the First Amendment is money spent by a group while communicating with its membership. Labor unions make major expenditures to educate their members and get them to the polls on election day through newsletters, passing out leaflets, paid staff members, transportation services, and large scale telephone banks in major cities. The full extent of such expenditures is not known because internal communication and voter mobilization costs are not required to be reported under the law. Informed observers, however, estimate these expenditures in the millions. For example, it is estimated that the $119 million in contributions made by unions to mainly Democratic candidates in 1996 were dwarfed by the value of the unions' in-kind services to their favored candidates.[8] Another largely unregulated area of campaign activity involves multimillion dollar expenditures by tax-exempt organizations such as the Sierra Club on the left and Citizens for Tax Reform on the right. These highly politicized groups engage in issue advertising and other forms of advocacy designed to benefit or damage the electoral prospects of various candidates. For example, the Sierra Club in 1996 spent approximately $3 million on an issue advocacy campaign that was outside the purview of the FEC on staff, grassroots organizing, mail, phone banks and radio/television advertising; while Citizens for Tax Reform sent out 17 million pieces of mail in the final days of the election.[9]

"Issue Advocacy"

In 1996 voters were bombarded with television advertising costing between $135 million and $150 million paid for by political parties and interest groups engaged in *issue advocacy*—defined by the FEC as "public advertisement, not sponsored by a federal office candidate or political committee, encouraging readers or listeners to take action to advance whatever public cause is being promoted." This type of advertising, which cannot contain "express advocacy" of the election or defeat of a candidate for federal office, is not regulated by FEC and, hence, there are no limits on how much parties and groups may spend on issue ads. Although these ads do not expressly advocate the election or defeat of specific candidates, they have been carefully crafted in such a way that the average viewer finds them almost indistinguishable from conventional ads for candidates. A particularly effective set of issue ads costing $15 million was run by the DNC in 1995 supporting President Clinton in his battles with the Republican controlled Congress. All told, the Democratic party spent $45 million on issue ads for the 1996 campaign.[10] A study by the Annenberg Public Policy Center found that 87 percent of the issue ads in 1996 named individual candidates and that they were significantly more negative than regular political commercials. The Annenberg Center also estimated that in 1998 interest groups and parties would spend at least $260 million on issue advocacy advertising.[11]

The growth of issue advocacy advertising by parties and interest groups has rendered the contribution and spending limits of the FECA virtually meaningless. Thus, in 1996, the AFL-CIO engaged in a $35 million television and voter education campaign aimed at vulnerable House Republicans; the U.S. Chamber of Commerce organized a $4.5 million ad campaign to counter that of the AFL-CIO; and the DNC and RNC each had multimillion dollar issue-oriented commercials designed to advance the electoral fortunes of Bill Clinton and Bob Dole. Party organizations have found issue advertising an especially attractive means of getting around contribution and spending limits in the FECA because issue ads can be funded using "soft money"—funds raised outside the restrictions of the FECA.

Not only has the growth of issue advocacy advertising created massive loopholes in the federal campaign finance laws, it has also worked to take control of campaign strategy out of the hands of the candidates. Because outside groups can enter campaigns and engage in saturation advertising without advance warning to the candidates, Rich Bond, a Republican campaign consultant, made the following observation concerning their impact upon the candidates: "It takes the planning and strategy of campaigns almost totally out of your control. You plan on 1,000 rating points [a measure of TV reach] for your close, and all of a sudden, there are 3,000 points from outside groups. It's like a space ship landing."[12] In effect, the issue content of the campaign can become that contained in the ads of competing interest groups rather than issues upon which the candidates seek to run.

Pragmatic Reasons Why Interest Groups Engage in Issue Advertising

Reason 1: To get around the low contribution limits of the Federal Election Campaign Act. With many Senate candidates spending over $10 million and increasing numbers of House candidates shelling out $1 million, PAC contributions of $5,000 seem to appear as mere drops in the proverbial bucket.

Reason 2: To gain greater control over the issue agenda of campaigns. Groups have found that the only way they can introduce their issues into public dialogue in most campaigns is to do it themselves and not to rely upon candidates—even friendly candidates. Issue ads become a "two for one" deal. Their sponsors get to advocate for a favored candidate while also advancing their own issue.

Reason 3: To control how the issue is pushed or communicated to the public. Once a group gives money to a candidate, the group loses control over how it is spent and what it buys. But with issue ads, the group controls the campaign product.

Reason 4: To control who spends their money. If money is given to candidates, it is the candidates that decide which pollsters, media consultants, and mail and phone vendors will get the fees. With group sponsored issue ads, the group determines who gets the business.

Source: Ron Faucheux, "The Indirect Approach," *Campaigns and Elections*, June 1998, p. 21.

"Soft Money"

The FECA contains major "soft money" loopholes that enable individuals, unions, and corporations to evade federal contribution limits or prohibitions and permit parties to exceed their spending limits in support of federal candidates. "Soft money" involves contributions, often in denominations in excess of $100,000, that go to national and state parties or auxiliary committees set up by the national Republican and Democratic parties. It is used for "party building"—activities such as voter registration drives, get-out-the-vote campaigns, generic advertising that urges voter support for a party's full slate of candidates rather than for specific candidates, and, as was noted previously, it was used extensively in 1996 by both parties for "issue advocacy" ads that were only thinly disguised commercials mainly for top-of-the-ticket candidates rather than those at the bottom.

A significant share of the soft money raised by the national parties is transferred to state and local parties. Thus, in the 1995–96 election cycle, the FEC reported that the DNC transferred $54.2 million to its state parties, while the RNC transferred $48.2 to GOP state units. State parties that receive these large transfers are expected to use the funds to implement national party electoral strategies. For example, in 1996, the DNC transferred $32 million to state parties in twelve battleground states in the presidential campaign. The state parties then paid for television advertising that had been developed and placed in the media by the DNC's media production company. The Republicans had a similar operation.[13]

As figure 7.2 demonstrates, soft money is by far the fastest growing source of campaign money. The $263.5 million in soft money raised by the two parties in the 1995–96 election cycle was triple the amount raised four years earlier. In the competition for soft money dollars, the Republican party, which raised $141.2 million, was more effective than the Democrats, who collected $122.3 million. The reason soft money is so popular with the parties is that it allows the parties to collect funds in large amounts from big donors who do not have to abide by the contribution limits that federal law imposes on other types of contributions, such as direct contributions to federal candidates. For corporations, labor unions, and other groups, soft money contributions are attractive, because the money can be taken directly out of their treasuries—something they cannot legally do in making direct contributions to federal candidates.

Figure 7.2
"SOFT MONEY": A FAST-GROWING SOURCE OF FUNDS

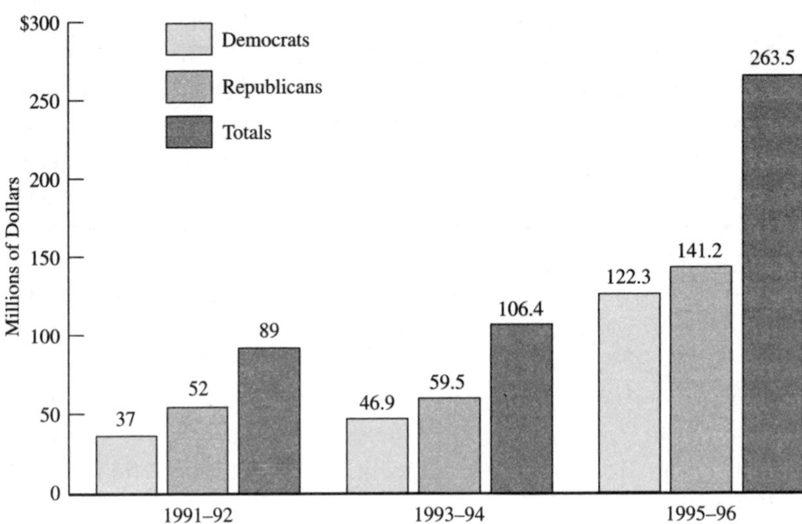

Source: Congressional Quarterly Weekly Report, April 5, 1997, p. 773. Used by permission.

Given the differing policy orientations of the two parties, soft money contributors allocate their funds between the parties in distinct ways. Labor unions give almost 100 percent of their soft money contributions to the Democratic party, while business organizations (corporations and trade associations) and ideological groups favor the GOP (see table 7.4).

Although soft money is the fastest growing source of political money and national level party committees have become increasingly dependent upon these types of financing, it should be kept in mind that soft money represents only a fraction of overall campaign contributions. Thus, in 1996, the Democrats raised just over

Table 7.4
Sources of Soft Money Contributions, 1995–96 Election Cycle

Type of Organization	Soft Money Totals	Amount to Republicans	Amount to Democrats	Percent Republican	Percent Democratic
Business	$203,502,742	$109,644,143	$92,855,342	54	46
Ideological	11,843,817	9,927,792	1,894,361	84	16
Labor	9,516,790	223,835	9,292,955	98	2
Other	3,773,456	1,826,203	1,907,753	48	51

Source: Center for Responsive Politics.

one-third of their money in soft dollars, while the Republicans collected about one-fourth of their funds in this manner.[14]

Public Financing of Elections

The Federal Elections Campaign Act authorizes public funding of general election campaigns for those presidential candidates who qualify and wish to accept the federal subsidy. Major party candidates (defined by the law as the nominees of parties receiving at least 25 percent of the popular vote in the last election) automatically qualify for public funding of their campaigns. Although public funding is not mandatory, a candidate who accepts it must agree to restrict expenditures to the amount of the federal grant and forego all private fund raising. The amount of public funding stipulated by the FECA of 1974 is $20 million, adjusted for inflation ($61.8 million in 1996). Minor parties' presidential candidates are also eligible for a proportionate share of public funding, provided their party received at least 5 percent of the popular vote for president in the previous election. Since the public financing funding features of the FECA first took effect in 1976, every major party candidate has chosen to accept public funding of his campaign. Acceptance of the federal funds removes from candidates the burden of private fund raising. Another reason why candidates elect to accept public funds is that they are fearful that failure to do so would alienate some voters and put them on the defensive by being charged with being beholden to special interests. Because presidential candidates receive saturation coverage by the news media, the spending limits which the public funding provisions of the FECA impose on candidates are not thought to create any major advantages for either party or for incumbents or challengers. Clearly, however, the use of public funding in presidential elections has tended to equalize the resources available to the Republican and Democratic parties.

The expenditure limits of the Act do affect the management and organization of campaigns. The presidential nominees' personal campaign committees, which are the recipients of public funding, must be organized in a highly centralized manner so that tight expenditure controls can be maintained in order to prevent a violation of the law through overspending. In addition, the nominees' campaign committees direct and coordinate party activities designed to assist the presidential ticket. As was noted above, the

FECA permits unlimited "party building" expenditures and thereby encourages voter mobilization activities by state and local parties and by auxiliary party committees created by the national committees. The presidential nominees' campaign committees, therefore, actively engage in coordinating the activities of state, local, and auxiliary party committees in their efforts to mobilize voters.

In addition to public funding of presidential campaigns, twenty-three states have public funding statutes for state elections. These statutes vary from state to state in terms of how the money for public financing of elections is raised, whether the funds are controlled by the candidates or the parties, and which races are eligible to be subsidized. Most plans involve taxpayer checkoffs of one or two dollars per income tax form, although six states use an add-on procedure in which taxpayers indicate on their tax forms a willingness to add a small contribution to the campaign fund. Checkoff plans tend to produce higher response rates from taxpayers than do add-on procedures. In most states, the contribution goes into a general campaign fund. However, in several states (including Arizona, Idaho, Iowa, Ohio, Virginia, and Utah) the citizens designate on the tax form which party is to receive their contribution.[15]

Public funding of campaigns may be accomplished indirectly by channeling funds through the state and county party organizations (e.g., in Arizona, Idaho, Iowa, New Mexico, Ohio, Utah, and Virginia). However, the more common practice among the states is for the funds to go directly to candidates. In four states (Kentucky, Minnesota, North Carolina, and Rhode Island), a combination of these allocation procedures is used. When the money goes through the party organization, the major consequence of public funding is to permit the party to engage more actively in a broad range of electoral activities. When the public subsidy goes to the candidates, Ruth Jones found that the public funding was more important to legislative candidates than statewide candidates, to state house of representatives candidates than state senate candidates, to Democratic candidates than Republicans, and to challengers than incumbents.[16] However, as campaign costs have escalated, public funding tends to be inadequate to finance campaigns at a level commensurate with candidates' needs. Nor does the evidence from a recent nationwide study provide any compelling evidence that state public funding programs have increased electoral competition, as was hoped by the reformers who pressed for adoption of public funding legislation. Public funding has not removed the advantages of incumbency; and it has not encouraged challengers to take on state legislative incumbents.[17] As the states have run up against antitax movements and fiscal constraints, the momentum for public financing of elections has diminished, and the reform movement has shifted its focus from replacing private money with public money toward attempts to restrict and disclose private sources of campaign money.

Public Funding Helped Jesse "The Body" Ventura Become the Governor of Minnesota

Minnesota's campaign finance reform law helped make possible one of the most surprising midterm election results of 1998—a former professional wrestler, Jesse Ventura, won the state's governorship. With his celebrity status, theatrics, tough-guy image, and anti-establishment populism, Ventura, the Reform party nominee, outdistanced his two major party opponents, Hubert H. "Skip" Humphrey, III, son of the state's most famous Democratic politician, and Paul Coleman, Republican mayor of St. Paul.

Ventura's low-budget campaign was aided by $400,000 in public funding, for which he qualified under Minnesota law by gaining over 5 percent of the vote in the primary election. With this money, Ventura moved beyond being a marginal candidate and was able to run comical and irreverent radio and television ads, including one that featured "The Body" posing as Rodin's "The Thinker."

His major party opponents also qualified for public funding, but in accepting public funds they were required to limit their campaign spending to $2.1 million. This prevented Humphrey and Coleman from bombarding the voters with television ads and running away with the election. With their spending limited, debates took on unusual importance. Believing that Ventura would drain votes away from the Republican candidate, Humphrey insisted that Ventura be included in the debates. However, Humphrey miscalculated. Ventura captured one-third of the Democrats while winning a quarter of the Republicans. As a result, Humphrey finished a distant third, and a former professional wrestler became Minnesota's Reform party governor.

Source: Jon Jeter, "Campaign Reform Helped 'The Body' Slam Rivals," *Washington Post*, November 5, 1998, p. A41.

Political Parties and the Federal Election Campaign Act

A key issue in congressional deliberations on regulating of campaign finance through public financing has been whether the national party organizations or the presidential candidates should receive the federal subsidy. Initially in 1966, Congress opted for party control of the funds. Senator Robert Kennedy (D-N.Y.) argued against this approach on the grounds that it would tend to concentrate power in the national party chairmen and diminish the role of state and local parties. Kennedy even envisioned the national chairmen becoming kingmakers under this system since he believed that they could control nominations and discipline state parties through their control of public funds allocated to the parties.[18] Such arguments apparently had an impact because in 1967 Congress suspended its earlier action and in the FECA of 1974 provided public funding to presidential candidates. By giving money to candidates, not parties, the FECA reinforces the decentralized qualities of the American party system and confirms the conception of the party as a candidate dominated structure. Candidates are given discretion to accept or reject federal campaign subsidies, and candidate organizations control the federal funds. Each candidate is required to set up a single central campaign committee which accepts all contributions or federal subsidies and makes expenditures. Under this system it is unlikely that a presidential campaign will ever be run through the national committees of the two parties. As David Price has noted, the FECA gives a modest role ($11.99 million in 1996) to the national committees in terms of campaign spending in presidential elections, but "it builds in the law the assumption that these committees are separate from and ancillary to the candidate's campaign organizations."[19]

Federal law also contains provisions that tend to depress state and local party participation in congressional, senatorial, and presidential campaigns. In presidential elections, strict expenditure limits on the campaign can cause presidential campaign managers to discourage state and local party involvement because such activity, unless it falls within the specially exempted category of voluntary, is counted against the candidate's spending limit. Such rules can cause candidate organizations to constrain state and local parties and to devote greater emphasis to television advertising.[20] State and local party activity in congressional and senatorial elections can also be depressed by the FECA's expenditure limits on parties. Expenditure limits apply to state parties and all their subunits (e.g., county and city organizations) collectively. Therefore, any advertising done by a local party unit to support congressional and senatorial candidates must be counted against the state party's expenditure limits. Representative David Price, a political scientist and former state chairman of the Democratic party in North Carolina, has concluded that "such complexity [in the law] invites evasion, but it also has an unmistakably chilling effect on party participation in federal campaigns."[21]

The FECA further weakened the parties' role in campaigns by enhancing the position of a rival type of organization—the PAC. The FECA permits corporations and unions to communicate with their stockholders, employees, and members on political matters, conduct voter registration and get out the vote drives among these groups, and set up political action committees. As a result of statutory changes which began in 1971, there has been an explosion in the number of PACs (3,844 in 1998) and in the amount of money they spend on campaigns, as well as their relative share of campaign expenditures. In the case of House elections, FECA treats parties as almost the equivalent of PACs by limiting party committee direct contributions to candidates to $5,000 per election, the same limits which are required of PACs.

The FECA, however, does contain provisions which are quite solicitous of parties. As noted previously, national party committees are permitted to make coordinated expenditures to support House and Senate candidates. In the case of the Senate, these expenditures can be substantial and have a major impact on the races. There are also special provisions pertaining to the national committees of major parties. These provisions include: (1) public funding for national party conventions; (2) authorizing the major party national committees to raise and spend $11.99 million (in 1996) over and above the public subsidy to support presidential candidates; and (3) permitting individuals to contribute up to $20,000 per year to the national committees, while limiting contributions to other multicandidate committees (PACs) to $5,000. State parties benefit from the FECA "party building" provisions that encourage the national parties to transfer funds or channel "soft money" contributions their way. This routing of resources to state parties enables these organizations to play a more significant role in campaigns. The national party organizations are major beneficiaries of the "soft money" loophole in the FECA, which enables them to collect millions of dollars which are used to defray operating expenses, engage in issue and generic advertising, and fund registration and get-out-the-vote drives in key states.

Even the public funding provisions of FECA have some positive implications for the Republican and Democratic parties. The law defines a major party as one receiving 25 percent of the vote in the last presidential election and make such parties' candidates eligible for the full quota of public funding. Given the remoteness of either major party's popular vote for president falling below 25 percent, it would appear that both the Republican and Democratic parties have an assured future with a federal subsidy for their presidential campaigns. Indeed, the FECA almost guarantees through its special treatment of major parties and the incentives it creates for them that these organizations will exist into the future to the virtual exclusion of all others.

Table 7.5

Funding Sources for House and Senate Candidates in General Elections, 1986–1996

		Percentage Distribution		
Year	Amount Raised by Candidates and Party Expenditures on Behalf of Candidates ($ Millions)	PACs	Party Contributions and Expenditures	Individuals and Other Sources
House				
1986	234.2	36	4	60
1988	249.0	40	4	56
1990	257.5	40	3	57
1992	332.0	36	5	59
1994	371.3	34	5	50
1996	460.7	25	5	60
Senate				
1986	208.6	21	9	70
1988	199.4	22	9	69
1990	191.0	21	7	72
1992	216.0	21	13	66
1994	291.7	15	8	58
1996	242.0	16	9	64

Source: Norman J. Ornstein, Thomas E. Mann, and Michael J. Malbin, *Vital Statistics on Congress 1997–1998* (Washington, D.C.: Congressional Quarterly, Inc., 1998), pp. 98–104. Used by permission.

The Rise of PACs

Political action committees are major competitors with the parties for influence over the campaign process. As previously noted, the FECA of 1971 and amendments of 1974 significantly expanded the role of PACs, especially corporate PACs. PACs are a type of "political committee" which the statutes grant the right to solicit and accumulate funds for distribution to candidates. The law provides an exemption for corporate PACs from the general rule against federal campaign contributions by corporations and federally insured institutions. These institutions may now use corporate funds to offset the costs of setting up a PAC and soliciting contributions to them from stockholders, administrative personnel, and their families. Labor union and trade association PACs are also given legal recognition by the law and given the right to solicit funds from their members. There are also independent PACs, organized by like-minded persons interested in

Figure 7.3

THE GROWTH OF POLITICAL ACTION COMMITTEES, 1974–1998

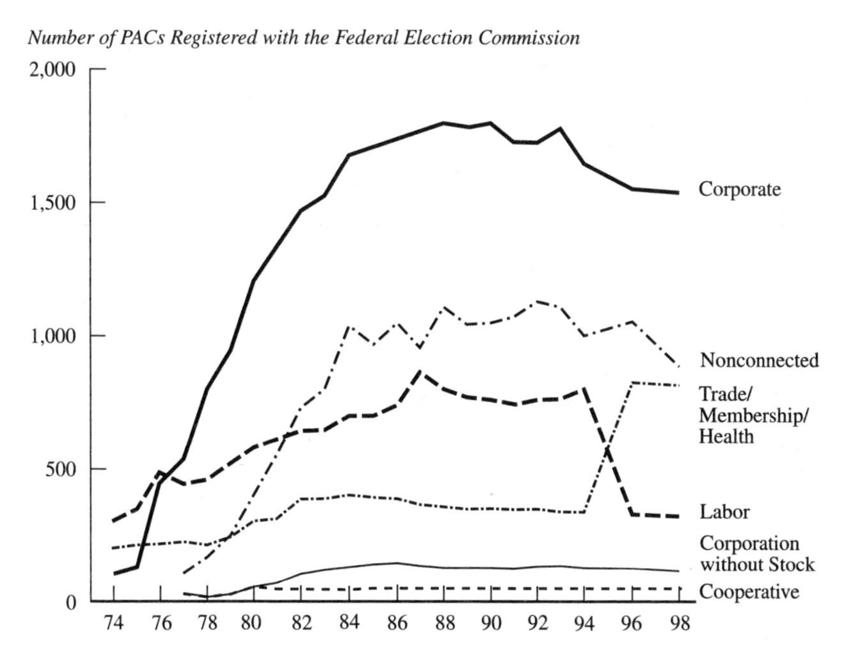

Source: Federal Election Commission.

promoting a particular ideology or policy position. All PACs must meet minimum statutory standards concerning the number of contributors and candidate recipients of PAC contributions.

Prior to the 1960s, PACs were largely a labor union phenomenon, patterned after the example of the AFL-CIO's Committee on Political Education (COPE), though the National Association of Manufacturers and the American Medical Association also maintained PACs. The statutory changes of the 1970s, however, spurred a literal explosion in the number of PACs which is revealed in figure 7.3. Not only has the number of PACs proliferated, but so has their role in campaigns. Their share of the escalating cost of campaigns jumped from 22 percent of House campaign expenditures in 1976 to an average of 34 percent between 1990 and 1996.

One of the most striking characteristics of PAC contribution patterns to House and Senate campaigns is their preference for incumbents (see table 7.6). Thus in the 1995–1996 election cycle, 69 percent of all PAC contributions went to incumbents, while 14 percent went to challengers, and 17 percent to open seat candidates. Since the Democrats until 1995 have had by far the largest share of incumbents in the House, they have received the largest share of PAC contributions to House candidates, while in the Senate the parties' share of the PAC monies in any given election year depends heavily upon the number of Republican and Democratic incumbents seeking reelection. Since the GOP won

Table 7.6

PACs Favor Incumbents!

Amount and Percent of PAC Contributions to Incumbents, Challengers, and Open Seat Candidates in House and Senate Elections, 1986–1996

(in millions of dollars)

Candidate Status	1986	1988	1990	1992	1994	1996
Incumbents	$96.2 69%	$118.2 74%	$125.8 79%	135.3 72%	$137.2 72%	$96.2 67%
Challengers	$19.9 14%	$18.9 12%	$16.2 10%	$22.9 12%	$19.0 10%	$31.6 15%
Open Seats	$23.8 17%	$22.2 14%	$17.1 11%	$30.7 16%	$33.4 18%	$39.8 18%

Source: Federal Election Commission data.

control of Congress in the 1994 elections, PACs (particularly business PACs) have been favoring Republicans with their largess. The GOP's PAC money went up $46.5 million between 1994 and 1996, while the Democrats' received $98.8 million, a drop of $18.8 million[22] (see table 7.7).

The full impact of PACs on political parties has not yet been determined. The conventional wisdom is that PAC growth has weakened the parties. However, there is evidence that both the Democratic and Republican parties have adapted to the PAC phenomenon. The parties solicit funds from PACs and encourage them to contribute directly to needy candidates. In an effort to channel PAC money into targeted races, the parties' national level committees have revealed the results of party commissioned polls to PAC directors, held special candidate receptions for PAC personnel, and set up candidate interviews with PAC representatives. Some PACs form close alliances with parties and become a dependable source of support for party candidates, for example, organized labor's relationship with the Democratic party.

Table 7.7

Amount and Percent of PAC Contributions Going to Republican and Democratic Candidates for the House and Senate 1986–1996 (in millions of dollars)

	1986	1988	1990	1992	1994	1996
Senate						
Democrats	$22.7 45%	$28.3 55%	$24.8 51%	$31.7 57%	$26.8 50%	$19.4 35%
Republicans	$27.4 55%	$23.4 45%	$23.9 49%	$23.9 43%	$26.7 50%	$36.1 65%
House						
Democrats	$56.1 63%	$68.4 66%	$73.3 67%	$88.1 67%	$90.7 67%	$79.4 50%
Republicans	$33.5 37%	$35.7 44%	$36.9 33%	$43.7 33%	$45.0 33%	$79.7 50%

Source: "PAC Activity Increases in 1995–1996 Election Cycle," Federal Election Commission Press Release, April 22, 1997.

The Electoral College

When voters within a state go to the polls and mark their ballots for the presidential candidate of their choice, they are in fact voting for a slate of presidential electors who will cast that state's electoral votes for president. The election of an American president is not a direct popular vote, but rather an indirect election process in which the voters select electors who in turn make the actual choice of a president. In designing this system, the Founders envisioned that the presidential electors would be a council of wise men from each state who would render an independent judgment on the best person to hold the nation's highest office. They also expected that the electoral college would, in effect, "nominate" presidential candidates in those instances when no candidate received an electoral college majority, because the House of Representatives would then choose a president from among the top three electoral college vote getters. The Founders also envisioned a nonpartisan selection process. Only the first two elections of George Washington came close to fulfilling the Constitution writers' expectations. Washington was indeed chosen by the electoral college on a nonpartisan basis. But in the ensuing elections, the contests for the president became highly partisan. Competing parties ran slates of candidates for the position of presidential elector within the states and these elector candidates were pledged to support their party's nominee for president and vice president.

Allocation of Electoral Votes among the States

Each state's allocation of electoral votes is determined by its representation in the Congress. An electoral vote is assigned to each state based upon its number of senators and representatives (e.g., California with two senators and fifty-two representatives has fifty-four electoral votes; Vermont with two senators and one representative has three electoral votes). The District of Columbia in accordance with the Twenty-third Amendment is entitled to three electoral votes.

Allocating a State's Electoral Votes: Winner-Take-All

In every state but Maine and Nebraska, the allocation of a state's electoral votes among the presidential candidates is on the basis of a winner-take-all system. The candidate who receives a *plurality* of the state popular vote for president receives *all* of that state's electoral votes, no matter how narrow the candidate's margin of victory. In Maine and Nebraska, the state's electoral votes are allocated on the basis of two electoral votes for the candidate gaining a plurality in the state-wide vote, and one electoral vote for the winner in each congressional district. Although an exception to the winner-take-all rule, Maine has consistently cast all its electoral votes for one presidential candidate, as did Nebraska when it initiated the district system for the 1992 presidential election.

Majority in the Electoral College Required for Election

To be elected president, a candidate must receive an absolute majority of the votes in the electoral college (i.e., 270 of the total 538 electoral votes). If no candidate for president receives an electoral college majority, the election is then thrown into the newly elected House of Representatives, which chooses from the three candidates who received the largest number of electoral votes. In making its selection, the House votes by state delegation, with each state having one vote and with a majority of the states required for election. When no vice presidential candidate has a majority of the electoral votes, the Senate chooses the vice president from between the two candidates with the largest number of electoral votes.

The House of Representatives has been required to choose the president only twice. The first time was after the election of 1800, when Thomas Jefferson and his vice presidential running mate, Aaron Burr, both received the same number of electoral votes. This tie vote occurred because electors could not differentiate in casting their two votes between which candidate they preferred for president and vice president under the Constitution as originally written. Rather, the candidate with the largest number of votes was elected president and the candidate in second place became vice president. This system of balloting, which was not well adapted to the emerging party system in which candidates for president and vice president ran as a ticket, resulted in the tie vote between Jefferson and Burr. The House ultimately resolved the tie in Jefferson's favor. In consequence of this bitter controversy, the Twelfth Amendment was added to the Constitution. It provided for electors to vote separately for the offices of president and vice president. The other instance of the House having to decide the election occurred in the election of 1824 when four persons received electoral votes: Andrew Jackson (99 votes), John Quincy Adams (84), William Crawford (41), and Henry

Clay (37). With the support of Henry Clay, Adams was selected as president by a majority of one vote.

Electoral College Tendency to Exaggerate the Popular Vote Margin of the Winning Candidate

In three instances, the presidential candidate who was the winner of the popular vote failed to gain a majority in the electoral college. In 1824, Andrew Jackson received a plurality of the popular vote in the eighteen states which chose their electors by popular vote (there were twenty-four states in the Union and in six the state legislatures chose the electors). The other cases of the popular vote winner not gaining an electoral vote majority took place in the 1876 contest between Samuel J. Tilden (Democrat) and Republican Rutherford B. Hayes, when Hayes was awarded disputed electoral votes of Oregon plus four southern states, and in 1888 when Grover Cleveland (Democrat) with a 95,096 popular vote plurality lost in the electoral college to Benjamin Harrison (Republican) by a 168 to 233 margin.

Most public discussion of the electoral college focuses upon the possibility of a recurrence of the 1888 outcome when the winner of the popular vote was not able to muster an electoral vote majority. In actual practice, however, the electoral college normally operates in such a way as to exaggerate the popular vote winner's margin of victory. For example, Richard Nixon's 43.4 percent of the popular vote was less than one percent greater than Hubert Humphrey's 42.7 percent. In the electoral college, however, Nixon's margin was a more comfortable 55.9 percent. A more striking example of the extent to which the winner of the popular vote can have his margin of victory exaggerated by the operation of the electoral college occurred in 1980 when Ronald Reagan received 50.7 percent of the popular vote and 90.9 percent of the electoral vote. This consistent pattern of the winning candidate's proportion of the electoral vote being greater than his popular vote percentage is shown in figure 7.4. Because the popular vote winner and the electoral vote winner have been the same since 1888, there has been little interest within the Congress in changing the electoral college system. It has been argued that the tendency of the electoral college to exaggerate the winning presidential candidate's margin of victory gives the president an opportunity to claim an electoral mandate to govern and implement the policies that were advocated in the campaign.

Encouraging Two-Party Politics

The electoral college system works to the advantage of the two major parties and the detriment of minor parties. The combination of a winner-take-all system to determine the allocation of the states' electoral votes and the requirement of a majority in the electoral college to be elected makes it almost impossible for third parties to win a presidential election. To win any electoral votes and have any impact on the electoral vote, a third party candidate must have voter support that is geographically

Figure 7.4

ELECTORAL COLLEGE EXAGGERATES THE WINNING CANDIDATES MARGIN OF VICTORY, 1976–1996

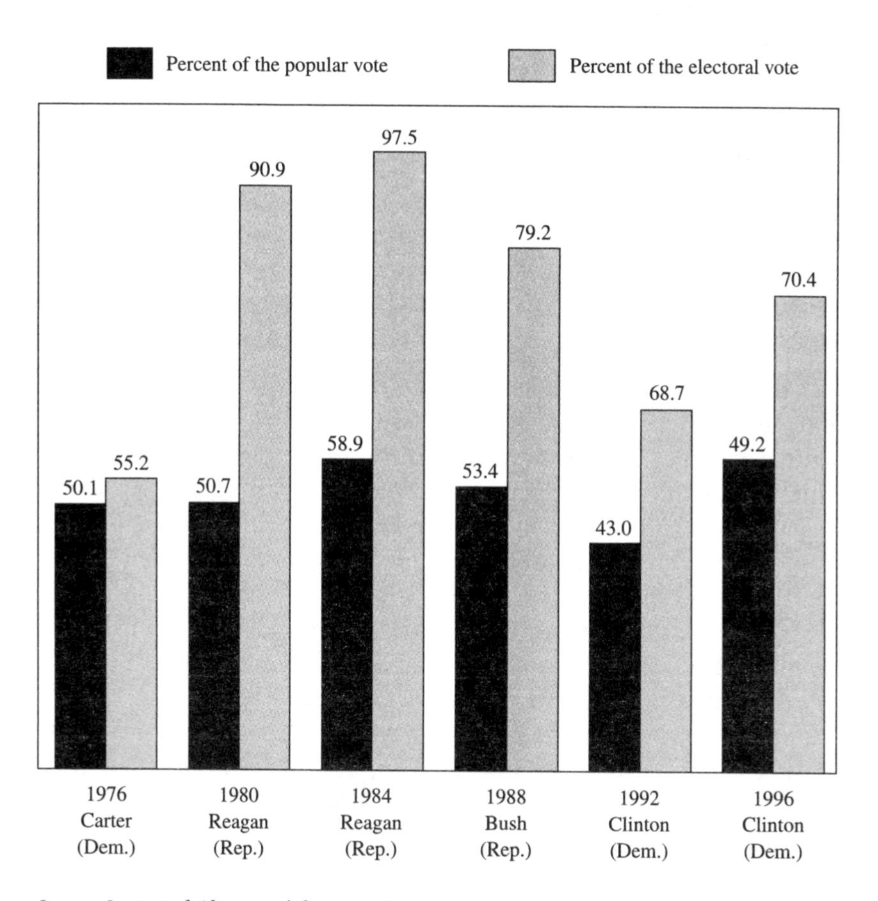

Source: Statistical Abstract of the United States, 1997, p. 271.

concentrated the way George Wallace's was in the southern states in 1968 or Strom Thurmond's was in 1948. When a third party candidate's support is more evenly spread across the country, as in the case of Ross Perot in 1992 and 1996, the candidate has virtually no hope of winning any electoral votes.

If the electoral college tends to be stacked against third parties winning elections, this does not mean that third parties are without influence. By taking votes that might otherwise have gone to one of the major party candidates, third parties can affect the outcome of the vote. Theodore Roosevelt's Progressive party in 1912 split the normally Republican majority in the country and enabled the minority Democratic candidate, Woodrow Wilson, to be elected. In recent elections, third parties have affected the distribution of electoral votes within particular states, but they have not affected the outcome of the election. For example, in 1992 a *Washington Post* analysis of exit poll data showed that had Perot not been in the race, Ohio would have been in the Bush column, but Clinton still would have won 349 electoral votes to Bush's 189.[23] Running on the Reform party ticket in 1996, Perot again had no effect on the presidential election result, although he did deprive President Clinton of a majority of the popular vote.[24]

Big versus Small State Advantages

Small states are mathematically overrepresented in the electoral college. This is because their overrepresentation in the House (every state is guaranteed one representative irrespective of population) and the Senate (each state has two senators irrespective of population) guarantees them overrepresentation in the electoral college. Nelson Polsby and Aaron Wildavsky have noted that after the 1990 census the seven states with three electoral votes each had 268,000 or fewer citizens per electoral vote, while all the states with thirteen or more electoral votes had 475,500 or more citizens per electoral vote.[25]

It is, however, the large, populous states, because of the winner-take-all system, that mainly benefit from the electoral college. California with fifty-four electoral votes has more electoral votes than the thirteen smallest states combined (six states with three electoral votes and seven states with four electoral votes). This means that narrow victories in large states yield a much higher return in terms of electoral votes than do large pluralities in small states. A vote in California holds the potential of influencing fifty-four electoral votes, while a vote in South Dakota can influence only three.

The critical nature of the big states to a presidential nominee can be seen by the data contained in table 7.8. The ten largest states have a combined total of 257 electoral votes (48 percent of the total), just 13 short of the 270 needed for election. Without carrying at least some of these large states, it is almost impossible for a candidate to be elected president. It is, therefore, small wonder that presidential candidates tend to concentrate their campaign efforts in those large states where they believe they have a chance of victory. Since these states are normally quite competitive between the two major parties, they are major battlegrounds in presidential elections. Because the electoral college makes large competitive states so important in presidential elections, it also benefits those groups that are geographically concentrated in these states.

Table 7.8

The Impact of the Big States and the Small States on the Electoral College[a]

State	Electoral Votes	Percent of Total Electoral College	State	Electoral Votes	Percent of Total Electoral College
Smallest States (13)			**Largest States (10)**		
Vermont	3	.56	California	54	10.00
Delaware	3	.56	New York	33	6.10
Montana	3	.56	Texas	32	5.92
South Dakota	3	.56	Florida	25	4.65
North Dakota	3	.56	Pennsylvania	23	4.28
Wyoming	3	.56	Illinois	22	4.09
Alaska	3	.56	Ohio	21	3.90
Maine	4	.74	Michigan	18	3.34
New Hampshire	4	.74	New Jersey	15	2.79
Rhode Island	4	.74	North Carolina	14	2.60
Nevada	4	.74	Total	257	47.67
Idaho	4	.74			
Hawaii	4	.74			
Total	45	8.36			

a. Based on 1990 census figures.

Partisan Implications: The GOP "Lock" on the Electoral College Is Picked in 1992

In the presidential elections of 1968, 1972, and the 1980s, Republican strength in the South and states west of the Mississippi (especially the Mountain States) led to a widespread belief that the GOP had a "lock" on the electoral college. This base of approximately 140 electoral votes had enabled such Republican candidates as George Bush in 1988 to focus their campaign resources on the key competitive states (e.g., Ohio, New Jersey, Connecticut, Michigan, and Illinois) that had large blocs of electoral votes. By holding their southern and western base and then concentrating their campaigns upon the big competitive states, GOP candidates in the 1980s had rolled up large electoral vote majorities (see figure 7.5). The GOP advantage in the South and West was so great during the 1980s that Democratic candidates such as Michael Dukakis (1988) were forced to virtually write off these regions as hopeless. With most of the southern and western electoral votes thus out of reach, Democrats faced the nearly impossible task of having to carry practically all the competitive states of the Northeast and Midwest.

The Republican "lock" on the electoral college was not, however, as secure as it appeared at first glance. Bush in 1988 carried fourteen states with only 55 percent or less of the popular vote. Included on this list were states rich in electoral votes: California (54), Pennsylvania (23), Illinois (22), and Ohio (21). Picking the so-called GOP "lock" on the electoral college was, therefore, feasible for the Democrats in 1992, provided there was a sufficient swing of national sentiment away from the Republicans.

In 1992 that is exactly what happened. George Bush's share of the popular vote fell from 53 percent to 37 percent and the GOP "lock" on the electoral college was picked. By carrying all the large states of the Midwest and Northeast, while making inroads into the GOP's southern base (Arkansas, Georgia, Louisiana, Tennessee) and western bastion (California, Colorado, Montana, Nevada, New Mexico), Bill Clinton won 370 electoral votes (69 percent of the total electoral vote); George Bush gained 168 (31 percent); and Ross Perot was shut out (see figure 7.5). The Democrats' ability to break the Republican "lock" on the electoral college continued in 1996. This election produced electoral college results that were similar to those of 1992, as Clinton won another overwhelming electoral college victory with slightly less than a majority of the popular vote.

Figure 7.5
PRESIDENTIAL ELECTORAL VOTE RESULTS, 1988 AND 1992

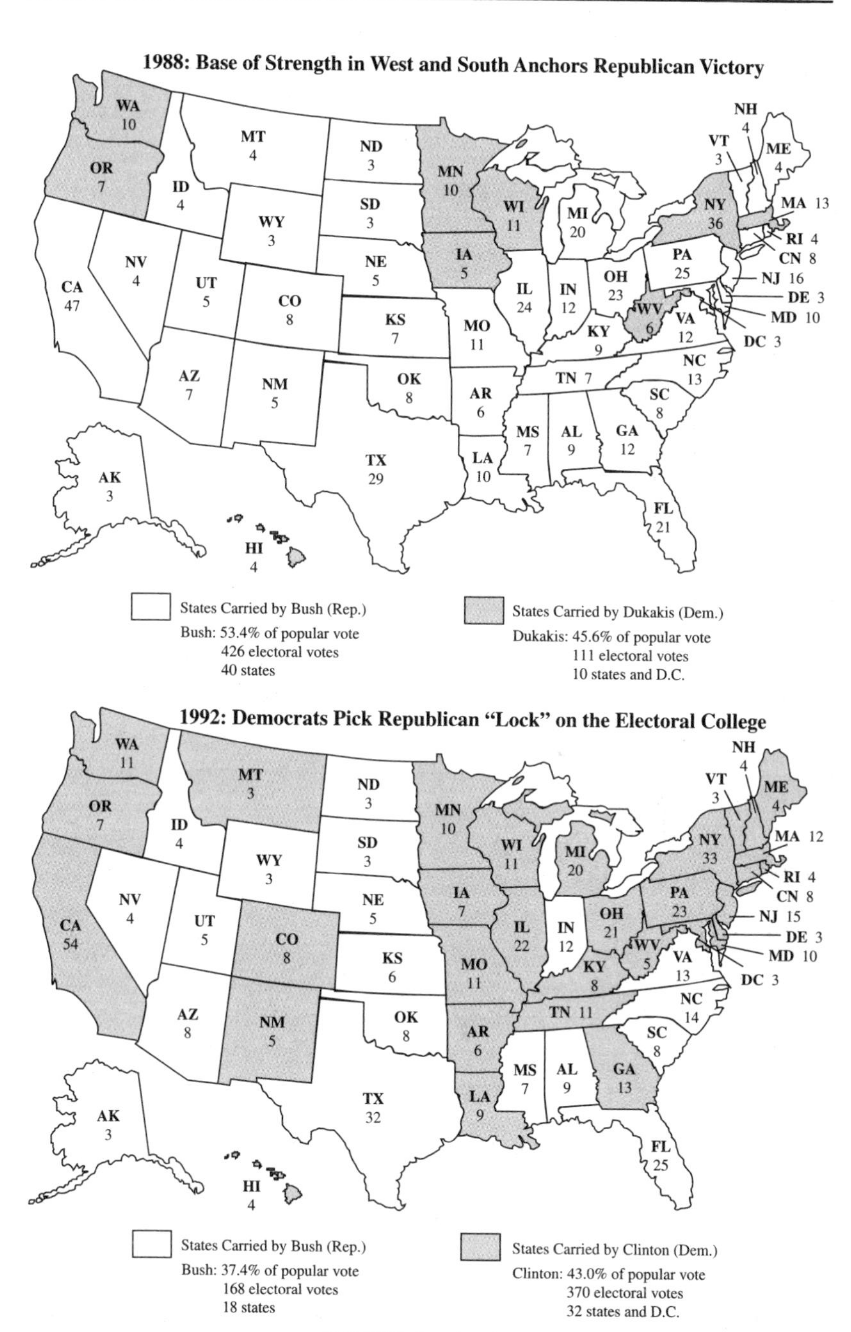

Four states switched party preference between 1992 and 1996: Florida and Arizona moved into the Democratic column, while Montana and Colorado shifted back to the GOP.

While the 1992 and 1996 elections at least temporarily shattered the notion of the GOP having a "lock" on the electoral college, they also demonstrated that even in years when national trends are running against the Republicans, the South and West constitute the party's critical base of support in presidential elections. The importance of the Democrats' base in the Northeast, upper Midwest and Northwest was also apparent. But what stands out most clearly is that the critical battlegrounds in electoral college politics continue to be the large competitive states like California, Florida, Ohio, Michigan, Illinois, New York, Pennsylvania, and Texas.

Reform: Direct Popular Vote versus the Electoral College

Most of the criticism of the electoral college has been concentrated upon the possibility that the winner of the popular vote might not win the electoral vote and the "undemocratic" character of the winner-take-all system of allocating electoral votes. Therefore, the great appeal of direct popular vote proposals is that such a system would assure victory to the popular vote winner, be more democratic, and be less complicated.

Interestingly, little attention is paid in popular debates about the electoral college to the advantages the system holds for large states. However, one effect of switching to a direct popular vote system of election would be to reduce the current special importance of the large states. Under a direct vote system, the vote in Delaware or Wyoming would be equivalent to the vote in California, since no electoral votes would be at stake.

However, there is a serious issue concerning the implications of a direct vote system for the nature of the American party system. One of the first questions that would have to be decided concerning a direct vote system would be the issue of how large a plurality of the popular vote would constitute victory. If a simple plurality is all that is required for election, then third party candidates would have little chance of winning and would remain a relatively minor force in American politics. However, the possibility of a candidate's being elected president with less than 40 percent of the votes (a distinct possibility in a simple plurality system—Clinton won with just 43.0 percent in 1992) has troubled many reformers. They have, therefore, tended to support the plan of the American Bar Association which would require a presidential candidate to receive at least 40 percent of the vote in order to be elected. Under this plan, if no candidate received the required 40 percent, there would be a runoff election between the top two presidential vote getters. Such a plan would greatly increase the potential influence of third parties and splinter groups. The possibility of a runoff election creates an incentive for any sizeable organized interest to contest the first election in order to demonstrate its public appeal and thereby put itself in a strong position to bargain with the major party candidates for support in the second election. It is easy to envision the emergence under this system of peace, right to life, women's, African-American, Hispanic, environmental, farmers, and other parties. The result could be splintering of the party system. Under the current electoral college system, such interests are forced to compromise with the major parties before the general election. As a result, the major parties tend to be centrist and moderate in orientation. Those interests that stay outside the fold during the general election are severely penalized because they have no hope of winning. The direct vote system with provisions for a runoff election would dramatically change the incentive structure of American politics and encourage minor parties and a splintering of the existing parties.[26]

Some have advocated a different type of reform—a proportional allocation of a state's electoral votes in accordance with each party's share of the popular vote. For example, if California voted 50 percent Republican, 45 percent democratic, and 5 percent for a third party candidate, the state's fifty-four electoral votes would be allocated proportionally so that the Republicans would receive twenty-seven electoral votes; the Democrats would get twenty-four; and the third party would win three. Such a system would substantially reduce the current advantage given to the large states by the winner-take-all allocation process. The proportional plan would also increase the likelihood of elections being thrown into the House of Representatives because no candidate gained a majority in the electoral college. For example, both the 1960 and the 1968 elections would have to have been decided by the House because neither major party candidate would have received an electoral vote majority.

Although reform plans abound, there appears little likelihood that the electoral college will be changed in the foreseeable future. The principal reason is that there is little interest in change so long as the electoral college operates (as it has since 1888) to produce a winner who has also won the popular vote. In addition, there are significant interests anxious to protect their advantages under the existing process. Small state senators are determined to retain their state's mathematical advantage under the electoral college and succeeded in getting the Senate to block a direct vote plan passed by the House in 1970. Organized interests concentrated in the large states have also opposed the direct vote reforms because they believe such changes would reduce their potential influence with presidents.[27]

The General Election Campaign

Each campaign is unique. They differ depending upon who the contending candidates are, the nature of the office being sought (executive, legislative, or judicial), the level of government (national, state, or local), the applicable campaign finance and election regulatory statutes, the campaign resources of the candidates, type of nominating campaigns that were conducted, the nature of the constituency, and the tenor of the times (e.g., which issues are salient to the voters). For the incumbent, the campaign is usually a matter of protecting one's inherent advantages of name familiarity and a favorable image while maintaining a favorable balance of campaign resources. For the challenger, who is often underfinanced, the campaign is frequently a time of frantic scrambling to accumulate adequate campaign resources and seeking to find the point of vulnerability in the incumbent's record. In every election cycle, elections are won and lost because of campaign decisions. For example, in 1984, Senator Walter Huddleston (D-Ky.) was forty-six points ahead in the polls and appeared headed for relatively easy reelection to a third term until the campaign of his opponent was ignited and the voters' interest captured by a series of imaginative campaign ads. These ads sought to portray the incumbent as a man who shirked his senatorial duties and obligations to his constituents by taking junkets to plush vacation spots at government expense. His challenger's television ads showed bloodhounds on the seemingly illusive senator's trail first at the Capitol, where he was nowhere to be found, and then at a posh Caribbean resort, where his trace was discovered. By the end of the campaign, Senator Huddleston had seen his comfortable lead disappear and on election night Kentucky had a new senator, Republican Mitch McConnell. Further evidence of the importance of campaign strategies was demonstrated by the 1992 presidential race in which the Clinton campaign was successful in keeping its message zeroed in on blaming the Bush administration for the economy's performance and the need for a new economic plan. The focused nature of its advertising, plus the use of a quick response technique to any charge made by the Republicans, enabled the Clinton organization to keep the campaign agenda on its chosen issue—the state of the economy. By contrast, Bush's message lacked focus; he wavered among claiming that the economy was better than his opponents asserted, blaming the Democratic Congress for the state of the economy, and attacking Clinton's character. The Bush campaign's unsuccessful search for campaign themes combined with unfavorable media coverage prevented it from being able to define the campaign agenda as it had so successfully done in 1988.[28]

In 1996, the Clinton campaign again was successful through advertising, campaign events, and speeches in setting the campaign agenda. It succeeded in framing the electorate's choice as a referendum on the Republican Revolution that followed the party's takeover of Congress after the 1994 elections. Clinton's message was that the Republicans were uncaring and insensitive and should not be trusted with America's future. By contrast, Republican Bob Dole did not find an issue that made an impact until the last weeks of the campaign, when he began to stress the issue of Clinton's character amid news media reports of Democratic campaign finance irregularities.[29]

When the Voter Decides

Most voters (normally around 60 percent) in presidential elections make up their minds about the candidate for whom they will vote before or during the nominating conventions (see table 7.9). A substantial portion of the electorate, however, does make its decision after the conventions and during the general election campaign. Therefore, the impact of the campaign can be significant. For example, a 1980 *New York Times* survey of voters who switched preferences or decided not to vote during the last four days of the campaign revealed that as a result of these last minute decisions

Table 7.9
When Voters Said They Decided on the Presidential Candidate for Whom They Would Vote, 1996

Before conventions	49%
During the conventions	13%
During campaign	34%
Don't remember, not ascertained	3%
Total	100%

Source: Center for Political Studies National Election Studies.

concerning whether to vote and candidate preference, Reagan registered a net gain of 1 percent, Carter a net loss of 6 percent, and Anderson a 2 percent loss.[30] The potential impact of late deciders was again evident in the 1992 presidential election. An unusually high proportion of voters (42 percent) who were surveyed as they left their polling places reported making their decisions only in the last two weeks of the campaign.[31]

Candidate Centered Campaigns in an Era of Technological Change

In the modern campaign, the candidate tends to be the focus of campaigns, not the party. Most candidates build a personal organization devoted almost exclusively to their own election rather than the election of the party ticket. These organizations recruit volunteers and raise funds independently of the party. Indeed, any campaign for a major office run by a party organization is now a rarity in American politics. The candidate organizations tend to utilize professionals for the various phases of the campaign. These campaign technicians—pollsters, media consultants, direct mail specialists, computer experts, targeting experts, and management specialists—operate as private entrepreneurs outside the regular party organization. Campaign consultants tend to work, however, only for the candidates of one party. There has grown up, therefore, two sets of consultants—one group works almost exclusively for Democratic candidates and another for Republicans. Candidates and consultants have found that it is extremely difficult to develop a relationship of trust and confidence unless it is understood from the beginning that both are on the same side politically. The partisan orientation of consulting firms is reinforced by the fact that the national party organizations, such as the national committees and the congressional campaign committees of both parties, each maintain approved lists of consultants whom they recommend to their parties' candidates.

Although the party organizations are seldom involved in the day-to-day management of campaigns, they can provide essential and timely financial support and in-kind contributions of services such as polls, computer analyses of voting patterns, and phone banks to contact voters. Indeed, the role of national party organizations in campaigns for the House and Senate has been growing rather than declining, especially in the case of the Republican party. Among state parties, most assist their gubernatorial nominees with money and/or in-kind services (e.g., staff, polls, voter mobilization programs), but increasingly they have turned over to legislative campaign committees principal responsibility for supporting legislative candidates. However, even with the increased organizational strength evidenced by state parties and legislative campaign committees in recent decades (see chapter 4), the level of state party support given to candidates is usually but a small proportion of the funds required, and it is the personal organization of the candidate that is in charge of the campaign.

The transfer of campaign emphasis from the political party to the candidate's organization has been made possible by a revolution in campaign techniques. The new techniques and technology of campaigning have unalterably changed how people run for public office. Instead of relying upon a hierarchical party organization and precinct committeemen to keep the pulse of public opinion and get out the vote on election day, the modern candidate utilizes an array of sophisticated and expensive techniques that require professionals for their implementation. Public sentiments are measured by public opinion polls. Polling normally begins with a *benchmark poll* taken well in advance of the election and designed to provide a preliminary reading of voter opinion and a baseline from which to measure shifts in public opinion. The benchmark poll is normally followed by a series of polls taken at periodic intervals. In well-funded campaigns for major offices, there are also *tracking polls* taken during the final days of the campaign. Tracking polls involve calling approximately one hundred to one hundred fifty voters on a daily basis and using a rolling three-day average to gauge last minute shifts of opinion. Some candidate organizations involved in close races have credited tracking with giving them the information they needed to make the important last minute adjustments in their campaigns and advertising that gave them their margin of victory. Survey research is now combined with demographic targeting techniques to sharpen the impact of campaign activities. For example, if polls reveal that a particular set of voters, such as blue collar workers of eastern and southern European heritage, are undecided about for whom to vote, it is important to be able to find these voters within the constituency. Computer analyses of census data can aid in the identification of where these voters reside. With these targeting data in hand, the campaign organization can develop an appropriate plan for directing the campaign's direct mail, phone banks, door-to-door canvassing, and media purchases. The close link between survey research and demographic targeting was summarized by Samuel Kernell, who observed:

> Just as benchmark surveys tell candidates who to appeal to and how, survey-driven targeting identifies where these receptive voters are to be found. Answering these "who," and "how," and "where" questions is indispensable for becoming a serious candidate.[32]

For the actual contacting of voters there are also new techniques. Direct mail specialists can enable candidates to rifle shot their appeals to selected voter groups with a message that is apt to strike a responsive chord with the group being courted. Television has supplanted the political party for national, statewide, and some congressional or local campaigns as the principal conduit between the candidate and the voters. Politicians have adapted to the television revolution by seeking to exploit its capacity to contact individual voters. Media consultants are hired in virtually all major campaigns to develop media advertising. Campaigns also have as one of their objectives the gaining of as much free exposure on newscasts and interview shows as possible. Publicity on hard news programs is particularly valuable because viewers are naturally more wary of candidate advertisements than of candidate images conveyed on regular news programs. Campaigns, therefore, are designed with the help of media consultants to capture as much news publicity as possible. As Austin Ranney has noted:

> One of the most valued tricks of the consultants' trade is knowing how to invent and stage campaign events that will serve *both* the broadcasters' need for good visuals and newsworthiness *and* the candidate's need for free and favorable exposure.[33]

A New Campaign Technology: Wooing Voters, Dollars, and Endorsements on the Net

In 1996 Senator Bob Dole made campaign history when he announced his Web site during a debate with President Clinton. By 1998 almost every candidate for major office and many local candidates as well maintained a Web site. These Web sites provided not only the traditional fare of candidate resumes and issue positions, but also encouraged supporters to donate money, to pass on e-mail endorsements to friends and newspapers, and to participate in the campaign via their computers. Among the innovative uses of Web sites and e-mail in the 1998 midterm elections were the following.

- Senator Barbara Boxer's (D-Calif.) director of technical operations e-mailed 3,000 of her supporters urging them to voice their opinions when her GOP opponent, State Treasurer Matt Fong, appeared on a virtual town hall meeting hosted by a Los Angeles affiliate of NBC. On her Web site, visitors could click on the "Get Involved" symbol and find out how to host a house party, send letters to newspaper editors, or pass on e-mail information kits to friends. Boxer even advertised her Web site on a dozen Web sites of California newspapers and magazines.
- Ohio's Republican gubernatorial candidate, Robert Taft, at his Web site urged supporters to type in their zip codes in order to receive a list of radio talk shows airing their locales so that they could call in and talk up Taft's candidacy.
- In Indiana, the Web site of Evan Bayh, the Democratic nominee for governor, was set up so that visitors could give their credit card numbers and make contributions to his campaign.

As more and more households go on line, it is anticipated that the campaigns in 2000 will more fully utilize the Web and do so in highly sophisticated ways.

Source: William Booth, "Netizen Kane?: More Politicians Use Web to Woo Voters, Donors, Volunteers," *Washington Post,* October 17, 1998, pp. A1, A10.

Among the gimmicks used by candidates to attract news coverage is the "walking" campaign. It was pioneered by Lawton Chiles who walked the length of the Florida peninsula to win a Senate seat in 1970, and by Dan Walker to become Illinois' governor in 1972. Bob Graham, with the help of media consultant Robert Squier, moved from being an obscure state senator to the Florida governor's residence by working one day each at one hundred mainly bluecollar jobs. The press gave him substantial publicity and Squier filmed Graham at his various jobs and made advertisements from the clips for later use in the campaign.[34]

A campaign innovation used extensively beginning in 1992 has been the use of "talk shows" as a means to reach the voters. Clinton was especially effective with appearances on such nontraditional candidate forums as "Larry King Live," MTV, and the Arsenio Hall and Phil Donahue shows. President Bush at first resisted appearing on what he characterized as these "weird talk shows," but he, too, eventually participated in the "talk show campaign." The candidates also brought their campaigns to America's breakfast tables as they were interviewed on early morning programs like "Today" and "Good Morning America."

The talk show format held advantages for Clinton, a candidate who was skilled in the informal give and take of voter forums and town hall meetings. Unlike the tough questions posed by national political reporters about campaign tactics, polls, and inconsistencies in policy positions, the less confrontational questions of the talk shows concerned how the candidates would solve problems on the minds of callers and members of a studio audience. This type of forum gave candidates a chance to reach voters on subjects they cared about without having their messages "stepped on" by reporters. Clinton, in particular, also sought to bypass the tough national media by using satellite hookups with local reporters in crucial media markets. Since local reporters tended to ask "softer" questions than the national media, the candidate could be more effective in conveying his intended message to voters.

In the 1980s and 1990s, a large share of candidates' budgets in statewide races was devoted to television advertisements. Indeed, in big states like California, campaigns have become largely television advertising campaigns, as the opposing candidates "debate" each other and seek to influence voters via 30-second television spots designed by media consultants. Often these media campaigns emphasize attack ads, featuring harsh criticism of an opponent's record and character. Criticism of an opponent, particularly one's record in public office, has always been a standard and legitimate part of American electoral politics. However, in recent elections television attack ads have, in the view of many close observers, crossed over the line between legitimate criticism of an individual's record and outright distortion. Increasingly, candidates' organizations have followed a strategy of responding quickly to such attacks either by seeking to correct a gross distortion or by launching an attack ad campaign of their own. As the *Washington Post's* Paul Taylor has commented: "When the cross-fire of these kinds of ads begins two rules of engagement stand out: Rebuttals rarely catch up with accusations, and issues rarely compete with character."[35] In this kind of atmosphere, candidates' media consultants, except for the candidates themselves, become the most prominent and often controversial participants in the electoral process.

The use of media, pollsters, direct mail specialists, computer analysis, and other modern techniques of campaigning requires a campaign plan, a high level of financial support, cash flow management, and skilled management. As a result, most major campaigns involve professional campaign managers and planners. The need for such services has increased the cost of campaigns. It also has encouraged candidate centered campaigning because no party organization is currently in a position to provide candidates with all the sophisticated services they need to run an effective campaign. In their striving to compete, candidates have gone out and personally raised the funds necessary to have access to needed campaign technology and professionals. In the process, the party organization has been largely bypassed and the dominant campaign organization has become the personal organization of the candidate. At the same time, a major new industry has developed—the campaign consultant industry. The parties themselves have even encouraged these trends by insisting that candidates whom they support financially hire professionals and use modern techniques as a condition for receiving national party contributions.

Incumbency

Incumbency normally carries with it advantages. The resources and privileges of public office enable incumbents to publicize themselves and build support through the positions they take and the decisions they make. Incumbents are better known than challengers and they have built-in ways of reaching the voters. Incumbent members of Congress stay in contact with their constituents through newsletters, surveys of constituent opinion, special targeted mailings, news releases, radio and television tapes, and meetings with constituent groups. Skilled incumbents use the rights and duties of public office in a way that projects the image of caring and conscientious legislators fulfilling their obligations to constituents. Voters often see these newsletters, office hours in the district, casework to help constituents having problems with the federal bureaucracy, and advocacy of programs to benefit the constituency as instances of members of Congress merely performing their official duties. By contrast, voters see challengers as "politicians" or "campaigners" interested primarily in winning votes on election day. The self advertisement efforts of all incumbent members of the House have meant that they are not only well known to their constituents, but they are normally thought of in positive terms. By contrast, most House challengers are not well known to the voters, who have difficulty making an evaluation of their qualifications.[36]

Incumbency is less of an advantage for senators than it is for House members. Senators normally are elected from more competitive constituencies than representatives. Incumbent senators can expect, because of the prominence of the office, that a major campaign will be run against them and that their opponents will receive substantial funding and free publicity. In the case of the House elections, voters frequently do not know much about the challengers because only a weak campaign is run on their behalf. Voters are, however, more likely to know the alternative choices before them in Senate elections. The incumbent advantage of senators is, therefore, reduced.

The pomp and circumstance of the presidency is impossible for any challenger to match. President Reagan's visit to the beaches of Normandy to commemorate the fortieth anniversary of D-Day in World War II provided a dramatic and emotional setting for an incumbent president seeking reelection in 1984. His trip to China also gave him major publicity advantages over his rivals. Indeed, the advantages of the presidency are so great that some incumbents adopt a "Rose Garden" strategy of campaigning. This involves staying close to the White House and arranging events for television in the Oval Office and the Rose Garden which show the president performing his responsibilities for the nation, while his opponent is out campaigning. During the 1976 presidential campaign, President Ford's advisors made full use of this technique after they discovered that his ratings in the polls were higher when he stayed in the White House than when he was on the road campaigning. And in 1980, President Carter for a time stopped campaigning for reelection outside the White House on the pretext that the Iranian hostage crisis required his full time attention at the White House.

Incumbent executives, especially the president and governors, are also in a position to claim credit for all the positive things that have occurred during their tenure. Presidents Eisenhower, Reagan, and Clinton therefore, were able to run on themes of peace and prosperity during their reelection campaigns of 1956, 1984, and 1996. Incumbency is, however, a two edged sword. Presidents can also be held accountable for the negative things that have happened while they have been in office. Presidents Ford (1976), Carter (1980), and Bush (1992) found that the voters were unforgiving about a faltering economy and foreign policy setbacks. It makes little difference that presidents cannot control all aspects of our domestic and international condition. They are still likely to be held accountable.

Incumbent senators and representatives have fewer problems than presidents with being held accountable for adverse conditions in the nation and world. Members of the Congress tend to be judged by their constituents not on the basis of the record of the institution of which they are members, but rather upon their own individual records. Therefore, they are somewhat insulated from voter resentment about the state of the union, provided they have used their incumbency to build voter trust.

A further advantage of incumbency, especially in the case of legislative campaigns, is the ease incumbents have in raising money. Incumbents consistently have more money to spend on their campaigns than do challengers in both House and Senate races. This pattern is illustrated in figure 7.6, which presents the mean expenditures in 1996 House races for incumbents and challengers of both parties. Incumbents had average expenditures that were more than $391,974 higher than those of challengers. Such summary numbers, however, mask the full extent of incumbent financial advantage in campaigns. Many challengers fall far below

Figure 7.6
MEAN EXPENDITURES OF U.S. HOUSE CANDIDATES, 1995–1996

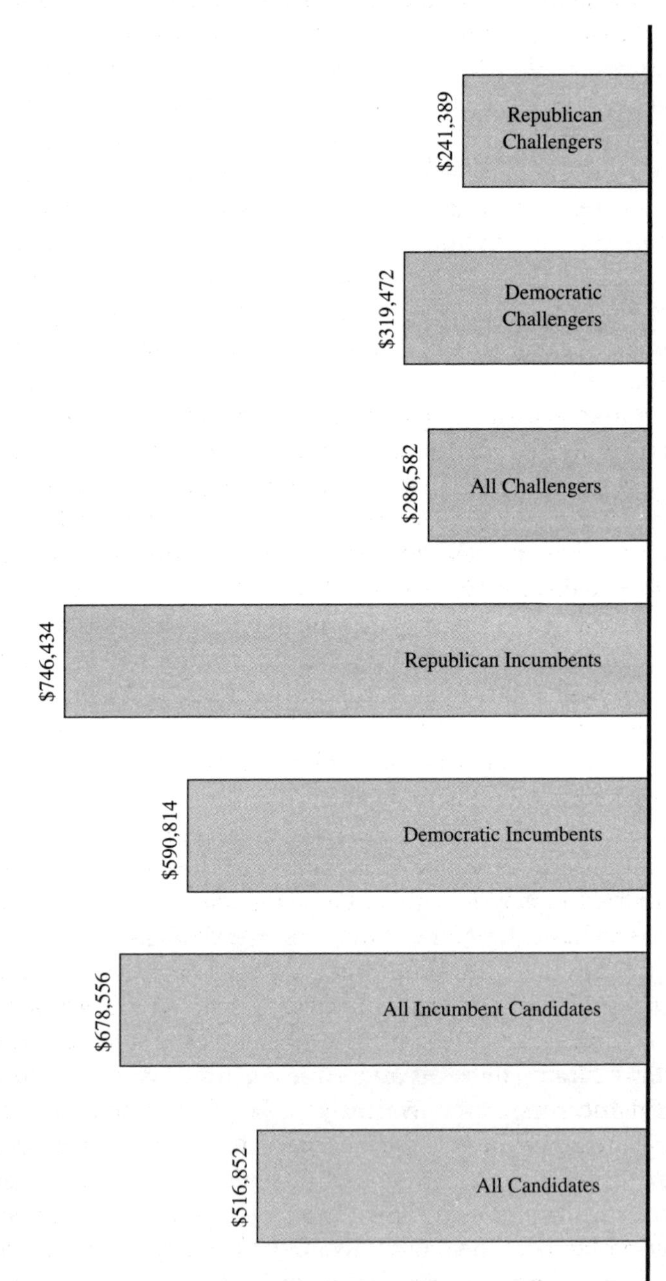

Source: Thomas E. Mann, Norman J. Ornstein, and Michael J. Malbin, *Vital Statistics on Congress 1997–1998* (Washington, D.C.: Congressional Quarterly, 1998), pp. 81–82.

the average expenditure figure cited in figure 7.6. For example, the Democratic challengers, who failed to gain 40 percent of the vote, spent an average of only $96,758 on their campaigns, while their incumbent GOP opponents had mean expenditures of $583,946. Similarly, the average spending by a Republican challenger who lost to a Democratic incumbent who gained more than 60 percent of the vote, was a mere $107,822, compared to a mean expenditure by the incumbent of $477,204.[37] Such financial advantages for incumbents affect the way they campaign. Incumbents are much more likely to have campaign staffs composed of paid professionals than are their opponents, who must rely more heavily on volunteer assistance.[38]

There is one particular set of candidates for whom incumbency has traditionally created severe difficulties. These are incumbent vice presidents seeking to succeed a president of their own party. Vice presidents running for president in their own right find themselves in a particularly restricted position in terms of campaign strategy. One of their claims to being qualified for the presidency is their service as vice president. Most claim that they were involved in the major decisions of the administration in which they served. The problem with such claims is that every administration after it has been in office for a time makes decisions that offend sizeable numbers of voters. This presents the vice president with a dilemma. If he gives unqualified support to the administration's policies, he risks losing the support of key voter groups. But if he suggests that he disagrees with some aspects of administration policy, he confesses to a lack of influence in the administration in which he claims to have been a key policy maker. And if he seeks to put distance between himself and the president, the vice president runs the risk of losing the support of the president's supporters. The liabilities inherent in the vice presidency were major problems for Richard Nixon in 1960 and Hubert Humphrey in 1968 as they sought the presidency. Walter Mondale found in 1984, four years after leaving office, that service in the vice presidency during the Carter administration was a serious drawback for his campaign.

Even George Bush, who became the first incumbent vice president to be elected to the presidency since Martin Van Buren in 1836, had to endure and overcome charges that he was a "wimp" because of his reluctance to distance himself from Reagan administration policies.

Majority versus Minority Party Status

Candidates have customarily placed differing emphasis on partisan themes depending on whether they were the nominees of the majority or minority party. Majority party candidates have normally stressed party-type appeals and sought to rally the faithful to turn out and vote because if the faithful respond to the call, then the party's candidate is assured of victory. As the dominant party in terms of the electorate's party identification since the Great Depression of the 1930s, the Democratic party nationally has emphasized partisan Democratic appeals to the electorate. Past accomplishments of the party and its heroes have been stressed along with negative characterizations of the Republicans (e.g., "the party of the rich"). Because pro-Democratic voters groups have tended to have lower rates of turnout than Republican leaning voters, special efforts have been made to mobilize Democrats to get to the polls on election day. The Democratic candidates have stressed their party's label in campaign literature and advertising. Thus when Democrats were faced with the prospect of sizeable defections to the independent candidacy of John B. Anderson in 1980, they urged their supporters not to "waste" their votes and thereby help the Republicans through a vote for Anderson.

The minority party Republicans have faced since the 1930s a quite different strategic problem. Just holding their party together and turning out its affiliates on election day would not bring the GOP victory. They not only have needed to turn out their own vote, but they have also had to win over substantial numbers of independents and dissident Democrats. As a result, most Republican presidential campaigns have downplayed partisan Republican appeals. Instead, the party has often blurred the differences between the parties and sought to capitalize upon a more compelling cue than partisanship for voters to use in making their choice. The nomination of a World War II hero whose appeal transcended partisanship, Dwight D. Eisenhower, in 1952 and 1956 was a particularly effective tactic. Exploitation of major differences within the Democratic party, as in 1968 and 1972, has also proven effective. Less successful have been the "me-too" campaigns of the 1940s and 1960, which offered little in the way of differences between the Republicans and their Democratic opponents. The successful Reagan campaigns of 1980 and 1984 used a combination of all these minority party strategies. The candidate was an attractive and amiable former movie actor, who was fond of quoting Democratic stars like Franklin Roosevelt, John F. Kennedy, and Harry Truman, while also dramatizing major policy splits among Democrats.

As party identification has declined in importance as a basis for voter choice in presidential elections, the significance of majority-minority status in determining campaign strategy has been reduced. In addition, surveys conducted in the 1980s and 1990s have revealed that the two major parties were approaching parity in terms of the party identification of the voters. If this division between the parties continues within the electorate, it will further reduce the impact of majority-minority party status on campaign strategy.

Debates

Debates have now become a standard part of presidential campaigns and candidates debates or forums are common in contests for other offices. The debate format is not neutral in its impact. The presidential debates have generally worked to the advantage of the challenger or less experienced candidate. Debates elevate the challenger to equal status with the president by putting both individuals on the same stage and making both respond to the same questions and to each other. The aura of the presidency tends to be temporarily removed from the incumbent as he faces his opponent one-on-one on a sparsely furnished stage. The incumbent's claims about the importance of experience tend to be diminished when the challenger acquits himself reasonably well against the president. A clear example of this occurred in 1976 when Gerald Ford, the experienced national politician, met Jimmy Carter, who had held no federal office. Carter was reasonably effective in his debates, but Ford's campaign suffered a serious setback because he left the mistaken impression that in his opinion Eastern Europe was not under the domination of the Soviet Union.

Since the media tends to hype the debates and give them prime time coverage, the candidates tend to see them as make-or-break events.[39] Extended negotiations, therefore, normally occur between the candidates' managers over the format of the debates—all aimed at preventing the opposition from gaining any procedural advantage. The wrangling over the number, timing, and format of the debates was particularly protracted in 1992, lasting until late September. This reflected the Bush camp's lack of enthusiasm for debating

Clinton, who was generally considered more articulate and practiced in the debate format. In addition, Bush's strategist James Baker believed that voters' decisions tend to be "frozen" as they await the debates. Baker hoped that by delaying an agreement on the debates, the Bush camp could narrow Clinton's lead in the polls. It was acknowledged, however, that the debates were inevitable because they are now such an institutionalized part of presidential elections.

The end result of the Bush-Clinton negotiations was a series of debates with formats that were helpful to Clinton's candidacy. Perot was allowed to participate because both Bush and Clinton anticipated that his presence would help their candidacies—Bush hoped that Perot would cut into Clinton's lead, and Clinton expected Perot to attack Bush's record on the economy and in the process reinforce Clinton's principal campaign theme. It was Clinton's expectation that proved closer to the mark than Bush's hope. The candidates' negotiators finally agreed to three different debate formats: the traditional questioning by a panel of reporters; a candidates' discussion led by a sole moderator; and questioning by an audience of undecided voters. The audience participation format was especially advantageous for Clinton who had gained experience and skill in responding to audiences during his nominating campaign.

In the predebate negotiations of 1996, the Clinton campaign was also successful in securing procedural arrangements that were to the president's advantage. Dole was trailing in the polls, and his campaign wanted four debates, with the last debate taking place close to election day. Seeking to avoid any unnecessary risks to their front-running status in the campaign, Clinton and his strategists wanted only two debates—one using their preferred town hall format, and both well before the election. In return for Clinton agreeing to exclude third-party candidate Ross Perot from the debates, Dole agreed to all of Clinton's debate demands. Dole feared that Perot's participation in the debates would boost Perot's vote and split the anti-Clinton voters. Presidential advisor, George Stephenopoulos, summed up how Clinton got the debate format he was seeking as follows.

> They [the Dole people] didn't have leverage going into negotiations. They were behind. They needed to make sure Perot wasn't in it. As long as we would agree to Perot not being in it, we could get everything else we wanted going in. We got our time frame. We got our length, we got our moderator.[40]

With a massive television audience (35 million to 45 million viewers per debate in 1996; 66 million in 1992), debates have the potential to damage or help presidential nominees. As a general rule, the candidate who is perceived to have "won" the debate tends to make a modest gain in the polls.[41] For example, George Bush had a net gain of 2.8 percentage points over Michael Dukakis after the second debate, which viewers believed Bush had won. In 1996, Clinton was generally perceived to have won the debates. By presenting a positive image of his record and policies while avoiding angry reactions to Dole's attacks, he was able to maintain his double digit lead in the polls after the debates.

There is little evidence that vice presidential debates have any consistent effect on the standings of the candidates. This was true even in 1988, when there was a lopsided public assessment that Democrat Lloyd Bentsen had bested Republican Dan Quayle in their debate.[42]

While the "winner" of the debates may receive a modest upward "bump" in the polls, it is unlikely that the "bump" will be of a sufficient magnitude to alter the course of the race unless the contest is extremely close going into the debate. The impact of the debates is further limited by the fact that, for many viewers, the debates tend to reinforce their preexisting candidate preferences. That is, most viewers think their preferred candidate won the debate, and those who are dissatisfied with their candidate's performance are likely to say that the debate was a tie.[43]

The history of televised debates also demonstrates that it is not so much the substance of what is said that matters as it is the image of the candidates that is conveyed. The press tends to judge the debates in terms of winners and losers and press judgments affect the public's assessment. Voters in general do not follow the content of the debates carefully and do not normally have great confidence in their ability to make judgments concerning the substance of the debate. They, therefore, tend to rely rather heavily on media commentaries on the debates. As a result, immediately after the event, there is frequently a rather even split between the candidates in the viewers' minds about who won the debate. However, after several days of press commentary there is usually a shift by the public in the direction of the verdict rendered by the press. A dramatic example of this tendency occurred in 1976 when viewers by a two-to-one margin said that Ford had won the second debate.

After heavy press coverage of Ford's gaffe regarding the Soviet domination of Eastern Europe, public opinion shifted two-to-one to Carter's advantage.[44] Similarly in the 1984 debates, there was a strong shift in the voters' judgment about who won the first Reagan-Mondale debate between the night of the debate and two days later. After extensive media discussion of Reagan's lackluster performance, the percent of voters saying he won the debate dropped from 34 to 17 percent and those saying Mondale won went from 43 to 66 percent.[45]

Issues

Throughout the years from the Great Depression in the 1930s until the 1980 election, Democratic candidates generally had a clear advantage over the Republicans when dealing with domestic issues. Through their sponsorship and expansion of a vast array of government programs, which Republicans frequently opposed, the Democrats were in a position to seek support from virtually every major group in American society. The party has also had a favorable image on economic issues. When asked which party they believed was best for the economy, employment, and jobs, voters from the 1930s to 1980 consistently favored the Democrats. As a result, in elections when pocketbook issues were salient (e.g., 1960, 1976), the Democrats were at a distinct advantage. Indeed, during much of this period, Republican candidates sought to downplay domestic issues and emphasize foreign policy concerns (1952—"Bring the boys home from Korea"; 1968—"End the war in Vietnam") or the general management of the government (1952—"the mess in Washington"). The public's perceptions of the parties changed significantly during the Carter administration and the 1980 campaign. For the first time since the 1930s, voters began to view the GOP candidate as best for the economy, no doubt reflecting the double digit inflation, rising unemployment, and high interest rates of the later years of the Carter administration.[46] The Republicans lost their economic policy advantage during the serious 1981–1982 recession that occurred during the first Reagan administration. However, an improved economy during 1984 and 1988 enabled the Republicans to achieve a favorable rating from the electorate in terms of their ability to handle the economy. But with most Americans believing that the economy was in the doldrums and the Republican Bush administration on the defensive, the Democrats regained the advantage on economic issues in 1992 and captured the White House for the first time since 1976. Basking in a vibrant economy of the 1990s, the Democrats retained their advantage on the economic issue in 1996, as well as on environmental, health care, education, and abortion issues. On other domestic issues—controlling government spending, welfare reform, taxes, promoting moral values—the GOP held the advantage.

With partisan advantage on the economy and domestic issues having shifted frequently between the two parties in recent elections, it is clear that American politics has emerged from the New Deal era and that neither party has a continuing lock on these issues. Rather, the electorate appears quite capable of venting its frustrations on either party, depending upon which one it holds responsible for the state of the nation. Thus an electorate which in 1992 banished the Bush administration from the White House for its seeming lack of sensitivity to the public's economic concerns turned right around two years later and gave the Republicans a resounding victory that included control of the Congress for the first time in over forty years. Then, amid the prosperity of 1996, the voters rewarded Bill Clinton with a second term and continued GOP control of Congress.

The Republicans' traditional disadvantage in domestic issues was partially offset by an advantage they carried regarding foreign policy. Voters during the period from the Korean War through 1972 tended to perceive the GOP as the party best for peace, though the party temporarily lost this advantage during the 1964 campaign. As a result, Republicans tended to be advantaged when foreign policy issues were highly salient, as during the Korean War in 1952 and the Vietnam War in 1968. Foreign policy issues also helped the GOP in 1972, when the Democratic nominee, Senator George McGovern (D-S.D.), and his policies of quick withdrawal from Vietnam, opposition to continued military support for the government of Vietnam, sharp cuts in defense spending, and a willingness to beg North Vietnam for release of American POWs caused deep divisions within the Democratic ranks.

The Republicans' historic advantage on foreign policy issues was lost to the Democrats during the 1976–1984 elections. During this period, voters perceived the Democratic party ahead of the GOP in terms of being best for peace (though the Republicans came out ahead on the party best for maintaining a strong defense). In

1988, the Republicans regained their advantage over the Democrats as the party whom voters perceived as best for handling nuclear arms agreements, dealing with the Soviet Union, dealing with international terrorism, and maintaining national security. Voters continued to prefer having Bush handle foreign affairs in 1992. The voters preference for Bush over Clinton was small consolation to the GOP, however, because few voters considered foreign policy a basis for making their decisions on election day. With no major crisis facing the nation, foreign policy was again a low salience issue in 1996.

A third cluster of issues involves social issues such as crime, traditional morality, law and order, abortion, race relations, and school prayer. These are issues that often stir deep emotions, and they tend to affect the parties in different ways. As a coalition of free market libertarians and social conservatives, the GOP can usually stay united so long as it concentrates on economic issues where both factions are in essential agreement on government's limited role. But when social issues come to the fore, the party risks serious schisms because the free marketers favor individual choice and the social conservatives favor government intervention.

Social issues also hold the capacity to split the Democratic coalition which contains traditional Democrats—often white middle-class southern voters—who do not share the enthusiasm which its liberal egalitarian elements have for such policies as affirmative action, cutting defense, protecting a woman's right to an abortion, or promoting gay rights.

Candidate Image

There are no hard and fast rules to guide candidates in terms of how to conduct their campaigns to achieve a favorable personal image, though homilies abound—appear decisive, don't appear trigger happy, the best defense is a strong offense, carry the attack to your opponent. Personal characteristics that voters believe are important tend to vary depending upon the condition in which the country finds itself. Thus Jimmy Carter's outsider, non-Washingtonian, peanut farmer, righteous image had substantial appeal to a nation reeling from the traumas of the Vietnam War and Watergate. Throughout the 1976 presidential campaign, Carter stressed these images to a public anxious for a president who radiated honesty and religious conviction. In the changed circumstances of 1980, as the country faced severe economic problems and foreign policy setbacks, effective leadership became the personal quality voters sought in a president. And effective leadership was what voters thought they were not getting from Carter, while they perceived Ronald Reagan to be a stronger leader. Again, in 1984 and 1988 leadership was the top rated presidential quality for the voters. In both elections, the Republicans gained substantial electoral advantage from the experience factor. Thus in 1988, CNN-*Los Angeles Times* exit polls showed 34 percent of the voters citing "more experience" as the basis for their vote choice, with 97 percent favoring Bush and only 3 percent favoring Dukakis. Dukakis was also hurt by the Bush campaign's portrayal of him as a liberal.[47] In 1996, Clinton had a generally favorable image with the public, although a significant number of voters questioned his integrity. Dole was perceived more negatively than positively, with concerns about his age bothering many voters.[48]

There is frequent commentary about how candidates can manipulate their images through skillful use of the mass media. In fact, however, candidate images are not easily created and altered. For example, candidates cannot control the topics that will be raised by their opponents or journalists, nor can they erase their past records. Candidates for major office that are not well known to the public have the greatest opportunity to create a favorable image during the early stages of their campaigns. While candidate image can be influential in affecting voter choice for high visibility races, such as those for president or governor, the impact of candidate image normally declines as one goes lower down the ballot, because these candidates are less well known and less visible.[49]

To a significant degree elections are about performance, as the voters render a verdict on an incumbent and the incumbent's party's record in office. That is, elections involve retrospective voting on the part of the citizenry. Abramson, Aldrich, and Rohde after analyzing National Election Study data between 1976 and 1992, emphasize this point when they concluded:

> The 1976 election, with its razor-edge for Carter, was a very narrow rejection of Ford's incumbency, and 1980 was a clear and strong rejection of Carter's. In 1984, Reagan won in large because he was seen as having performed well. In 1988, Bush won in large because Reagan was seen as having performed well—and people thought Bush would stay the course. In 1992 Bush lost because of the

far more negative evaluation of his administration and of his party than had obtained in any other recent election except 1980 . . . an election in which the incumbent lost the election.[50]

The Campaign and Governance

Although candidates can vary their campaign strategies and can hire experts to devise the seemingly most effective strategy, all are restricted by conditions over which they have little or limited control—election laws, the state of the economy, international conditions, campaign resources, public images of the parties, and the partisan division of the electorate between Republicans and Democrats. Candidates, therefore, must tailor their campaigns to fit conditions or run the risk of defeat or a serious decline in electoral support.

The impact of the campaign, however, goes well beyond its importance in terms of influencing voter decisions (the topic of chapter 8). The campaign also affects the behavior of public officials after the election. Perceptions of the public, of societal problems, and of important interest groups that must be accommodated are influenced by campaign experiences. Obligations to the public in terms of campaign pledges to key constituency groups often mean that public officials feel honor bound to pursue particular policies once in office. Many elected officials recruit key staff personnel from their campaign organizations. But most importantly, the outcome of the campaign determines which party will control the government and by how large a margin. Which party holds power influences the direction of public policy.

Suggestions for Further Reading

Abramson, Paul R.; Aldrich, John H.; and Rohde, David W. *Change and Continuity in the 1992 Elections.* Washington, D.C.: CQ Press, 1994.

Biersack, Robert; Herrnson, Paul S.; and Wilcox, Clyde, eds. *Risky Business: PAC Decisionmaking in Congressional Elections.* Armonk, N.Y.: M.E. Sharpe, 1994.

Herrnson, Paul S. *Congressional Elections: Campaigning at Home and in Washington,* 2nd ed. Washington, D.C.: CQ Press, 1998.

Jamieson, Kathleen Hall. *Packaging the Presidency: A History and Criticism of Presidential Campaign Advertising.* 2nd ed. New York: Oxford University Press, 1992.

Holbrook, Thomas M. *Do Campaigns Matter?* Thousand Oaks, Calif.: Sage, 1996.

Nelson, Michael, ed., *The Elections of 1992.* Washington, D.C.: CQ Press, 1993.

Polsby, Nelson W., and Wildavsky, Aaron. *Presidential Elections: Strategies in American and Electoral Politics.* 9th ed. Chatham, N.J.: Chatham House, 1996.

Rozell, Mark, and Wilcox, Clyde. *Interest Groups in American Campaigns: The New Face of Electioneering.* Washington, D.C.: CQ Press, 1999.

Salmore, Stephen A., and Salmore, Barbara G. *Candidates, Parties, and Campaigns.* 2d ed. Washington, D.C.: CQ Press, 1989.

Sorauf, Frank J. *Inside Campaign Finance: Myths and Realities.* New Haven, Conn.: Yale University Press, 1992.

Thurber, James A., and Nelson, Candice J., eds. *Campaigns and Elections, American Style.* Boulder, Colo.: Westview Press, 1995.

West, Darrell M. *Air Wars: Television Advertising in Election Campaigns, 1952–1996.* 2nd. ed. Washington, D.C.: CQ Press, 1997.

Notes

1. *Smith v. Allright,* 321 U.S. 649 (1944).

2. V. O. Key, Jr., *Politics, Parties, and Pressure Groups,* 5th ed. (New York: Crowell, 1964), P. 644.

3. Michael Weisskopf, "The Professional Touch," *Washington Post,* November 8, 1994, p. A3.

4. John F. Harris, "Clinton's Campaign Consultants Reaped Millions from TV Ads," *Washington Post,* January 4, 1998, p.A4.

5. Jon Jeter, "Campaign Reform Helped 'The Body" Slam Rivals," *Washington Post,* November 5, 1998, p. A41.

6. Gary C. Jacobson, *The Politics of Congressional Elections,* 4th ed. (New York: Longman, 1997), p. 104. On the impact of campaign spending, see also Paul Herrnson, *Congressional Elections* (Washington, D.C.: CQ Press, 1998), ch 9.

7. Guy Guliotta and Ira Chinoy, "Outsiders Made Erie Ballot a National Battle," *Washington Post,* February 10, 1997, p. A10.

8. Alan Greenblatt, "Labor Wants Out of the Limelight after Glare of Probes, Backlash," *Congressional Quarterly Weekly Report,* March 29, 1998,pp.788–789.

9. Eliza Newlin Carney, "Stealth Bombers," *National Journal,* August 16, 1997, pp. 1640–1643.

10. Allison Mitchell, "Building a War Chest: How Clinton Financed His Plan," *New York Times* (national edition), December 27, 1996, pp. A1, A12.

11. David S. Broder and Ruth Marcus, "Wielding Third Force in Politics," *Washington Post,* September 27, 1997, pp. A1, A6; David E, Rosenbaum, "Groups Spending $260 Million on Ads to Promote Agendas, *New York Times* (national edition), October 15, 1998, p. A21.

12. Ibid., p. A6.

13. Jill Abramson and Leslie Wayne, "Democrats Used the State Parties to Bypass Limits," *New York Times* (national edition), October 2, 1997, p. A4.

14. Larry Makinson, *The Big Picture: Money Follows Power Shift on Capitol Hill* (Washington, D.C.: Center for Responsive Politics, 1997), p. 3.

15. Michael. J. Malbin and Thomas L. Gais, *The Day After Reform: Sobering Campaign Finance Lessons from the American States* (Albany, N.Y.: Rockefeller Institute Press, 1998), pp. 52–54; 66–70.

16. Ruth S. Jones, "Financing State Elections," in Michael J. Malbin, ed., *Money and Politics in the United States: Financing Elections in the 1980s* (Chatham, N.J.: Chatham House, 1984), p. 203.

17. Malbin and Gais, *The Day After Reform*, pp. 136–138; see also Kenneth R. Mayer and John M. Wood, "The Impact of Public Financing on Electoral Competitiveness: Evidence from Wisconsin 1964–1990," *Legislative Studies Quarterly* 15 (February 1995): 69–88.

18. *Congressional Record* (daily edition, 89th Congress, 1st Session, April 4, 1967), pp. S4590–4592.

19. David E. Price, *Bringing Back the Parties* (Washington, D.C.: CQ Press, 1984), p. 243.

20. Ibid., pp. 244–245.

21. Ibid., p. 245.

22. "PAC Activity Increases in 1995–96 Election Cycle," Federal Election Commission press release, April 22, 1997.

23. E. J. Dionne, "Perot Seen Not Affecting the Vote Outcome," *Washington Post*, November 8, 1992, p. A36.

24. Paul R. Abramson, John H. Aldrich, and David W. Rohde, *Change and Continuity in the 1996 Elections* (Washington, D.C.: CQ Press, 1998), p. 248..

25. Nelson W. Polsby and Aaron Wildavsky, *Presidential Elections: Strategies of American Electoral Politics*, 9th ed. (Chatham, N.J.: Chatham House, 1996), p. 292.

26. Ibid., pp. 294–295.

27. For further discussions of electoral college reform, see Lawrence D. Longley and Alan G. Braun, *The Politics of Electoral College Reform* (New Haven: Yale University Press, 1972); Wallace S. Sayre and Judith H. Parris, *Voting for President* (Washington, D.C.: Brookings Institution, 1970); Thomas E. Cronin, "The Direct Vote and the Electoral College: The Case of Messing Things Up?," *Presidential Studies Quarterly* (Spring 1979), pp. 178–188; Alexander M. Bickel, *Reform and Continuity: The Electoral College, The Convention, and the Party System* (New York: Harper Colophon Books, 1971).

28. Darrell M. West, *Air Wars: Television Advertising in Election Campaigns,*

1952–1992 (Washington, D.C.: CQ Press, 1993), pp. 121–123.; On the impact of campaigns, see Stephen A. Salmore and Barbara G. Salmore, *Candidates, Parties, and Campaigns*, 2d ed. (Washington, D.C.: CQ Press, 1989).

29. Darrell M. West, *Air Wars: Television Advertising in Election Campaigns, 1952-1996*, 2d ed. (Washington, D.C.: CQ Press, 1997), pp. 141–142.

30. Adam Clymer, "Poll Shows Iran and Economy Center among Late-Shifting Voters," *New York Times*, Nov. 16, 1980, pp. 1, 32.

31. Data from exit polls conducted by Voter Research and Surveys, reported in *American Enterprise*, January/ February, 1993, p. 106.

32. Samuel Kernell, "A Primer on Demographic Targeting," *Election Politics* 1 (Winter 1983–84): 18.

33. Austin Ranney, *Channels of Power: The Impact of Television on American Politics* (New York: Basic Books, 1983), p. 114.

34. Ibid., p. 115.

35. Paul Taylor, "Armed with Distortions, Candidates Attack," *Washington Post*, Sept. 21, 1990, pp. Al, A10.

36. Jacobson, *The Politics of Congressional Elections*, pp. 28–34 and ch. 5.

37. Mann, Ornstein, and Malbin, *Vital Statistics on Congress, 1997–1998*, pp. 88–89.

38. Edie N. Goldenburg and Michael W. Traugott, *Campaigning for Congress* (Washington, D.C.: CQ Press, 1984), p. 21.

39. For a thorough analysis of the impact of presidential debates and of the scholarly literature on debates, see Thomas M. Holbrook, *Do Elections Matter?* (Thousand Oaks, Calif.: Sage, 1996), ch. 5.

40. David S. Broder, "Campaigns Without Shame," *Washington Post*, September 24, 1997, p. A21.

41. Holbrook, *Do Elections Matter?* p. 114.

42. Ibid.

43. Ibid., p. 123.

44. Thomas E. Patterson, "Television and Election Strategy," in Gerald Benjamin, ed., *The Communications Revolution in Politics* (New York: Academy of Political Science, 1982), p. 31.

45. Kathleen A. Frankovic, "The 1984 Election: The Irrelevance of the Campaign," *P.S.* 18 (Winter 1985): 43.

46. William Schneider, "The November 4 Vote for President: What Did It Mean?" in Austin Ranney, ed., *The American Elections of 1980* (Washington, D.C.: American Enterprise Institute, 1981), p. 231; *Gallup Poll Index*, Report No. 181, Sept. 1980, p. 19.

47. "Explaining Their Vote," *National Journal*, Nov. 21, 1988, p. 2844.

48. Abramson, Aldrich, and Rohde, *Change and Continuity in the 1996*

Elections, p. 163.

49. William H. Flanigan and Nancy H. Zingale, *Political Behavior of the American Electorate*, 9th ed. (Washington, D.C.: CQ Press, 1998), pp. 166–170.

50. Paul R. Abramson, John H. Aldrich, and David W. Rohde, *Change and Continuity in the 1992 Elections* (Washington, D.C.: CQ Press, 1994), p. 216.

8 POLITICAL PARTIES AND THE VOTERS

CHAPTER EIGHT

When the party nominating processes have narrowed the list of candidates and the campaign maneuverings have ended on election eve, it is the voter who decides the fate of the parties and their candidates. Parties cannot survive or exercise significant influence on the affairs of state without substantial voter support, because modern democratic governments derive their legitimacy through free elections. The nature of the party-in-the-electorate, therefore, is crucial to understanding the parties' role in the political process. Which voters will actually turn out and go to the polls on election day? How strong is the pull of partisanship in determining voter choices? Which party will benefit from the short term influences of current issues and candidates' images? The electoral fate of the parties is tied up in the answers to these questions, which are the focus of this chapter.

Voter Turnout

Although free elections are critical to the functioning of the republic, a relatively low proportion of the American electorate actually took advantage of its right to the franchise in 1996. The U.S. Bureau of the Census reported that in 1996, 48.9 percent of the voting age population cast ballots.[1] This figure constituted a decrease of 6.2 percent over 1992 and reflected the general downward trend in turnout since 1960.

Voter turnout varies significantly depending upon the timing of the election and the offices being contested. There is also substantial variation among the states in their rates of voter turnout.

Figure 8.1 demonstrates that voter turnout is substantially higher in presidential election years than it is in midterm elections for the House of Representatives. Presidential elections are characterized by saturation news coverage and intense campaigns. As a result, voters receive more stimuli to vote in these years than they do in midterm congressional elections. Since 1952, the fall-off in turnout from presidential elections to the next midterm congressional election has averaged 17.6 percent. Turnout also varies between offices being contested. As is shown in figure 8.1, there is a fall-off in voter participation between presidential balloting and voting for the House of Representatives in presidential election years.

Figure 8.1
VOTER TURNOUT IN PRESIDENTIAL AND HOUSE ELECTIONS, 1952–1996

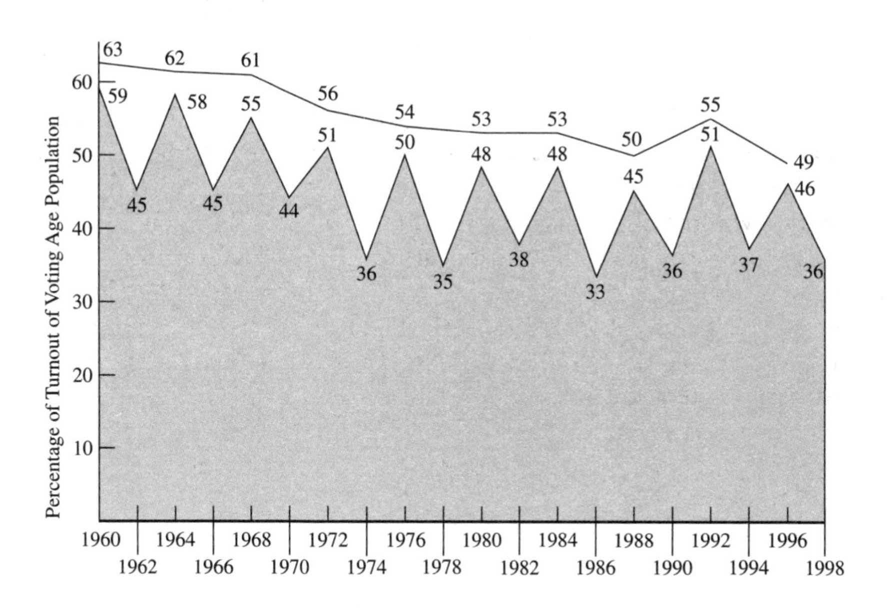

Source: Statistical Abstract of the United States, 1997, p. 289; 1998 data is from the Committee for the Study of the American Electorate.

Among the states, there are major differences in rates of turnout (see table 8.1), with southern and southwestern states having the lowest levels of voter participation. Political scientists have found that these varied turnout rates are related to both the political and the demographic characteristics of the states. Interparty competition is highly correlated with turnout: as the chances that either party may win goes up, the people are more likely to vote.[2] Campaign spending can also increase turnout because as more money is spent voters are provided with more information about the candidates, which increases the likelihood that they will vote.[3]

Turnout is also affected by the socioeconomic makeup of the state population. The following characteristics are associated with higher levels of election day turnout: high incomes, high status occupations, high levels of educational achievement, middle age Jewish heritage, Catholicism, and being white. A study has shown that more than half of the variation among the states in voter turnout was caused by differences in race, age, income and educational level.[4] Differences in state registration requirements can also cause differential turnout rates. The restrictiveness of these regulations varies tremendously. For example, North Dakota has no registration requirements; Wisconsin requires registration only in urban areas; Maine, Minnesota, and Wisconsin permit registration at the polls. It has been estimated that if every state had registration laws as permissive as those in the most permissive states, turnout would rise by 9 percent.[5] With passage of the so-called "Motor Voter" law in 1993 by Congress, states are now required to implement a series of measures designed to make registration easier: registration of individuals applying for driver's licenses; registration by mail; and registration at designated government agencies, for example, public assistance offices and state-funded agencies serving persons with disabilities. During the first year that the law was in effect, the number of registered voters increased by 9.2 million, of which approximately 3.4 million can be attributed to citizens registering through new procedures mandated by the Motor Voter law.

Who Votes?

Demographic Characteristics. The two personal characteristics that are most closely related to voter turnout are *age* and *education* (see table 8.2). As age increases, so does turnout. Young

Table 8.1
Presidential Turnout Rates, 1992, 1996
(percent of voting age population)

1996 Rank	1992	1996	Percent Change, 1992-1996
National	*55.2*	*48.9*	*–6.3*
1. Maine	72.0	64.5	–7.5
2. Minnesota	71.6	64.3	–7.3
3. Montana	70.1	62.9	–7.2
4. South Dakota	67.0	61.1	–5.9
5. Wyoming	62.7	60.1	–2.6
6. Vermont	67.5	58.6	–8.9
7. Idaho	65.2	58.2	–7.0
8. New Hampshire	63.1	58.0	–5.1
9. Iowa	65.3	57.7	–7.6
10. Oregon	65.7	57.5	–8.2
11. Wisconsin	69.0	57.4	–11.6
12. Alaska	65.4	56.9	–8.5
Louisiana	59.8	56.9	–2.9
14. Kansas	63.0	56.6	–6.4
15. Connecticut	63.8	56.4	–7.4
16. North Dakota	67.3	56.3	–11.0
17. Nebraska	63.2	56.1	–7.1
18. Massachusetts	60.2	55.3	–4.9
19. Washington	60.2	54.7	–5.5
20. Michigan	61.7	54.5	–7.2
21. Ohio	60.6	54.3	–6.3
22. Mississippi	61.5	54.2	–7.3
Missouri	62.0	54.2	–7.8
24. Colorado	62.7	52.0	–10.7
Rhode Island	58.4	52.0	–6.4
26. New Jersey	58.4	51.0	–7.4
27. Utah	65.1	50.3	–14.8
28. Oklahoma	59.1	49.9	–9.2
29. Delaware	55.2	49.6	–5.6
30. Illinois	58.9	49.2	–9.7
31. Pennsylvania	54.3	49.0	–5.3
32. Indiana	55.2	48.9	–6.3
33. Florida	50.2	48.0	–2.2
34. Alabama	55.2	47.7	–7.5
35. Kentucky	53.7	47.5	–6.2
Arkansas	53.8	47.5	–6.3
Virginia	52.8	47.5	–5.3
38. Tennessee	52.4	47.1	–5.1
39. Maryland	53.9	46.7	–7.2
40. New York	50.9	46.5	–4.4
41. New Mexico	51.6	46.0	–5.6
42. North Carolina	50.1	45.8	–4.3
43. Arizona	52.4	45.4	–7.0
44. West Virginia	52.8	45.0	–7.8
45. California	49.1	43.3	–5.8
46. Georgia	46.9	42.6	–4.3
47. Dist. of Col.	49.6	42.3	–7.3
48. South Carolina	45.0	41.5	–3.5
49. Texas	49.1	41.2	–8.9
50. Hawaii	41.9	40.8	–1.1
51. Nevada	50.0	39.3	–9.7

Source: Statistical Abstract of the United States, 1997, p. 290.

Table 8.2
Participation in National Elections, 1996

Characteristic	Percent of Persons Reporting That They Voted in 1996
Male	52.8
Female	55.5
White	56.0
Black	50.6
Hispanic	26.7
Age	
18-20	31.2
21-24	33.4
25-34	43.1
35-44	54.9
45-54	62.3
55-64	67.8
65-74	70.1
School years completed	
8 years or less	28.1
High school	
1-3 years	33.8
4 years	49.1
College	
1-3 years	60.5
4 years or more	73.0
Employed	55.2
Unemployed	37.2
Not in labor force	54.1

Source: Statistical Abstract of the United States, 1997, p. 288. Bureau of the Census, *Voting and Registration in the Election of November 1996* (June 1998).

people tend to have a low rate of turnout compared to those in the over-sixty age bracket. The low rate of turnout among eighteen- to twenty-year-olds has undoubtedly contributed to the decline in overall turnout that occurred in the 1970s, because the extension of the franchise to these persons significantly expanded the pool of eligible voters. This pattern of abstaining from voting reflects the unsettled character and mobility of young people's lives. Registration requirements, residency rules, military service, and moving all create hurdles to political participation among the young. It should be noted, however, that by age thirty-five most people have become at least occasional voters and that only a small portion of the middle aged and older public remain outside the voting public. It is estimated that only 5 percent of the electorate could be classified as habitual nonvoters.[6]

Education is the most important influence on voter turnout. The higher the level of educational attainment, the greater the likelihood of voting. Better educated persons are more likely to vote because they tend to be better able to see the relevance of politics in their lives and the things they care about, are more interested in politics, and more skilled in dealing with registration requirements. Higher levels of educational attainment are associated with better paying jobs. However, income has only slight impact on turnout when other factors such as education, age, race, sex, and region are held constant.

There are also racial differences in turnout races. A higher proportion of whites than blacks votes, and blacks are more frequent voters than Hispanics. The lower turnout rates of blacks and Hispanics tend to reflect the lower age and educational levels of these minorities. Beginning in the 1980s women began to have slightly higher turnout rates than men, reversing the traditional pattern of higher male turnout. Political scientists have not developed a widely accepted theoretical reason for women voting at a higher rate than men, but it is clear that women can be expected to remain a majority of the American electorate.

Partisan Implications. Voters are generally of a higher socioeconomic level than nonvoters; they are also more apt to be better educated, middle aged, and white. In partisan terms, this pattern of turnout means that Republicans are slightly more likely to turn out and vote than are Democratic voters. As a result, get-out-the-vote campaigns aimed at maximizing turnout have been a standard emphasis of Democratic campaigns. Increased voter turnout, however, is not necessarily the key to Democratic electoral success. Thus the analyses of Abramson, Aldrich, and Rohde have shown that under any reasonable scenario increased turnout would not have led to Democratic victories in 1980, 1984 and 1988. In those elections, the Democrats' problem was not low turnout, but high levels of defection to the GOP by the party's voters. Turnout may have made a modest contribution to Clinton's victory, since the 1992 increase in turnout was somewhat greater among Democrats than Republicans. However, just as the Democrats were damaged more by defections than low turnout in the 1980s, their 1992 victory was attributable more to conversions (one in six Clinton voters voted for Bush in 1988) than it was to increases in turnout.[7] In

1996, voters who considered themselves Democrats had lower turnout rates than did Republican identifiers. Had Democrats turned out at the same level as Republicans and supported their party's ticket at the same level as voting Democrats, President Clinton's share of the popular vote would have increased an estimated 1.6 percentage points.[8] While this would not have changed the outcome of the election, it would have given Clinton a popular vote majority.

Just as the evidence in presidential elections indicates that there is no consistent pattern of partisan advantage attached to the turnout rate, research on gubernatorial and senatorial elections presents similar findings. As each party's core of partisans has shrunk in recent decades and peripheral voters have dealigned themselves from the parties, the effects of turnout on election outcomes has become generally small and unreliable.[9]

The Role of Personal Attitudes. Legal impediments, such as restrictive registration laws, can hold down participation in elections. To make voting easier and more convenient, some have even suggested making election day a national holiday. Although 50 percent of nonvoters in one survey reported that they would be likely to vote if it were done on a holiday, there is reason to doubt their good intentions. If these persons are not now sufficiently interested in politics to vote, there is every reason to believe that they would take a holiday from both work and voting if given the opportunity. Nonvoting is not primarily a matter of legal impediments; it is rather caused by personal attitudes—a lack of interest, low sense of civic obligation, and weak feelings of partisan affiliation. Nonvoters are also more likely than voters to believe that elections do not make a difference. The importance of personal attitudes can be seen in table 8.3. Likely voters are more apt to be partisans and to see a difference between the parties. They also have a sense of civic obligation and feel guilty if they do not participate in elections. Likely voters also have a greater sense of confidence in their ability to understand politics and the willingness of public officials to pay attention to the wishes of the people.

The Impact of Voter Mobilization. One of the problems with the research findings that have been summarized to this point is that they make it appear that voter turnout is a deterministic function of the personal characteristics of voters or the demographic properties of electorates. There are, of course, differences in the propensities of various subgroups of the population to vote, but the extent of electoral participation is also influenced by such factors as the amount of campaign spending, the level of interparty competition, and the intensity of the campaign. Political parties and candidate organizations through their campaign activities are able to influence turnout as they mobilize the electorate.

When the outcome of an election is a foregone conclusion with one party or candidate assured of election, voter participation is apt to be adversely affected. A clear example of this tendency for an absence of competition to depress turnout occurred in the South, where the entrenched Democratic party was assured of general election victories. As a result, voter turnout tended to be lower in the noncompetitive general elections than in the primaries, where meaningful contests for the Democratic nomination were likely to occur. However, as the Republican party has become a powerful force in southern politics, turnout in general elections has increased substantially.

Table 8.3
Attitudes toward Voting and Politics

Attitude	Percent Voting
Very interested in campaign	89%
Not much interested in campaign	36
Perceives election as close	78
Does not perceive election as close	69
Cares about the outcome of the election	84
Does not care about the outcome of the election	51
Strong Republican or Democrat	86
Independent	61
Believes people should not vote if they do not care	68
Believes people should vote anyway	85
Thinks politics is too complicated	72
Thinks politics is not too complicated	86
Feels he/she doesn't "have a say"	65
Feels he/she does "have a say"	81
Feels public officials don't care	70
Feels public officials do care	82

Source: National Election Study, 1992.

An indicator of the intensity of a campaign is the level of spending in which the parties and candidates engage to mobilize voters. Studies of campaign spending in gubernatorial and state legislative races have demonstrated that spending increases electoral involvement, but that, after a certain threshold is reached, additional increments of spending produce increasingly smaller payoffs in terms of voter turnout.[10]

Is Nonvoting a Social Disease?

A commonly expressed view is that America's seemingly high rate of nonvoting is symptomatic of a civic disorder that endangers the republic. Unfavorable comparisons between turnout rates in the United States and other Western democracies are frequently cited as evidence of decay in the American body politic. It is necessary, however, when considering these cross-national comparisons to keep in mind that other nations compute turnout rates as a percentage of registered voters going to the polls. By contrast, American turnout rates are normally calculated as a percentage of the voting age population. As a result, most of the free world can boast of higher turnout rates than the United States. However, when turnout in the United States is computed on the basis of registered voters, instead of voting age population, the rate is a respectable 85 percent. In addition, Americans have more opportunities to vote than do citizens of other democracies because of the frequency and varied types of elections in the United States—primaries and general elections for national, state, and local offices, state and local referenda, and recall elections. British political scientist Ivor Crewe emphasized this point when he observed:

> Turnout rates provide only a limited perspective on the amount of electoral participation. Turnout cannot measure the frequency of elections. Although turnout in the United States is below that of most other democracies, American citizens do not necessarily do less voting; in fact, they probably do more. No country can approach the United States in frequency and variety of elections. Only one other country—Switzerland—can compete in the number and variety of local referendums. Only Belgium and Turkey hold party "primaries" in most parts of the country.[11]

There is no compelling evidence to indicate that America's relatively low rate of turnout results in distortions of the citizenry's will. In general, nonvoters have candidate preferences much like those of voters.[12] Thus, analyses by sociologist Ruy Teixeira reveal that if all the eligible citizens had actually voted in the presidential elections from 1964 to 1988, the outcomes would have remained the same (table 8.4). This does not mean that turnout never makes a difference in election results. But it does mean that relatively unusual conditions must be present for turnout to play a determining role in election outcomes. These conditions include the following factors: an extremely close election; a large turnout; a large group of nonvoters with heavily lopsided candidate preferences available for mobilization. Although this combination of conditions is not often present, they were present in 1983 when Harold Washington was elected as Chicago's first African-American

Table 8.4

What If We Had an Election and Everybody Came? Self-Reported Voters and Nonvoters, by Presidential Vote of Preference, 1964–1988

Vote or Preference	Nonvoters	Voters	Voters and Nonvoters
1964			
Democratic vote or preference	79.7	67.4	70.0
Republican vote or preference	20.3	32.4	29.9
Other vote or preference	0	0.2	0.1
1968			
Democratic vote or preference	44.6	40.9	41.7
Republican vote or preference	40.4	47.6	46.0
Other vote or preference	15.0	11.5	12.2
1980			
Democratic vote or preference	46.8	39.4	41.1
Republican vote or preference	45.1	50.8	49.5
Other vote or preference	8.2	9.8	9.4
1984			
Democratic vote or preference	38.6	41.4	40.8
Republican vote or preference	61.2	57.7	58.4
Other vote or preference	0.3	0.9	0.8
1988			
Democratic vote or preference	44.4	46.6	46.0
Republican vote or preference	54.3	52.3	52.8
Other vote or preference	1.3	1.2	1.2

Note: The National Election Study (NES) did not ascertain the presidential preference of nonvoters in 1972 and 1976.

Source: Ruy A. Teixeira, *The Disappearing American Voter* (Washington, D.C.: Brookings, 1992), p. 96. Reprinted by permission.

mayor. In that election African-Americans voted overwhelmingly (99 percent) for Washington and their historically low turnout shot up by 30 percent.[13]

Even though nonvoting in America is perhaps less a symptom of an ailing polity than it might appear at first glance, reasons for concern still exist. With educated, affluent, and influential groups having the highest turnout rates, universal suffrage does not provide the kind of counterweight to power and wealth once envisioned by its advocates. Indeed, the research of Hill and Leighley has shown that, where the poor have higher levels of turnout, welfare benefits are more generous than in states with low turnout among the poor.[14] A high incidence of nonvoting also can threaten the legitimacy of democratic government and cause people to withdraw their support from the government. Large blocs of nonvoters with weak ties to established political leaders and parties could, therefore, pose a threat to political stability.

Party Identification

Voters' electoral choices reflect the interaction of enduring attitudes and beliefs and more transitory factors such as current issues and candidate images. The most important long-term influence is *party identification*—a feeling of attachment to and sympathy for a political party.[15] It is considered a long-term and continuing influence on voter choice because one's party identification is not likely to undergo frequent changes in response to changing events or life circumstances. Unlike issues and candidate images which vary from year to year, a voter's party identification is quite stable.

Party identification is measured in public opinion surveys by asking voters a question such as the following: "Generally speaking, do you think of yourself as a Republican, Democrat, or Independent?" Scholars also attempt to probe voters to determine the strength of voters' partisan commitments and have developed the following seven point scale.

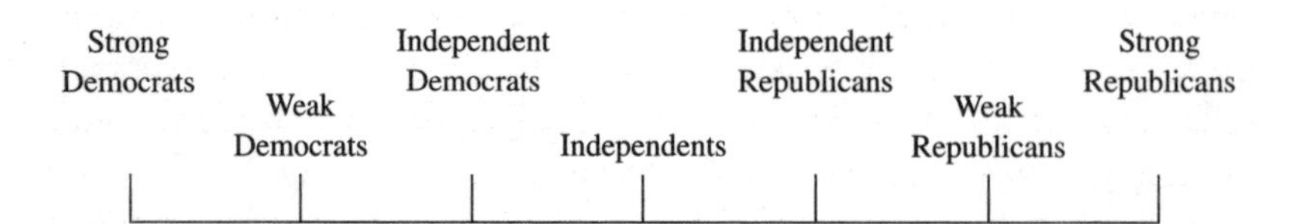

Table 8.5 shows that between 1952 and 1996 approximately three-fourths to two-thirds of the American electorate held a partisan identification, with the Democrats maintaining a consistent advantage over the GOP.

Party identification tends to be acquired at an early age. Studies of grade school children have shown that by fourth grade most students have a partisan preference.[16] This sense of partisanship is usually devoid of an informational or policy content—that is, young children know little about the candidates and issue differences between the parties. Children's sense of partisan affiliation is usually acquired through their families; they tend to imitate the behavior of their parents even when the adults are not actively seeking to persuade their children to adopt their viewpoints. Learning party identification is not, therefore, a conscious activity; it is an informal family centered process. As Herbert Asher has noted, "One reason why the family is so crucial is that other agents of political learning, such as teachers and school curricula, studiously avoid getting enmeshed in partisan questions."[17]

Although partisanship is normally learned in childhood, there is substantial stability in most people's party affiliations. However, changing life circumstances and real-world events, as well as policy preferences, can cause some voters to change their party preference.[18] For example, President Reagan's popularity in 1981 coincided with an increase in Republican identifiers. A downturn in the economy in late 1981 and 1982 produced a decline in the president's popularity and a shift to the Democrats among party identifiers. Then, during 1984–85, the surging popularity of the president and an improved economy produced an increase in the proportion of voters identifying with the GOP. Clearly, party identification does respond to short-term influences, though the dominant pattern has been one of relative stability in individuals' party orientation.

Partisanship and Vote Choice

The strength of party identification is related to both voters' patterns of turnout and loyalty to their parties. As the strength of commitment to a party increases, so does the likelihood that a person will turn out and vote. Strong partisans, therefore, have higher rates of turnout than weak partisans, who in turn are more likely to vote than independents. As would be expected, independents and weak

Table 8.5
Party Identification in the United States, 1952–1996

	1952	1956	1960	1964	1968	1972	1976	1980	1984	1988	1992	1996
Strong Democrats	22%	21%	20%	27%	20%	15%	15%	18%	17%	18%	17%	19%
Weak Democrats	25	23	25	25	25	26	25	23	20	18	18	20
Leaning Democratic	10	6	6	9	10	11	12	11	11	12	14	13
Independent	5	9	10	8	11	13	15	13	11	11	12	9
Leaning Republican	7	8	7	6	9	11	10	10	12	13	13	11
Weak Republicans	14	14	14	14	15	13	14	14	15	14	15	15
Strong Republicans	14	15	16	11	10	10	9	9	12	14	11	13
Apolitical	3	4	3	1	1	1	1	2	2	2	1	1
Total	100	100	100	100	100	100	100	100	100	100	101 *	102 *

*Does not sum to 100% due to rounding.

Source: National Election Study Surveys

partisans are less likely to support one party consistently than are strong Republicans and Democrats, who have a high degree of party loyalty.[19]

In most post–World War II presidential elections, Republican voters have exhibited a higher degree of loyalty than Democrats, although the degree of party loyalty is heavily influenced by such factors as the appeal of the candidates in a given election. Thus, few Republicans defected from Eisenhower in the 1950s, Nixon in 1972, or Reagan in 1980–1984, and Democrats were loyal to Johnson in 1964. But when candidate appeal has ebbed, partisans of both parties have defected in large numbers—for example, Republicans from Goldwater (1964) and Democrats from McGovern (1972), Carter (1980), Mondale (1984), and Dukakis (1988). The pattern of Democratic presidential candidates being hit hardest by partisan defections came to at least a temporary halt in 1992 and 1996. Thus, in 1996, Bill Clinton won because he held his own among Democratic identifiers and did better than usual among independents who lean toward the Republicans and weak Republicans[20] (see table 8.6).

The Decline in Party Voting

Studies consistently have demonstrated that party identification is a major determinant of how people vote. However, there is substantial evidence that partisanship is having a reduced impact on voters' decisions. Voters are engaging in ticket splitting with increased frequency—that is, voting for one party's candidate in one race, but voting for the other party's candidates in contests for different offices. Table 8.7 shows that at the turn of the century, ticket splitting between presidential and congressional candidates was unusual, but that by the 1960s it was commonplace for almost one-third of the nation's congressional districts to have split outcomes between the presidential and congressional outcomes. Further evidence of the increasingly candidate-centered nature of electoral politics can be found in the high incidence of split-ticket voting and split-party victories when a state holds gubernatorial and senatorial elections simultaneously. Between 1980 and 1996, there were 135 instances when states held gubernatorial and senatorial elections in the same year. In almost half (46 percent) of those elections, a governor and a senator from different parties were elected within the states.[21]

Table 8.6
Presidential Voting of Party Identifiers, 1996

	Dole	Clinton	Perot
Strong Democrat	2%	94%	4%
Weak Democrat	11	83	6
Leaning Democrat	7	74	18
Independent	47	29	24
Leaning Republican	66	23	11
Weak Republican	71	19	10
Strong Republican	96	3	1

Source: National Election Study, 1996. Used by permission.

Table 8.7
Congressional Districts with Split Results for President and U.S. Representative, 1900-1996

		Districts with Split Results[b]	
Year	Districts[a]	Number	Percentage
1900	295	10	3.4
1904	310	5	1.6
1908	314	21	6.7
1912	333	84	25.2
1916	333	35	10.5
1920	344	11	3.2
1924	356	42	11.8
1928	359	68	18.9
1932	355	50	14.1
1936	361	51	14.1
1940	362	53	14.6
1944	367	41	11.2
1948	422	90	21.3
1952	435	84	19.3
1956	435	130	29.9
1960	437	114	26.1
1964	435	145	33.3
1968	435	139	32.0
1972	435	192	44.1
1976	435	124	28.5
1980	435	143	32.8
1984	435	196	45.0
1988	435	148	34.0
1992	435	100	23.0
1996	435	110	25.5

a. Before 1952 complete data are not available on every congressional district.

b. Congressional districts carried by a presidential candidate of one party and a House candidate of another party.

Source: Norman J. Ornstein, Thomas E. Mann, and Michael J. Malbin, *Vital Statistics on Congress, 1997–1998* (Washington, D.C.: Congressional Quarterly, Inc., 1998), p. 71. Used by permission.

As shown in table 8.6, the Democrats have consistently held an advantage over the Republicans in terms of party identifiers. However, that advantage has narrowed since the 1960s and it is an advantage that is made even smaller by the tendency of Republicans to have higher rates of turnout than Democrats. The permanence of the increasingly close partisan balance between Republican and Democratic identifiers is, of course, difficult to assess. There is a strong probability, however, that it will endure because it reflects realignments in the partisanship of major population groups—the erosion of Democratic strength among white southerners and Catholics—and the declining size of unions in society.

While studying the shifts in party identification that have occurred during and after presidential campaigns, Seymour Martin Lipset has identified a pattern of voters shifting their party identification to bring it into harmony with their vote preference. These voters who shift in response to candidate preference plus the sizeable proportion of citizens claiming to be independents documents "that a large part of [the electorate] can be easily moved from one party to another."[22] Since voters' partisanship responds to political events and conditions, Morris Fiorina has suggested that party identification should be considered a sort of "running tally" of past experiences—a summary expression of political memory.[23] With voters becoming less than permanently wedded to a particular party, the electorate has become increasingly susceptible to mobilization by either party, and subject to the impact of short-term influence like candidate appeal and issues.

Candidates and Issues

Party identification has been a long-term and enduring influence upon voter choices, but its impact can be modified by the short-term and changing influences of candidates and issues. Candidate images are especially important when the candidates' personalities, political styles, backgrounds, and physical appearances are given a high level of media coverage, as in presidential elections. In the 1950s, Dwight Eisenhower was a candidate with exceptional personal appeal that increased the Republican percentage of the vote substantially. During most of the elections since 1952, candidate appeal has been a plus factor for Republican presidential tickets (1964, 1992, and 1996 were the exceptions). In 1980, doubts about both candidates—Carter for his record as president, Reagan because of uncertainty about him as a president—meant that candidate image was of negligible effect. In 1984 Reagan benefited from a strong leader image and had the good fortune to run against Democrat Walter Mondale, whom voters perceived as weak. In 1988, candidate image again benefited the Republicans, as George Bush was viewed more favorably than Michael Dukakis. However, Bush's image deteriorated dramatically before the 1992 elections, while voters gave Bill Clinton a favorable evaluation overall. And again in 1996, Clinton was rated more favorably than his Republican opponent, although not as favorably as in 1992.

In some elections a candidate gains a major advantage over an opponent because the opponent has a particularly unfavorable image with the voters. Striking examples of unfavorable images were the 1964 election when Republican Barry Goldwater was perceived as "trigger happy" and impulsive, and the 1972 election when only one-third of the voters thought the Democratic nominee, Senator George McGovern (S.D.), sufficiently trustworthy to be president, while 60 percent gave a trustworthy rating to President Richard Nixon.[24]

Normally, candidate image has a reduced impact upon voter choice the farther down one goes on the ballot to less visible and less well-known candidates. A candidate's personal qualities may still be important in terms of obtaining a nomination, winning party or interest group endorsements, and putting together a campaign staff. But they are apt to have limited influence on voter decisions simply because the voter is less apt to be aware of them.[25]

The impact of issues on voter choice varies depending upon conditions and candidates. In the 1964–1972 period—a time of controversial candidates, the civil rights movement, and Vietnam war—there was an increased correlation between attitudes on issues and vote choice.[26] In the 1980s through 1996, however, the issue positions of presidential candidates had a lesser impact on voters. For example, aside from the improved state of the economy, there were no issues in 1996 that were particularly influential. However, people with varying issue positions did have different candidate preferences. Thus, persons favoring an increase in government services, government help for minorities, cuts in defense spending, a pro-choice position on abortion, and government health insurance were supportive of Clinton over Dole.

There are characteristics of electoral behavior that work against issues determining voter decisions. Widespread lack of knowledge concerning the stands taken by candidates on various issues exists within the electorate. Some voters, therefore, project to their favored candidate their own personal issue positions, irrespective of the actual issues stands of the candidate. Some voters may adopt an issue position because their preferred candidate has taken that position. In addition, voters may not feel intensely about some issues, even though they are subject to substantial debate during the campaign. Voters' ability to cast their ballots based upon issues is also affected by the campaign strategies of the candidates, who may or may not engage in issue oriented campaigns. There are several factors that need to be present for issues to have an impact on voters: (1) voters must be informed and concerned about an issue; (2) the candidates must be distinguishable from each other on this issue; and (3) the voters must perceive the candidates' stands in relationship to their own issue position.[27]

In 1996 a significant number of voters could not meet these conditions. Eleven percent had no opinion on government spending versus cutting government services and an additional 4 percent could not locate the candidates' positions on this issue; there were similar proportions of the electorate who could not locate themselves or the candidates on the issue of defense spending. The conditions for issue voting are most likely to be met and voters tend to care most intensely about an issue when they are suffering or perceive a threat, and normally economic threats are the easiest for them to understand. By contrast, foreign policy threats are more difficult to comprehend. The higher salience and hence electoral payoff attached to economic issues lay behind the well-publicized reminder, "It's the economy, stupid," which was tacked to the wall of Clinton's campaign headquarters in 1992.

The 1972 presidential election was an instance in which voter perceptions of candidate positions on issues appeared to play a significant role in voter choices. The National Election Study revealed that voters saw Nixon as being closer to their own personal issue positions than was McGovern on eleven of fourteen issues. There was also a close correlation between the voters' perception of which candidate was closest to them on the issues and their actual vote choice.[28] The 1972 election also illustrates how candidate images can become intertwined with issue concerns of the voters and how these images of candidates can make the impact of issues more pronounced. McGovern's issue problems were compounded by his general image. His ideas were thought by 75 percent of the people to be "far out" and "impractical." He was perceived as liberal by 31 percent of the voters and as radical by another 31 percent, while only 17 percent considered themselves liberal and only 1 percent thought of themselves as radical. Peter Natchez has summarized how McGovern's image affected perceptions on his issues positions.

> His "indecisiveness" and "extremism" fed on each other; his indecisiveness created an aura of impracticality around the issue positions he was trying to develop; his search for the right issues made him seem indecisive.[29]

Another way of viewing issue voting is in terms of voters rendering a verdict on the past performance of the candidates and their parties, rather than in terms of candidates' promises for the future. This type of retrospective voting is especially important when an incumbent is running for reelection.[30] In 1980, for example, President Jimmy Carter was widely perceived to have been less than effective as president—particularly with regard to his handling of the economy, but also in foreign affairs (e.g., the Iranian hostage crisis). For many voters this was a more salient concern than their closeness to the candidates on various issues. The essence of retrospective issue voting was captured by candidate Reagan during his debate with President Carter when he asked the voters if they were better off than they had been four years before. In contrast to the negative verdict rendered on the performance of the Carter administration in 1980, the voters were more positive about the record of the Reagan administration in 1984. Voters gave Reagan a 58 percent positive to 46 percent negative rating for his handling of the economy and 86 percent of those giving him a positive rating also voted for him. In 1988, the Republicans again benefited from a favorable assessment of Reagan's stewardship of the economy. The GOP margin of victory was narrower, however, because Reagan got somewhat less positive marks in his second term and Bush had lower ability to win the support of those approving of Reagan's performance. But in 1992, when Bush was running for reelection on his own record, only about two voters in five approved of his performance and he was ousted from the White House. By contrast, in

1996, Bill Clinton, as the incumbent president, was given a generally positive performance evaluation by the voters. This, combined with the absence of any advantage for the Republicans in terms of their being perceived as better able to deal with the voters' concern, helped Clinton gain reelection.[31]

The relative importance of various issues to the voters is subject to dramatic changes from election to election (see table 8.8). In the 1950s, foreign affairs was the most salient issue for America because of the Korean war and the cold war. During the early 1960s issues of race relations gained prominence. The Vietnam War pushed foreign policy concerns to the fore again in the mid-1960s along with the so-called social issues of urban riots, campus unrest, drugs, and law and order. During the mid-1970s through the early 1990s, an unsteady economy made economic issues the most salient. Issue saliency is extremely important in elections because a candidate to be effective must be perceived favorably by the voters on the issues that are currently important to them. It does little good for a candidate to be well perceived on an issue of modest importance to the voters if that candidate is viewed unfavorably on the issue that is really on their minds. For example, in the 1992 presidential election, economic issues were most salient. Therefore, it

Table 8.8
The Changing Public Perception of the Country's Most Important Problem: Presidential Election Years, 1936–1996

Year	Most Important Problem Facing the Country
1936	Unemployment
1940	Keeping out of war
1944	Winning war
1948	Keeping peace
1952	Korean war
1956	Keeping peace
1960	Keeping peace
1964	Vietnam, race relations
1968	Vietnam
1972	Vietnam
1976	High cost of living, unemployment
1980	High cost of living, unemployment
1984	Unemployment, fear of war
1988	Economy
1992	Economy
1996	Noneconomic issues (crime, education, morals, health care)

Source: Gallup Poll Surveys.

did George Bush and the Republicans little good to be perceived more favorably than the Democrats on foreign policy issues.

The short-term influences of candidate image and issues can work either to reinforce partisan inclinations of voters or cause them to defect from their party. For example, dissatisfaction with the performance of the Ford Administration on the economy tended to reinforce the loyalty of Democrats to their party in 1976. But in 1980 and 1984, Democrats defected in large numbers as economic and social issues drove a wedge between them and their party. In 1992, it was the GOP which was hit hardest by defections due to economic issues and an unfavorable candidate image. Again, in 1996, Clinton benefited from GOP defections as he did better than usual among Republican leaners and moderate Republicans.

Social and Economic Bases of Partisanship and Voting

In the United States, lines of partisan conflict tend to cross-cut social and economic cleavages in society. The parties tend, therefore, to be broad coalitions embracing a wide variety of interests. Indeed, both parties draw significant levels of electoral support from virtually every major socioeconomic group in society. The only significant exception is black voters, who since 1964 have voted Democratic in overwhelming proportions (84 percent in 1996). Although both parties can expect at least some backing from just about every socioeconomic group, the two parties do not gain equal proportions of support from each group. There are distinctive patterns in the voting behavior of various groups, and the Republicans and Democrats have different bases of support.

Economic and Class Differences

As income, education, and occupational status go up, the likelihood of an individual's voting Republican increases (see table 8.9). Lower income persons, blue-collar workers, and people from labor union households have constituted a traditional base of Democratic support, while professional/managerial personnel, and college educated, nonunion household members have tended to be Republicans. While these patterns have been present in presidential elections since the New Deal realignment of the 1930s, it is important to note that a significant proportion of the voters in each of these categories consistently depart from their group's normal partisan inclination. For example, Republicans can normally expect to receive about 33–40 percent of the labor union household vote, and Democrats customarily gain a similar share of the professional/managerial voters and the college educated.

Since 1952, analysts have observed a decline in class based differences between the parties. Indeed, the United States is regarded as unusual among Western-style democracies for the relatively low impact that social class has upon voting behavior. In most European democracies, it has much greater consequence. The relatively weak impact of social class on voting is attributable in significant degree to American cultural values of freedom and individualism that stress getting ahead based upon ability and hard work rather than through class solidarity. Successful candidates, therefore, normally do not seek to exploit class-based issues. Bill Clinton, in 1996, for example, campaigned as a moderate, supporting free trade (which was opposed by labor leaders) and on welfare reform.[32]

Although class based voting in the United States is not strong, the Democrats, since the 1930s, have done better than the Republicans among voters with lower incomes and education levels and among union members. Table 8.9 shows that, in 1996, Clinton clearly fared better among the poor than among the affluent. Interestingly, the Democrats do well at both the upper and lower socioeconomic levels in that their economic policies appear to appeal to less-well-off Americans, and those with advanced degrees—especially well-educated women—seem to reject Republican emphasis in recent campaigns on traditional values. At the same time, Republican traditional values appeals may have attracted working-class support. The downward trend in class based voting is dampened when the analysis is expanded to include African Americans, because they are disproportionately working class and overwhelmingly Democratic. However, blacks vote Democratic mainly because they are black not because they are working class. Thus, both working- and middle-class blacks voted overwhelmingly Democratic in 1992 and 1996.

Although class based voting seems to be on the decline in the nation as a whole, this is not true in the South, where a quite different pattern is emerging. Through the 1950s, virtually all southerners, irrespective of their socioeconomic status, were Democrats. Since that time, the middle class has become increasingly Republican, while the working class, especially the black working

Table 8.9
Voting Patterns of Political and Socioeconomic Groups, 1996 Presidential Election (percent of vote)

	Clinton (Dem.)	Dole (Rep.)	Perot (Ind.)
Democrats	84	10	5
Republicans	13	80	6
Independents	43	35	17
Liberals	78	11	7
Moderates	57	33	9
Conservatives	20	71	8
First-time voters	54	34	11
Whites	43	46	9
African-Americans	84	12	4
Hispanics	72	21	6
Asian-Americans	43	48	8
Men	43	44	10
Women	54	38	7
Age			
18-29	53	34	10
30-44	48	41	9
45-59	48	41	7
60+	48	44	7
Region of residence			
East	55	34	9
Midwest	48	41	10
South	46	46	7
West	48	40	8
Family income			
Under $15,000	59	28	11
$15,000–29,999	53	36	9
$30,000–49,999	48	40	10
$50,000–74,999	47	45	7
$75,000–99,999	44	48	7
over $100,000	38	54	6
Union household	69	30	9
Education			
Less than high school	59	28	11
High school graduate	51	35	13
Some college	48	40	10
College graduate	44	46	8
Postgraduate	52	40	5
White Protestant	36	53	10
Catholic	53	37	12
Jewish	78	16	3
Married	44	46	9
Not married	59	31	9

Note: Percentages may not add to 100 because of rounding.

Source: Voter Research and Surveys exit polls.

class, has remained strongly Democratic. As a result, class based voter alignments in the South have been intensified, while they have been reduced in the North. In both regions, however, class based voting is relatively weak.[33]

Religious Differences

Religion, like class, has been a traditional basis of partisan alignment since the New Deal period. Catholics have tended to be Democrats and white Protestants to be Republicans. John Petrocik and Frederick Steeper estimated in the mid-1980s that the normal white Protestant vote was 70 percent Republican.[34] The growth of Republican voting among Fundamentalist/Born-again Christians has been particularly strong in the 1980s and 1990s. Catholic support of Democratic presidential candidates declined in the 1970s and 1980s, but rebounded in 1996 as Clinton carried the Catholic vote by a substantial margin.

Like regionally based party loyalties, those which are religiously based frequently have their roots in historical circumstances. Prior to 1928, Catholics were less apt to vote Democratic than in succeeding years. But in 1928, Governor Al Smith of New York became the first Roman Catholic to be nominated for president by a major party. The 1928 campaign featured an intense anti-Catholic backlash that helped convert many Catholics to the Democratic cause. Religious cleavages were again activated in 1960 with the nomination of an Irish Catholic, John F. Kennedy, as the Democratic standard-bearer. In that election, 80 percent of Catholic voters voted Democratic, compared to the 50 percent that had cast ballots for the Democratic nominee, Adlai Stevenson, in 1956. Economic and educational status does affect the extent to which Catholics prefer the Democratic party. Higher status Catholics are less likely to be Democrats than lower status Catholics, but the two parties have a differential appeal to Catholics and Protestants that rests upon historical events interacting with cultural differences. The tendency of Catholics to be more Democratic than Protestants is not simply a reflection of class differences.[35]

Jewish voters have been overwhelmingly Democratic since the New Deal era. The allegiance of Jewish voters to the Democratic party has held firm even though substantial proportions of the Jewish population have achieved middle and upper-middle-class status. Antisemitism and discrimination against Jews

Table 8. 10
The "Churched" and the "Unchurched": Church Attendance and Voting Behavior, 1992 and 1996

Attendance	1992 Democrat	1992 Republican	1996 Democrat	1996 Republican
Once a week/month	46%	52%	45%	55%
Less than once a month	57%	40%	60%	40%

Source: Los Angeles Times, survey, November 5, 1996, reported in *The Public Perspective,* December/January 1997, p. 26.

have tended to cause them to identify with the less advantaged and be supportive of liberal social welfare policies. This type of policy orientation has made them pro-Democratic, irrespective of income, class, or educational attainment. In the 1980s and 1990s Jewish voters' Democratic proclivities were further encouraged by the appeals made by Republicans to fundamentalist Christian groups and their endorsement of these groups' positions on issues of social policy (e.g., support for prayer in public schools).

One of the most striking developments is the emerging relationship between the frequency of church attendance and voting behavior. As is shown in table 8.10, Republicans fared much better in 1992 and 1996 among the "churched" portion of the electorate than they did with the "less churched" and "unchurched."

Gender Differences

Gender has not been a source of partisan division in the United States until recently. However, beginning in 1980 a pattern emerged of women being less likely to vote Republican than men, and the term "gender gap" entered the political vocabulary. The gender gap reflects the fact that since the 1960s women have encountered new types of problems as they have entered the work force in expanded numbers and as the numbers of single-parent, female-headed households has increased. The impact of these changes can be seen in the fact that family status has now become a variable influencing voting behavior. In 1996 married voters narrowly favored Dole, while those who were single, divorced or separated, or widowed all strongly backed Clinton by a margin of almost 30 percentage points (see table 8.9).

In 1992, Clinton was a clear beneficiary of the gender gap (see table 8.9). The Voter Research and Surveys exit polls show that he narrowly lost to Dole among men (45-44 percent), but had a 54 to 38 percent point advantage among women. He did particularly well among single women (62 percent) and younger women in the twenty-one to twenty-nine-year-old age group (58 percent), those with a college degree (53 percent), and suburban women (53 percent). However, his percentage among married women was substantially smaller (48 percent).

Although most discussion has focused upon the movement of women in the Democratic direction, the gender gap has always had another component—the movement of men toward the Republicans. Indeed, except for 1992, men have given GOP presidential candidates a higher percent of their vote in every election since 1980, with the margin reaching a high of 25 percent when Reagan topped Mondale 62 to 37 percent in 1984.[36]

Regional Differences

Periodically, major issues have emerged in American political history that have pitted one section of the country against another. These conflicts have had a lasting impact on party loyalties and voting habits. Because the first Republican president led the Union during the Civil War and a Republican Congress forced Reconstruction upon the South, the region became overwhelmingly Democratic in its political sympathies after the Civil War and up until the latter half of the present century.

In the South, the small town, white, Protestant, middle-class conservatives that in other regions could have been expected to provide the core of support for the Republican party were Democrats. They elected Democrats to Congress and supported virtually every Democratic presidential nominee from the post-Reconstruction period until the 1950s. An exception occurred when the Democrats nominated Governor Al Smith of New York, whose Catholicism pushed many southerners into the Republican camp for one election. Starting in the 1950s, however, the GOP began to win significant proportions of the southern vote for president and since 1968 the Republicans have won a plurality of the white southern vote in every presidential election.

The change in the voting patterns of the South has been caused by the in-migration of middle class northerners who have carried their Republicanism with them. These transplanted Republicans are particularly evident in the growing suburban areas of cities such as Dallas, Houston, and Atlanta. Another factor creating a change in the partisan orientation of the South is the declining support for the Democratic party among young white southerners, who are less influenced by the traditions of the South than older generations. Conclusive evidence of the realignment of southern white voters was revealed in the 1994 midterm elections in which the GOP won a majority of the House seats from southern and border states. The Republicans also held a majority of the Senate seats from the states of the old Confederacy after the 1994 elections.

The plains states and the mountain states have also shown a distinctive partisan orientation. These regions have tended to be the core areas of Republicanism, particularly in recent presidential elections. Through most of their history they have been predominantly rural and characterized by relatively high economic and cultural homogeneity. William Schneider has described Nebraska and Kansas as archetypal farm belt states

> overwhelmingly agricultural and white Anglo-Saxon Protestant, and not marked by major class or cultural stratification. For example, the largest foreign-stock group in Nebraska, Kansas, and the Dakotas is German, but the Germans in these states are mostly Protestants, whose culture is close to that of their Protestant neighbors.[37]

Schneider has also observed that the farm belt and mountain states never experienced the same level of internal class conflict as did the northeast, south, and progressive states during the late nineteenth and early twentieth centuries. These areas have not been immune to protest movements (e.g., populism), but a leftward leaning class constituency never developed because protest movements were confined to a native-stock agrarian milieu. However, there is a sense of sectional protest in the farm belt and mountain states that tends to be directed against the federal government (e.g., claims by western ranchers and timber and mining interests that the Clinton administration through its land use and natural resources policies was waging a "war on the West"). Republicans have successfully appealed to the powerful anti-Washington sentiment in western states.

Racial Differences

After the Civil War and before the 1930s, black Americans were overwhelmingly Republican. They supported the party of Lincoln.

During the Depression and New Deal era, they shifted toward the Democrats. Their support for Republican candidates remained substantial, however, as Eisenhower received 39 percent of the black vote in 1956 and Nixon gained 25 percent four years later. In the 1964 presidential election between Barry Goldwater and President Lyndon Johnson, the images of the parties became sharply differentiated on civil rights issues, with the Democrats clearly perceived as the more liberal of the parties. In that election, blacks voted overwhelmingly for the Democratic candidate and have continued to do so in succeeding elections. It is estimated, for example, that even though Ronald Reagan scored a landslide victory in the country as a whole in 1984, he won only 9 percent of the black vote. A growing black population, higher levels of voter turnout, and massive support for Democratic candidates have meant that blacks constitute an expanding and increasingly important share of the Democratic vote. Strong black support is now essential for Democratic electoral victories in national, state, and many local contests.

Voters of Spanish heritage also show a strong but less pronounced tendency to support Democratic candidates. Whereas Dole lost the black vote to Clinton 12–84 percent in 1996, his losing margin among Hispanic Americans was 21–72 percent. There are significant differences among Hispanics in their political preferences. Mexican Americans tend to be Democrats, but Cuban Americans, who have done relatively well economically in this country, tend to be Republicans for economic as well as foreign policy reasons. Because Hispanics are one of the fastest growing segments of the population, their political impact on elections, especially in the Southwest, is likely to be profound and results in both parties investing resources to win their allegiance.

Another growing population group is Asian Americans, who are expected to double their population in the United States between 1980 and 2000. Thus far this new Asian immigrant group has been disproportionately professional, educated, and socially active. In 1996, they voted 48 percent Republican and 43 percent Democrat. The emergence of new racial voter groups, such as the Asian Americans, plus the prominence of black and Hispanic voting blocks means that American politics will have significant racial dimensions into the foreseeable future. Interestingly, these groups are likely to manifest highly distinctive voting patterns at the very time that European ethnicity has declined as an important force in American politics, as the later European immigrant populations have been assimilated.

The Socioeconomic Composition of the Parties

Although both parties have significant levels of support among virtually every major socioeconomic group in American life, significant changes have occurred since the 1950s in the profiles of the Republican and Democratic parties based upon people's party identification (see table 8.11).

The three largest elements of the Democratic coalition in the late 1950s were northern union members, white southerners, and Catholics, with blacks contributing 9 percent of the party's core support and Jews 4 percent. The core of the Republican vote was white Protestants living outside the South. The parties had developed a new look by the late 1970s. The Democrats had become less southern and more black and northern union members were a smaller proportion of the party's support. Blacks had moved from 9 percent of the party's identifiers in the 1950s to 20 percent by 1996.

By 1996 black Republicans became even more rare and southerners constituted 34 percent of the identifiers compared to only 15 percent in the late 1950s. As Petrocik and Steeper have observed, "What had once been the party of Northern white Protestants was transformed into a national party by virtue of its growing Southern constituency."[38]

Clearly, the electoral landscape of the 1990s is significantly changed from that of the 1930s through the 1950s. Whereas in the New Deal years, women and men voted almost identically, today they show significant differences in party preferences. The New Deal Democratic coalition has been seriously undermined, particularly by the defections of white southerners and to a lesser degree by defections among Catholics and labor union households. Northern white protestants remain strongly Republican, with "born-again Christians" joining their ranks. Black voters have come to constitute an enlarged and especially loyal base of Democratic voters and at the same time, the growing Hispanic population remains heavily Democratic. These significant changes in socioeconomic group party preferences and the demonstrated ability of the Republicans to win the presidency in five of the last eight elections indicate that the era of the normal Democratic majority in presidential elections is now past.

Table 8.11

Profiles of Democratic and Republican Party Coalitions, 1950s–1996

	Democrat Party Identifiers (Percent)							
	1950s	1960s	1970s	1980	1984	1988	1992	1996
White Protestants	18	20	17	16	17	15	16	16
Catholics	14	16	17	14	14	14	14	12
Northern union households	22	16	19	17	16	14	12	14
White southerners	31	26	23	23	22	23	20	22
Jews	4	4	3	5	3	4	3	3
Blacks	9	13	16	18	17	22	22	20
Hispanics	1	2	2	3	7	5	11	10
All others	2	2	3	4	5	3	2	3
Total	100	100	100	100	100	100	100	100

	Republican Party Identifiers (Percent)							
	1950s	1960s	1970s	1980	1984	1988	1992	1996
White Protestants	51	50	43	37	38	37	38	32
Catholics	10	12	12	14	14	16	14	13
Northern union households	16	11	14	16	12	12	10	10
White southerners	15	21	23	22	25	25	23	34
Jews	1	1	1	1	1	2	1	.3
Blacks	5	2	2	3	2	4	3	3
Hispanics	0	—	1	2	4	2	7	5
All others	2	3	3	5	5	3	4	4
Total	100	100	100	100	100	100	100	101.3*

*Does not add up to 100 due to rounding.

Source: John R. Petrocik, "Issues and Agendas: Electoral Coalitions in the 1988 Election," paper presented at the annual meeting of the American Political Science Association, Aug. 31–Sept. 3, 1989; 1992 and 1996 data provided by Petrocik. Used by permission.

Election Outcomes

The discussion of voting behavior has dealt thus far with the forces influencing individual voter choices and the patterns of voting by socioeconomic groups. Elections, however, are played out as contests for specific offices, in different constituencies, at various times. Office, constituency, and timing factors, therefore, combine to produce diverse patterns of election outcomes.

Presidential Elections

Despite the fact that Democrats have enjoyed a substantial advantage in party identification in the period of 1956–1996, the Republicans have been most successful in capturing the presidency (see figure 8.2). In eleven presidential elections held during this

Figure 8.2

REPUBLICAN AND DEMOCRATIC PERCENTAGE OF POPULAR VOTE FOR PRESIDENT, 1956–1996

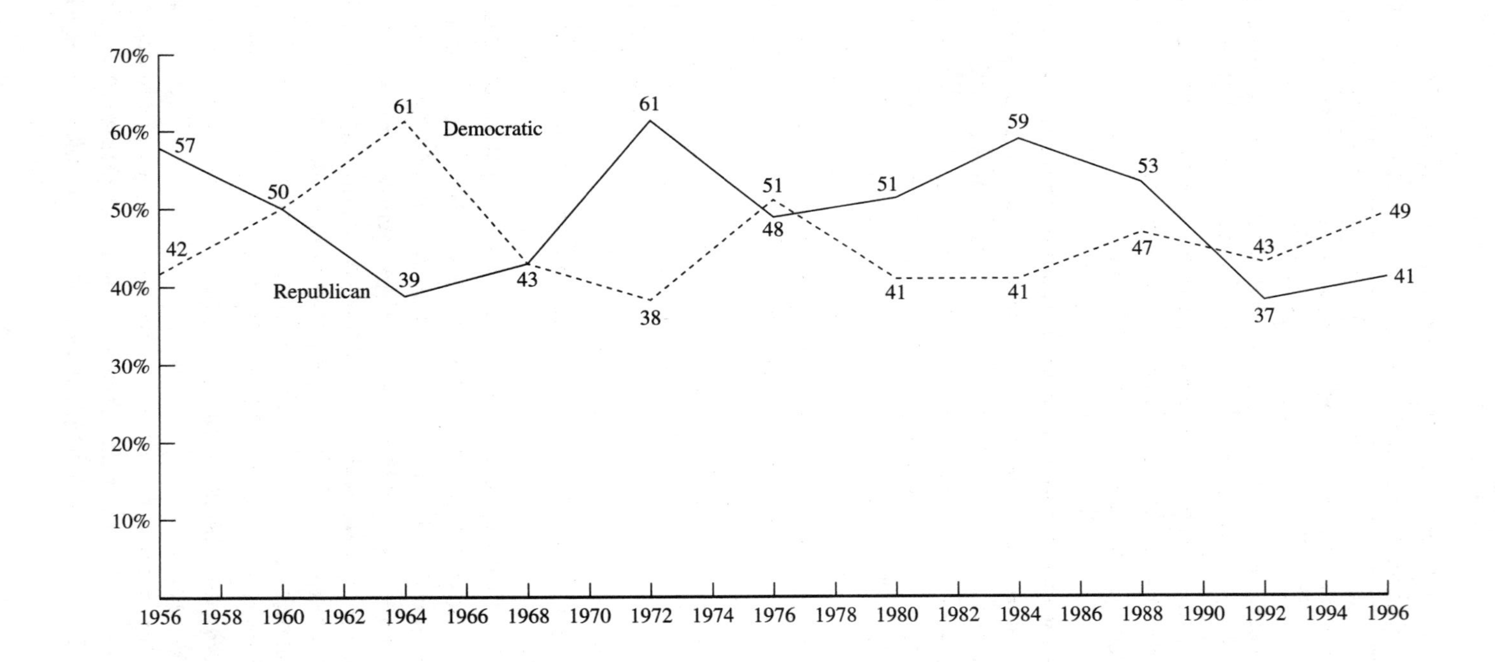

Source: Statistical Abstract of the United States, 1996, p. 271.

period, the Republicans have won six times and the Democrats five. The GOP has been victorious in five of the last eight presidential contests. Obviously, short-term factors of candidate image, issues, and party image have overridden the normal Democratic advantage in party identifiers to produce this pattern of outcome in presidential elections. Among the most dramatic aspects of this pattern is the changing allegiance of the South in presidential elections.

In 1952 and 1956 the Democratic nominee's strongest region was the South. Indeed, the only states carried by Adlai Stevenson against Dwight Eisenhower were states of the old Confederacy or border states. The South was also critical for John F. Kennedy's election in the 1960s. However, none of these Democratic candidates was able to win all the states of the Confederacy, as had been the pattern in the 1930s and 1940s. In 1968 only one southern state, Texas, was carried by the Democratic ticket as the third party candidacy of Alabama Governor George Wallace swept five deep South states and Nixon won the balance. In his 1972 bid for reelection, Nixon carried every southern state for the GOP. Jimmy Carter, a native southerner, was the last Democratic nominee to carry this region and he accomplished this feat in 1976 without majority support of white southerners. In 1980 Ronald Reagan carried every southern state but Carter's native Georgia, and in 1984 and 1988 the GOP swept all the states in the region. In 1992 and 1996, the South continued to be the GOP's strongest region in presidential elections, although Clinton brought four states of the old Confederacy back into the Democratic fold in both of those elections.

The twenty-one nonsouthern states west of the Mississippi have also shown a strong proclivity to vote Republican. Between 1968 and 1988 the Republican candidate never carried fewer than sixteen of these states, and in 1984 Reagan won all but Walter Mondale's home state of Minnesota. In 1992 and 1996, Clinton made major inroads into this previously GOP stronghold carrying California (with its rich lode of fifty-four electoral votes), Washington, Oregon, Minnesota, Missouri, Iowa, New Mexico, Hawaii, and Nevada. In 1996, he even picked up traditionally Republican Arizona.

In each of its presidential victories between 1956 and 1988 the Republicans were beneficiaries of major internal splits within the dominant Democratic party. Democrats are divided on such

Figure 8.3

REPUBLICAN AND DEMOCRATIC PERCENTAGE OF SENATE SEATS, 1956–1998

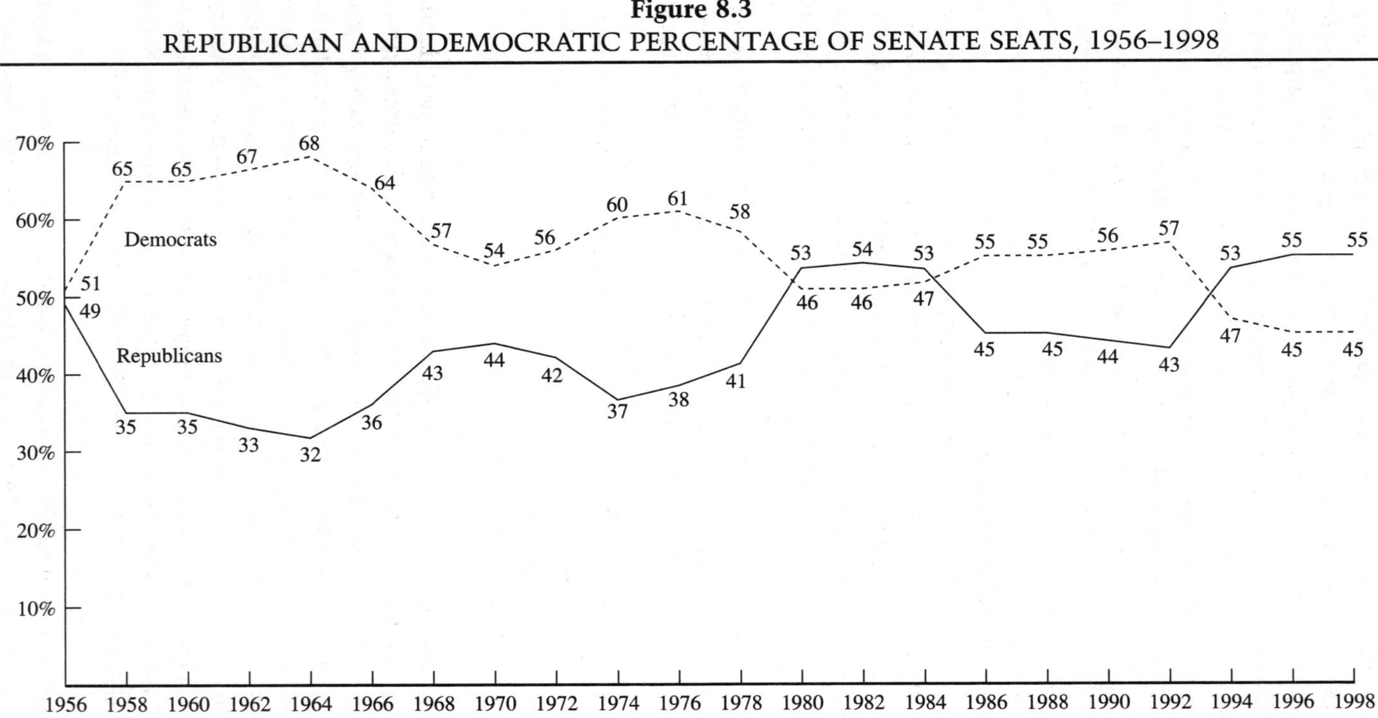

Source: Statistical Abstract of the United States, 1994, p. 279; 1997, p. 279; and *Congressional Quarterly Weekly Report*, November 7, 1998, p. 2994. Used by permission.

matters as affirmative action, crime, abortion, school prayer, and national defense issues that have become more important than they were in the 1940s through the early 1960s. At the same time, the old New Deal agenda of national government responsibility for the social welfare of individuals and the regulation of the economy has either lost its salience or the perceived "superiority" of the Democrats on these issues for the party's traditional voters has become less obvious.[39] These changes have given the GOP the opportunity to compete effectively in presidential elections. At the same time, the declining importance of partisanship for most voters has eased the difficulty for the traditional minority party in mobilizing an electoral majority.

The decline of partisanship within the electorate, however, presents opportunities for the Democrats as well as the GOP. A less partisan electorate is a volatile electorate that is capable of mobilization by either party, provided it has the right mix of conditions, issues, and candidates working in its favor. With the Democrats and Republicans approaching a rough parity in surveys of party identification, and party considerations playing a diminished role in voter choices, claims that there now exists a Republican majority in presidential elections would appear to be questionable. Clearly, the Democratic loss of the South has meant that the party has lost its normal majority, but that loss is not the same as saying there is now a Republican presidential majority.

Elections to the Senate

Whatever advantages the Republicans may have had in presidential contests had been substantially offset by Democratic domination of the Congress. Until the 1994 midterm elections, which gave Republicans control of both the House and Senate, the voters had denied the party control over both chambers for forty years. Democratic dominance had been so pervasive and persistent that there had even been talk of the GOP being a "permanent minority" in the House.[40] During its forty years in the congressional wilderness, the Republicans did achieve temporary majority status in the Senate during the Reagan era from 1981 through 1986 (see figure 8.3).

Regional Patterns. Some of the same regional patterns that are detectable in presidential elections are also present in senatorial elections. In state-wide elections for the Senate, the GOP dominated the once Democratic delegations from the South and from the Mountain states going into the 1996 elections.

Democratic control of the Senate as recently as 1960 was anchored by the party's dominance of southern politics which enabled it to control all twenty-two seats in states of the old Confederacy. As a result, southerners constituted the largest regional bloc within the Senate Democratic party in 1960—making up 33.8 percent of the party membership (see table 8.12). The next largest group of Democratic senators were from the Mountain states (twelve seats; 18.5 percent). The party was, therefore, a strongly southern and western oriented party. The Republicans, by contrast, drew strength mainly from Plains, Middle Atlantic, and New England areas. In the over thirty years between 1960 and 1996, the senatorial parties have been transformed.

Table 8.12

Composition of Republican and Democratic Parties in the U.S. Senate, by Region, 1960–1998

		Republicans		Democrats	
Region	**Year**	**Seats Held**	**Percent of Party Membership in Senate**	**Seats Held**	**Percent of Party Membership in Senate**
South	1960	0	0	22	33.8
	1998	14	25.5	8	17.8
Border	1960	4	11.4	6	9.2
	1998	6	10.9	4	8.9
New England	1960	7	20.0	5	7.7
	1998	6	10.9	6	13.3
Mid Atlantic	1960	6	17.1	2	3.1
	1998	3	5.5	5	11.1
Midwest	1960	3	8.6	7	10.8
	1998	5	9.1	5	11.1
Plains	1960	9	25.7	3	4.6
	1998	5	9.1	7	15.6
Mountain	1960	4	11.4	12	18.5
	1998	11	20.0	5	11.1
Pacific Coast	1960	2	5.7	8	12.3
	1998	4	7.3	6	13.3

Source: Norman J. Ornstein, Thomas E. Mann, and Michael J. Malbin, *Vital Statistics on Congress 1996–1997* (Washington, D.C.: Congressional Quarterly, Inc., 1998), pp. 17–18; and *New York Times*, November 5, 1998, (national edition), p. B4.

After the 1994 elections, the Senate Democratic party became substantially less southern and western in membership. Southern states constituted less than 20 percent of the party's membership and Mountain state senators were but 10.6 percent. Whereas in 1960, these two regions had elected a majority (52.3 percent) of the Democratic senators, by 1994 they were electing less than one-third (29.7 percent). By contrast, the Senate GOP membership clearly reflected the party's growing strength in the South and Mountain regions. Over 45 percent of GOP senators in 1994 represented either southern or Mountain states.

Incumbency. Senate incumbents can generally be expected to be reelected. In the elections held (see table 8.13) between 1960 and 1998, on average 81.7 percent of the incumbents seeking reelections were winners. The incumbent reelection rate for senators,

Table 8.13

Senatorial Incumbent Reelection Rates, 1960–1998

		Sought Reelection				
Year	Retired	Total	Defeated in Primaries	Defeated in General Election	Total Reelected	Reelected as Percentage of Those Seeking Reelection
1960	5	29	0	1	28	96.6
1962	4	35	1	5	29	82.9
1964	2	33	1	4	28	84.8
1966	3	32	3	1	28	87.5
1968	6	28	4	4	20	71.4
1970	4	31	1	6	24	77.4
1972	6	27	2	5	20	74.1
1974	7	27	2	2	23	85.2
1976	8	25	0	9	16	64.0
1978	10	25	3	7	15	60.0
1980	5	29	4	9	16	55.2
1982	3	30	0	2	28	93.3
1984	4	29	0	3	26	89.6
1986	5	28	0	7	21	75.0
1988	6	27	0	4	23	85.2
1990	3	32	0	1	31	96.9
1992	7	28	1	4	23	82.1
1994	8	26	0	2	24	92.3
1996	13	21	1	1	19	90.5
1998	4	30	0	3	27	90.0

Source: Norman J. Ornstein, Thomas E. Mann, and Michael J. Malbin, *Vital Statistics on Congress, 1996–1997* (Washington, D.C.: Congressional Quarterly, Inc., 1998), p. 62; *Congressional Quarterly Week Report*, November 7, 1998, p. 2994.

however, is substantially below that of members of the House of Representatives. This was particularly true during the 1976–1980 period when less than 65 percent of incumbents were successful in retaining their seats. The relatively high levels of incumbent senator defeat reflect several factors: (1) the generally higher levels of interparty competition that exist in state-wide constituencies as compared to the smaller and more demographically homogeneous House districts; (2) the higher levels of campaign resources plowed into challenger races for the Senate; and (3) the higher visibility of Senate contests. A substantial proportion of Senate incumbents, however, are normally elected by wide margins. In the elections from 1980 through 1998, slightly more than half of the incumbents (nineteen of thirty in 1998) gained at least 60 percent of the popular vote in their states.

Presidential Elections and Senate Outcomes. Senate election outcomes show substantial independence from presidential results. It is not unusual for states to have split outcomes between their presidential and senatorial votes. For example, in 1996, 26 percent of the states had split results between the presidential and senatorial elections. The tendency of voters to split their tickets between presidential and senatorial candidates has meant that the party winning the presidency is frequently unable to register a net gain of Senate seats. In five of the eleven presidential elections since World War II, the party of the winning presidential candidate has actually lost Senate seats (see table 8.14). The most dramatic postwar instance of presidential coattails occurred in 1980 when the Republicans picked up twelve seats and secured control of the upper chamber for the first time since 1954.

The outcome of Senate elections, of course, is conditioned by the fact that only one-third of the Senate is up for election in any presidential year. The extent to which national trends assist the party of the winning presidential candidate, therefore, is influenced by which one-third of the Senate is up for election that year. For example, the opportunities for the GOP to pick up seats in 1980 were enhanced by the fact that the Democrats were defending twenty-four seats and the Republicans only ten and those ten were relatively safe because they had survived the strong swing to the Democrats during the Watergate election of 1974. Some of these Democrat incumbents, therefore, were vulnerable in 1980 because they had benefited from the unusually heavy Democratic vote in 1974. The Constitution's requirement of staggered terms for senators makes unlikely a consistent pattern of gains in the Senate for the party of the winning presidential candidate.

Senatorial Elections at Midterm. As in the case of House elections, the president's party customarily loses seats during midterm elections (see table 8.14). This pattern of outcomes, however, is less pronounced in the case of Senate elections than it is for House elections. In about one-third of the Senate midterm elections since the

Table 8.14

Presidential Party Gains/Losses in Senate Seats in Presidential and Midterm Elections, 1946–1998

Year	Party Winning Presidency	Net Seats Won/Lost
1946	(Democrat elected in 1944)	– 9 Dem.
1948	Democrat	+ 9 Dem.
1950		– 6 Dem.
1952	Republican	+ 1 Rep.
1954		– 6 Rep.
1956	Republican	+ 1 Dem.
1958		– 13 Rep.
1960	Democrat	+ 2 Rep.
1962		+ 3 Dem.
1964	Democrat	+ 1 Dem.
1966		– 4 Dem.
1968	Republican	+ 6 Rep.
1970		+ 2 Rep.
1972	Republican	+ 2 Dem.
1974		– 5 Rep.
1976	Democrat	No Change
1978		– 3 Dem.
1980	Republican	+ 12 Rep.
1982		+ 1 Rep.
1984	Republican	– 2 Rep.
1986		– 8 Rep.
1988	Republican	No Change
1990		– 1 Rep.
1992	Democrat	No Change
1994		– 10 * Dem.
1996	Democrat	– 2 Dem.
1998	Democrat	No Change

*Includes Senator Richard Shelby (Ala.) who switched immediately following the 1994 elections.

Source: Norman J. Ornstein, Thomas E. Mann, and Michael J. Malbin, *Vital Statistics on Congress, 1996–1997* (Washington, D.C.: Congressional Quarterly, Inc., 1998), pp. 54–55; *Congressional Quarterly Weekly Report,* November 7, 1998, p. 2994.

Civil War, the president's party has actually gained seats. The outcome at midterm is influenced not only by national political trends and the state of the economy, but by which particular set of senators is up for election. An important factor influencing the extent to which there is a net shift of seats from one party to the other is the number of seats each party is defending as it goes into the election. If the president's party is defending a relatively large number of seats, the likelihood of major losses by his party is enhanced. For example, in the 1994 senatorial midterm elections, there were twenty-two seats being defended by the Democrats and thirteen by the GOP. These circumstances, plus careful targeting of national party resources to open seat contests and races where incumbents were seriously threatened, enabled the Republicans to emerge from the election with a net gain of ten seats.

Elections to the House of Representatives

Consequences of the Single Member District-Plurality System. The single member district-plurality system of election has meant that a party's percentage of the House membership will not necessarily be proportionate to its national popular vote for Congress. If one party's voters tend to be concentrated in districts that it wins overwhelmingly and if the opposition party tends to win most of the marginal districts by narrow margins, then the composition of the legislative chamber is not apt to reflect accurately the share of the total vote received by either party. A disparity between popular votes and a party's share of the legislative seats is an inevitable consequence of the uneven manner in which adherents of the two parties are scattered across the country and the way boundary lines are drawn. Of course, overt gerrymandering of congressional district lines designed to enhance the advantage of one party or the other can magnify the disparity between seats won and a party's share of the national two party vote.

Table 8.15 shows the extent to which disparity exists between the national popular vote for Congress and the partisan distribution of seats within the House. Since 1960, it has been the Democrats that have been advantaged by the single member district-plurality system of election. Even more dramatic disparities can exist between a party's percentage of the state popular vote for House candidates and the share of the seats it wins in a state's congressional delegation. Examples of instances in which both the Democrats and Republicans have benefited from this disparity are shown in table 8.16. The alternative to a single member district-plurality system is a system of proportional representation using multi-member legislative districts. Under proportional representation a party receives a share of legislative seats from a given constituency that corresponds to its percentage of the vote. Proportional representation, however, provides incentive to develop a multiplicity of parties because each is assured of some legislative representation if it can meet some minimum threshold requirement to qualify for electing legislators. The single member district system tends to give one party a majority in the national legislature, whereas proportional representation frequently leads to situations in which no party has a legislative majority and cross-party coalitions must be formed to organize a government.

Regional Patterns. Changes in regional voting patterns are reflected in the makeup of parties in the House just as they are with the Senate parties. In 1960 almost 40 percent of the House Democratic membership came from the South (see table 8.17). By 1994, southern Democrats constituted only 29.9 percent of the membership and the Pacific Coast contingent had become more important. As southern influence in the House Democratic party has declined, it has grown significantly among the Republicans. Southern Republicans moved from being an insignificant segment of the party (3.5 percent) in 1960 to the largest regional contingent after the 1994 elections. This shift was symbolized in 1995 by the selection of Newt Gingrich of Georgia to be Speaker of the House and Richard Armey of Texas to be the Majority Leader. Further evidence of the rising importance of the South in the House Republican party is the fact that Florida had one of the largest Republican state delegations after the 1998 elections. The Florida GOP delegation (fifteen members) was outranked only by California with twenty-four. The rise of the South in the House Republican party has been accompanied by a significant decline in the proportion of the party membership coming from the Midwest, Mid-Atlantic, and Plains regions.

Table 8.15
Popular Vote for the House of Representatives and Percentage of Seats Won, 1960–1998

Year	Democratic Candidates: Percentage of All Votes	Democratic Candidates: Percentage of Seats Won	Republican Candidates: Percentage of All Votes	Republican Candidates: Percentage of Seats Won	Difference between Democratic Percentage of Seats and Votes Won
1960	54.4	60.0	44.8	40.0	+ 5.6
1962	52.1	59.4	47.1	40.6	+ 7.3
1964	56.9	67.8	42.4	32.2	+ 10.9
1966	50.5	57.0	48.0	43.0	+ 6.5
1968	50.0	55.9	48.2	44.1	+ 5.9
1970	53.0	58.6	44.5	41.4	+ 5.6
1972	51.7	55.8	46.4	44.2	+ 4.1
1974	57.1	66.9	40.5	33.1	+ 9.8
1976	56.2	67.1	42.1	32.9	+ 10.9
1978	53.4	63.7	44.7	36.3	+ 10.3
1980	50.4	55.9	48.0	44.1	+ 5.5
1982	55.6	61.8	42.9	38.2	+ 6.2
1984	52.1	58.2	47.0	41.8	+ 6.1
1986	54.5	59.3	44.6	40.7	+ 4.8
1988	53.3	59.8	45.5	40.2	+ 6.5
1990	52.9	61.4	45.0	38.4	+ 8.5
1992	50.9	59.3	46.5	40.5	+ 8.4
1994	45.5	46.9	52.4	52.9	+ 1.1
1996	48.5	47.6	48.9	52.2	– 0.9

Source: Norman J. Ornstein, Thomas E. Mann, and Michael J. Malbin, *Vital Statistics on Congress, 1997–1998* (Washington, D.C.: Congressional Quarterly, Inc., 1998), pp. 52–53.

Table 8.16
Popular Vote for the House Compared to Percentage of Seats Won in Selected States, 1994

State	Democrats: Percent of Popular Vote for Congress	Democrats: Percent of Seats Won	Democrats: No of Seats Won	Republicans: Percent of Popular Vote for Congress	Republicans: Percent of Seats Won	Republicans: No of Seats Won
California	50	52	27	45	48	25
Iowa	45	0	0	50	100	5
Kansas	41	0	0	56	100	4
New Hampshire	45	0	0	50	100	2
New Jersey	48	38	5	50	62	8
Oklahoma	37	17	1	61	83	5
Texas	46	60	18	53	40	12
West Virginia	88	100	3	12	0	0

Source: Statistical Abstract of the United States, 1997, pp. 275, 280.

Table 8.17
Composition of the Republican and Democratic Parties in the U.S. House of Representatives, by Region, 1960–1998

		Republicans		Democrats	
Region	**Year**	**Seats Won**	**Percent of Party Membership in House**	**Seats Won**	**Percent of Party Membership in House**
South	1960	6	3.5	98	37.5
	1998	71	31.8	54	25.6
Border	1960	6	3.5	32	12.3
	1998	19	8.5	13	6.2
New England[a]	1960	14	8.2	14	5.4
	1998	4	1.8	18	8.5
Mid Atlantic	1960	44	25.7	43	16.5
	1998	34	15.2	52	24.6
Midwest	1960	51	29.3	35	13.4
	1998	37	16.6	37	17.5
Plains	1960	25	14.6	6	2.3
	1998	13	5.8	9	4.3
Mountain	1960	4	2.3	11	4.2
	1998	17	7.6	6	3.3
Pacific Coast	1960	21	12.3	22	8.4
	1998	30	13.4	39	17.6

a. Independent elected in Vermont.

Sources: Statistical Abstract of the United States; New York Times (national edition), November 5, 1998, pp. B8–9.

Incumbency. The pattern of incumbents gaining reelection is stronger in the House than in the Senate. Normally, over 90 percent of the House incumbents gain reelection. In 1986 the figure reached a postwar high of 98.3 percent, a reelection rate that was reached again in 1998. And even in 1994, when the Republicans won control of the House while ousting thirty-five incumbent Democrats, incumbents enjoyed an overall reelection rate of 92 percent. House incumbents benefit from the relatively homogeneous nature of their districts when compared to the larger and more socially diverse statewide constituencies of senators. The distinctive socioeconomic character of individual House districts frequently gives a clear advantage to the candidate of one party or the other (e.g., predominantly black inner city districts are safely Democratic as are most big city districts with concentrations of blue-collar workers of eastern and southern European heritage; middle- and upper-middle-class suburban/small town districts are normally strongly Republican).

Incumbents are in a position to engage in extensive self-advertisement (e.g., mass mailings, constituent surveys, press releases, radio and television tapes, constituent service, town hall meetings) designed to project a favorable image. Of particular benefit to incumbents is the fact that major campaign efforts are not normally made on behalf of their challengers. Through skillful use of the advantages of public office, incumbents in most House districts are able to make their constituencies relatively safe for themselves for extended periods of time. Major struggles for control of the House, therefore, are fought out in the small proportion of districts in which incumbents are considered electorally vulnerable and in open seats, where no incumbent is seeking reelection. The advantages of incumbency are illustrated by the fact that between 1980 and 1996, on average, three-fourths of House incumbents received at least 60 percent of the vote. These healthy reelection margins which House members in the aggregate pile up tend to mask the fact that a large proportion of the representatives have had at least one close election in their congressional careers. In the 105th Congress (1997–1998), 54 percent had had an election in which they won by 55 percent or less of the vote.[41] The sense of electoral insecurity which such elections can generate causes most members to work constantly to maintain a relationship of trust with their constituents.[42]

The Historic 1998 Midterm Elections: The President's Party Gains Seats in the House, But Incumbents Still Win!

Post-1998 election commentary focused upon the fact that, for the first time in a midterm election since 1934, the party of the president gained seats in the House of Representatives. This surprising outcome made 1998 an historic election. However, in one important respect, the 1998 midterm House elections were anything but exceptional. Incumbents won in all but a handful of races as the following numbers demonstrate.

	Republicans	Democrats	Independents	Total	Percent
Incumbents Reelected	206	188	1	395	98.3%
Incumbents Defeated	6	1	0	7	1.7%

Presidential Elections and House Outcomes. Normally the party winning the presidency registers a net gain of House seats in presidential election years. Post–World War II exceptions to this pattern of the party winning the presidency not picking up House seats occurred in 1956, 1960, 1988, and 1992 (see table 8.18). The advantages of incumbency and the tendency of voters to split their tickets between presidential and congressional races have reduced the likelihood of major shifts in the partisan composition of the House after a presidential election.

A much commented upon aspect of the 1984 presidential election landslide for Republican Ronald Reagan was the inability of the GOP to make large scale gains in the House (the Republicans scored

Table 8.18

Presidential Party Gains/Losses in House Seats in Presidential and Midterm Elections, 1946–1998

Year	Party Winning the Presidency	Net Seats Won/Lost
1946	(Democrat elected in 1944)	– 55 Dem.
1948	Democrat	+ 75 Dem.
1950		– 29 Dem.
1952	Republican	+ 22 Rep.
1954		– 18 Rep.
1956	Republican	+ 2 Dem.
1958		– 48 Rep.
1960	Democrat	+ 22 Rep.
1962		– 4 Dem.
1964	Democrat	+ 37 Dem.
1966		– 47 Dem.
1968	Republican	+ 5 Rep.
1970		– 12 Rep.
1972	Republican	+ 12 Rep.
1974		– 48 Rep.
1976	Democrat	+ 1 Dem.
1978		– 15 Dem.
1980	Republican	+ 34 Rep.
1982		– 26 Rep.
1984	Republican	+ 14 Rep.
1986		– 5 Rep.
1988	Republican	– 2 Rep.
1990		– 8 Rep.
1992	Democrat	– 10 Dem.
1994		– 52 Dem.
1996	Democrat	+ 9 Dem.
1998		+ 5 Dem.

Sources: Norman J. Ornstein, Thomas E. Mann, and Michael J. Malbin, *Vital Statistics on Congress, 1997–1998* (Washington, D.C.: Congressional Quarterly, Inc., 1998), pp. 54–56; *Congressional Quarterly Weekly Report,* November 7, 1998, p. 2990.

a net gain of only fourteen seats). Obviously, the president's coattails did not have sufficient pulling power to bring into office with him significant numbers of additional Republican representatives. Many voters split their tickets between presidential and House elections. In Alabama, for example, all five Democratic incumbent representatives won reelection by at least 60 percent of the vote, while Reagan was carrying the state for president by a 60 percent margin. The growing independence of presidential and House election outcomes (see table 8.18) reflects the declining importance of partisanship as a decisional cue for voters in House races.

Congressional elections expert Gary Jacobson has concluded that a necessary condition for long presidential coattails is that "serious congressional candidates of the president-elect's party anticipate a good year well in advance and so position themselves to take advantage of the electoral benefits that later flow from the top of the ticket."[43] This clearly occurred in 1980 as GOP strategists anticipated a good year and succeeded in recruiting strong candidates for races in Democratic-held districts. The prospects of a strong showing for Republican candidates enabled them to raise substantial campaign warchests and mount major campaign efforts. Strong candidates with sufficient campaign resources were the key to the GOP gain of thirty-four House seats in the Reagan presidential victory of 1980. Jacobson's analysis reveals that only six House seats would have shifted to the Republicans in 1980 "if every Republican had enjoyed merely the average vote swing from 1978 to 1980 of three percentage points" in favor of the GOP. Victorious Republican challengers instead averaged an increase of 13 percent over the vote that candidates of their party had received in 1978.[44] Without the strong campaigns of these GOP challengers, the Reagan coattails in 1980 would in all likelihood have been virtually undetectable.

In 1984, the Republicans had greater difficulty taking advantage of the national trend which favored their party. The party's inability to dislodge incumbent Democrats in the 1982 midterm elections produced a lingering "bad memory" for some potentially strong GOP challengers who decided to bypass the 1984 House elections. Republican recruitment efforts were also hampered by the uncertain state of the recession racked economy during 1983, when most serious candidates had to make their decisions about whether to enter House election contests.

The GOP also had difficulty recruiting strong challengers to Democratic incumbents for the 1988 House elections because of the decline in President Reagan's popularity due to the Iran-Contra affair, an uncertain economy in 1987, and polls in early 1988 showing the Democrats ahead of the Republicans. In addition, the Republicans were hurt by a shortage of Democratic open seats, which normally provide the best opportunity for a party to take seats away from the opposition.[45] Clearly, a large number of attractive, well-funded challengers and a substantial number of open seats are necessary conditions for major gains in House elections during presidential years.

Presidential coattails are also encouraged if congressional candidates are able to give voters a reason to connect the presidential vote and the congressional vote. This occurred in the presidential landslides of 1980 and 1964. In 1980, Republican congressional candidates were able to tap the public discontent with the general drift of political life as they joined Reagan in asking voters to "Vote Republican, for a change!" Similarly, Democratic candidates in 1964 campaigned on the theme of completing the agendas of the New Deal, John F. Kennedy, and Lyndon B. Johnson. They also exploited the unpopularity of Barry Goldwater's policies by linking Republican congressional candidates with their party's presidential nominee. In both of these elections, the winning party gained landslide presidential victories with substantial coattails while advocating major changes in national policy.

By contrast in the presidential reelections of 1956, 1972, 1984, 1988, and 1996 there was an absence of coattails. Each election took place during a period of relative prosperity and improved international conditions. The emphasis of the winning campaigns, therefore, was upon continuity not change. Campaigns which stress continuity, however, give little rhetorical advantage to challengers seeking to dislodge incumbents. In 1984 and 1988, for example, Republicans seeking to oust Democrats had great difficulty blaming their opponents for obstructing progress, and Democrats sought to claim some of the credit for the good times. The 1996 election was almost a mirror image of 1984. With the Republicans in control of Congress, their incumbents asserted that they had at least equal claim with President Clinton to credit for economic prosperity. In these circumstances Democratic challengers found it hard to find a compelling campaign issue. Thus, the nature of the campaign themes and the issues that are salient to the voters also have a bearing on the extent of presidential coattails. The absence of a coattail effect for the Democrats (a loss of ten seats) in 1992 can be attributed to Clinton's winning only 43 percent of the popular vote in a three-way race for the presidency against Bush and Perot, plus redistricting that was favorable to the Republicans in several states.

House Elections at Midterm. Since the Civil War, in every midterm election, except for 1934 and 1998, the president's party has lost House seats. The 1934 exception to this pattern occurred in the midst of the realignments of the early New Deal Era. The unanticipated and historic five seat Democratic gain in 1998 occurred amid controversy over a special prosecutor's allegations of possible perjury and obstruction of justice by President Clinton in connection with his affair with a White House intern and the initiation of presidential impeachment proceedings by the Republican controlled House of Representatives. In achieving their unexpected gains in the House, the Democrats were aided by voters who tended to perceive the Democrats as being stronger than the Republicans on such issues as education, health care, and Social Security. In addition, solid majorities of voters expressed approval of the president's job performance and opposition to impeachment, even though they overwhelmingly disapproved of Clinton's behavior. The Democrats also benefited from voter mobilization efforts, which resulted in a greater turn out of blacks and union household members who voted heavily Democratic.

A variety of explanations have been offered for the tendency of the president's party to lose House seats in midterm elections (see table 8.18). One factor influencing the extent of loss by the president's party in the House is that of the strength of the president's coattails in the previous election.[46] If a president sweeps a large number of candidates from his party into office with him, there is apt to be a sizeable bloc who will face difficult reelection bids at midterm when the president is not on the ballot. Those who are highly vulnerable are likely to fail in reelection. Thus in 1964, the Lyndon Johnson Democratic landslide coincided with a net gain of thirty-seven Democratic seats in the House. In the 1966 midterm election, many of these newly elected Democrats lost their seats as the GOP registered a major net gain of forty-seven seats. However, if the presidential candidate lacks coattails and fails to carry House members of his party into office with him, the president's party is likely to suffer only minimal losses at midterm because few incumbents owe their previous election to presidential coattails. Such a pattern occurred in 1960 when John F. Kennedy ran behind most of his party's House candidates and the Democratic party actually lost twenty-two seats. As a result, few Democrats seeking reelection in 1962 owed their election to presidential coattails and Democrats sustained a loss of only four seats in the 1962 midterm elections.

The extent of midterm losses by the president's party also involves more immediate influences than the strength of presidential coattails in the previous election. Two such influences are presidential popularity and the state of the economy. Edward Tufte has analyzed the relationship of these factors to the vote received by candidates of the president's party in House midterm elections.[47] He discovered that both a decline in presidential popularity and a downturn in the economy correlated strongly with a fall-off in the popular vote for the president's party. While presidential popularity and economic conditions have significance for House elections at midterm, these kinds of aggregate national statistical analyses do not take fully into account the fact that House elections are decided by voters making choices among specific candidates in various congressional districts. Thus in 1982, the Republicans were able to hold their losses in the House to twenty-six seats, even though the depressed state of the economy and President Reagan's declining presidential popularity would have predicated a loss of much more substantial magnitude. The inability of aggregate statistics to explain the extent of loss at midterm by the president's party has led political scientists to explore the consequences of strategic decision making by political activists.

Gary Jacobson and Samuel Kernell have suggested that economic conditions and the state of presidential popularity have their impact on the outcome of House races twelve to eighteen months in advance of the election when political leaders in both parties are making key decisions that will affect the outcome of specific House contests.[48] It is during this time that candidates make decisions about whether to run or not. If circumstances seem adverse for a party, promising challengers may conclude that they should wait and run when circumstances seem more likely to yield victory. Similarly, incumbents may elect to retire rather than face tough races when conditions are not favorable to their party. Or if conditions look good for a party, its incumbents are apt again to stand for reelection and it is easier to recruit strong challengers to run in districts held by the opposition. Contributors make similar calculations about the worth of investing in campaigns based upon assumptions concerning the possibility of a winnable race. Over a year in advance of an election, therefore, decisions are made about who the candidates will be, whether they will be well funded, and whether the party should adopt an offensive strategy designed to win seats from the opposition or adopt a defensive strategy that seeks to channel resources into retaining the party's existing seats. These decisions by political leaders go a long way toward determining the types of contests that will be waged in congressional districts across the nation.

An example of the effects of strategic decisions by political leaders on midterm elections can be seen in 1994. Sensing that President Clinton's relatively low approval ratings, widespread discontent with government, and worries about the economy would provide an opportunity for major gains, Republicans successfully recruited strong candidates to challenge Democratic incumbents and to run in the unusually large number of open seat contests—fifty-two (thirty held by Democrats) in the House and nine (six held by the Democrats) in the Senate as well as to challenge incumbent Democrats. The Republican National Committee even borrowed $5 million so that it could pump resources into targeted races. While the Republicans were thus in an offensive mode, the situation for the Democrats was exactly the reverse. Faced with less than favorable conditions, an unusually large number of Democratic incumbents did not seek reelection and the party was forced into a defensive posture that was not able to withstand the GOP tidal wave.

Gubernatorial and State Legislative Elections

Democratic Dominance before 1994. Despite setbacks in presidential politics, the Democratic party has dominated gubernatorial and state legislative elections during most of the post–World War II era. Between 1956 and 1994, the GOP has controlled a majority of the nation's governorships only twice—following the 1968 and 1994 elections (see figure 8.4) and the party never controlled

Figure 8.4
PARTY CONTROL OF GOVERNORSHIPS (PERCENT)

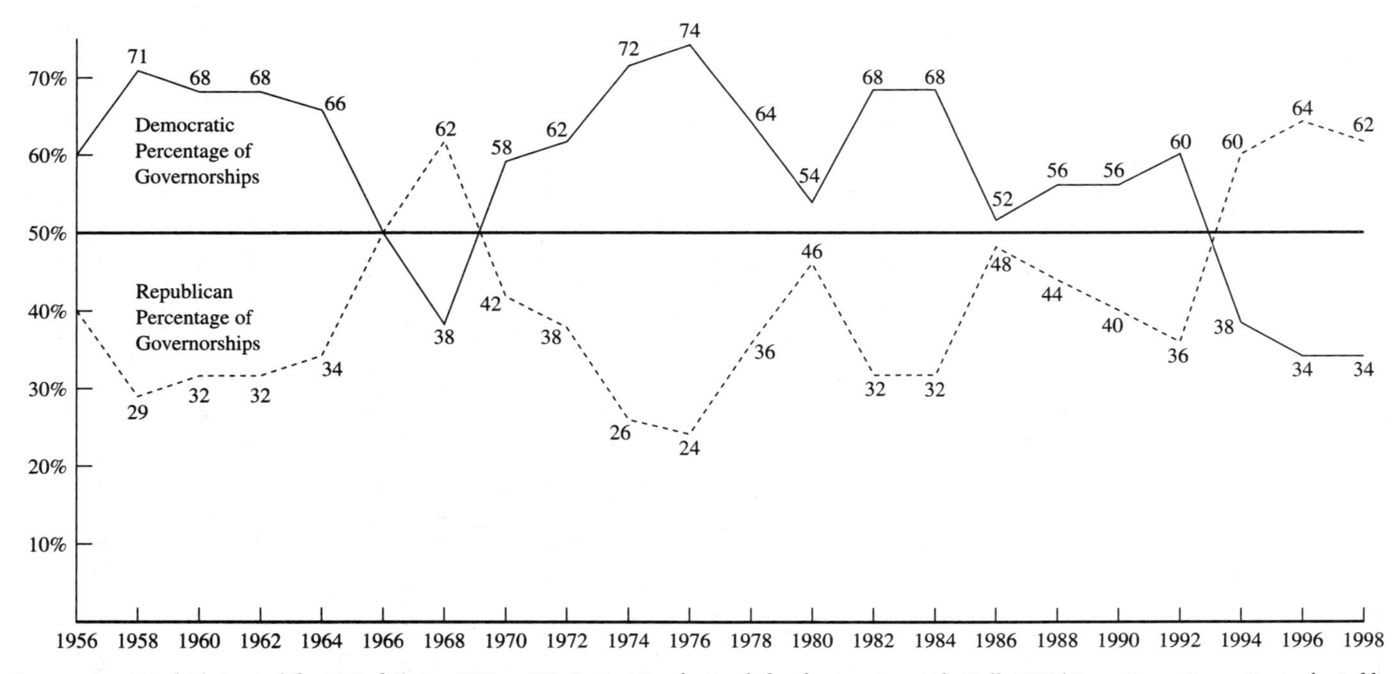

Sources: Statistical Abstract of the United States, 1997, p. 283; Regina Dougherty, el al., eds. *America at the Polls 1996* (Storrs, Conn: Roper Center for Public Opinion Research, University of Connecticut, 1997), p. 32; *Congressional Quarterly Weekly Report*, November 7, 1998, p. 3000.

both state legislative chambers in a majority of the states. The post–World War II pattern of Republicans winning the largest share of presidential elections and Democrats tending to dominate governorships and state legislatures (as well as House elections) created a two tiered political system. Analysts considered this two tiered system to be a reflection of voters' differing expectations for governmental institutions and their perceptions of which party was best able to operate those institutions. Thus, voters seemed to expect the House of Representatives and state officials to protect specific government programs from which they derived benefits. In protecting those benefits, they saw the Democrats as doing a better job than the GOP. At the same time, voters viewed the presidency as the office responsible for protecting broad national interests, and for this responsibility they favored the Republicans in most postwar presidential elections.[49] However, the 1992 and 1994 elections, which brought a Democrat to the White House and Republicans into control of Congress and a majority of governorships, have turned this theory on its head. Ensuing elections will determine whether the 1992–1998 elections were aberrations or the beginning of a new political era.

Regional Patterns. With the exception of Democrats in the South from 1960 until 1994, there has been no consistent pattern of regional party dominance of governorships. Rather, party fortunes within regions have shown substantial variation over relatively short periods of time (see table 8.19). For example, Republican control of the five midwestern governorships has ranged from zero to five between 1960 and 1980 and stood at four after the 1994 and 1998 elections. Even before the 1994 GOP sweep the South had not escaped the rising tide of interparty competition. Every southern state but Georgia had elected at least one Republican governor between 1966 and 1998.

One of the most interesting patterns of regional voting during the Reagan-Bush era was the ability of the Democrats to win governorships in the Mountain states, one of the GOP's areas of greatest strength in presidential elections. Between 1980 and 1990 the Democrats never held less than five of the eight governorships in this region and after the 1982 elections they held all eight. Clearly, Democratic governors were able to differentiate themselves from their national party and effectively appeal to voters.

Table 8.19
Party Control of Governorships by Region, 1960–1998

Region	1960		1970		1980		1990			1998		
	Rep.	Dem.	Rep.	Dem.	Rep.	Dem.	Rep.	Dem.	Ind.	Rep.	Dem.	Ind.
New England	4	2	4	2	1	5	4	1	1	3	2	1
Mid Atlantic	1	3	3	1	3	1	1	3	0	3	1	0
Midwest	0	5	3	2	5	0	4	1	0	4	1	0
Plains	4	2	1	5	5	1	3	3	0	4	1	1
South	0	11	2	9	4	7	3	8	0	7	4	0
Border	0	5	2	3	1	4	1	4	0	2	3	0
Mountain	5	3	3	5	1	7	3	5	0	8	0	0
Pacific Coast	2	3	3	2	3	2	1	3	1	0	5	0
Totals	16	34	21	29	23	27	20	28	2	31	17	2

Sources: Statistical Abstract of the United States, 1990, p. 258; Everett Carll Ladd, ed., *America at the Polls, 1994* (Storrs, Conn.: Roper Center for Public Opinion Research, 1995), p. 13; *New York Times* (national edition), November 5,1998, pp. B1–B7.

The most distinctive pattern of regional voting for state legislative elections exists in the South, which has been overwhelmingly dominated by the Democrats. Whereas the Republicans have been able to compete effectively for governorships in most of the South since the mid-1960s, their progress toward competitiveness in state legislative elections has been much slower.

After becoming a growing presence in southern legislatures during the 1980s and early 1990s, Republicans scored major breakthroughs in 1994. For the first time since Reconstruction, the GOP won southern legislative majorities in the Florida Senate and North Carolina House. And in 1998, the GOP won control of both chambers in Florida, which became the first state of the old Confederacy since Reconstruction to have both a Republican legislature and governor.

Although the Republicans after 1994 were capable of being a decision making force in most southern legislatures, there were still states of the old Confederacy with only a corporal's guard of Republican legislators (e.g., Arkansas and Louisiana), or where the GOP held less than one-third of the seats (Alabama House, Mississippi House and Senate).

Incumbency. Incumbent governors tend to be more vulnerable to defeat than are U.S. senators or representatives. While incumbent representatives are returned at a 90 percent rate and senators at approximately the 80 percent level, governors since the 1950s have been reelected at an over 70 percent level. The higher level of gubernatorial vulnerability arises from the fact that governors are normally central figures in every controversial policy dispute within their states. There is also a public perception that governors have extensive power and are capable of handling state problems. Governors are likely, therefore, to be held accountable for the state of their states, especially when conditions become less than favorable.

Evidence is emerging that incumbency is becoming a major advantage for state legislators.[50] As state legislatures have developed into more professionalized institutions—annual sessions, higher pay, larger staffs, fewer voluntary retirements—the job of the legislator has become virtually a full time job in many states. Full time legislators have extensive opportunities to engage in self-advertisement through use of their perquisites of office and normally have a much easier time raising campaign funds. In addition, they often enjoy the support of party caucus staffs and aggressive legislative campaign committees. As a result, defeating incumbent legislators has become more difficult. The National Conference of State Legislatures has reported that from 25 to 65 percent of the incumbent legislators in some states run unopposed in both the primary and general elections. In many states, incumbent legislators' reelection rates rival the 90+ percent level now prevalent in the U.S. House of Representatives. In Wisconsin, for example, State Assembly incumbents achieved an average reelection rate of over 98 percent in 1992–1996, and, in 1994, 1996, and 1998 100 percent of incumbent state senators won reelection. If this trend toward incumbent advantage continues it may substantially retard partisan shifts in control of state legislative chambers.

Although incumbency carries with it significant advantages, its influence is not as pervasive in gubernatorial and state legislative elections as it is in congressional and senatorial elections. In state contests, the extent of partisan strength in the electorate and the capacities of the parties and their candidates to mobilize their supporters through campaign spending and other voter mobilization activities are important factors in determining the share of the vote each party receives. The Republicans, who have been the minority party in most states, can generally increase their share of the vote in gubernatorial races through higher levels of spending. By contrast, the electorally stronger Democrats quickly reach a point of diminishing returns from campaign spending.[51] In state legislative elections, challengers in both parties tend to benefit more than incumbents through increased expenditures.[52]

Professionalized Legislatures. As a part of the 1970s movement to reform state legislatures, salaries were increased, and additional staff and other resources were provided to legislators. This process of legislative professionalization made legislative service virtually a full-time job in many states. Research by Morris Fiorina has shown that the trend toward fulltime legislators tended to advantage the Democrats by making legislative service more attractive to the party's pool of potential candidates. By contrast, the pool of persons from whom the GOP recruited its candidates tended to find that fulltime legislative service was incompatible with another career, thereby hurting the party's candidate recruitment efforts and contributing to the Republicans' minority status in most state legislatures since the 1970s.[53]

Presidential Elections and State Election Outcomes. Gubernatorial elections have shown a marked independence from national trends in presidential years. In six of the twelve elections between 1952 and 1996, the party of the winning presidential candidate has actually lost governorships (1956, 1960, 1964, 1972, 1988, and 1996). Even in landslide years, such as 1964 and 1972, the party of the successful presidential candidate has sustained a loss of governorships (see table 8.20). Similarly, in the 1988 Republican presidential victory for Bush the party lost two governorships. These data evidence the increased incidence of ticket splitting between presidential and gubernatorial elections since the turn of the century.

In the period 1896–1908, presidential and gubernatorial results within the states coincided in 89.5 percent of the elections.[54] This pattern continued into the 1920s. For example, in 1920 the Republicans won the governorship in each of the twenty-eight nonsouthern states carried by their presidential nominee, Warren G. Harding. By contrast, only 66 percent of the results coincided in the presidential elections from 1976 to 1992. Recently, the Democrats have been the least effective in capturing governorships while winning the presidency. Between 1952 and 1996, the party scored a net gain in governorships only twice, in 1976 and 1992. The GOP, by contrast, has more frequently registered gubernatorial gains when it was also winning the presidency (though the party's average gain has been only one governorship—see table 8.20).

State legislative elections are affected by presidential coattails. James Campbell has demonstrated that the presidential vote within a state consistently and positively influences the percentage of legislative seats gained by the party winning the presidency.[55] However, when partisan control of state legislative chambers is analyzed, it is apparent that there is substantial variation across the states in the impact of presidential campaigns. It is not unusual for the party of the winning presidential candidate to fail to gain control of additional legislative chambers or to actually lose control of chambers in presidential years. In six of eleven elections since 1950, the party winning the presidency has failed to achieve a net gain in legislative chambers and in five instances the winning party actually sustained a net loss (see table 8.21).

State Elections at Midterm. Midterm gubernatorial elections are highly susceptible to national trends. Indeed, proportionate changes in partisan control of governorships are likely to be greater at midterm than switched party control of seats in the Congress. There is a general pattern of the president's party losing governorships during midterm elections. In every midterm election between 1950 and 1998, the president's party has lost governorships, except 1962, 1986 and 1998. The average midterm loss has been 4.7 governors, with the Republicans and Democrats both averaging a loss of four to five seats (see table 8.20).

The sole instance of the president's party gaining governorships in the post–World War II era occurred in 1986 when the GOP scored a net gain of eight governorships. With President Reagan riding a wave of popularity, the economy relatively strong, and an absence of foreign policy disturbance, local issues and candidate images dominated the 1986 elections. The Republicans in these circumstances were advantaged because they were defending only nine governorships while the Democrats were forced to defend twenty-seven. In addition, fifteen Democratic governors were not seeking reelection, thereby removing the Democrats' incumbent advantage factor.

One irony of the normal pattern of presidential party losses at midterm is that elections for governor seem more susceptible to national trends than do elections to the United States House of Representatives. A further irony in this pattern is that reformers have succeeded in shifting most gubernatorial elections from presidential to midterm years on the grounds that state elections should be fought on state issues rather than be contaminated by national issues and trends. It is apparent from the data presented in table 8.20 that voters have foiled the reformers' objective. Instead, national trends appear to have a greater impact on midterm gubernatorial elections than on those occurring simultaneously with presidential elections.

The reason for this pattern is that in presidential years, gubernatorial candidates are not the most prominent persons on the ballot. But at midterm, they are the most visible candidates seeking public office. Governors, as has been noted, are widely perceived to be powerful officials involved in their states' major policy conflicts and are likely to be held accountable for conditions within their states. As the candidate at the top of the ticket, the governor stands

Table 8.20

Results of Gubernatorial Elections in Presidential and Midterm Election Years, 1950–1998

		Governorships at Stake					Election Result			Gain/Losses	
Year	Party Winning Presidential Election	Total	Rep.	Dem.	Ind.	Republican Percent of Major-Party Vote	Rep.	Dem.	Ind.	Rep.	Dem.
1950		33	15	18	0	53.1	25	23	0	+ 6	– 6
1952	Rep.	31	15	16	0	47.0	30	18	0	+ 5	– 5
1954		33	23	10	0	47.2	21	27	0	– 9	+ 9
1956	Rep.	30	15	15	0	46.8	19	29	0	– 2	+ 2
1958		33	13	20	0	44.1	14	35	0	– 5	+ 6
1960	Dem.	27	12	15	0	46.5	16	34	0	+ 2	– 1
1962		35	14	21	0	50.0	16	34	0	No change	
1964	Dem.	25	7	18	0	45.2	17	33	0	+ 1	– 1
1966		35	14	21	0	53.1	25	25	0	+ 8	– 8
1968	Rep.	21	8	13	0	47.3	31	19	0	+ 6	– 6
1970		35	24	11	0	48.6	21	29	0	– 10	+ 10
1972	Rep.	18	8	10	0	49.7	19	31	0	– 2	+ 2
1974		35	11	24	0	43.6	13	36	1	– 6	+ 5
1976	Dem.	14	6	8	0	50.8	12	37	1	– 1	+ 1
1978		36	9	26	1	47.8	18	32	0	+ 6	– 5
1980	Rep.	13	3	10	0	50.0	23	27	0	+ 5	– 5
1982		36	16	20	0	45.6	16	34	0	– 7	+ 7
1984	Rep.	13	7	6	0	51.7	16	34	0	+ 1	– 1
1986		36	9	27	0	46.6	24	26	0	+ 8	– 8
1988	Rep.	12	8	4	0	50.6	22	28	0	– 2	+ 2
1990		36	16	20	0	44.9	20	28	2	– 2	No change
1992	Dem.	12	6	6	0	42.4	18	30	2	– 2	+ 2
1994		36	13	21	2	53.6	30	19	1	+ 12	– 11
1996	Dem.	11	4	7	0	46.1	32	17	1	+ 2	– 2
1998		36	24	11	1		31	17	2	– 1	No change

Table 8.20 (continued)

Summary		
Midterm elections		
Average number of governorships lost by:		
President's party	4.7	
Republicans	4.4	
Democrats	5.0	
Presidential election years		
Average gain/loss for party of winning presidential candidate		+1.0
Average gain/loss when winning presidential party is Republican		+1.6
Average gain/loss when winning presidential party is Democratic		0

Sources: John F. Bibby, "State Elections at Midterm," in Thomas E. Mann and Norman J. Ornstein, eds., *The American Elections of 1982* (Washington, D.C.: American Enterprise Institute, 1983), p. 115; John F. Bibby, "State Elections: What 1984 Means for 1986," *Public Opinion* 8 (Feb./March, 1985): 52, 54; post-election issues of *Congressional Quarterly Weekly Report*, 1986–1998.

Table 8.21
Party Control of State Legislatures, 1950–1998

Year	Republicans Control Both Houses	Split Control	Nonpartisan Legislature	Democrats Control Both Houses	Net Number of Chambers Gained/Lost: Republicans	Net Number of Chambers Gained/Lost: Democrats
1950	22	4	2	20	+9	−9
1952	26	2	2	18	+2	−2
1954	20	6	2	20	−8	+8
1956	17	6	2	23	−6	+6
1958	7	8	2	32	−18	+18
1960	14	5	2	29	+9	−9
1962	18	6	2	24	+9	−9
1964	7	9	2	32	−19	+19
1966	17	7	2	24	+18	−18
1968	20	8	2	20	+7	−7
1970	16	8	2	24	−8	+8
1972	16	8	2	24	No change	
1974	4	8	1	37	−24	+24
1976	4	10	1	35	+2	−2
1978	11	8	1	30	+12	−12
1980	15	5	1	29	+5	−5
1982	11	5	1	33	−8	+8
1984	11	10	1	28	+5	−5
1986	10	11	1	28	−3	+3
1988	7	13	1	29	−4	+4
1990	5	13	1	31	−4	+4
1992	8	16	1	25	+7	−7
1994	19	12	1	18	+18	−18
1996	18	11	1	20	−5	+5
1998	16	11	1	21	−3	+3

Summary

Midterm elections[a]

Average number of chambers lost by:

President's party	10.5
Republicans	10.4
Democrats	10.5

Presidential election years[b]

Average gain of chambers by:

Party of winning presidential candidate	1.3
Republicans	1.3
Democrats	1.0

a. In each midterm election since 1950 except 1998, the president's party lost control of legislative chambers.

b. In five of eleven presidential election years the winning presidential candidate's party did not have a net gain in legislative chambers.

Sources: John F. Bibby, "State House Elections at Midterm," in Thomas E. Mann and Norman J. Ornstein, eds., *The American Elections of 1982* (Washington, D.C.: American Enterprise Institute, 1983), p. 123; National Conference of State Legislatures data.

exposed as the most readily available target of voter discontent, since the president is not on the ballot. The pattern of governors of the president's party being blamed for adverse conditions was particularly apparent in the 1994 midterm elections when the Democrats sustained a net loss of twelve governorships. Democratic candidates that year found themselves constantly on the defensive because of the public discontent with government and continuing worries about the economy.[56]

Midterm elections for state legislatures also show a consistent pattern (except for 1998) of the president's party losing legislative seats and suffering a net loss in control of state legislative chambers[57] (see table 8.21). On average, the president's party has lost eleven legislative chambers in the midterm elections since 1950. As is true of gubernatorial elections, shifts in partisan control of legislative chambers tend to be greater in midterm elections than in presidential elections.

Voters, Elections, and Control of Government

Election results reflect the decisions of voters influenced by long-term affiliations with either the Republican or Democratic party and more short-term considerations relating to candidates and issues. The voters' electoral choices produce a wide array of different patterns of partisan control over governmental offices. These patterns of party control mirror the effects of regional diversity, incumbency, economic conditions, campaign effort, and the timing of elections. Those who assume governmental office as a result of elections constitute the party-in-government. It is these partisan leaders who carry major responsibility for the enunciation of party policy and for shaping the public's image of the party. They are also responsible for the content of governmental policies that affect the nation and the world. The role of the party-in-government and its impact on policy making are the concerns of the following chapter.

Suggestions for Further Reading

Abramson, Paul R.; Aldrich, John H.; and Rohde, David W. *Change and Continuity in the 1996 Elections*. Washington, D.C.: CQ Press, 1998.

Asher, Herbert B. *Presidential Elections and American Politics* 4th ed. Pacific Grove, Cal.: Brooks/Cole, 1992.

Campbell, Angus; Converse, Phillip E.; Miller, Warren E.; and Stokes, Donald E. *The American Voter.* New York: Wiley, 1960.

Campbell, James. *The Presidential Pulse of Congressional Elections.* Lexington: University of Kentucky Press, 1993.

Flanigan, William H., and Zingale, Nancy H. *Political Behavior of the American Electorate.* 9th ed. Washington, D.C.: CQ Press, 1998.

Herrnson, Paul S. *Congressional Elections: Campaigning at Home and in Washington.* Washington, D.C.: CQ Press, 1998.

Jacobson, Gary C. *The Electoral Origins of Divided Government.* Boulder, Colo.: Westview Press, 1990.

_______. *The Politics of Congressional Elections.* 4th ed. New York: Longman, 1997.

Keith, Bruce E.; Magleby, David B.; Nelson, Candice J.; Orr, Elizabeth; Westlye, Mark C.; and Wolfinger, Raymond E. *The Myth of the Independent Voter.* Berkeley: University of California Press, 1992.

Miller, Warren E., and Shanks, J. Merrill. *The New American Voter.* Cambridge, Mass.: Harvard University Press, 1996.

Nelson, Michael. *The Elections of 1996.* Washington, D.C.: CQ Press, 1997.

Rosenstone, Steven and Hanson, John Mark. *Mobilization, Participation, and Democracy in America.* New York: Macmillan, 1993.

Tate, Katherine. *From Protest to Politics: The New Black Voters in American Elections.* Rev. ed. Cambridge, Mass.: Harvard University Press, 1994.

Wattenberg, Martin P. *The Rise of Candidate-Centered Politics: Presidential Elections of the 1980s.* Cambridge, Mass.: Harvard University Press, 1991.

_______. *The Decline of American Political Parties, 1952–1992.* Cambridge, Mass.: Harvard University Press, 1994.

Wayne, Stephen. *The Road to the White House, 1996.* New York: Saint Martin's, 1997.

Notes

1. *Statistical Abstract of the United States,* 1997, p. 289.

2. M. Margaret Conway, *Political Participation in the United States,* 2nd ed. (Washington, D.C.: CQ Press, 1991), p. 80.

3. Robert Jackson, "The Mobilization of U.S. State Electorates," *Journal of Politics* 59 (1997): 520–537; and Samuel Patterson and Gregory Caldeira, "Getting Out the Vote: Participation in Gubernatorial Elections," *American Political Science Review* 77 (Sept. 1983): 675–689.

4. Jae-On Kim, John R. Petrocik, and Stephen Enokson, "Voter Turnout among the American States: Systematic and Individual Components," *American*

Political Science Review 69 (March 1975): 107–123.

5. Raymond E. Wolfinger and Steven J. Rosenstone, *Who Votes?* (New Haven, Conn.: Yale University Press, 1980), p. 41. For a cross-national analysis of factors influencing turnout, see G. Bingham Powell, "American Turnout in Comparative Perspective," *American Political Science Review* 80 (March, 1986): 17–43.

6. William H. Flanigan and Nancy H. Zingale, *Political Behavior of the American Electorate,* 9th ed. (Washington, D.C.: CQ Press, 1998), p. 41.

7. Paul R. Abramson, John H. Aldrich, and David W Rohde, *Change and Continuity in the 1992 Election* (Washington, D.C.: CQ Press, 1994), pp. 123–128.

8. Paul R. Abramson, John H. Aldrich, and David W. Rohde, *Change and Continuity in the 1996 Elections* (Washington, D.C.: CQ Press), pp. 87–88.

9. Jack N. Nagel and John E. McNulty, "Partisan Effects of Voter Turnout in Senatorial and Gubernatorial Elections," *American Political Science Review* 90 (December 1996): 780–793

10. Gregory A. Caldeira and Samuel C. Patterson, "Contextual Influences on Participation in U.S. State Legislative Elections, " *Legislative Studies Quarterly* 7 (Aug. 1982): 359–381; Samuel C. Patterson and Gregory A. Caldeira, "Getting Out the Vote: Participation in Gubernatorial Elections," *American Political Science Review* 77 (Sept. 1983): 675–689; see also Gregory A. Caldeira, Samuel C. Patterson, and Gregory A. Markko, "The Mobilization of Voters in Congressional Elections, " *Journal of Politics* 47 (May 1985): 490–509

11. Ivor Crewe, "As the World Turns Out," *Public Opinion* 4 (Feb./March 1981): 52.

12. See John R. Petrocik, "Voter Turnout and Electoral Preference," in Kay Schlozman, ed., *Elections in America* (Boston: Unwin Hyman, 1987), pp. 261–292; Abramson, et al., *Change and Continuity in the 1992 Elections,* ch. 4.

13. Ruy Teixeira, *The Disappearing American Voter* (Washington, D.C.: Brookings, 1992), pp. 94–97.

14. Kim Quaile Hill and Jan E. Leighley, "Lower-Class Mobilization and Policy Linkage in the U.S. States," *American Journal of Political Science* 39:75–86.

15. A classic statement of the concept of party identification is contained in Angus Campbell, Phillip E. Converse, Warren E. Miller, and Donald E. Stokes, *The American Voter* (New York: Wiley, 1960); see especially pp. 121–128.

16. Fred I. Greenstein, *Children and Politics* (New Haven, Conn.: Yale University Press, 1965), p. 71.

17. Herbert B. Asher, *Presidential Elections and American Politics,* 5th ed. (Pacific Grove, Cal.: Brooks/Cole, 1992), p. 69.

18. Morris P. Fiorina, *Retrospective Voting in American National Elections* (New Haven, Conn.: Yale University Press, 1981); Richard G. Niemi and M. Kent Jennings, "Issues and Inheritance in the Formation of Party Identification,"

American Journal of Political Science 35 (November 1991): 970–988.

19. Flanigan and Zingale, *Political Behavior of the American Electorate,* pp. 68–74.

20. Abramson, Aldrich, and Rohde, *Change and Continuity in the 1996 Elections,* p. 172.

21. For more complete data on split ticket voting in gubernatorial and senatorial elections, see William J. Keefe, *Parties, Politics, and Public Policy in America,* 8th ed. (Washington, D.C.: CQ Press, 1998), p. 201.

22. Seymour Martin Lipset, "The Elections, The Economy and Public Opinion," *P.S.* (Winter 1985): 35.

23. Morris P. Fiorina, "An Outline for a Model of Party Choice," *American Journal of Political Science* 78 (August 1977): 601–624.

24. For a summary of the impact of candidate image on voting in recent elections, see Flanigan and Zingale, *Political Behavior of the American Electorate,* pp. 166–170.

25. Ibid., pp. 169–170.

26. Norman Nie, Sidney Verba, and John R. Petrocik, *The Changing American Voter* (Cambridge, Mass.: Harvard University Press, 1976), ch. 10; Flanigan and Zingale, *Political Behavior of the American Electorate,* pp. 173–178. See also J. Merrill Shanks and Warren E. Miller, "Policy Direction and Performance Evaluation: Complementary Explanations of the Reagan Elections," a paper presented at the annual meeting of the American Political Science Association, Aug. 29–Sept. 1, 1985; and Warren E. Miller and Merrill Shanks, "Performance, Policy, Partisanship—and Perot," a paper presented at the annual meeting of the American Political Science Association, Washington, D.C., September 1993.

27. Abramson, et al., *Continuity and Change in the 1996 Elections,* pp. 129–130.

28. Arthur H. Miller, Warren E. Miller, Alden S. Raine, and Thad A. Brown, "A Majority Party in Disarray: Policy Polarization in the 1972 Election," *American Political Science Review* 70 (Sept. 1976): 760.

29. Peter B. Natchez, "Issues and Voters in the 1972 Elections," in *University Programs Modular Studies* (Morristown, N.J.: General Learning Press, 1974), p. 5. See also Asher, *Presidential Elections,* pp. 146–147.

30. Arther H. Miller and Martin P. Wattenberg, "Throwing the Rascals Out: Policy Performance Evaluations of Presidential Candidates," *American Political Science Review* 79 (June 1985): 359–373. See also Morris Fiorina, *Retrospective Voting in American National Elections* (New Haven, Conn.: Yale University Press, 1981).

31. Abramson, et al., *Continuity and Change in the 1996 Elections,* pp. 143–163.

32. Abramson, et al., *Change and Continuity in the 1996 Elections*, pp. 97–99; Flanigan and Zingale, *Political Behavior of the American Electorate*, pp. 101–103.

33. Flanigan and Zingale, *Political Behavior*, pp. 101–102.

34. John R. Petrocik and Frederick T Steeper, "Realignment and 1984: New Coalitions and New Majorities?," *Election Politics* 2 (Winter 1984–85): 5.

35. John R. Petrocik, *Party Coalitions: Realignments and the Decline of the New Deal Party System* (Chicago, Ill.: University of Chicago Press, 1981), pp. 65–66.

36. Jody Neuman, "The Gender Story: Women as Voters and Candidates in the 1996 Elections," in Regina Dougherty, et al., *America at the Poll 1996* (Storrs, Conn.: Roper Center for Public Opinion Research, 1997), pp. 102–106.

37. William Schneider, "Democrats and Republicans, Liberals and Conservatives," in Seymour Martin Lipset, ed., *Party Coalitions in the 1980s* (New Brunswick, N.J.: Transaction, 1981), pp. 203–204.

38. Petrocik and Steeper, "Realignment and 1984," p. 7.

39. Ibid., p. 8.

40. William F. Connelly, Jr., and John J. Pitney, Jr., *Congress' Permanent Minority? Republicans in the U.S. House* (Lanham, Md.: Littlefield Adams, 1994).

41. Norman J. Ornstein, Thomas E. Mann, and Michael J. Malbin, *Vital Statistics on Congress*, 1997–1998 (Washington, D.C.: Congressional Quarterly, 1998), p. 69.

42. See David R. Mayhew, *Congress: The Electoral Connection* (New Haven, Conn.: Yale University Press, 1984), ch. 2; Richard Fenno, Jr., *Homestyle* (Boston, Mass.: Little, Brown, 1978).

43. Gary C. Jacobson, "Congress: Politics after a Landslide without Coattails," in Michael Nelson, ed., *The Elections of 1984* (Washington, D.C.: CQ Press, 1985), p. 217.

44. Ibid.

45. Gary C. Jacobson, "Congress: A Singular Continuity," in Michael Nelson, ed., *The Elections of 1988* (Washington, D.C.: CQ Press, 1989), pp. 128–131.

46. Barbara Hinckley, "Interpreting Midterm Elections," *American Political Science Review* 59 (Sept. 1967): 694–700. For a thorough analysis of midterm elections, see James E. Campbell, *The Pulse of Congressional Elections* (Lexington: University of Kentucky Press, 1993).

47. Edward Tufte, "Determinants of the Outcome of Midterm Congressional Elections," *American Political Science Review* 67 (Sept. 1975): 812–826.

48. Gary C. Jacobson and Samuel Kernell, *Strategy and Choice in Congressional Elections* (New Haven, Conn.: Yale University Press, 1981).

49. Gary C. Jacobson, *The Electoral Origins of Divided Government, 1946–1988* (Boulder, Colo.: Westview Press, 1990), ch. 6; see also Byron E. Shafer, ed., *The End of Realignment* (Madison: University of Wisconsin Press, 1991), ch. 3.

50. Malcolm E. Jewell and David Breaux, "The Effect of Incumbency on State Legislative Elections," *Legislative Studies Quarterly* 13 (Nov. 1988): 477–494; Malcolm E. Jewell, "State Legislative Elections: What We Know and Don't Know," *American Politics Quarterly* 22 (1994): 483–509.

51. Samuel C. Patterson, "Campaign Spending in Contests for Governor," *Western Political Quarterly* 35 (Dec. 1982): 469–474; see also Samuel C. Patterson and Gregory A. Caldeira, "The Etiology of Partisan Competition," *American Political Science Review* 78 (Sept. 1984): 691–707.

52. Gregory A. Caldeira and Samuel C. Patterson, "Bringing Home the Votes: Electoral Outcomes in State Legislative Races," *Political Behavior* 4 (1982): 33–67.

53. Morris P. Fiorina, "Divided Government in the American States: A Byproduct of Legislative Professionalism?" *American Political Science Review* 88 (June 1994): 304–316.

54. Larry Sabato, *Goodbye to Good-time Charlie: The American Governorship Transformed*, 2d ed. (Washington, D.C.: CQ Press, 1983), p. 139.

55. James E. Campbell, "Presidential Coattails and Midterm Losses in State Legislative Elections," *American Political Science Review* 80 (March 1986): 45–63.

56. The impact of the national economy on gubernatorial and legislative elections is analyzed by John E. Chubb, "Institutions, the Economy and the Dynamics of State Elections," *American Political Science Review* 82 (March 1988): 133–154; see also Lonna Rae Atkeson and Randall W. Partin, "Economic and Referendum Voting: A Comparison of Gubernatorial and Senatorial Elections," *American Political Science Review* 89 (March 1995): 99–107; Richard G. Niemi, Harold W. Stanley, and Ronald J. Vogel, "State Economies and State Taxes: Do Voters Hold Governors Accountable?" *American Journal of Political Science* 39 (Nov. 1995): 936–957.

57. Campbell, "Presidential Coattails"; John F. Bibby, "State House Elections at Midterm," in Thomas E. Mann and Norman J. Ornstein, eds., *The American Elections of 1982* (Washington, D.C.: American Enterprise Institute, 1983), pp. 121–125.

PARTIES IN THE GOVERNMENT

CHAPTER
NINE

In national and state government, Republicans and Democrats "make the major decision about who pays and who receives."[1] Only leaders of these two major parties have occupied the Oval Office in the White House since the Civil War; only an occasional independent ever gains election to the House or Senate, and those that do quickly associate themselves with one of the major parties for organizational purposes and committee assignments; since 1942 only five people have been elected to governorships as third party candidates or independents (most recently Angus King of Maine in 1994 and 1998, and Jesse Ventura of Minnesota in 1998); and following the 1998 elections only 19 (.003 percent) state legislators out of 7,375 were elected as independents or minor party candidates (not including the nonpartisan unicameral legislature of Nebraska). American government is organized on a partisan basis. Presidents and governors customarily appoint fellow members of their party to key posts within their administrations and to judicial vacancies. In Congress and most state legislatures, key leadership posts go to members of the majority party and committees are aligned to give the dominant party numerical control. Partisans and partisanship pervade American government. Even so, American parties face major obstacles in guiding the policy making machinery.

The party-in-government must operate within a constitutional order that was designed to make coordinated and cooperative action difficult. Federalism and separation of powers were conceived as checks and balances on organized factions, not as facilitators of cooperation. American parties are divided geographically by federalism, which creates thousand of separate constituencies in which elected officials can operate with relative autonomy. Separation of powers divides the parties functionally and reduces the need for cooperation among party leaders in the executive and legislative branches. In a parliamentary system, legislators who fail to support their party's prime minister run the risk of forcing the cabinet to resign and the calling of new parliamentary elections. American legislators, however, are not required to support the policies of a president or governor of their party in order to maintain partisan control of the executive branch or to preserve their own positions in the legislature. Separation of powers assures executives of fixed terms of office irrespective of which party controls the legislature, and imposes no special obligations of loyalty to the executive's policies upon the party's legislators.

Within America's separation of powers system, there exists a *"separation of party organizations"*[2] as well. When President Bill Clinton is called the leader of the Democratic party, or President George Bush was said to be the leader of the Republican party, there is an implication that these men head a single organizational entity. But American parties are not of this type. There is a "presidential party" composed of presidential appointees to the executive branch, national convention delegates, the national committee, and the president's personal campaign organization. There is also a "congressional party" with fully organized structures in both chambers that operates quite autonomously from the presidential party. In addition, there are gubernatorial and legislative parties in the states.

The separateness of these organizations is particularly noticeable in terms of nominations. Presidents play no significant role in the selection of party nominees for the House and Senate. Rather, they are chosen by their districts and states in primary elections. Presidents may encourage particular individuals to seek party nominations, but they cannot prevent others from running nor guarantee the nomination to their favorite candidates.

In a similar manner, representatives and senators have only the most limited influence upon presidential nominations. The largest proportion of national convention delegates are selected by presidential primaries in which congressional endorsements are of scant value. Nor are congressional leaders in a strong position to win presidential nominations for themselves. Winning a presidential nomination requires virtually full time campaigning for two to four years—time that is not available to a senator or representative with major congressional leadership responsibilities. As Austin Ranney has observed, members of Congress have about "as little power over whom their party nominates for the presidency as the president has over whom his party nominates for the House and Senate."[3] The separateness of the presidential and congressional parties stemming from the lack of centralized control of the nominating process was cogently stated by Richard E. Neustadt.

> What the Constitution separates, our political parties do not combine. The parties are themselves composed of separate organizations sharing public authority. The authority consists of nominating powers. Our national parties are confederations of state and local institutions, with a headquarters that represents the White House, more or less, if the party has a President in office. These confederacies manage presidential nominations. All other public offices depend upon electorates confined within the states. All other nominations are controlled within the states. The President and congressmen who bear one party's label are divided by dependence upon different sets of voters. The differences are sharpest at the stage of nomination. The White House has too small a share in nominating congressmen, and Congress has too little weight in nominating Presidents for party to erase their constitutional separation. Party links are stronger than is frequently supposed, but nominating processes assure the separation.[4]

Presidents have even less influence over the selection of congressional leaders than they do over nominations. Representatives and senators strongly resent presidential intrusion into their leadership selection processes. As a result, even expressions of support by presidents are rare and there are no verified instances of presidents seeking to oust a speaker, floor leader, or whip.[5] Just as presidents do not influence selection of congressional party leaders, representatives and senators do not exert significant influence upon the organization of the White House staff which normally consists of principal and closest advisors to the president.

The existence of a separate and distinct "presidential party" alongside a "congressional party" has, in the words of Theodore J. Lowi, provided the basis for a "*real* separation of powers" within the government. That is, the separation of organizations within the parties reinforces and makes meaningful the separation of powers created by the writers of the Constitution.[6]

The separateness of the presidential and congressional parties at the national level is replicated in most of the states, where distinct gubernatorial and legislative party structures normally exist. just as the national constitutional provisions for separation of powers make a unified party difficult to achieve, similar provisions in state constitutions cause party fragmentation. Yet for all their diffuseness, American parties do have a center of gravity. They tend to be executive centered coalitions.[7] The president is the only party leader with a truly national constituency and it is his nomination and general election campaigns that are the chief activities of the national party. His visibility makes him and his policies the symbols of the party to the mass electorate. The leverage derived from his visibility and mass support enhance the ability of the president to lead the government and persuade others in public office to support his policies. Even with all the difficulties that confront any president seeking to exert party leadership, his position is infinitely stronger than that of any competing party leader. In state government, governors tend to enjoy a similar level of prominence to that of presidents in national politics.

The President as Party leader

Presidential leadership involves exerting influence over the national party organization, the Congress, the executive branch, and even the judiciary. In his relations with each of these institutions, the resources of the president are substantial, but he operates under severe constraints imposed by the Constitution and the party system.

The President and the National Party

A president needs to assert dominance over his party's organizational structure lest it become an independent power center during his administration or be used by rivals working against his policies and renomination. Of particular importance is controlling the national committee. It is the most inclusive party organization in the country because its membership includes representatives of all the state parties and key party constituencies. It operates a year-round headquarters, staffed by professionals in contact with political leaders around the country, and it has resources that can be used to underwrite White House political activities—polls, fund-raising expenses, and presidential travel. The national committee also exerts substantial influence over presidential nominations through its role in developing national party rules, administering those rules, and handling the arrangements for national conventions. These activities require that presidential interests be protected within the national committee.

Although he has no formal role in the national committee, the president's informal influence over the selection of the national chairman is nearly total. His "recommendations" are customarily accepted without dissent. For example, even with the Watergate scandals washing over the Nixon Administration and threatening to sink it, the president was able to designate George Bush as Republican National Committee chairman.

Presidents are anxious to have the national committee chairman act as the president's agent rather than as the committee's agent with an agenda and constituency of his or her own. The fate of two recent Republican National Committee (RNC) chairmen is illustrative. After the GOP lost the 1976 elections, William Brock, a former Tennessee senator, was elected by the RNC to be its chairman. His tenure is widely viewed as one of the most successful in the party's history as the RNC instituted an impressive array of fund raising, candidate recruitment, and candidate and state party support programs that are credited with helping the party achieve major gains in the 1978 and 1980 elections. Brock, however, was viewed during the 1980 presidential primaries as something less than a Reagan enthusiast by the candidate's key advisors, who sought Brock's ouster as national chairman. While Ronald Reagan himself declined to have Brock dismissed, the Reagan dominated national convention in 1980 adopted a rules change requiring that the national committee officers be elected immediately after the convention and in January of each odd numbered year thereafter. Although the Reagan forces permitted Brock to be reelected after the 1980 convention, they installed as RNC deputy chairman and chief operating officer, Drew Lewis, the Reagan campaign chairman in Pennsylvania. And in January, 1981, the White House passed the word that Nevada state GOP chairman, Richard Richards, was the presidential choice for RNC chairman. Richards was duly elected without opposition. (Brock, however, was given the cabinet rank post of U.S. States Trade Representative and later appointed secretary of Labor in the Reagan administration.)

After two years on the job and amidst rumors of White House dissatisfaction with his performance, Richards was replaced in a major overhaul of the national party that was dictated by the White House. The president wished to have his friend and confidant Senator Paul Laxalt (Nev.) head the national committee. RNC rules, however, required that the RNC chairman serve in a full time capacity—something that was impossible for Laxalt because of his Senate duties. To overcome this obstacle, the White House arranged for Laxalt to assume the newly created post of party General Chairman, while having the RNC elect Frank Fahrenkopf, the state chairman in Nevada, to the national chairmanship.

President George Bush, like his predecessor, controlled the selection of GOP national chairmen. His first chairman was Lee Atwater (1989–1991), a close political advisor who managed Bush's presidential campaign in 1988. When Atwater developed a fatal illness and was forced to resign, Bush in 1991 tapped Secretary of Agriculture Clayton Yuetter to replace him. Since Yuetter had had relatively little campaign experience, it was clear that he was expected to serve as a spokesperson for the administration and to follow White House direction. In preparation for his 1992 reelection campaign, Bush selected campaign consultant Rich Bond to replace Yuetter.

Democratic presidents have also controlled the selection of Democratic National Committee (DNC) leaders. President Clinton installed his campaign manager David Wilhelm as his first national party chairman. However, when the White House found his leadership to be wanting, Wilhelm was shoved aside in favor of former House Democratic Whip Tony Coelho (D-Calif.), who served as the coordinator of the DNC's 1994 campaign efforts. After the election, the president selected Senator Christopher Dodd (D-Conn.) to be party General Chairman. In this position, Dodd was expected to be a spokesperson for the president and the party, as well as a counter force to RNC Chairman Haley Barbour on television interview programs. To complement Dodd's appointment, long time South Carolina National Committee member Donald Fowler was selected to be DNC chairman with responsibility for day to day running of the party headquarters. When Dodd and Fowler stepped down following the 1996 election, Clinton designated their replacements—Colorado Governor Roy Romer as general chairman and fund raiser Steven Grossman as national chairman. For the party controlling the presidency, national committee subordination to the White House is almost complete, as presidential interests are given priority.

The leadership of the national committees customarily finds it necessary to work under the supervision of White House aides charged with responsibility for protecting the president's political interests. In the Reagan White House, this responsibility was formalized by the designation of one of the president's key aides as the assistant to the president for political and government affairs. Edward Rollins, who held this post during most of Reagan's first term, left the White House staff temporarily to manage the president's renomination and general election campaigns and then reassumed his White House post after the 1984 election. President Bush relied more on the RNC to handle political business (especially while Lee Atwater was RNC chairman), but he maintained a White House Office of Political Affairs, and the influence of his chief of staff on the RNC was substantial. Clinton has also used the White House Office of Political Affairs to coordinate White House and DNC activities. His deputy chief of staff, Harold Ickes, played a major role in directing the 1996 presidential campaign.

White House personnel and political operatives have also assumed responsibility for handling administration patronage appointments. This reflects an unwillingness on the part of presidents and their supporters to place their executive appointments at the disposal of the party organization for purposes of party building. There is instead an emphasis on building a personal organization supportive of the president. The creation of personnel and political offices in the White House, operating with substantial autonomy from the national committees, is a departure from past practice when the national committees were the chief patronage dispensing agents. Until 1953, when Dwight Eisenhower stopped the practice, the national party chairman had in a few instances even served simultaneously as postmaster general and handled the vast patronage available to the party within the postal system.[8] The reform of the postal service in the 1970s has removed the agency from the patronage system and precluded national committee involvement in its hiring practices.

National committees have also seen their presidential campaign roles restricted since the 1960s. National party chairmen formerly served as the campaign managers of presidential reelection campaigns and the campaigns were run out of the national committee headquarters. The last national chairman charged with responsibility for a presidential reelection campaign was Leonard Hall, who as RNC chairman managed the 1956 Eisenhower campaign. Since then incumbent presidents have set up their own personal campaign organizations and relegated the national committee to a supportive role. The Federal Election Campaign Act encourages this separation of the national committee from the presidential campaign committee responsible for the receipt and expenditure of funds, while also permitting separate national committee spending on presidential campaigns that are receiving public financing.

The assumption of traditional party functions by the White House staff and the subordination of the national committee to the White House have made being national chairman of the president's party a frequently frustrating experience. Based on his experiences as RNC chairman under President Richard Nixon in 1972, Senator Bob Dole (R-Kans.) commented, "When your party's in power, the chairman doesn't have any decision-making role." Kenneth Curtis, Carter's first DNC chairman, in announcing his resignation described the party chairmanship as "this lousy job" and Reagan's first chairman, Richard Richards, expressed similar sentiments of frustration when he announced in 1982, amidst rumors that he was being pushed out, that he would not seek a second term. He also complained about the White House staff acting as a buffer between the president and the party. "If I had my choice, I would not have a political shop in the White House," he stated.[9]

While the president and his chief aides exercise impressive influence over their party's national committee, national committees do have an element of autonomy in their operations. The programs of assistance that they operate for the benefit of state parties and candidates develop constituencies that expect continued support. This is particularly true within the Republican party which because of its superior financial resources has developed a wide range of support programs for state parties. It is doubtful that any president could discontinue these RNC activities now that they are well established without seriously undermining his position with his party. It is interesting to note, for example, that even though key Reagan supporters wanted Bill Brock removed as national chairman as soon as Reagan won the GOP nomination in 1980, the Reagan dominated RNC continued and even expanded programs of support for state parties and candidates that were initiated by Brock. RNC efforts to strengthen state parties were also maintained by the Bush dominated RNC. And it was a failure to provide sufficient support to congressional Democrats and state parties that created pressures outside the White House for President Clinton to replace DNC Chairman Wilhelm in 1994.[10]

There is also an expectation that national chairmen will conduct their operations in a fair manner when handling national convention arrangements in instances when an incumbent president is being challenged for his party's nomination. When President Gerald Ford was challenged in 1976 by Ronald Reagan and President Jimmy Carter faced opposition from Senator Edward Kennedy in 1980, Mary Louise Smith of the RNC and John C. White of the DNC both sought to convey an image of neutrality in national committee operations relating to the convention, even though both were acknowledged supporters of their incumbent presidents.

As was noted in chapter 4, governors frequently exert influence over their state party committees which is at least as pervasive as that of the president over the national committee. Like presidents, governors work to prevent their state committees from becoming competing or hostile centers of power within the party. Unlike the national committee-presidential relationship, however, there have periodically been instances of alienation and conflict between governors and state party committees. The most common pattern, however, has been for governors to play a substantial role in the selection of state chairmen, to be consulted on state party issues, and to assist the party in such activities as fund raising and candidate recruitment.

Presidential Nominations and the Building of Governing Coalitions

The pattern of national committee subordination to the president and his staff and the tendency of presidents to set up their own personal political operations within the White House is a reflection of the changed process of coalition building involved in gaining presidential nominations. As noted in chapter 6, winning a presidential nomination involves intense personal campaigning and an organization equipped to contest presidential primaries and party caucuses which are open to almost any interested citizen. It is no longer a process of forging a coalition from amongst state and local party leaders, governors, senators, congressmen, mayors, and interest groups aligned with the party. Prior to the 1970s, candidates for presidential nominations were required to build electoral coalitions around party leaders and elected officials. In the process of their negotiations with these leaders, presidential candidates became well acquainted with many of the people who would be important to them once they entered the Oval Office. In effect, presidents began to forge a governing coalition while they sought their party's nomination. The changes in the nominating process, which have substantially diminished the power of party and elected officials, have had the effect, according to Austin Ranney, of separating "the process of building the coalition needed for the nomination from the process of building the coalition needed for governing."[11] Presidential leadership of the government, already made difficult by the constitutional restrictions of federalism and separation of powers, is made even more difficult by the nature of the nomination process. *Washington Post* columnist David Broder noted the consequences of the changed nominating process for governance while comparing the experiences of John F. Kennedy and Jimmy Carter.

> Kennedy ran in four contested primaries in 1960. Contrast four with the thirty-four that await anyone who wants the nomination in 1980. After Kennedy won West Virginia, he still had to persuade the leaders of his party—the governors, the mayors, the leaders of allied interest groups—particularly organized labor—that they could stake their reputations on his qualities as the best man to be the standard bearer for the party. Contrast that with Jimmy Carter, who never had to meet, and in fact, in many cases, did not meet, those similar officials until after he had achieved the Democratic nomination.
>
> The significance of the difference for the presidency is that in one case, a man, if he is elected, comes with the alliances that make it possible for him to organize the coalitions and support necessary to lead a government.
>
> In the present nominating system, he comes as a fellow whose only coalition is whatever he got out of the living rooms of Iowa (precinct caucuses). If there is one thing that Jimmy Carter's frustration in office ought to teach us, it is that the affiliation and commitment that is made on Iowa caucus night and New Hampshire primary day is not by itself sufficient to sustain a man for four years in the White House.[12]

The difficult leadership position in which an American president finds himself upon entering the White House is quite different than that of most chief executives in other Western style democracies. In the United Kingdom, for example, the leader of the opposition party is in an officially recognized governmental position. The opposition leader stands ready to assume the prime ministership in the event the cabinet is forced to resign or his party wins a national election. His governing coalition is already in place and he is, therefore, in a stronger position than an American president to exert leadership over the government. American presidents, by contrast, only assume leadership of their party upon winning a presidential nomination and they continue to hold the leadership only if they can win the general election.[13]

The Party, the President, and Congress

The president's policy making powers are shared with the Congress even in areas like international relations and national security. Much of what a president can accomplish in terms of policy-making requires the cooperation of the Congress. In gaining policy influence with the Congress, presidents are constantly required to use the kinship which they share with their party colleagues in the legislature. These partisan ties, however, are not of a truly binding character and tensions always exist between the president and Congress.

Sources of Presidential-Congressional Differences

Electoral Bases. The circumstances of elections to the Congress and presidency carry the seeds for conflict between the president and his fellow partisans on the Hill. As noted previously, presidents are nominated and elected without the development of mutual obligations between the president and the congressional party. He owes them nothing for his victory. But by the same token, members of the Congress also perceive that they got there largely through their own efforts. With the president having no real control over his party's congressional nominations, presidential leverage with legislators is fractured early in the electoral process.

Nor does the president derive substantial influence over members of Congress from the general election process.

Presidential coattails are becoming rather threadbare as voters increasingly split their tickets in presidential and congressional contests.[14] Neither George Bush in 1988 nor Bill Clinton in 1992 and 1996 had coattails of any significance. Bush ran ahead of his party's successful House candidates in only twenty-six districts, and Clinton ran ahead in but four districts in 1992 and twenty-seven in 1996.[15] This declining influence of coattails has weakened the position of the president vis-à-vis the Congress because it has diminished the perception among members that they owe their election at least in part to the president's popularity and that they should, therefore, support his policies.

The differing constituencies of members of Congress as compared to presidents and the timing of elections also creates differing perspectives. Legislators are ultimately responsible to the constituents in their states or districts. No matter how pressing national problems may be, reelection requires attention to local or state interests. Representatives and senators have few electoral incentives to view issues from a national perspective. By contrast, the president has a national constituency and is forced to take a more comprehensive view of issues than is required of legislators. Further tension is introduced into presidential-congressional relations by the staggered timing of elections. Because senators are elected for six year overlapping terms, only one-third of the senators are ever elected simultaneously with the president. Those that are elected with the president know their next reelection campaign will be fought during a midterm election when the president is not on the ballot. House members, of course, are also on a different election schedule than presidents. Their two year terms require them to run without the president on the ballot during midterm elections. The staggered timing of elections means that the president, senators, and representatives must confront the voters at different times and under divergent circumstances. They are, therefore, apt to view their electoral mandates quite differently.

Institutional Bases. Complementing the electoral bases for differences between the president and Congress are institutional sources of tension. The executive branch is organized on a relatively hierarchical basis with the president in charge and held accountable for its actions. Presidents with their sweeping responsibility for policy development and implementation are forced to consider the trade-offs that must be made among various policies and to take a comprehensive national view of policy. The hierarchical character of the executive enhances the president's ability to propose policies that are comprehensive and consistent in character.

By contrast, the Congress is structured in a more decentralized manner. Major decision-making responsibilities are delegated to committees and subcommittees, which often have memberships that are not particularly representative of their parent chambers. Senators and representatives tend to gravitate toward committees which have special significance for their constituencies (e.g., westerners to the Natural Resources committees, farm state legislators to the Agriculture committees, and urban legislators to the Banking Committee or committees with jurisdiction over labor and education issues). Committees, therefore, often become centers of narrower interest concerns than are found among leaders of the executive branch. Differences between the branches are further encouraged because Congress considers issues serially—one at a time—rather than in a comprehensive manner. That is, Congress often considers issues with little reference to other related policies. The decentralized power structure of Congress and its reliance on the committee/subcommittee system for detailed review of policy proposals make it almost impossible for the institution to consider policies in as integrated and comprehensive a manner as the executive branch.[16]

The relatively hierarchical structure of the executive branch and the more decentralized character of Congress also cause the president and legislators to have a different sense of accountability to the voters.[17] Because presidents are so visible and responsible for the development and implementation of a full range of policies, they are held accountable for the performance of the government as a whole. The representatives and senators are substantially less visible and the decentralization of power within Congress makes it virtually impossible to hold any of its members accountable for the actions of the Congress, let alone the national government. Legislators, therefore, are evaluated on the basis of their own records, not the performance of the government as a whole. This frees them to engage in activities that will enhance their standing with constituents, irrespective of the national implications of those actions. Many even campaign by running against the Congress and its record, knowing full well that individually they will not be judged by Congress' institutional record.[18] This difference in public accountability between presidents and legislators means that presidents normally have a much greater sense of urgency for dealing with national problems than do members of the Congress. Presidents know that they will be held accountable for national ills, but legislators find themselves less likely to be held responsible.

Presidents also operate on a different time perspective than do legislators. Whereas the president's term in office is fixed and he has a limited time to accomplish his objectives and establish his place in history, representatives and senators normally think in terms of lifetime careers in the Congress. Presidents are concerned about problems of the moment—passing proposals that are of high priority. Congressmen, instead, worry about how to advance their long term influence in the chamber, promote the policies to which they attach importance, and maintain electability within their constituencies.[19]

Presidential leadership of Congress is also made more difficult because of the separation of powers system which makes possible divided partisan control of the presidency and Congress. Indeed, in the years since the first Eisenhower election in 1952, divided government has been more common than single party control (see table 9.1). Except during Eisenhower's first two years in office, Republican presidents have consistently had to face a Congress in which at least one chamber was controlled by the Democrats. Democratic presidents have been more fortunate. Until the Republican sweep in the 1994 midterm elections left President Bill Clinton facing a Republican controlled Congress, every Democratic president starting with Harry Truman in 1948 had the benefit of a Democratic Congress. Separation of powers has had similar consequences for state government. Between 1952 and 1998 only Georgia did not experience divided government at least once. In some states, it has been a common occurrence (e.g., Illinois, Michigan, New York, Ohio). Following the 1998 elections twenty-six states had divided partisan control between the governor and at least one house of the state legislature.

Table 9.1
Single Party versus Divided Control of the National Government, 1952–2000

Single Party Control of Government	Divided Government
Republican President,	*Republican President/*
Senate and House	*Democratic Senate and House*
1953–54 Eisenhower	1955–56 Eisenhower
	1957–58 Eisenhower
Democratic President,	1959–60 Eisenhower
Senate and House	1969–70 Nixon
1961–62 Kennedy	1971–72 Nixon
1963–64 Kennedy/Johnson	1973–74 Nixon/Ford
1965–66 Johnson	1975–76 Ford
1967–68 Johnson	1987–88 Reagan
1977–78 Carter	
1979–80 Carter	*Republican President and Senate*
1993–94 Clinton	*Democratic House*
	1981–82 Reagan
	1983–84 Reagan
	1985–86 Reagan
	Republican President
	Democratic Senate and House
	1987–88 Reagan
	1989–90 Bush
	1991–92 Bush
	Democratic President,
	Republican Senate and House
	1995–96 Clinton
	1997–98 Clinton
	1999–2000 Clinton
Total Years of Single Party Control of Government: 16	*Total Years of Divided Party Control of Government: 34*

Party Loyalty as a Basis for Presidential-Congressional Cooperation

While the tensions between the president and Congress are substantial, the extent of conflict can be overstated. Partisanship does provide a basis for cooperation and for keeping inevitable conflicts within reasonable bounds. The claims of party loyalty are important within the Congress. Studies of roll call voting have consistently found that the best single predictor of the way members of Congress will vote is their party affiliation.[20] With major portions of the congressional agenda determined by presidential policy initiatives, the party membership that the president shares with congressional colleagues is of substantial importance in promoting cooperation between the executive and legislature. Table 9.2 presents evidence of the extent of support received by presidents from their congressional party members and the opposition. In the forty years between 1954 and 1994, presidents have been able to count upon their party members in Congress supporting them at least two-thirds of the time, and periodically the level of support reached the 80 percent range (see table 9.2). Presidential influence can even cause legislators of the president's party to alter their previous voting patterns on roll calls. For example, Republicans have shown a tendency to increase their support for foreign aid when there is a Republican in the Oval Office. Similarly, support for hikes in the debt ceiling are affected by which party controls the presidency, especially for Republicans who are more likely to support the increases if a member of their party occupies the White House. Support for budget deficit reductions in the 1980s and 1990s has also been affected by party control of the presidency. In the 1980s, Republican senators took the lead in efforts to control the deficit while Republican Ronald Reagan was in the White House. But in 1993, when there was a return to unified Democratic control of the government, the Democrats found that they had to act alone to pass Clinton's deficit reduction plan.[21]

Table 9.2

Average Level of Congressional Support for the President's Position, 1954–1996 (percent)

		Members of the President's Party			Members of the Opposition Party		
Year	**President**	**Party**	**House**	**Senate**	**Party**	**House**	**Senate**
1954–60	Eisenhower	Rep.	68%	80%	Dem.	54%	52%
1961–63	Kennedy	Dem.	83	75	Rep.	41	47
1964–68	Johnson	Dem.	81	71	Rep.	49	56
1969–74	Nixon	Rep.	73	73	Dem.	53	50
1974–76	Ford	Rep.	65	72	Dem.	41	48
1977–80	Carter	Dem.	69	74	Rep.	42	52
1981–88	Reagan	Rep.	68	79	Dem.	33	44
1989–92	Bush	Rep.	69	77	Dem.	30	42
1993–94	Clinton	Dem.	76	87	Rep.	43	36
1995–96	Clinton	Dem.	75	82	Rep.	30	33

Sources: Norman J. Ornstein, Thomas E. Mann, and Michael J. Malbin, *Vital Statistics on Congress, 1997–1998* (Washington, D.C.: Congressional Quarterly, Inc., 1998), pp. 208–209. Used by permission.

In seeking to influence the Congress, presidents tend to work closely with the elected party leadership of their party in the House and Senate. Party leaders on the Hill are normally quite supportive of presidential policy initiatives because they have a stake in his legislative successes. If the president fails in gaining adoption of his legislative program, they also fail. Through acting as presidential spokesmen on Capitol Hill and as conduits for communication between the White House and the Capitol, party leaders gain influence and leverage with their congressional colleagues. They, therefore, zealously guard their prerogatives as the principal presidential contact persons within the Congress. Presidents also benefit from working through the party leadership in Congress. As David Truman has pointed out:

> The clock provides no hours for the cultivation of rank-and-file legislators which direct leadership of the Congress would require. . . . If the agenda . . . [the President] . . . sets is to emerge in a product he favors, he must have the information and means for day-to-day assessment, if not actual guidance of Congressional activity. The elective leaders wield no monopoly here, but standing as strategic communications points, they are, for the President as much as for their legislative associates, an important source of intelligence, entirely aside from their capabilities as facilitators or obstructors of his program. . . . Relations with the leaders of the Congressional party can be supplemented . . . but no substitutes have appeared on which he can rely with equal confidence. To the degree that the mechanism of the Congressional party is relied upon, however, it must be taken as it is, with the leaders it has produced.[22]

Although the presidential-congressional leader relationship is in Truman's words "collaborative and mutually useful," it is not necessarily smooth. The most important constituency of congressional party leaders is not the president, but their legislative colleagues. To hold their leadership positions, they must protect the interests of their congressional colleagues. Thus it was widely reported that Robert Dole (R-Kan.) was selected by Senate Republicans to replace Howard Baker (R-Tenn.) as majority leader in 1984 because his GOP colleagues considered him sufficiently independent and tough minded to stand up to presidential and White House staff pressures. Dole's willingness to criticize publicly the Reagan and Bush White House and initiate policy proposals not necessarily blessed by the president demonstrates that this confidence was not misplaced. Similarly, House Democratic Minority

Leader Richard Gephardt (Mo.) demonstrated substantial independence from the Clinton White House after the 1994 midterm elections ceded control of Congress to the Republicans. After his selection as leader, Gephardt stated that he and his Democratic colleagues would "try to work in tandem with the White House," but then added that "House Democrats are an independent organization."[23] He then followed up this declaration of independence by twice in January 1995 upstaging President Bill Clinton. By just forty-eight hours, he beat the president to the punch in unveiling a middle-class tax cut proposal; and he also dramatically called for a flattening and simplifying of income tax rates.[24] And in 1998, as Clinton faced the greatest crisis of his presidency, charges by Special Prosecutor Kenneth Starr that he had committed impeachable offenses, Gephardt and Senate Democratic Leader Daschle (S.D.) were both highly critical of the president's behavior in the Monica Lewinski scandal and his legal stratagems to avoid charges of perjury.

In seeking to influence Congress, recent presidents have expanded the resources of the White House. Eisenhower created an Office of Congressional Relations in the White House to complement the formal party structures. Since then, this office has become one of the key units in the White House. It has a contingent of personal presidential lobbyists, who are dispatched daily to the Capitol to win votes for the administration's program. The Office of Congressional Relations also seeks to coordinate its activities with those of the congressional liaison personnel in each of the agencies of the executive branch.

More recently, starting with the Nixon administration, an Office of Public Liaison has been set up within the White House. Under the leadership of Anne Wexler during the Carter administration, this office became an effective mobilizer of grass roots constituency and interest group pressures on Congress. This practice was intensified under the Reagan administration and continued by Bush and Clinton.

As the numbers in table 9.2 demonstrate, presidents can rarely expect nearly unanimous support for their programs from party colleagues in Congress. Even if such support were forthcoming, it could be insufficient to pass legislation, because the president's party does not necessarily control the Congress. It is, therefore, often necessary for presidents to build bipartisan legislative coalitions. The recurring need for support on both sides of the aisle tends to dampen partisan conflict and forces bipartisan consultation on the formulation of legislation. It also permits members of both parties to claim credit for presidential policy initiatives that have support among legislators' constituencies. A dramatic example of a president having to rely on a bipartisan coalition to pass high priority legislation occurred in 1993. Even though the Democrats controlled both the White House and Congress, President Clinton needed a majority of Republican representatives to gain approval for the North American Free Trade Agreement (NAFTA), after a majority of his own party's legislators abandoned him on this issue. Similarly, the historic 1997 agreement to balance the budget came about only through bipartisan bargaining and agreement between a Democratic president and a Republican controlled Congress.

Of course, the need for bipartisan support may create difficulties for the president within his own party. To the extent that he negotiates and makes deals with the opposition party in order to build legislative majorities, the president runs the risk of alienating his loyal supporters. Loyalists in the president's party often perceive that White House largesse seems to be flowing toward members of the opposition party, whom they view as less deserving than themselves. But if the president fails to accommodate some elements in the opposition, he is likely to leave his governance responsibilities unfulfilled. Balancing the need for both party loyalty and bipartisanship support is a constant juggling act which presidents are compelled to perform.[25]

Does United or Divided Party Control of Government Really Make a Difference in Lawmaking?

The discussion of party influence on presidential-congressional relations thus far has stressed that united party control of the government eases the president's burden in gaining congressional approval of his legislative agenda. Left as yet unanswered, however, is the question of whether or not united party control of the government is really critical to the passage of major, innovative legislation. Interestingly, exhaustive research by David R. Mayhew of major policy enactments from 1946 through 1994 reveals that there has been no great difference in the amount of major initiatives passed during periods of united versus divided party control of the government.[26] The basic reason for this unexpected finding is that lawmaking is affected by a variety of forces over and above party control of government and these forces tend to "even out" lawmaking across both conditions of united and divided party control.

Regardless of the conditions of party control, it is generally difficult "to pass laws by narrow congressional majorities; refractory committees, lack of party discipline, presidential veto threats, looming filibusters, or the sheer complexity of Capitol Hill can intrude."[27] The constancy of legislative action across Congresses is also attributable to the more or less random occurrence of world and domestic events that can rapidly trigger major legislative enactments, such as the Marshall Plan (after the start of the Cold War), the Gun Control Act of 1968 (after the assassinations of Dr. Martin Luther King, Jr., and Robert F. Kennedy), the Coal Mine Safety Act (after a West Virginia mine disaster), and the Federal Election Campaign Act of 1974 (after the Watergate scandals). The public mood can affect lawmaking in similar ways under conditions of both united and divided government. As Mayhew has observed, "nothing stands out more in the postwar record than the surge of hyper-legislating that extended from roughly 1963 through 1975–1976"[28] during Johnson (united party control) and Nixon-Ford (divided party control) administrations. The thrust toward increased government spending and regulation of this era had widespread public support as Congress enacted such measures as the Occupational Safety and Health Act (OSHA) in 1970, the Clean Air Act of 1970, the Supplementary Security Income (SSI) program in 1972, the Water Pollution Control Act of 1972, and the Federal Election Campaign Act of 1974. In addition, there is great variability in presidents' skills as legislative leaders. It is probably no accident that unusually ambitious programs were enacted during the mid-1960s while a "consummate wheeler dealer," Lyndon Johnson, was in the White House. Jimmy Carter, who maintained an "outsider" stance toward Congress and the Washington community, had larger Democratic majorities in the House than did Johnson but it did him little good. When it came to mobilizing votes in Congress or winning public support, no recent president has been in the same league with Johnson or Ronald Reagan.[29]

The absence of a surge in significant lawmaking when united party control of the government was restored after Bill Clinton's election in 1992 reflects impact of the factors noted in the previous paragraph. The difficulties inherent in the legislative process doomed several presidential initiatives. For example, a Republican filibuster in the Senate killed Clinton's economic stimulus package. Divisions within the Democratic party helped defeat presidential proposals for health care reform and gays in the military. Nor was there an activist public mood to support the kind of activist government that Clinton espoused during his first two years in office. Congressional productivity has also been affected by the heightened partisanship that now characterizes the Congress, especially the House. This intensified partisanship has led to bitter partisan battles within Congress and to confrontations (e.g., two government shutdowns due to disagreement over the budget in 1995) and periodic legislative deadlocks between the Democratic Clinton administration and the GOP controlled Congress.

The Party, the President, and the Executive Branch

For a president to influence the direction of national policy requires more than influence with Congress. He must also exert influence *within* the executive branch because it is here that policy initiatives are developed and implemented. Government organization charts often depict the president at the pinnacle of the executive branch with direct control over the far-flung departments and agencies. Most presidents, however, have found organizational chart depictions of their power illusionary. A multitude of factors contribute to making it difficult for presidents to exercise effective control over the executive establishment.

Each agency and department has a separate congressionally enacted statutory mandate governing its organizational structure, policies, and budgets. Presidents and their appointees within the agencies must operate within the constraints imposed by these statutes. In addition, each agency has its own permanent civil service staff. These persons are committed to the mission of the agency and often have developed a policy orientation and style of operation—a bureaucratic culture—that even presidents find almost impossible to alter. Conservative presidents are normally highly suspicious of bureaucrats who administer liberal programs and insist on maintaining these programs when the president sees no need for them. Liberal presidents often complain about the bureaucracy for different reasons. They see the bureaucracy as being unwilling to break out of its traditions and move in new directions. President John F. Kennedy, for example, in a mood of frustration is said to have once referred to the State Department as a "fudge factory." The federal bureaucracy is, however, essential for the successful administration of presidential policies. Presidents of either ideological stripe must, therefore, reconcile their style of operation with this relatively independent force within their administrations.[30] The programs administered by the various agencies develop a clientele of beneficiaries who have ties to the civil service and to the congressional committee members involved in passing agency authorizations and appropriations. These clientele groups are normally prepared to mobilize political influence to protect their interests within the agency. Therefore, cabinet secretaries charged with carrying out presidential policies are confronted frequently with having to cope with the combined influence of their department's bureaucracy, clientele groups, and attentive congressmen and senators. Since any of these forces has the political resources to make the life of a cabinet officer difficult in the extreme, there is a tendency on the part of many department heads to come to an accommodation with these interests. However, to the extent that they become responsive to these so-called "iron triangles," the president loses influence over his cabinet officers. Presidents and White House staff are constantly concerned that cabinet secretaries will become more responsive to pressures arising within their departments than they are to presidential initiatives. The cross-pressures operating upon department heads were once captured in somewhat exaggerated form by President Coolidge's vice president, Charles Dawes, who quipped that "the members of the Cabinet are a President's natural enemies."[31]

Presidential leadership of the executive branch has become more difficult in recent decades because of what Hugh Heclo calls "policy congestion." As the involvement of the government in society and the world has expanded, the policy concerns of the government have become more complex. One government program has implications for another and one issue impinges on another. This interaction of federal programs is now pervasive and results in overlap and layering. In domestic programs, overlap results because federal assistance to state and local governments, profit and nonprofit groups, and individuals is administered by a variety of agencies, and recipients may receive assistance from several agencies.

But no one is responsible for supervising the cumulative effects of each agency's programs. The layering stems from attempts to impose crosscutting requirements on all programs (for example, rules against discrimination based on race, sex, or age). With each of these crosscutting requirements administered by a different agency, there is no one department responsible for supervising their cumulative effect. The interrelatedness of issues, Heclo notes, is illustrated by the ways in which consideration of highway policy has changed since the 1950s when Eisenhower proposed building the interstate highway system. At that time, it was debated and then executed as a highway program with only modest attention given to nonhighway type concerns. Today if such a program were proposed anew, the implications of the interstate system for a whole range of nonhighway uses would be considered, for example, private car versus mass transportation, energy conservation, economic development, minority hiring of construction workers, and urban development.[32]

"There are," Heclo concludes, "more issues to be coordinated affecting any given agency, and there are more agencies in need of coordination for any given issue." As a result, the president, "rather than simply deciding on the government agenda, is increasingly involved in sorting out relationships among agendas—for economic management, international affairs, social policy, intergovernmental relations, and so on."[33] The end product of his synthesis is apt to appear diffuse and unfocused. Presidents operate within a system in which

> one unrelinquishable value interferes with another and . . . no final choice can be made between the environment and profitability, between social compassion and economic competition, or between the risks of peace and those of war.[34]

As a result, the executive branch has difficulty speaking with one voice, and presidents who seek to balance these conflicting values often appear ambiguous and undecisive.

The massive expansion of governmental programs in the 1960s and 1970s has also spawned additional organized interests capable of political mobilization to protect their special policy interests. They range from grass-roots neighborhood organizations, to state and local government officials who administer federal programs, to Ralph Nader's Raiders, to conservative public interest law firms, to high priced Washington lawyers maneuvering to protect their client's interests. There are now more interests to be reconciled by a president seeking to coordinate governmental policy.

A traditional means used by presidents to exercise some control over the sprawling executive branch has been the appointment of fellow partisans to policy-making positions. For example, among high level executive appointees requiring Senate confirmation, such as assistant secretaries of departments, Nixon appointees were 81 percent Republican. Under Reagan and Bush the percentages of fellow Republicans in top rank positions rose to 97 and 100 percent.[35] President Clinton's White House continued the practice of seeking to gain control of the executive branch by appointing Democratic partisans as it sought to create a competent staff for its administration while also responding to the claims and demands of campaign workers, contributors, and the diverse groups, movements, and constituencies that had brought it electoral success.

By centralizing appointment decisions in the White House Personnel Office, presidential control and bureaucratic responsiveness to the White House have been increased. At the same time, there have been unintended and potentially less than desirable consequences. White House centralization of personnel decisions has permitted job seekers, interest groups, campaign contributors, and members of Congress to press their claims more directly upon the White House staff, moved more conflicts into the White House, and caused conflict between the appointments staff and administrative units.[36]

Given the loose nature of American parties, appointment of fellow partisans does not assure a president that his appointees will be inclined to follow faithfully his policy initiatives. As previously noted, cabinet members often find it necessary to make an accommodation with their staffs, clientele groups, and congressional committees. In addition, prominent party leaders appointed to the cabinet have their own networks of supporters and are likely to be inclined toward periodic spells of independence.

White House staff operate in a quite different environment than do presidential appointees to the departments and agencies. In the White House, the president and his key aides reign supreme. Actions taken to facilitate presidential objectives bring rewards, not responsiveness to Congress, interest groups, or the civil service. Presidents have, therefore, tended to expand the size of the White

House staff as a mechanism to monitor and supervise the rest of the executive branch. Of course, increasing the size of the White House staff in itself creates problems of control and the potential for elements of the staff to engage in activities that create embarrassments for the administration. For Republican presidents, the Office of Management and Budget (OMB) has been a key control and coordinating agency. Democratic presidents, who have had a greater interest in expanding governmental programs, have tended to rely more heavily on the domestic policy staff at the White House.[37] In both Republican and Democratic administrations, however, there is heavy reliance on the domestic and foreign policy staffs in the White House because of their responsiveness to presidential concerns. The creation of policy development and evaluation staffs within the White House, of course, creates tensions between the senior officials of the departments and their counterparts in the White House. Conflicts over policy and scrambling for influence with the president became so intense during the Carter administration that Secretary of State Cyrus Vance resigned after many disputes with National Security Advisor Zbigniew Brzezinski. Though less dramatic, the Reagan, Bush, and Clinton administrations too have seen their share of conflicts between White House staffers and agency heads. For example, Reagan's secretary of state, George Shultz, had difficulties regarding policy and access to the president with the president's national security advisors; Bush's Environmental Protection Agency head, William Reilly, had well-publicized policy disputes with White House Chief of Staff John Sununu; and Secretary of State Warren Christopher has been in periodic disagreement with Clinton White House staffers over both policy and the structure of foreign policy initiatives.

Recent presidents have followed a variety of strategies designed to achieve control over the executive branch. During his second term, Nixon adopted a strategy of appointing relatively "faceless individuals with no independent political clout of their own to cabinet positions and then planting a Nixon White House operative within each department at a high level in order to monitor the department for the White House.[38] This experiment in White House control, however, collapsed as the Watergate crisis overtook the Nixon presidency.

Reagan's unusual success in controlling his administration can be attributed to four factors.[39] First, he and his key staff members dramatically limited their policy priorities and focused upon economic issues. The president was, therefore, perceived as rising above the policy congestion with a clear agenda for action. Second, the Reagan administration entered the White House with a program. It was, however, not so much a party program as it was a program developed by conservative policy activists. The Heritage Foundation, a conservative, Washington-based think tank, for example, produced a 1,080 page compilation of 1,270 policy recommendations for the administration. After the first year of the Reagan administration, the Foundation claimed that 61 percent of its recommendations had been acted upon.

A third factor in the administration's management strategy was finding a body of like-minded people to staff the executive branch. Loyalty to Reagan and to his conservative philosophy were essential prerequisites for appointment. For example, John Kessel's comparative study of White House personnel has revealed that Reagan appointees were not only highly conservative, but they showed a greater level of agreement with each other than did the staffs of Presidents Nixon and Carter.[40]

Unlike Presidents Nixon and Carter, who allowed their department heads to have a free hand in filling subordinate positions, job applicants in the Reagan administration were checked out by the White House personnel office for their loyalty to the president's objectives. Indeed, the Reagan White House even went so far as to fill many of its subcabinet posts with conservative loyalists before cabinet officers were designated. As Bert Rockman, an expert on executive politics, has observed, Reagan "cabinet officers provided the administration's public face, but the subcabinet officials in particular were chosen for their commitment to the goals of the White House."[41]

The final factor contributing to presidential control of the executive branch during the Reagan administration was a concerted effort to reinforce central rather than department loyalties among leaders of the executive branch. Initial policy proposals for the various departments were developed by transition teams of conservative activists from outside the government. The newly appointed heads, therefore, were given little time or opportunity to try and develop their own policy directives. In addition, much of the negotiation with the Congress on key issues was handled by White House staff personnel, not the various department heads.

The administration also made extensive use of the cabinet councils—policy groups composed of cabinet members dealing with related policy matters and key White House staff members (e.g., the cabinet council on economic affairs).

Reagan's successors, George Bush and Bill Clinton, have had less centralized administrations, less ideologically oriented personnel policies, and more diffuse policy objectives. Clinton, in staffing his administration, stressed gender, and racial and ethnic diversity. This severely limited his ability to put people speedily in place and also made it difficult to build a team founded on clear and coherent directions.[42] In all administrations, however, the party in the executive branch is used primarily for purposes of governing and not for the building up of the party organizations. The party in the executive, of course, is also a resource that can be used to help secure the president's renomination and reelection. It is not, however, an institution over which the party organization exerts substantial influence.

The Party, the President, and the Judiciary

The president and his White House staff can exert direct pressure upon the Congress and the executive branch. Party and presidential influences upon the judiciary, however, follow a much more indirect route—largely through the process of appointing federal judges. Presidents normally select approximately 90 percent of their judicial nominees from within the ranks of their own party. The impact of these appointments on judicial policy-making can be profound. Together, Ronald Reagan and George Bush, between 1981 and 1992, appointed 70 percent of all the federal judges. This is an impact on the federal judiciary exceeded only by Franklin Roosevelt, who appointed 75 percent of the federal judges. During the Reagan and Bush administrations, therefore, the federal bench was transformed from being predominantly Democratic to one with a Republican majority. One of the lasting legacies of the Reagan and Bush presidencies, therefore, has been a conservative Republican influence on the federal bench.[43] Even though President Clinton made 129 appointments to the federal courts during his first two years in office, the Republican domination of the courts continued. As of 1994, Clinton's appointments had brought the percentage of Republican appointed judges down from 70 to 60 percent. It is expected that Clinton can create a predominantly Democratic federal branch by the end of his second term.[44]

In making federal district and court of appeals appointments, presidents are forced to share power with their party's senators. The practice of senatorial courtesy enables senators of the president's party to block federal appointments within their own states if they disapprove of the nominee. To a significant degree, therefore, the initial screening of judicial candidates is done by senators of the president's party from the state in which the appointment is to be made. Because federal judicial appointments are among the most prized patronage plums at the disposal of a president and his party, there is often substantial jockeying for influence among home state senators of the president's party, the justice Department, White House staff, concerned interest groups, bar associations, state party organizations, and presidential supporters from the state where the appointment will be made. The ultimate decision on a judicial nomination is a presidential prerogative. However, disputes between the Justice Department and senators of the president's party over judicial appointments within their home state can become rancorous if the president declines to nominate the individual preferred by a senator. In such cases, Senate colleagues are likely to rise in defense of senatorial courtesy by stalling all pending judicial nominations.

In those states in which there is no senator of the president's party, presidents normally give substantial weight to the recommendations of House members of the president's party, governors, and campaign officials. To a significant degree, any administration is dependent upon knowledgeable people within the states in making judicial appointments because the Justice Department and the White House staff do not have detailed knowledge of the legal fraternity in the various states.

In selecting nominees for the Supreme Court, the president has substantially more leeway than in making appointments to the federal district courts or the courts of appeals. The practice of senatorial courtesy does not operate in the confirmation process, though it is essential for presidents to nominate candidates capable of securing the necessary votes for confirmation by the full Senate. The direction of national judicial policy can be dramatically changed through Supreme Court appointments. The reliable liberal majorities that existed on the Warren Court have ceased to exist because between 1969 and 1992 Presidents Nixon, Ford, Reagan, and Bush were able to appoint a majority of the justices.

Because of the Supreme Court's potential to affect controversial public policy issues like abortion, affirmative action, and presidential war powers, it is not surprising that Court appointments can become an issue in presidential campaigns. For example, Ronald Reagan's conservative ideological approach to Court appointments caused his 1984 Democratic opponent, Walter Mondale, to charge that Christian-right minister Jerry Falwell would be picking Supreme Court nominees in a second Reagan administration. Judicial politics was also prominent in Clinton's presidential campaigns, as he pledged that his judicial appointees would be pro-choice. Judicial politics expert Sheldon Goldman has observed accurately that "when we elect a president, we're electing a judiciary."[45]

Parties in Congress

The congressional environment has not been conducive to high levels of party unity or strong policy leadership by the parties. The party leadership of Congress has been forced to adapt to the fact that members of the House and Senate are individually responsible for their own renomination and reelection. Since the congressional party organizations can guarantee members neither safe seats nor extensive campaign resources in return for loyalty on roll call votes, members frequently assume a highly independent orientation when voting on the House and Senate floor. They must protect themselves with their constituents, irrespective of party policy positions.

As was noted previously, the separation of powers systems further reduces the incentives for party loyalty within the party of the president. Unlike a parliamentary system, members of Congress who desert their president on key votes do not risk losing control of the executive branch or the calling of new congressional elections. The Constitution assures both the president and members of Congress fixed terms in office, even when presidential programs lack congressional support.

The parties of Congress also have to contend with the committee/subcommittee system, which has major responsibility for the development of policy proposals. Strong congressional committees and subcommittees result in power over various aspects of public policy being scattered among hundreds of House and Senate subcommittees and committees. With each committee and subcommittee zealously guarding its jurisdiction and prerogatives, policy development and coordination by congressional party leaders is extremely difficult.

Although electoral forces and institutional arrangements operate to frustrate party influence within Congress, evidence of partisanship abounds in the organizational structure, decision making, and social life of Congress. It is not, however, an all pervasive or disciplined type of partisanship. Partisanship is, however, an ever present influence that has grown stronger since the mid-1980s as an electoral realignment has occurred in the South. This realignment has resulted in a decline in the proportion of conservative southern Democrats in Congress and a corresponding increase in conservative southern Republicans. In the process, both the Democratic and Republican congressional parties have become more ideologically homogeneous and, therefore, more unified and the Congress more susceptible to partisan influences.

Evidence of Partisanship

Congress is organized on a highly partisan basis. Members of the majority party hold the key leadership posts—Speaker of the House, Majority Floor Leader of the Senate, and all committee and subcommittee chairmanships in each chamber. By holding these positions, the majority party maintains procedural control of the Congress. This enables the majority party leadership to determine which bills will be scheduled for action, as well as when they will be on the agenda and under what conditions. With majority status there are other benefits—additional staff assistance to facilitate action on policies supported by the members of the party, and committee ratios of Democrats to Republicans that assure the majority party of at least a numerical advantage in each committee and subcommittee. In the House, for example, the majority party has set the ratio of majority to minority members of key committees, such as Rules, Ways and Means, and Appropriations, at a level that assures the majority party of control on most issues. These majority party advantages often make life in the minority a frustrating experience. In the 1980s and until 1994, when they gained control of the House after forty years in the wilderness of minority status,

Republicans grew increasingly frustrated. With the combative Newt Gingrich (Ga.) as their leader, a group of junior Republican members decided to forego attempts to win minor concessions from the majority Democrats through cooperation and compromise. Instead, they adopted a highly confrontational style on the House floor designed to raise issues that could be used in the next election. A leader of these aggressive and highly conservative Republicans explained their actions as follows.

> There is . . . a sense of trying to force confrontation as a . . . permanent way for the Republican minority to operate. More confrontation rather than cooperation. . . . Another way to put it from our perspective would be that we receive absolutely none of the benefits for helping you guys [Democrats] pass your bills. We're never going to be committee chairmen as long as we're in the minority. We're never going to move up, we're never going to be subcommittee chairmen, and as long as we don't have that option, we'll confront instead of cooperate.[46]

With the Congress under the control of Republicans after the 1994 elections, it was the Democrats' turn to feel the frustrations that go with minority status, especially in the House of Representatives. As the House Republicans exhibited a high degree of party unity and now exercised the same sorts of powers that the Democrats had previously used to severely limit minority party influence over legislation, Democrats complained about being shut out of a meaningful decision-making role.

The parties tend to loom large in the minds of junior members because it is through the congressional party organizations that members receive their committee assignments. Assignment to preferred committees is often essential, especially in the House, if members are to achieve such congressional career goals as reelection, power in the chamber, or policy influence.[47] During the days immediately after their first election and before they have even taken the oath of office, members-elect must campaign among their senior party colleagues for support in gaining good committee assignments. Thus at the beginning of their life in the Congress, they are confronted with the importance of partisanship. Often the leadership will impress upon members the importance of loyalty before granting assignment to a key committee.

The party leadership is also important as a source of needed information—the legislative schedule, the expected outcome of a roll call, the position of the president on a key amendment, the strategy of interest groups on an issue, and the electoral consequences of a yea or nay vote. The party leaders are obviously not the only source of information on such matters, but with their larger staffs and wide range of political contacts, they are an important source of political intelligence for rank and file members.The leadership can also be extremely useful in helping members acquire the financial resources for reelection campaigns.

The social contacts of a member of the Congress tend to be within their own party. The physical layout of the two chambers encourage this. The House and Senate floor arrangements feature a center aisle with the Democrats on one side, the Republicans on the other. One's seatmates, with whom one shares information, political gossip, and small talk, are fellow partisans. The same pattern holds true in the committee and subcommittee meetings rooms, where the seating arrangement divides the members of the two parties. Even the cloakrooms off the House and Senate floors are segregated along party lines. Republicans go to the Republican cloakroom and Democrats to the Democratic cloakroom when they wish to get a cup of coffee, make a phone call, or just relax. The social life of the Congress, therefore, tends to reinforce the organizational partisanship of the institution.

Partisanship is also encouraged because of the ideological bonds that exist among party members in Congress. Most national legislators share strong ideological affinities. Through their political socialization processes, fellow partisans come to develop compatible ideological orientations. They are also likely to have a common interest in supporting similar voter groups and interest groups.

The extent of partisanship in the Congress may also be seen in member voting patterns on House and Senate roll calls. Figure 9.1 shows the percentage of time between 1960 and 1996 that a majority of voting Republicans have aligned themselves against a majority of voting Democrats on roll call votes in the House and Senate. The percentage of party votes in the two chambers has ranged between a high of 64 percent in the 1994 House to just 27 percent in the House during 1970 and 1972. When viewed in historical perspective, the level of partisan division portrayed in figure 9.1 constitutes a decline from the period around the turn of the century when over 70 percent of House roll calls involved a majority from each party voting on opposite sides.[48] Similarly, the current

Figure 9.1
PARTY VOTES IN THE CONGRESS, 1960–1996 (PERCENT OF ALL ROLL CALLS)

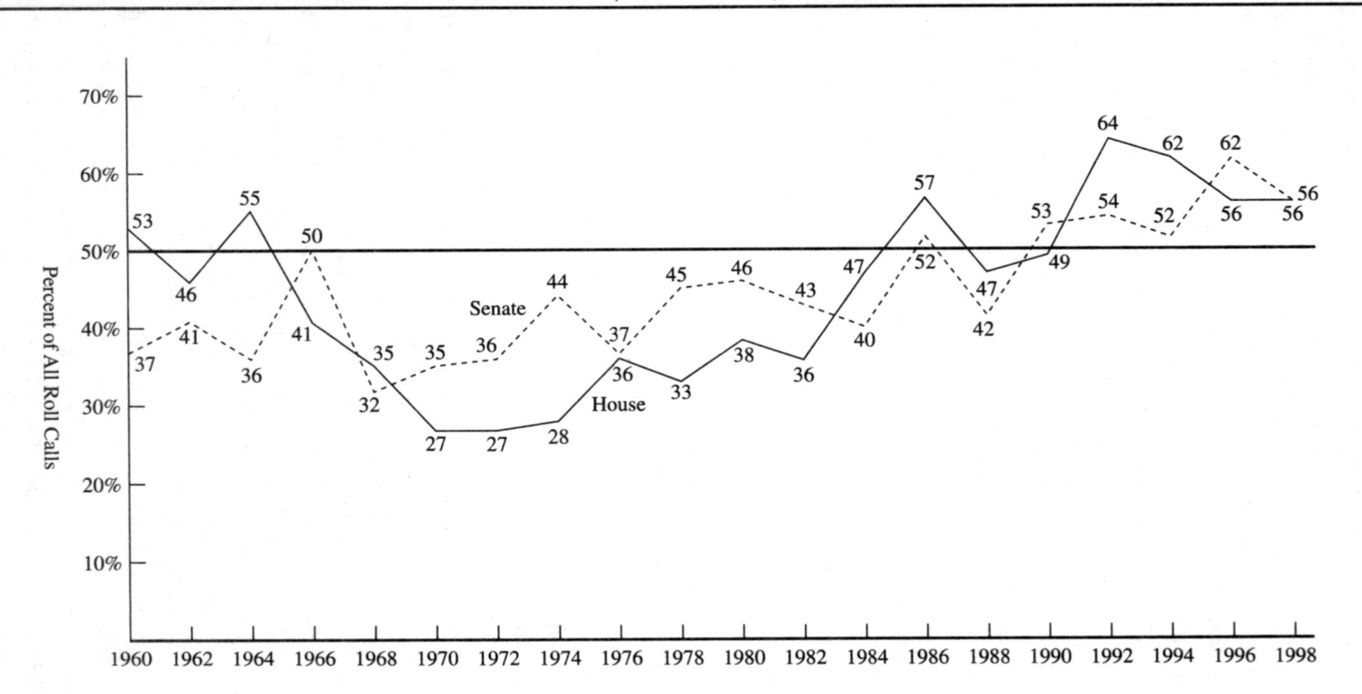

Note: Data indicate the percentage of recorded votes on which a majority of voting Democrats opposed a majority of voting Republicans.

Source: Norman J. Ornstein, Thomas E. Mann, and Michael J. Malbin, *Vital Statistics on Congress, 1997–1998* (Washington, D.C.: Congressional Quarterly, 1998), p. 210. Used by permission.

levels of partisan voting in Congress appear low when compared to the more intense partisanship found in other Western democracies. However, with each chamber holding between 800 to 1,000 roll calls during each Congress (a two year period) and with many of the bills being of a minor or noncontroversial character, the data in figure 9.1 give evidence of substantial partisan division within the House and Senate. It is also clear that the extent of party-line voting has increased substantially since the late 1970s, reaching thirty-year highs during the Bush and Clinton administrations.

The extent of partisanship in Congress can be explored further by examining the degree of party unity on those roll calls which pit a majority of Democrats against a majority of Republicans. Figures 9.2 and 9.3 show the percentage of Republicans and Democrats voting in agreement with a majority of their party colleagues on issues that divided the two parties. These 1960–1996 data reveal that average party unity scores for a session of the Congress have rarely dipped below 70 percent and frequently have climbed into the 80+ percent range. Like the data on the extent of partisan roll calls, the party unity scores can be viewed from different perspectives. On the one hand the data show substantial evidence of partisanship and party loyalty that has been trending upward since the mid-1980s. But at the same time, the data also demonstrate that the parties are far from unified and that substantial divisions exist within both parties.

The extent of these internal party cleavages are portrayed in table 9.3, which shows that almost a quarter of Senate Democrats and over one-third of Republican senators voted against a majority of their party colleagues on at least 20 percent of Senate roll call votes in 1997. Party opposition scores in the House are lower, but still reveal internal divisions within both parties. There are even members of both parties that vote in opposition more often than in agreement with a majority of their party colleagues. For example, in 1997, three Democratic representatives voted in opposition to their party colleagues on over 60 percent of the partisan roll calls, with Representative James Trafficant (D-Ohio) racking up a 77 percent party opposition score. In the Senate, three Republicans—Arlen Specter (Penn.), James Jeffords (Vt.), and Olympia Snowe (Me.)—each voted in opposition to their fellow Republicans over 40 percent of the time. Clearly, the two congressional parties are anything but monolithic in their policy orientations. It should, however, be kept in mind that both the Republican and Democratic parties on Capitol

Figure 9.2
PARTY UNITY IN THE HOUSE OF REPRESENTATIVES, 1960–1996

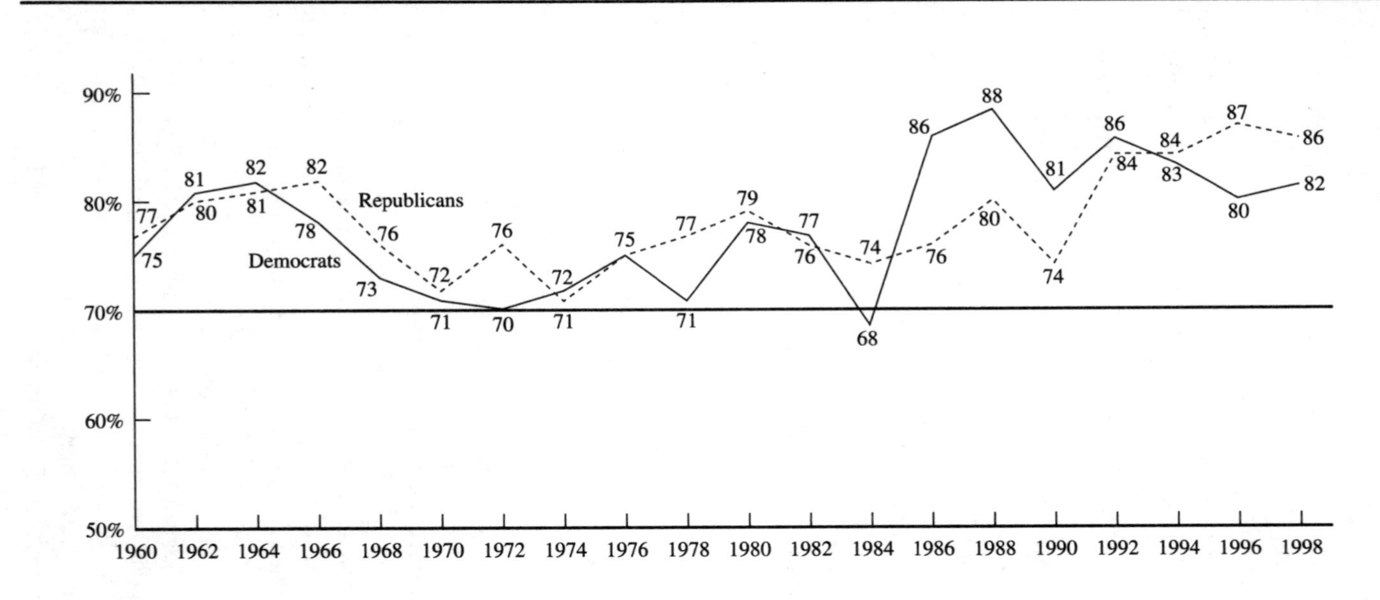

Note: Data show percentage of members voting with a majority of their party on roll call voters on which a majority of voting Democrats oppose a majority of voting Republicans.

Source: Norman J. Ornstein, Thomas E. Mann, and Michael J. Malbin, *Vital Statistics on Congress, 1997–1998* (Washington, D.C.: Congressional Quarterly, 1998), pp. 212–213. Used by permission.

Figure 9.3
PARTY UNITY IN THE SENATE, 1960–1996

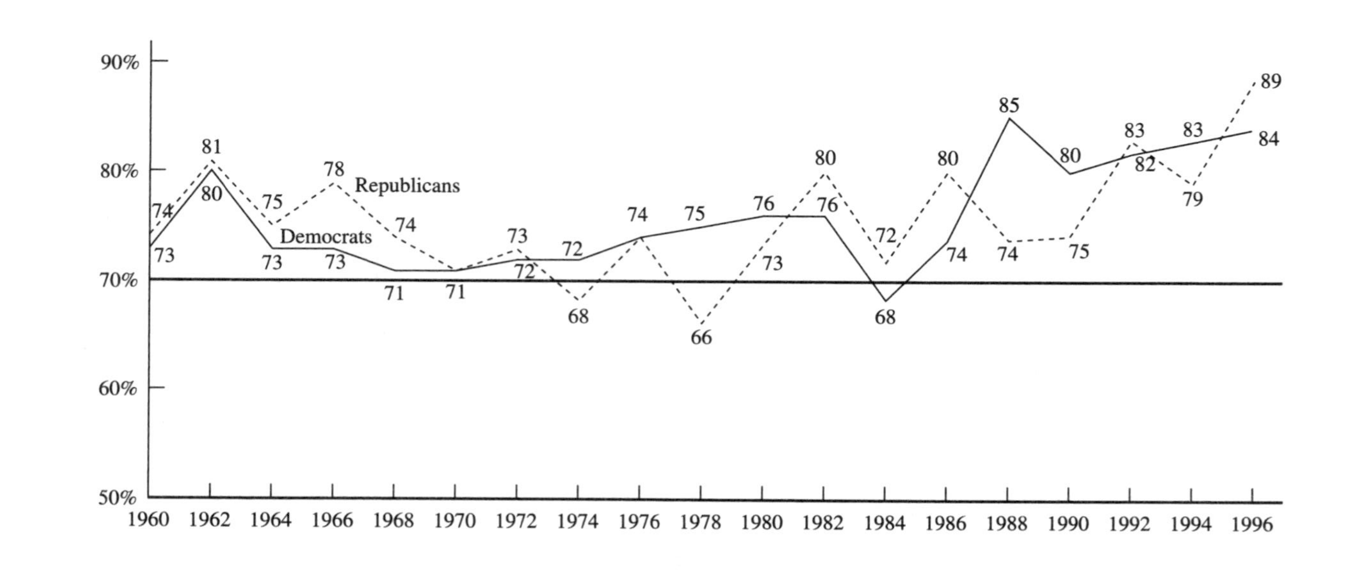

Note: Data show percentage of members voting with a majority of their party on roll calls on which a majority of voting Democrats oppose a majority of voting Republicans.

Source: Norman J. Ornstein, Thomas E. Mann, and Michael J. Malbin, *Vital Statistics on Congress, 1997–1998* (Washington, D.C.: Congressional Quarterly, 1998), pp. 211–212. Used by permission.

Hill have become substantially more unified in recent years, especially the Republicans. The research of William Keefe has shown that even the most conservative wing of the congressional Democratic party, the southern Democrats, is more liberal than the most moderate wing of the congressional Republican party, the northeastern Republicans.[49] Partisan clashes that strained the customary civility of congressional life and were so evident during the Bush and Clinton administration reflect the partisan polarization that now characterizes policymaking in both the House and Senate.

Even so, the internal cleavages that exist within the congressional parties and the resulting lack of party unity mean that legislative majorities must frequently be forged with bipartisan coalitions. President Clinton was able to win approval of the North American Free Trade Agreement (NAFTA), a priority item on his legislative agenda, only because a majority of the House Republicans, led by Newt Gingrich (Ga.), supported the agreement, while a majority of Democrats voted in opposition. Even Democratic Majority Leader Richard Gephardt (Mo.) and Democratic Whip David Bonior (Mich.) opposed the president on NAFTA.

One of the most influential and enduring cross-party coalitions in the postwar years has been the so-called conservative coalition of Republicans and conservative southern Democrats. Table 9.4 shows the frequency with which this coalition has appeared since 1960 as well as its success rate. When it has appeared, the coalition normally scored legislative victories. It was a critical factor in President

Table 9.3

Extent of Roll Call Voting Against a Majority of Their Party Colleagues, 105th Congress, 1997

	Voting against a Majority of Their Party on 20 Percent or More of Roll Calls		
	Number	**Percent**	**Number of Party Members in the Chamber**
Senate			
Democrats	12	27	45
Republicans	8	15	55
House			
Democrats	48	23	206
Republicans	18	8	228

Source: Derived from data prepared by *Congressional Quarterly Weekly Report,* January 3, 1998, pp. 35–37. Used by permission.

Table 9.4
Conservative Coalition Appearances and Victories in Congress, 1960–1997

	House		Senate	
Year	Appearances	Victories	Appearances	Victories
1960	20%	35%	22%	67%
1961	30	74	32	48
1962	13	44	15	71
1963	13	67	19	44
1964	11	67	17	47
1965	25	25	24	39
1966	19	32	30	51
1967	22	73	18	54
1968	22	63	25	80
1969	25	71	28	67
1970	17	70	26	64
1971	31	79	28	86
1972	25	79	29	63
1973	25	67	21	54
1974	22	67	30	54
1975	28	52	28	48
1976	17	59	26	58
1977	22	60	29	74
1978	20	57	23	46
1979	21	73	18	65
1980	16	67	20	75
1981	21	88	21	95
1982	16	78	20	90
1983	18	71	12	89
1984	14	75	18	94
1985	13	84	11	93
1986	11	78	20	93
1987	9	88	8	100
1988	8	82	10	97
1989	11	80	12	95
1990	10	74	11	95
1991	9	86	14	95
1992	10	88	14	87
1993	7	98	10	90
1994	7	92	10	72
1995	13	100	9	95
1996	51	100	38	97
1997	8	92	9	100

Note: Appearances refers to the percentage of all roll call votes in the House or Senate on which a majority of voting southern Democrats and a majority of voting Republicans opposed a stand taken by a majority of northern Democrats.

Sources: Norman J. Ornstein, Thomas E. Mann, and Michael J. Malbin, *Vital Statistics on Congress, 1997–1998* (Washington, D.C.: Congressional Quarterly, Inc., 1998), pp. 214–215; *Congressional Quarterly Weekly Report,* January 3, 1998, p. 21. Used by permission.

Reagan's successful push for major budgetary reductions and tax law changes during his first year in office and it continued to be important on foreign and defense policy issues during his second term.

Although the cross-party conservative coalition has in the past been a major force in congressional decision making, the data in table 9.4 show that by the late 1980s it had become a shadow of its former self. It now appears much less frequently than in the 1960s and 1970s. The coalition did see a brief rebirth during 1996 when President Clinton and the Republican Congress managed to declare a truce after their budgetary confrontations in 1995 that led to two shutdowns of government. However, the following year, partisan polarization reasserted itself and the conservative coalition appeared less than 10 percent of the time (see table 9.4). The decline of the conservative coalition reflects heightened party unity and increased intensity of partisan conflict divisions since the late 1980s within Congress (see figures 9.2 and 9.3).

This increase in party line voting in Congress has been caused by more policy oriented Democratic and Republican congressional leaders and the divisiveness of such issues as the budget, defense versus social program spending, and social issues. These and other issues have increasingly pitted a president and his congressional colleagues against an opposition party controlling one or both chambers of Congress. Intensified partisan conflict also reflects the changing composition of the two parties in Congress. As partisan realignment has occurred among southern voters, Republicans have won an increasingly larger share of the region's House and Senate seats. This has meant that the Republican membership has become more southern and more conservative. At the same time, the Democratic membership has become less southern, and those Democrats elected from the South are often heavily dependent upon black voters and less likely to be conservatives (often dubbed "Boll Weevils"). Further contributing to the intensified partisanship of Congress is the growing number of Republicans from generally conservative western state constituencies. The net effect of these membership changes has been to make each party's membership more homogeneous ideologically and thereby to sharpen partisan divisions within Congress.[50]

Although partisanship is a pervasive influence within Congress, parties must compete with other powerful forces—the president, interest groups, and constituency interests—for members' votes. In this competition, the parties do not always prevail.

The special character of the congressional party was captured by political scientist David B. Truman. After identifying the distinctive voting patterns of the members of the two parties as well as deep intraparty schisms, he concluded that congressional parties were *mediate groups.* He wrote:

> The party labels do distinguish different patterns of attitude and value and different systems of interaction. . . . Moreover, they have a marked degree of stability and structure. . . . Yet, the degree of cleavage . . . in both parties indicates that the parties constitute a different and perhaps special type of group. They have a vitality and persistence as organizations despite internal divisions which in most other groups would be a prelude to dissolution, secession, or ostracism. . . . [The congressional party] is mediate and supplementary in function. That is, from the viewpoint of the members it does some things of importance, and its failures may be of considerable consequence to them. On the other hand, retention of their status as senators [and representatives] is not so completely dependent upon it—unlike the management of a corporation, the members of a labor union, or the components of a military organization—that its risks are entirely their risks or its failures necessarily theirs.[51]

Party Organization in the House

Because of its large size (435 members), the House has rules that strictly regulate the processing of legislation and limit the effectiveness of dilatory tactics. These rules, which bring an element of order to the chamber and enable it to fulfill its legislative responsibilities, also have the effect of severely limiting the power of the minority party and individual members. In the House, the majority party, if it is reasonably united, is in a position to work its will on most issues and minority party and individual members have only the most restricted powers of delay and obstruction. These procedural rules strengthen the position of the party leaders, especially the Speaker and majority floor leader, who tend to dominate the setting of the House agenda.

The Speaker of the House. The most prominent and influential member of the House is its Speaker, who serves as both its presiding officer and the leader of the majority party. Early in this century, the speakership was brought to the zenith of its power by the legendary and autocratic Joseph G. Cannon ("Uncle Joe") an Illinois Republican, who served as Speaker from 1903 to 1911. He dominated his party and the House through his extensive formal powers, which he used aggressively to assure that his faction of the Republican party controlled the House. These powers included serving as presiding officer of the House, control of member committee assignments, designation of committee chairmen, whom he both appointed and removed, and regulation of the work schedule of the House through his chairmanship of the Committee on Rules. Cannon, however, lost his majority on procedural issues within the House during 1910 and 1911. In a revolt of Progressive Republicans and Democrats, the Speaker was stripped of his position as chairman of the Rules Committee, his power to make committee assignments, and some of his powers to recognize members on the floor. The modern Speakers do not have as extensive formal powers as those that were available to Cannon and must lead their parties and the House by relying more heavily on informal means—persuasion, bargaining, and negotiation.

In the 1970s, the Democrats made a series of rule changes that vested some renewed formal power in the Speaker. The Speaker was made chairman of the Steering and Policy Committee, which made committee assignments for Democratic members. This gave the Speaker the ability to exert a significant impact on the careers of rank and file members and to influence the composition and therefore the policy orientation of committees. The Speaker was also given authority to name Democratic members of the Rules Committee and through the Rules Committee to control the flow of the legislation to the floor as well as the procedures under which bills were considered by the House. As the presiding officer of the House, the Speaker is also in a position to make strategically important parliamentary rulings. Backed by a relatively cohesive party membership, these formal powers in the hands of an aggressive speaker, like Jim Wright (D-Tex., 1986–1989) or Newt Gingrich (1995–1998), provide the bases for strong and policy oriented party leadership.

When the Republicans took control of the House after the 1994 elections, they too vested Speaker Newt Gingrich (Ga.) with increased influence over committee assignments and control over which Republicans would serve on the powerful House Rules Committee. He used these powers to select committee chairmen (who would support his legislative agenda), sometimes in violation of the seniority principle. And, like his Democratic predecessors, he used the Rules Committee to develop procedures for consideration of legislation that would severely limit the influence of the

Figure 9.4
PARTY LEADERSHIP POSITIONS IN THE 106TH CONGRESS, 1999–2000

House of Representatives

Speaker
(Nominated by the Republicans and elected by the full house)

Majority Party (Republicans)	**Minority Party** (Democrats)
Floor Leader	Floor Leader
Whip	Whip
Conference Chairman	Caucus Chairman
Policy Committee Chairman (Committee helps develop party policy.)	Policy Committee Chairman (Position held by minority floor leader. Committee helps develop party policy.)
Steering Committee Chairman (Position held by the Speaker. Committee makes Republican committee assignments.)	Steering Committee Chairman (Position held by minority floor leader. Committee makes Democratic committee assignments.)
Chief Deputy Whip	Chief Deputy Whips (4)
National Republican Congressional Committee Chairman (Committee recruits and supports Republican House candidates.)	Democratic Congressional Campaign Committee Chairman (Committee recruits and supports Democratic House candidates.)

Senate

President Pro Tempore
(Most senior member in terms of service in the majority party)

Majority Party (Republicans)	**Minority Party** (Democrats)
Floor Leader	Floor Leader
Whip	Whip
Conference Chairman	Conference Chairman (Position held by minority floor leader.)
Policy Committee Chairman (Committee consults on policy research.)	Policy Committee Chairman (Position held by minority floor leader. Committee consults on policy.)
	Policy Committee Co-Chairman
Conference Secretary	Conference Secretary
Committee on Committees Chairmen (Committee makes Republican committee assignments.)	Steering and Coordination Committee (Committee makes Democratic committee assignments.)
Chief Deputy Whip	Chief Deputy Whip
	Technology and Communications Committee Chairman (Develops methods of communicating party message)
National Republican Senatorial Committee Chairman (Committee recruits and supports Republican senatorial candidates.)	Democratic Senatorial Campaign Committee Chairman (Committee recruits and supports Democratic senatorial candidates.)

minority party. With the generally unified backing of his party colleagues, especially among junior members who credited him with masterminding the end of forty years of Democratic control over the House, Gingrich emerged as the most powerful Speaker since Cannon. In the first one hundred days of the 104th Congress in 1995, the Gingrich-led Republicans succeeded in gaining House passage of an almost unprecedented amount of major legislation that was contained in their ten-point campaign manifesto, the Contract with America.[52]

Even though recent Democratic and Republican speakers have been able to centralize power to a degree that was unknown in the House from the 1950s through the 1970s, there is one political reality with which all Speakers must cope. This is the fact that their power is only as great as their colleagues will permit. When significant numbers of their party colleagues become disenchanted and withdraw support out of concern for policy outcomes and/or electoral survival, then the power of the Speaker is threatened.[53] Thus, in 1997, Speaker Gingrich, who had been hailed as the strongest Speaker since Joseph G. Cannon (1903–1911) was threatened by a revolt led by the most conservative members of his party, who believed he was failing to deliver on the conservative agenda and was too accommodating to President Clinton and party moderates. Gingrich was able to quell this attempted coup, but he was left in a weakened position due to factionalism between moderates and conservatives within his own party's ranks, each of whom could exert power leverage on the Speaker because his party's majority in the House was only eleven seats. When the GOP lost five seats in 1998, Gingrich's position was further weakened, and with only a six seat majority in the Chamber, he chose to resign.

A further limitation of the power of the Speaker is the committee system. Committees and subcommittees each have their own subject matter jurisdictions and have traditionally operated with substantial autonomy from party leaders.

The Floor Leaders. Within the majority party, the Speaker's principal associate is the floor leader. He normally acts as the key party spokesman and strategist on the House floor. With the Speaker, he helps to plan the legislative schedule of the House. He carries major responsibilities for persuading his colleagues to support party leadership positions on House votes and must also spend time talking with his colleagues to gauge members' sentiments on various issues.

The minority floor leader is the highest ranking position within his party. He is responsible for serving as party spokesman and defender on the floor, developing legislative strategy to advance the minority goals, building bridges to dissident members of the opposition, and keeping in touch with the sentiments of his party colleagues. When his party controls the presidency, the minority leader has the responsibility of acting as a spokesman for the White House and for advancing its legislative program. During the Reagan and Bush administrations Republican leader Robert Michel of Illinois often found that serving the needs of the White House and his colleagues was extremely difficult. On the one hand, it was frequently necessary to make concessions to the majority Democrats in order to fashion a majority on the House floor. But such concessions frequently were not well received by his own hard core partisans who were seeking confrontations with the opposition to develop issues for the next election. House leader Richard Gebhardt (Mo.) has faced similar problems and has frequently asserted his own and his Democratic colleagues' opposition to policies of the Clinton White House, including such key issues as welfare reform and trade. The minority leader with the president of his own party is constantly torn by his party's obligations to govern, thereby downplaying partisanship, and the party's desire for majority status.

The Whips. Both parties have assistant leaders known as whips. The term derives from the English hunt, where the job of the whip was to keep the dogs together. Similarly, the duty of the party whips is to encourage party discipline. The whips do not have the formal authority to "whip" their colleagues into line. Rather, they are responsible for conveying to rank and file members the party position on issues, persuading them to support it, and making advance nosecounts to determine the likelihood for success of a leadership position on the floor. Each party has an elaborate whip organization composed of a deputy whip and regional whips responsible for contacting and persuading their colleagues. just before key party votes and during the roll calls, whips can be seen roaming the floor rounding up votes for their side and standing by the doors of the chamber signaling members how to vote as they enter the House chamber from their offices and committee rooms.

The Policy Committees. Party policy committees function as agencies to gauge party sentiments and to identify the party position on issues before they come to the House floor for a vote. For example, if there is substantial disagreement within a policy committee concerning what should be the party's position on an issue, this absence of a consensus will probably cause the leadership not to take a formal party position on an issue. On the other hand, policy committee endorsement of a position on a bill tends to strengthen the leadership's position in winning party members' support for their viewpoint. The policy committees play a role of providing policy guidance to members, but they do not have the power to bind members to support their positions. Nor do the policy committees customarily seek to involve themselves in the deliberations of the standing committees. The policy committees instead enter the process at the stage when legislation has emerged from committee and is being scheduled for floor action. Therefore, they are not agencies for the development of a party program. The Congress and its parties are too decentralized for them to play such a role.

The Steering Committees. Each party has a Steering Committee which is responsible for making committee assignments for party members. For the majority party, the Steering Committee also nominates members to serve as committee chairmen, while in the minority party it nominates members to be ranking minority members of committees. These nominations must be confirmed by their full party membership. By serving as chairman of their party's Steering Committee, the Speaker and Minority Leader exert a profound influence over the committee assignments and chairmanships and in the process strengthen their leverage with party colleagues.

Party Caucuses and Conferences. Party caucuses or conferences include all the members of the party in a chamber. The most important work of the party caucuses is done at the beginning of a new Congress when they meet to organize their parties in the House. It is at these meetings that party leaders are elected and party rules are adopted. In addition, these organizational meetings customarily ratify decisions of the steering committees concerning committee assignments and chairmanships or ranking minority member positions on the committees. Major intraparty struggles periodically erupt over the selection of leaders, which can affect the future course of the party. House Democrats have been less inclined to have contested elections for leadership positions than the Republicans. Democratic leaders have tended to move through a series of subordinate positions before becoming Speaker. For example, Thomas Foley served apprenticeships as whip and majority leader before being elected to the Speakership upon the retirement of Jim Wright (D-Tex.) in 1989. By contrast, minority Republicans have had a series of revolts that have toppled the minority leaders—for example, Gerald Ford (R-Mich.) ousted Charles Halleck (R-Ind.) after the election debacle of 1964, and Halleck successfully challenged Joseph Martin (R-Mass.) after a similar GOP electoral disaster in 1958.

Party caucuses are held on an almost weekly basis throughout a congressional session to allow members to express their sentiments on issues facing the House and to rally partisan support for leadership positions on key votes. Like the policy committees, however, the caucuses do not make decisions that are binding on their members in terms of how they shall vote on the floor. Only rarely have the caucuses in recent years sought to instruct committee members concerning action on legislation being considered by a committee. Every member of the caucus is also a member of at least one standing committee and, therefore, has a stake in maintaining the autonomy and power of the committees. Strong expressions of sentiment in the caucus can, however, affect the actions and strategy of the party leadership.

The Democratic caucus has played a major role in reshaping the procedures of the House of Representatives. Through changes in party and House rules initiated in the caucus during the 1970s, the seniority system for selection of committee chairmen was modified, members were restricted to one subcommittee chairmanship, subcommittees gained substantial autonomy from full committee chairmen, the Steering Committee gained the power to make committee assignments from the Democratic members of the Ways and Means Committee, the Speaker acquired the power to nominate Democratic members to the Rules Committee, and had his power to refer bills to committee strengthened. As a consequence of the Democrats' caucus mandated rules changes in the 1970s and similar rules adopted by the Republican Conference, the party leadership in both parties has been strengthened and power has been considerably centralized in the once highly decentralized House.

Informal Party Groups. In addition to the regular party organizational structure that has just been described, there also exists within the House a series of informal party groups which can work under some circumstances to reinforce party unity and at other times to cause fragmentation. An important set of groups within each party are the state party delegations which vary in size and in the formality of their organizations. Some meet regularly to discuss their position on legislation and to share information. As communications networks, state delegations can be used by both the leadership and dissident factions to line up support for floor votes. State delegations are particularly active during the time early in a Congress when committee assignments are being made. The various delegations lobby to get their members on key committees and often engage in complicated multidelegation bargaining schemes in order to secure the best possible assignments for their members.

Within both parties there are class clubs which are organized on the basis of the Congress or year in which a member was first elected. Freshmen class clubs are the most active as they seek to promote junior members' interests with the leadership and assert some influence through coordinated actions. As members gain seniority and positions of influence in the committee system and party organizations, however, they normally find the class clubs of limited usefulness.

There are also a series of ideologically oriented groups within each party which seek to pressure their parties' leadership to adopt policies compatible with the groups' views. The most successful and oldest of these ideologically oriented groups is the Democratic Study Group (DSG). It is a liberal group of Democrats that is virtually a party organization within a party organization. It has its own fund raising mechanism, whip system, research operation and staff. Much smaller and less structured groups of moderate and conservative Democrats also operate in the House. The New Democratic Coalition, with about forty members, has as its goal moving the Democratic caucus to a more centrist policy orientation. Leaning somewhat to the right of the New Democrats is a smaller group, the Blue Dog Democrats, who have tried to play a brokering role on budgetary issues. The relatively small size of these moderate groups and their rather ad hoc character have limited their influence within the party. Additional and increasingly important subgroups among the House Democrats are the Black and Hispanic Caucuses.

The Republicans also have policy oriented subgroups. The Republican Study Committee, a group of conservative Republicans, patterned their operations after the DSG. Their aggressiveness made them an important force within the House GOP. Like the Democrats, the Republicans also have a moderate group, the Tuesday Lunch Bunch, which seeks to steer the GOP toward centrist course of policy. In the 104th Congress, two other factional groups, the Family Caucus and the Conservative Action Team (CATs) were launched to counter the moderates. It was the leaders of these groups, who believed that Speaker Gingrich was too accommodating to the moderates and the president, that led the abortive coup against the Speaker in the summer of 1997.

Both GOP and Democratic leaders enlist the support of interest groups allied with their parties to mobilize the votes of members on key votes on the House floor. In the 1980s and 1990s, the House Democratic leaders increasingly formalized these activities by designating specific staff aides to work with groups such as organized labor as their primary responsibility. Republican leaders work closely with a dramatically different set of allied groups than the Democrats that include the National Federation of Independent Businesses, the National Rife Association, and the Christian Coalition. The Thursday Group of about a dozen groups with substantial memberships at the grass roots has met weekly with the GOP conference chairman to plan strategy for gaining support for GOP policies. The Republican leadership has also worked with single purpose coalitions on key policy issues. For example, Project Relief consisted of 350 industry groups dedicated to regular relief.[54]

Party Organization in the Senate

Whereas the average member of the House is a relatively anonymous figure, except in his or her own constituency, senators are much more visible and are frequently national figures. They represent major commonwealths. Most importantly, there are only one hundred senators. The smaller size of the Senate means that it can function with rules that permit the individual senators much greater leeway and influence. As a result, the average senator has significantly more formal power than the average representative. For example, much of the work of the Senate is done under unanimous consent agreements developed and negotiated by the majority leader. By refusing to agree to a unanimous consent request, an individual senator can hold up the work of the Senate until concessions are made to him. Senators also have available to them the filibuster or its threatened use as means of gaining leverage with their colleagues. The Senate's closure rule requires the votes of sixty senators to cut off debate. This means that a determined band of senators can often block action on legislation to which they are strongly opposed or at least gain concessions in return for dropping their filibuster. In comparison to the House, influence is more widely dispersed in the Senate and each member is more equal in power. Formal leadership positions (e.g., majority or minority floor leader, committee chairmanships) are important, but they are less important in the modern individualistic Senate than in the more hierarchical House.[55]

Unlike the House, the Senate's presiding officer is not a key party leader. The vice president is constitutionally empowered to preside, but he rarely does except when his vote may be needed to break a tie or when he may be called upon to make an important parliamentary ruling. As a nonmember of the Senate and a figure with limited power in the White House, the vice president is not normally an important factor in Senate decision making. Nor is the position of president pro tempore an influential position. By tradition this post is awarded to the majority party's most senior member in terms of Senate service. Senator J. Strom Thurmond (R-S.C.) became president pro tempore in 1995. Senator Thurmond's Senate influence stemmed, however, not from his position as president pro tempore, but from his seniority on the Armed Services Committee. Like the vice president, the president pro tempore rarely presides over the Senate. This task is instead delegated to freshman senators as an apprenticeship task. It is not an onerous duty because the Senate rules are relatively simple, unlike the complex House rules which give substantial advantage to the party controlling the presiding officer.

The Floor Leaders. The key leaders of the Senate are the party floor leaders. The majority floor leader is responsible for the Senate schedule, which he handles mainly through negotiated unanimous consent agreements. This procedural prerogative gives the leader some bargaining advantage with colleagues. He also acts as his party's chief spokesman and legislative strategist. But much more than in the House, the leader has only limited formal powers. His influence rests upon his ability to find a compromise position and then persuade a majority of the senators to support his position. The minority floor leader serves his party in a capacity similar to that of the majority leader, except he has no responsibility for developing the schedule of Senate business.

Senate floor leaders are also responsible for steering presidential programs through the Senate when their party controls the presidency. This normally involves juggling the interests of fellow party members in the Senate and the concerns of the White House, while keeping lines of communication open to opposition party senators whose votes may be needed to build a majority. With senators on a different reelection schedule and often holding different policy priorities than the president, the majority leader can easily become ensnarled in intraparty and institutional rivalries. In addition he must negotiate with the House leadership, whose views are apt to depart from those of the Senate or president. For example, GOP Floor Leader Robert Dole, as a spokesman and strategist for the Senate GOP, on occasion found himself at odds with the White House during the Reagan and Bush administrations. And after the Republicans took control of Congress in 1995, he was placed in the awkward position of running for his party's presidential nomination while mediating between the aggressively conservative House Republican leadership and the generally more moderate Senate Republicans.

The Whips. Each party has a whip who serves as an assistant floor leader. In both parties, the whip appoints a series of deputy whips to work with him in counting votes prior to key roll calls, persuading members to support the party position, and communicating leadership positions to the membership.

The Policy Committees. Senate policy committees do not make policy for the parties. The Republican party committee meets on a weekly basis for luncheon to discuss matters of mutual interest, but not to take positions on issues. It also has a staff which does research for the leadership and individual members, but it is not involved in the development of party policy. The Democratic Policy Committee has been used as an advisory body to the floor leader and has assisted him in scheduling Senate business when the party was in the majority.

The Committees on Committees. Each party has a committee on committees (called the Steering Committee in the Democratic party) to handle member committee assignments. In making these appointments, the Republicans have tended to rely heavily upon seniority as a criterion for selection, while the Democrats have had a more open process in which candidates for committee posts waged campaigns to secure coveted assignments. Compared to the House, a larger share of Senate issues are resolved on the floor than in committee. As a result, the committee assignment process is of somewhat less importance to the individual senators than it is for House members. Senate rules permit each senator substantial opportunities to have an impact on floor deliberations, whereas the restrictive House rules do not permit rank and file members equivalent chances to influence the decisions of the full House.

The Conferences. The party conferences in the Senate are used primarily to organize the parties at the beginning of each new Congress. At these meetings the leadership is elected and party rules are adopted. Senate party conferences meet irregularly to discuss legislative issues. These meetings provide the leadership with a sense of where their membership stands on an issue, but the sessions are not used to arrive at a party position or to intervene in the work of standing committees.

Congressional Parties and National Party Organizations

The congressional parties operate with substantial autonomy from their national committees. The principal constituencies of the national committees are the state party organizations and the president, when a party holds the White House. Congressional party leaders, especially when the party does not control the presidency, zealously guard their prerogatives as policy spokesmen for the party and show little deference to, or interest in, the work of the national committees. When out-party national chairmen have set up policy advisory committees to develop party positions on issues, these committees have been most successful when they were dominated by congressional leaders, as was true of the Republican Coordinating Committee of the period between the 1964 and 1968 elections.[56] However, when policy advisory committees have sought an independent policy development role, they have often been treated with disdain or ignored by the party leadership of Congress. Thus Speaker Sam Rayburn and Senate Majority Leader Lyndon B. Johnson of Texas paid little heed to the activities of the Democratic Advisory Council appointed by Democratic National Chairman Paul Butler after the 1956 elections. Further evidence of the distance between the national committees and the congressional party members was the decision of several key Democrats (including House Caucus Chairman Richard Gephardt and Senators Sam Nunn of Georgia and Lawton Chiles of Florida) after the 1984 presidential election defeat to form a policy advisory council in direct competition to that appointed by DNC Chairman Paul Kirk.[57]

The national committee's separation from the congressional parties is also revealed by the existence in both parties of autonomous House and Senate campaign committees. Conscious that their constituency is members of the House and Senate, the congressional and senatorial campaign committees go about their business of seeking to elect representatives and senators, and leave presidential election politics and aid to state candidates to the national committees.

Nor do the congressional and senatorial campaign committees seek to enforce party loyalty or ideological purity by bestowing their campaign support only on incumbents who have adhered to the party line on roll call votes, or to nonincumbents who have pledged to do so. Rather, the campaign committees have granted aid to candidates on strictly electoral criteria: Which candidates are the strongest? Which races does the party have the best chance of winning? Which incumbents are in tough reelection contests? Given the diversity of viewpoints represented in the congressional and senatorial parties, it would be almost impossible for the campaign committees to enforce party discipline without causing bitter and counterproductive intraparty disputes. The campaign committees, therefore, function principally as candidate recruiters, fund raisers, and campaign professionals rather than as party policy makers or enforcers of party discipline.

Parties and Policy in the Congress

Political parties are the most inclusive institutions within the Congress. As such, they constitute Congress' strongest integrating and centralizing influence. For members of the president's party, this integrating force is often reinforced by the influence of the White House and its legislative program. But even with the parties' very substantial influence, the policy-making process of Congress cannot be characterized as party government, where disciplined parties with agreed upon programs confront each other.

Congressional parties operate in an environment in which forces of decentralization are intense. Strong standing committees and their relatively autonomous subcommittees create multiple centers of influence over specific aspects of public policy. The centralizing influence of the parties is further weakened by the fact that most representatives and senators are what might be termed independent political entrepreneurs. They are personally responsible for the well-being of their own political enterprises. The party organization and the congressional parties did not get them nominated and elected, though they may have helped. Members are, therefore, unwilling to submit to any kind of party discipline that might jeopardize their electoral positions and their careers. If the congressional parties are relatively weak, it is, as David Mayhew has noted, because that is the kind of parties that the members want. They want parties that will be of assistance to them in securing their policy goals, but which will not impose burdens of discipline to party policy line that could cost them the support of their constituents.[58]

The party leadership of Congress recognizes their colleagues' need for substantial freedom in making policy decisions. They also appreciate the power realities of the committee/subcommittee system. Party leaders, especially in the Senate, must supplement their formal powers with informal techniques to build legislative majorities one issue at a time. Occasionally they can enlist the support of outside forces like the administration or interest groups to reinforce party unity (though these same outside forces can also be an influence for party disunity). And frequently they must seek votes on the other side of the aisle to forge a majority. It is an endless process of bargaining, negotiation, and compromise.

Many have lamented the absence of strong and disciplined parties in the Congress on the grounds that it prevents the voter from being able to hold a party responsible at the polls for the policies of the government. It should be noted, however, that the level of party unity in Congress mirrors the lack of unity that also exists in the party-in-the-electorate. The electoral coalitions that elect Republicans and Democrats are diverse and contain conflicting and contradictory elements. Furthermore, the American constitutional system of separation of powers, which permits divided party control of government, would be extremely difficult to operate if the parties were highly unified and disciplined. In a circumstance in which one party controlled the White House and another held the Congress, disciplined parties could be a prescription for stalemate and deadlock. Relatively weak parties introduce an element of flexibility into the system and permit the government to act, even though neither party controls the government.

A Party-Influenced Government, But Not a Party-Dominated Government

The political parties' role in government is a paradoxical one. On the one hand, party influence is pervasive in the organizing of both the executive branch and the Congress, and partisan considerations are constantly in evidence in the selection of federal judges. In addition, shared partisanship between members of Congress and the president does much to facilitate cooperation and bridge the gap created by a constitutional separation of power. Party affiliation has also been shown to be the single best predictor of how representatives and senators will vote on congressional roll calls. Despite this evidence of party influence, there also exists evidence of the parties' limited capacity to control American governmental institutions. Presidents have consistently found it difficult to maintain effective control over the far-flung executive establishment, including the White House staff, even though key policy-making posts are occupied by persons from the president's party. In Congress, the absence of strict party discipline has been shown to be even more pronounced. American government and policy making, therefore, is party influenced, but it is not party dominated. The looseness of the American party system gives governmental officials substantial flexibility and independence in shaping public policy.

Suggestions for Further Reading

Baker, Richard A., and Davidson, Roger H., eds. *First among Equals: Outstanding Senate Leaders of the Twentieth Century.* Washington, D.C.: Congressional Quarterly, 1991.

Cox, Gary W, and McCubbins, Matthew D. *Legislative Leviathan: Party Government in the House.* Berkeley: University of California Press, 1993.

Dodd, Lawrence C., and Oppenheimer, Bruce I., eds. *Congress Reconsidered.* 6th ed. Washington, D.C.: CQ Press, 1997.

Jones, Charles 0. *The Presidency in a Separated System.* Washington, D.C.: Brookings, 1994.

———. *Passages to the Presidency: From Campaigning to Governing.* Washington, D.C.: Brookings, 1998

Krehbiel, Keith. *Pivotal Politics: A Theory of U.S. Lawmaking.* Chicago, Ill.: University of Chicago Press, 1998.

Mayhew, David R. *Divided We Govern: Party Control Lawmaking, and Investigations, 1946–1990.* New Haven, Conn.: Yale University Press, 1991.

Milkis, Sidney N. *The President and the Parties: The Transformation of the American Party System since the New Deal.* New York: Oxford University Press, 1993.

Peters, Ronald M., Jr. *The American Speakership: The Office in Historical Perspective.* Baltimore, Md.: Johns Hopkins University Press, 1990.

Rohde, David W. *Parties and Leaders in the Postreform House.* Chicago, Ill.: University of Chicago Press, 1991.

Sinclair, Barbara. *The Transformation of the United States Senate,* Baltimore, Md.: Johns Hopkins University Press, 1989

———. *Legislators, Leaders, and Lawmaking: The U.S. House of Representatives in the Postreform Era.* Baltimore, Md.: Johns Hopkins University Press, 1998.

Notes

1. Sarah McCally Morehouse, *State Politics, Parties and Policy* (New York: Holt, Rinehart, and Winston, 1981), p. 29.

2. Austin Ranney, "President and His Party," in Anthony King, ed., *Both Ends of the Avenue: The Presidency, the Executive Branch, and Congress in the 1980s* (Washington, D.C.: American Enterprise Institute, 1983), p. 137.

3. Ibid., p. 138.

4. Richard E. Neustadt, *President Power and the Modern Presidents: The Politics of Leadership* (New York: Free Press, 1990), pp. 29–30.

5. Ranney, "President and His Party," p. 139.

6. Theodore J. Lowi, "Party, Policy, and the Constitution in America," in

William Nisbet Chambers and Walter Dean Burnham, eds., *The American Party Systems: Stages of Development* (New York: Oxford University Press, 1975), p. 248; see also Leon D. Epstein, *Political Parties in the American Mold* (Madison: University of Wisconsin Press, 1986), pp. 80–89.

7. Paul Allen Beck, *Party Politics in America,* 8th ed. (New York: Longman, 1997), p. 383; Epstein, *Political Parties,* pp. 80–89.

8. Cornelius P. Cotter, "Eisenhower as Party Leader," *Political Science Quarterly* 98 (Summer 1983): 261. The development and extent of White House control over executive branch appointments is analyzed by C. Calvin Mackenzie, "Partisan Presidential Leadership: The President's Appointees," in L. Sandy Maisel, ed., *The Parties Respond: Changes in the American Party System* (Boulder, Colo.: Westview Press, 1990), ch. 13.

9. David Broder, "At White House Order," *Washington Post,* Jan. 1, 1991, A17; *New York Times,* Oct. 5, 1982, p. A24; Paul Taylor and Lou Cannon, "RNC's Embattled Richards Quits: Timing and Performance Questioned," *Washington Post,* Oct. 10, 1982, p. A5.

10. Dan Balz, "Party's Top Soldier Keeps Marching Even as White House Sounds Taps," *Washington Post,* August 11, 1994, p. A18.

11. Ranney, "President and His Party," p. 143.

12. *Choosing Presidential Candidates: How Good Is the New Way,* John Charles Daly, moderator, AEI Forums (Washington, D.C.: American Enterprise Institute, 1979), p. 7.

13. Ranney, "President and His Party," pp. 141–142.

14. See John A. Ferejohn and Randall L. Calvert, "Presidential Coattails in Historical Perspective," *American Journal of Political Science* 28 (Feb. 1984): 127–146; Randall L. Calvert and John A. Ferejohn, "Coattail Voting in Recent Presidential Elections," *American Political Science Review* 77 (June 1983): 407–419.

15. Norman J. Ornstein, Thomas E. Mann, and Michael J. Malbin, eds., *Vital Statistics on Congress,* 1997–1998 (Washington, D.C.: CQ Press, 1998), p. 72.

16. George C. Edwards, III, *Presidential Influence in Congress* (San Francisco, Cal.: W.H. Freeman, 1980), pp. 42–45.

17. Ibid., p. 45.

18. Richard E. Fenno, Jr., "U.S. House Members in Their Constituencies: An Exploration," *American Political Science Review* 71 (Sept. 1977): 914.

19. Nelson W. Polsby, *Congress and the Presidency*, 4th ed. (Englewood Cliffs, NJ.: Prentice-Hall, 1986), pp. 193–194.

20. For classic studies of the importance of party in roll call voting, see Julius Turner, *Party and Constituency: Pressures on Congress* (Baltimore, Md.: Johns Hopkins University Press, 1959); David B. Truman, *The Congressional Party* (New York: Wiley, 1959). See also Samuel C. Patterson and Gregory A. Caldeira, "Party

Voting in the United States Congress," *British Journal of Political Science* 18 (Jan. 1988): 111–131.

21. David Mayhew, "The Return of Unified Party Control Under Clinton: How Much of a Difference in Lawmaking?" in Bryan D. Jones, ed., *The New American Politics: Reflections on Political Change and the Clinton Administration* (Boulder, Colo.: Westview Press, 1995), p. 118.

22. Truman, *Congressional Party*, pp. 297–298.

23. Burt Solomon, "At Both Ends of the Avenue . . . Democrats Pander and Fall," *National Journal*, January 7, 1995, p. 38.

24. Todd S. Purdum, "White House Sees Gephardt as Straining Party Relations," *New York Times*, January 17, 1995, p. Al.

25. Polsby, *Congress and the Presidency*, pp. 194–196.

26. Mayhew, "The Return to United Party Control Under Clinton:' in Bryan D. Jones, ed., *The New American Politics: Reflections on Political Change and the Clinton Administration* (Boulder, Colo.: Westview Press, 1995), pp. 111–121, and David R. Mayhew, *Divided We Govern: Party Control, Lawmaking, and the Investigations 1946–1990* (New Haven, Conn.: Yale University Press, 1991).

27. Mayhew, "The Return to Unified Party Control Under Clinton:' p. 112.

28. Ibid., p. 113.

29. Ibid.

30. Francis E. Rourke, "The Presidency and the Bureaucracy: Strategic Alternatives," in Michael Nelson, ed. *The Presidency and the Political System* (Washington, D.C.: CQ Press, 1984), p. 340.

31. Quoted in Neustadt, *Presidential Power*, p. 39.

32. Hugh Heclo, "One Executive Branch or Many?" in Anthony King, ed., *Both Ends of the Avenue: The Presidency, the Executive Branch, and Congress in the 1980s* (Washington, D.C.: American Enterprise Institute, 1983), pp. 32–33.

33. Ibid., pp. 33–34.

34. Ibid., p. 34.

35. Bert A. Rockman, "The Federal Executive: Equilibrium and Change," in Jones, ed., *The New American Politics*, p. 162.

36. Norman C. Thomas and Joseph A. Pika, *The Politics of the Presidency*, 4th ed. rev. (Washington, D.C.: CQ Press), 1997, pp. 252–253; and Thomas J. Weko, *Politicizing the Presidency: The White House Personnel Office, 1948–1994* (Lawrence: University of Kansas Press, 1995), pp. 149–151, 157.

37. David E. Price, *Bringing Back the Parties* (Washington, D.C.: CQ Press, 1984), p. 176.

38. Rockman, "The Federal Executive: Equilibrium and Change," p. 160.

39. Heclo, "One Executive Branch or Many?" pp. 42–47.

40. John H. Kessel, "The Structures of the Reagan White House," *American*

Journal of Political Science 28 (May 1984): 235.

41. Rockman, "The Federal Executive: Equilibrium and Change," p. 160.

42. Ibid, p. 160.

43. See David M. O'Brien, "The Reagan Judges: His Most Enduring Legacy," in Charles O. Jones, ed., *The Reagan Legacy* (Chatham, N.J.: Chatham House, 1988), p. 62; Neil A. Lewis, "Unmaking the G.O.P. Court Legacy," *New York Times*, August 23, 1993, p. A9.

44. Joan Biskupic, "Despite 129 Clinton Appointments, GOP Judges Dominate U.S. Bench," *Washington Post*, October 14, 1994, p. A20.

45. Howard Kurtz, "Reagan Transforms the Federal Judiciary," *Washington Post*, March 31, 1985, p. A4.

46. Quoted in John F. Bibby, *Congress Off the Record: The Candid Analyses of Seven Members* (Washington, D.C.: American Enterprise Institute, 1983), p. 29.

47. For the most thorough analysis of member goals and committee politics, see Richard F. Fenno, Jr., *Congressmen in Committees* (Boston, Mass.: Little, Brown, 1983).

48. David Brady, Joseph Cooper, and Patricia Hurley, "The Decline of Party in the U.S. House of Representatives, 1887–1968," *Legislative Studies Quarterly* 4 (Aug. 1979): 383–386.

49. William J. Keefe, *Parties, Politics, and Public Policy in America*, 8th ed. (Washington, D.C.: CQ Press, 1998), pp. 240–241; see also David W. Rohde, *Parties and Leaders in the Postreform House* (Chicago, Ill.: University of Chicago Press, 1991).

50. For a concise analysis of the reasons for the increased partisanship within Congress, see Barbara Sinclair, "Evolution or Revolution? Policy-Oriented Congressional Parties in the 1980's," in L. Sandy Maisel, ed., *The Parties Respond: Changes in the American Party System* 3rd ed. (Boulder, Colo.: Westview, 1998), ch. 12.

51. Truman, *Congressional Party*, p. 95.

52. On the centralization of power in the hands of the Republican House leadership after the 1994 election, see John H. Aldrich and David W. Rohde, "The Transition to Republican Rule in the House," *Political Science Quarterly* 112 (Winter 1997–1998): 541–568; see also Lawrence W. Dodd and Bruce I. Oppenheimer, eds., *Congress Reconsidered*, 6th ed. (Washington, D.C.: CQ Press, 1997), pp 29–60.

53. See Charles O. Jones, "Joseph G. Cannon and Howard W. Smith: An Essay on the Limits of Leadership in the House of Representatives," *Journal of Politics* 30 (August 1968): 617–646.

54. Barbara Sinclair, "Transformational Leader or Faithful Agent? Innovation and Continuity in House Majority Party Leadership: The 104th and 105th Congresses," unpublished paper prepared for the Annual Meeting of the American

Political Science Association, Washington, D.C., August 28–31, 1997, pp. 21–22; and Barbara Sinclair, *Legislators, Leaders and Lawmaking* (Baltimore, Md.: Johns Hopkins University Press, 1995), pp. 236–240.

55. Barbara Sinclair, *The Transformation of the US. Senate* (Baltimore, Md.: Johns Hopkins University Press, 1989), chs. 5–7.

56. See John F. Bibby and Robert J. Huckshorn, "Out-Party Rebuilding Strategy: Republican National Committee Rebuilding Politics, 1964–1968:' in Bernard Cosman and Robert J. Huckshorn, eds., *Republican Politics, The 1964 Campaign, and Its Aftermath for the Party* (New York: Praeger, 1968), pp. 218–223.

57. Phil Gailey, "Dissidents Defy Top Democrats; Council Formed," *New York Times*, March 1, 1985, pp. 1, 9.

58. David R. Mayhew, *Congress: The Electoral Connection* (New Haven, Conn.: Yale University Press, 1974), pp. 97–105.

A CONCLUDING NOTE: AMERICAN PARTIES—DISTINCTIVE, DURABLE, ADAPTIVE, AND USEFUL

CHAPTER TEN

Throughout this brief exploration of American political parties, four strands of thought have consistently been a part of the discussion. American parties are distinctive, durable, adaptive, and useful to the republic.[1] These parties are unlike any others in Western democracies—they are organizationally weaker, lacking in substantial internal cohesion, without a mass dues paying membership, unable to control their own nominating processes, and heavily regulated by statute. They operate under severe handicaps—obstacles of a constitutional and political nature. The constitutional barriers of separation of powers and federalism make unified and disciplined parties extremely unlikely. Historical events (e.g., Civil War, Depression, patterns of immigration and migration) have created partisan loyalties in the electorate that meld together in the same party elements of disparate views and backgrounds. Progressive reforms like the direct primary have weakened the parties' capacity to control nominations, and civil service reforms have taken away much of the patronage that was used to sustain them. Competing political organizations such as interest groups, candidate organizations, campaign consultants, and PACs have gained seemingly increased influence both in campaign politics and governmental decision making. At the same time, voters seem less inclined to make their choices on election day on the basis of partisan considerations.

In the changing patterns of American party politics, many have perceived a general pattern of party decline, and a few have even envisioned an age of partyless politics in the near future.[2] Others see signs of party revival in such phenomena as the increased strength of the national party organizations and heightened party unity in Congress.[3] Of course, it is dangerous to predict the future and determine whether the revivalists or the seers of decline are correct. However, based upon past history, it is probably safe to predict that American parties will maintain their record of proven durability and adaptability to changing and even hostile conditions.

The evidence of their durability and adaptability is striking. For over 140 years the same two parties—the Republicans and Democrats—have dominated electoral politics. This is a record of durability unmatched in any other Western style democracy. Remarkably, these two parties compete against each other across the nation, despite the obstacles of regional diversity and federalism. They have adapted to the Progressive era reforms which stripped them of control over nominations and patronage, and they have adapted to the more recent reform environment of public funding of presidential elections and some state elections. The rise of political action committees has not put parties out of business. Instead, the parties have sought to coordinate and channel PAC contributions. As campaigns became more professionalized, technical, and expensive, the parties increased their fundraising potential through such techniques as direct mail and hired their own technical experts to provide in-kind services to candidates. At both the national and state levels there is evidence of increased party organizational strength compared to that which existed in the 1960s.[4]

Party identifiers continue to constitute approximately two-thirds of the voters, and the decline in party identifiers seems to have stabilized since the mid-1970s. Parties organize the Congress, state legislatures, the White House, and state administrations. They exert substantial influence on the decision making processes at the national and state levels.

But if American parties have a record of adaptability and durability, they also have a record of only modest strength. Defection rates among party identifiers in elections are frequently high—over 20 percent. Party organizations are insufficiently strong to nominate preferred candidates and then run their campaigns. The party-in-government is often fragmented and unable to hold together enough to enact a coherent program. The American system is not one of party government like that of the British. It should be noted, however, that the Congress took on a much more partisan tone starting in the late 1980s as party unity increased.

The picture of political parties in America that emerges, therefore, is a contradictory one—durability and adaptability combined with modest organizational strength, declining voter commitment, and frequent lack of internal cohesion among public office holders. The political parties of the United States constitute a unique response to the American constitutional system, demography, culture, and historical events. But for all their acknowledged weaknesses, parties remain and are likely to remain the principal agents for recruiting leaders, making nominations, contesting elections, bridging the gulf created by separation of powers, and providing a link between the citizenry and their government.

Notes

1. The distinctiveness of American political parties and their persistence are major themes of Leon D. Epstein's comprehensive and insightful analysis of the American party system. See Leon D. Epstein, *Political Parties in the American Mold* (Madison: University of Wisconsin Press, 1986).

2. Walter Dean Burnham, *Critical Elections and the Mainsprings of American Politics* (New York: Norton, 1970). See also David Broder, *The Party's Over* (New York: Harper and Row, 1972); and William Crotty, *Parties in Decline* (Boston, Mass.: Little, Brown, 1984).

3. See, for example, Paul S. Herrnson, *Party Campaigning in the 1980s* (Cambridge, Mass.: Harvard University Press, 1988); and Xandra Kayden and Eddie Mahe, *The Party Goes On* (New York: Basic Books, 1985).

4. Cornelius P. Cotter and John F. Bibby, "Institutional Development of Parties and the Thesis of Party Decline," *Political Science Quarterly* 95 (Spring 1980): 1–28; Kayden and Mahe, *The Party Goes On*; and Cornelius P. Cotter, James L. Gibson, John F. Bibby, and Robert J. Huckshorn, *Party Organizations in American Politics* (New York: Praeger, 1984).

Index to References

Index